Plato's *Statesman* Revisited

Trends in Classics – Supplementary Volumes

Volume 68

Plato's *Statesman* Revisited

Edited by
Beatriz Bossi and Thomas M. Robinson

DE GRUYTER

ISBN 978-3-11-060463-4
e-ISBN (PDF) 978-3-11-060554-9
e-ISBN (EPUB) 978-3-11-060491-7
ISSN 1868-4785

Library of Congress Control Number: 2018961056

Bibliographic information published by the Deutsche Nationalbibliothek
The Deutsche Nationalbibliothek lists this publication in the Deutsche Nationalbibliografie;
detailed bibliographic data are available on the Internet at http://dnb.dnb.de.

© 2018 Walter de Gruyter GmbH, Berlin/Boston
Editorial Office: Alessia Ferreccio and Katerina Zianna
Logo: Christopher Schneider, Laufen
Printing and binding: CPI books GmbH, Leck

www.degruyter.com

Contents

Part VII: **Bonds and Virtues**

Introduction

This book consists of a selection of papers presented at the *II International Spring Plato Seminar* (25-26 April 2016, Facultad de Filosofía, Universidad Complutense de Madrid) on Plato's *Politicus*[1] and some papers by other authors who were invited to contribute to this volume (namely, A. Larivée, M. Migliori and D. White). Inspired by Melissa Lane's conference on the same dialogue at Princeton University during her stay for three months in 2015, B. Bossi thought that it was due time for a second conference on one of Plato's dialogues in Spain, and that it would be a good follow up to organize it too on the *Politicus*. The aim of the conference was, like that of the first, held on Plato's *Sophist* (Benasque, 2009), the promotion of Plato studies in Spain; it offered us the opportunity to look afresh at one of Plato's most severely overlooked political dialogues, with discussions among a number of international scholars of distinction in the field taking place. This time, in the context of a bilingual seminar devoted to this topic at the Facultad de Filosofía of the UCM during the previous term, the conference included the participation of seven students whose papers were selected to take part in the conference.

Readers will find in this volume papers by scholars from the Anglo-Saxon orbit (Rowe, Blyth, White, Robinson) as well as from Italy (Giorgini, Palumbo, Migliori, Casertano, Motta, Candiotto), Spain (Zamora, Monserrat, Sánchez, Bossi), the French orbit (Larivée, El Murr), and Brazil (Peixoto, Vale dos Santos).

The papers included fall into seven categories that attempt to follow the order of the subjects as they are presented in the dialogue: 1.) two general papers dealing directly with the place of the *Statesman* in Plato's philosophy; 2.) two papers dealing with the difficulties arising from consideration of the ostensible aim of the dialogue, the definition of the art/science of government; 3.) a number which tackle the question of the interpretation of the myth and its reception; 4.) some discussing specific issues such as the art of measuring, weaving the polis, and the status of women; 5.) two papers focused on the problematic comparison between the statesman and the sophist; 6.) one paper contrasting the statesman's wisdom with the limits of the law; and finally 7.) three papers discussing the role which bonds and virtues play in several Platonic dialogues.

---

1 As this volume is presented to the community of scholars in English, for practical purposes we have decided to entitle the volume 'Plato's *Statesman* Revisited' (rather than Plato's *Politicus* Revisited) but we have respected the authors' choice of either title (and their interpretations of its meaning) in their respective papers. We are grateful to D. Blyth for his valuable help in the editing of this volume.

https://doi.org/10.1515/9783110605549-001

The volume opens with a strong and significant paper by A. Larivée which argues that the frustration the dialogue has generated is due mainly to an anachronistic expectation. The main problem of the dialogue, she claims, is that the statesman is an intangible, absent figure whose elusive political science has an enigmatic relationship with dialectic. The need for this science, she argues, is the message of this protreptic dialogue addressed to philosophers. It aims at encouraging them to pursue this political science passionately, badly needed as it is and still to be developed at the time Plato was writing. She concludes that Aristotle saw himself as a pioneer in that regard, and that his *Politics* could be considered as a sound proposal taking inspiration in Plato's *Politicus*. M. Migliori reflects on the major triad comprising the *Republic*, *Statesman* and *Laws*, in order to call attention to some key progressive points in Plato's politics. The contribution of the *Statesman*, he suggests, is to explain the significance of the 'utopian' model, the imitative nature of human polities, and the weight of the two pillars of human politics: the law and the statesman. The models of the *Republic* and the *Laws* are not to be implemented but constitute 'regulating principles'. The more theoretical philosopher-king of the *Republic* becomes a sensible single man ruling according to the laws 'by science or by opinion' while still imitating 'the divine', in a more down to earth *Statesman* (301a10–b3).

The second section deals with more specific problems. D. El Murr argues that, though it might seem that, by making political science *theoretical* and detached from a specific conception of 'practice' (equated with manual production) Plato runs the risk of purging political science of effectiveness, he manages to connect it to action through the notion of *prescription,* which El Murr regards as 'a distinctive conceptual innovation that the dialogue must be credited for in the history of political thought'. In addition, he seems to suggest that only a political science 'with such a high epistemic requirement' can take action and transform the social fabric. G. Casertano examines 277e–279a to reflect on the problematic relation between 'correct' and 'true' on the one hand, and between δόξα and ἐπιστήμη on the other. He argues that in our dialogue 'there is an identification, or at least a fluctuation' in the use of these terms. Unlike other dialogues where these terms are clearly opposed, the ἐπιστήμη of the king/statesman is also called δόξα, though it is described as the 'true opinion of a daemonic being'. Casertano finds the complete identification of 'correctness' and the 'kingly science' problematic arguing that, if the law is not set up by the true king (who does not need it) and every written law must be mere 'imitation' of the truth, it is unclear who else could produce it.

The third section is devoted to the interpretation and reception of the myth. D. White claims that the myth does serious philosophical work in the context of

Plato's dialogue, for it affects the results of collection and division and the difficult relation between part and class. The very notion of a paradigm as a methodological device originates within the myth, which constitutes a way to approximate the nature of statecraft, as it evokes a vision of the good. The creator of the cosmos referred to as "the god" cannot be either Cronus or Zeus, but, he submits, is the one who rectifies aberrations, as he weaves together the disparate epochs into a single, uniform cosmos. When read as a whole, he suggests, the dialogue's accessible interrelations are informative about the intricacies of methodology. On the other hand, D. Blyth observes that the Visitor's god in the myth deserves close comparison with Aristotle's prime mover not only because he is ontologically independent, explicitly divine and an ongoing intermittent cause of movement (unlike the demiurge in the *Timaeus*) but because the god of the myth, like Aristotle's god, he suggests, could be interpreted as physically unmoved, contemplating within himself the first principle(s) of being, and as a teleological contemporaneous cause of an everlasting cosmos as well. He finds support for his thesis at *Sophist* 248e–249a, which, as he understands it, can be read as making the claim that the forms must essentially be actively contemplated by intellect, and concludes that this might be the source of Aristotle's closely analogous conception of a *self-contemplating* intellect. Following the route of hermeneutical unity taken by Proclus, J.M. Zamora tackles the problem of the consistency between the myth in the *Statesman* and the one narrated in the *Timaeus*. According to Proclus' allegorical interpretation, the realm of Kronos (dialectic providence) represents the intellectual order of the gods, and corresponds to the intelligible world, while the realm of Zeus (the demiurge by antonomasia and the 'source of nature' identified with the 'prime destiny') represents reason operating in the physical world. He suggests that Kronos is for Zeus an 'intelligible intellect', and Zeus is for Kronos an 'intellectual intellect', but both preside over alternate cycles, and represent two permanent levels of reality. A. Motta closes this section also focusing on the legacy of the *Statesman* in Neoplatonism, arguing that their reading of the myth emphasizes cosmological and theological harmony. Whereas from the modern point of view the myth seems to be offering a parallel between the macrocosm and the human cosmos in order to explore political issues, she claims that the Neoplatonists employ it as an example and as an image in order to understand the intelligible proportions that govern the movement of the heavenly bodies, as well as the reflection of this movement in different realms; in their view, each text is envisaged as the visible side of something invisible that cannot be easily disclosed to everyone.

    J. Monserrat opens the fourth section dealing with the interpretation of the passage on measure. He argues that the question of learning to make appropriate and timely choices with due measure occupies the central pages of the *Statesman* because content and form go together, and calculating the appropriate method of research requires the same skill as deciding what is due in discourse and action. Due measure, he suggests, must be kept in memory to stop rationality in thought, word or deed from unravelling its own thread. He claims that due measure is not a method, but a new guiding principle for *logos*. G. Vale dos Santos discusses the image of weaving as a metaphor for thinking. As government is analogous to weaving, weaving is analogous to thinking, even when Plato does not claim this explicitly. Thinking, being a woven 'product' that articulates identities and differences, founds the governance of the city by articulating characters and measures for the common good. On the same question, N. Sánchez Madrid rejects the view that the choice of the weaving paradigm constitutes an arbitrary shift driven more by aesthetics than logic, as she claims that the weaving passage suggests that an effective theoretical knowledge is implied in the political *techne* which should imitate *phronesis* as portrayed by women at weaving. The ability to articulate heteronomous characters manifests itself as 'the hidden treasure of political theory', and, she suggests, 'matches the discovery process of Poe's purloined letter', for if it did not highlight the linkage between human thinking and weaving as one of its material translations, the knowledge of how to rule *poleis* would remain an entangled matter. In order to support her view, Sánchez Madrid compares the plots of both *Lysistrata* and the *Statesman* as they tackle the humble female art of weaving as an expression of reflective wisdom, concluding that the reproach of Lysistrata seems to have left 'some deep traces in Plato', for the political 'weaving' of characters and *technai* has its roots in a female 'intelligence which unfolds on the material world'. The section closes with a less optimistic, more general paper by T.M. Robinson which compares the 'Revolutionary' Plato to the 'Traditionalist' one when dealing with the role of women in society in the *Republic, Timaeus, Statesman*, and *Laws*. After highlighting both the revolutionary indications (women admitted as philosopher-rulers just as much as men) and the negative attitudes (such as taking a woman to be either naturally a 'coward' or 'unjust', or assuming reincarnation in the body of a woman to be the proper punishment for an immoral man) in the former two dialogues, when it comes to the *Statesman*, Robinson wonders why women apparently do not feature among the *epistemones politikoi* of the paradigmatically good society. He explores the reason for this, and concludes that the traditionalist Plato must have taken the lead again (which is in tune with the *Laws*, where though women receive equal education, they do not have access to the highest political offices).

L. Palumbo opens the sixth section by exploring the mimetic art of *visual writing*, which, in her view, enables the reader to experience his own resistance, empathy and mistakes, so as to 're-cognize' himself. After analysing the function of the myth, which *becomes* a model if, and only if, we are able to see how humans should imitate the movement of the cosmos, she considers the role of the wise statesman. While written laws are just 'imitations' of truth, the constitution that derives from the work of the expert would be the truest. All other forms of government are adulterations supported by counterfeits who are of all sophists the greatest ones, and the true rivals of Plato's mimetic art built on visual enchanting words. L. Candiotto deals with the difficulty of separating Socrates from the sophists. She argues that, since they share the same doxastic realm of expertise and some other features (such as Socrates being described as like an *atopos* satyr or magician) which are also detectable in 'the chorus of sophists' at 291a1-c6, they can easily be confused. Candiotto concludes that the separation of Socrates from the sophists is a *catharsis* of political urgency which takes place through the purification of rhetoric at the service of the statesman.

In the next section, M. Peixoto tackles the problem of the reason for the Stranger's insistence on mitigating the necessity of laws and on founding good government only on the wisdom of the king. After considering antecedents in Democritus and Antiphon, she argues that inflexible unquestionable laws cannot replace the statesman's experience (analogous to the doctor's and the captain's) because they are meant to reduce change to fixity and complex diversities to a minimal common denominator. She concludes that the virtue of phronesis would be, for the politically wise man, the equivalent of the laws, for the unwise.

The final section of the book begins with an enlightening general discussion by G. Giorgini of the differences the *Statesman* introduces, with regard to the *Republic* and the *Laws*, on the unity of virtue (which he takes as running counter to the Socratic view), education and the eugenic policy. The analogy with the art of weaving is, he suggests, very significant, not because it appeals to a female task (which in poetry had acquired a connotation of ruse and deceit, typically attributed to women) but because weaving together *opposing* virtues means that *differences* are to be taken into account and combined in due measure (performing a philosophical task). Against Protagoras, he argues, Platonic political science is not for everyone, but for a very few selected specialists who should be able to unite theoretical truth and practice, the idea of the good with its historical implementation. Instead of regarding the Stranger's views on virtue as eliminating the Socratic thesis of the unity of virtue, B. Bossi argues that the thesis of the essential involvement of wisdom in virtue proposed in the *Protagoras* and stated in the *Phaedo* is compatible with the thesis of non-involvement in the *Politicus*, if different meanings of 'virtue' are distinguished as operating at different levels. She defends a general consistent Platonic view of virtue throughout these dialogues, and suggests that the peculiar contribution of the *Politicus* is the dynamic perspective, for Plato offers new strategies to imagine the path from 'good temperament' to 'good character', and to 'genuine virtue' based on 'divine true opinion', instead of regarding these stages as statically stuck in a hierarchical pyramid. The volume closes with a paper by C. Rowe focused on three questions: what kind of *andreia*, and what kind of *sôphrosunê* belong to those virtuous citizens by the time the king takes them over from the state educators; why Plato should choose these two particular types as the sphere of operation for the royal weaver's skill; and what relationship should be entertained between the city of the *Politicus* and those of the *Republic* and the *Laws*. In response to the first one, he argues that they must be neither mere natural virtues nor fully developed ones, but something in between, ready to be mixed (presumably without 'philosophy and intelligence'). On the second question, he suggests that the reason is the existence of two fundamentally opposed tendencies, the very ones identified by Socrates in the *Republic*. In response to the third question, his proposal is that the best city Plato has in mind in the *Politicus* is *mutatis mutandis* the same as the best city he constructs in the *Republic* and in the *Laws*, and that the differences are to be explained by the different contexts. The novel aspect of the *Politicus* is, in his view, the framing of the problem of the conflict between the moderate and the courageous in terms of character-types, rather than, as in other places, in terms of internal conflicts of desires and beliefs.

Finally, we should like to mention the names of the students whose papers were selected to be presented during the Seminar, together with a very brief summary of their theses. Yalda Chamani Ballesteros talked about 'Plato's Silence', as a strategy to provoke the reader with puzzles. Inspired by F. Martínez Marzoa, Ignacio González Olmedo reflected 'On the two Aspects of the *Diairesis* in Plato's *Politicus*' in order to contribute to the understanding of the failure of this method in the dialogue. Carlos Marqués Delgado ('On the Neoplatonic Interpretation of the Myth of the *Politicus*: A Criticism to Modernity') argued against an interpretation of Plato as a dualist between theoretical and practical rationality. Andrea Moresco focused 'On the Intermediate Ontological Status of Due Measure in Plato's *Politicus*' which the politician should take into account in his practice, and argued that it could be taken as a contingent, though normative, image of the Form of Measure. Rosa Pérez Valdivieso reflected on 'Plato's Views on Women: Why a Female Paradigm for an Exclusive Male Activity?' to suggest that Plato might have appreciated not only the weaving of pieces of fabric but women's capacity to reconcile opposing temperaments among the members of the polis. Inspired by the paradigm of the shepherd and the description of the age of Kronos as a kind of Paradise, Michael Teofilov presented a paper entitled: 'Adumbrating Christian Views in Plato's *Politicus*?'. Paula L. Vega Martínez ('Plato and Aesthetics') reflected on the aesthetic dimension of Plato's political projects inasmuch as the wise statesman is able to shape collective identities. We are grateful to the Dean of the Faculty of Philosophy, Prof. Rafael Orden Jiménez, for his kind and hospitable welcoming of the participation of the students.

Last but not least, we shared two lively (and musical) Seminar dinners in Platonic *koinonia*.

The Editors, Spring 2018

Part I: **Defining the Place of the *Statesman***

Annie Larivée
Taking Frustration Seriously. Reading Plato's *Statesman* as a Protreptic to Political Science

Notwithstanding the *Laws*, the *Statesman* is probably the most unloved Platonic dialogue. This situation is often attributed to the text's apparent lack of unity, but so many other aspects of the dialogue are likely to create perplexity – and, possibly, irritation, if not exasperation – that the most honest hermeneutic attitude might be to acknowledge this negative reaction and take it seriously. This is what I intend to do here. Instead of fighting or ignoring the frustration felt by most readers of the *Statesman*, I want to explore the possibility that it stems neither from a gross hermeneutic negligence on their part, nor from a failure on Plato's part as an intelligent and skilled author, but is rather due mainly to an anachronistic expectation towards the text. In what follows, I will put forward an interpretative hypothesis which, I believe, does justice to this experience of frustration and helps to explain many of the perplexities modern readers encounter while reading the *Statesman*. My proposal will also lead to a better appreciation of the colossal – though grossly overlooked – significance of the *Statesman* from a historical point of view.

1 Fully acknowledging the problems

Unlike most other dialogues where the dramatic setting subtly echoes the ideas under discussion, the *Statesman* seems to present us with an odd clash between *logos* and *ergon*. Indeed, while promoting weaving as the most adequate paradigm to illustrate political expertise, the *Statesman* itself looks more like a colourful patch-work composed of a series of 'beaux morceaux' than an artfully woven fabric.[1] Many interpreters have tackled the problem of the unity of the *Statesman* (be it the unity of the two great themes of the dialogue, method and politics, or unity of argument), clearly hoping that solving this difficulty would reconcile readers with the text.[2]

---

1 E.g., the division of sciences, the myth of cosmic reversals, the definition of humans as featherless bipeds, the distinction between *eidos* and *meros*, the digression on right measure, the one on paradigms, the paradigm of weaving, etc. – the list of gems is long.
2 See for example Rowe (1995b) 14, Lane (1998) 2, 202, and more recently, El Murr (2014) 77 ff.

https://doi.org/10.1515/9783110605549-002

Although this endeavour is certainly worthwhile, it is not sufficient. Once the issue of unity is settled, so many problems persist that the temptation to blame them on authorial failure is strong.[3] After all, it is probably fair to say that not all Platonic dialogues can be celebrated as masterpieces, and the *Statesman* could just be one of the less remarkable texts Plato happened to write while engaging in what Socrates describes in the *Phaedrus* as an intelligent form of *paidia*. Interpreters who embrace a developmental approach can also 'explain' the *Statesman*'s apparent weaknesses by arguing that the dialogue represents a still inchoate or transitional stage in the evolution of Plato's political ideas between the *Republic* and the *Laws*.[4] A viable strategy for more charitable interpreters is to regard incongruities present in the text as purposeful training devices meant to develop the reader's critical mind and philosophical abilities.[5] This would be in harmony with the Stranger's declaration to the effect that the most important outcome of an inquiry like the one they are pursuing in the dialogue is to make one διαλεκτικωτέρος and εὑρετικώτερος (285d, 286e–287a). That approach can certainly help to account for particular methodological flaws or discrepancies, but it does not suffice to alleviate the frustration triggered by more fundamental difficulties that are often downplayed by commentators. Since I believe that fully acknowledging those problems is the very key to their solution, I will start by bringing them to attention in order to fully appreciate their significance and gravity. My priority at this stage is not to engage in minute textual analysis and to attempt to solve those tensions by offering substantial solutions. Rather my aim is to take a step back, paint these sources of perplexity with broad brush strokes and let them be, so to speak.

The following list of problems is far from being exhaustive; I am limiting myself to four major obstacles encountered in the interpretation of the *Statesman*. I focus on the problems – or perhaps I should call them *enigmas* – that I take to be the most crucial. They are intertwined and can be regarded as crucial insofar as they seem to threaten the dialogue's very raison d'être.

---

3 Rowe (1995a) 9–10, Klosko (2006) 200. For negative judgements made by past interpreters, see Lane (1998) 1–2. It is tempting to believe that Isocrates is alluding to Plato's *Statesman* when he refers to texts on the same topic as his own which raised high expectations while still in the making but disappointed once shared with the world (*To Nicocles*, 7).
4 See, for example, Kahn (1995), Annas (1995) xxii, Klosko (2006) 216.
5 I am not just thinking, here, of interpreters who see the *Statesman* as a form of scholastic Academic exercise designed to train students in dialectics. Rosen's ironic and highly critical reading of the dialogue shows how it can be a substantial philosophical exercise for the contemporary reader. Neither a 'gymnastic' approach nor a developmental one is fundamentally incompatible with the view I am be offering here.

a. The *Politikos* as an intangible, absent figure

The discussion pursued in the *Statesman* is supposed to aim at portraying a *man*: the 'political' or 'royal' man (πολιτικὸς, βασιλικὸς ἀνήρ). So much is announced by the Stranger at the very beginning of the dialogue (258b3), an objective that is reiterated in the very last line (311c7–8). Of this *man*, however, we learn very little. Throughout this long and convoluted discussion that is supposedly about him, he remains mysteriously faceless, intangible, hidden. Given the fact that this man is presented by the Stranger as being something like a *nomos empsychos*, the elusiveness of his portrayal seems especially problematic.[6]

This situation may be due to the method adopted by the Stranger. The results of his colossal dialectical inquiry, however patient and laborious, are in great part *negative*. Indeed, although the declared objective is to portray a specific figure (the 'political' or 'royal' man), this figure ends up being approached indirectly – i.e. through an identification of what the πολιτικὸς/βασιλικὸς ἀνήρ is *not*. He *is not* a provider of the pastoral kind responsible for his herd's τροφή. We learn so much from the lengthy description of the different leadership conditions under the reign of Cronos and that of Zeus (275e). Although they share the same denomination, he is also *not* to be confused with the head Priest of the *polis*, the βασιλεύς, one of the three ἄρχοντες at the time, in Athens (290d–e). Although their skills are precious and he makes use of them, he is also *not* to be confused with the figures of Chief of war, of the Judge or the Orator (304e–305e). And he has nothing in common with the myriad of "sophists" involved in public affairs, those "so-called politicians' ("...τοὺς πολιτικοὺς λεγομένους", 303c, "...τὸν περὶ τὰ τῶν πόλεων πράγματα χορόν", 291b–c). Perceiving those he should not be confused with is certainly useful to avoid misidentification, but it does not allow us to precisely distinguish the concrete qualities of the royal man.

True, we do learn positive things about him. Although this is not explicitly discussed, the terms as well as the gender used for pronouns and adjectives suggest that this figure is male (ἀνήρ, i.e., a man, not a woman).[7] This man possesses an expertise (ἐπιστήμη/τέχνη), and it is precisely the possession of this 'political' or 'royal' expertise that makes *him* political, royal. As the holder of this expertise,

---

6 Like the ship captain, the 'law' provided by the πολιτικός is nothing else than his own expertise, 297a2. In other words, he *is* the law; he embodies it, hence the reference to the ideal of the *nomos empsychos*. Although the expression is not found in the *Statesman*, the germ of this Hellenistic ideal is present. See Aalders (1969), and more recently, Ramelli (2006).

7 In light of the *Republic*'s second wave, this seems to call for an explanation. I plan to tackle that issue in another text.

he is not directly involved in action, but rather, issues prescriptions. These prescriptions are not simply relayed by him, they emanate from his own intelligence. His expertise is a form of ἐπιμέλεια, and his role is to provide collective care to a specific type of social animals: humans. The description that emerges from the dialectical inquiry is not entirely negative and un-informative. It does shed light on very basic features – the function of care among others – that tend to be forgotten and serve as corrective when corrupt leaders act as predators and neglect their very reason for existing. But given the level of generality of such a description, the insight it provides remains rather thin.

Further on in the inquiry, however, one element of comparison emerges that gives the reader's imagination something more substantial to feed on: the paradigm of weaving. Describing the political man as a weaver amounts to suggesting, albeit implicitly, something about his preferences and his character. Namely, that he values unity, connectedness, and that he is committed to creating the conditions for harmonious relationships between citizens to flourish. In light of traditional militaristic understanding of political leadership, there is something subversive about this proposition. One could even suggest that since weaving was a function conventionally reserved for women, this move on Plato's part also seems to promote something like a "feminization of politics".[8] At the very least, it evokes a caring style that focuses on the *protection* of the social whole by promoting ὁμόνοια, φιλία, collaboration, close ties and solidarity, while diffusing motives for inner divisions, rivalry and wars of conquest. That being said, in order to avoid anachronism, we should keep in mind that the general spirit of the fabric metaphor is reminiscent of the *Republic*'s conception of leadership as guardianship – there is something paternalistic about it. Training an elite class capable of safeguarding the political body seems to be the key idea: the πολιτικός will weave spirited and moderate citizens together in order to form a tight fabric that will envelop and protect the whole *polis*, slaves included. In other words, it is not the *polis* that is compared to the 'fabric', strictly speaking. It is the ruling class of the chief magistrates: the bold and moderate ἄρχοντες are the protective textile that envelops and preserves the *polis*.[9] The paradigmatic figures of the physician and of the ship captain, often evoked to describe the πολιτικός even though they are

---

8 See Larivée (2012) 288-91. For a different view, see Lane (1998) 164–71.
9 τοῦτο δὴ τέλος ὑφάσματος εὐθυπλοκίᾳ συμπλακὲν γίγνεσθαι φῶμεν πολιτικῆς πράξεως τὸ τῶν ἀνδρείων καὶ σωφρόνων ἀνθρώπων ἦθος, ὁπόταν ὁμονοίᾳ καὶ φιλίᾳ κοινὸν συναγαγοῦσα αὐτῶν τὸν βίον ἡ βασιλικὴ τέχνη, πάντων μεγαλοπρεπέστατον ὑφασμάτων καὶ ἄριστον ἀποτελέσασα ὥστ' εἶναι κοινὸν τούς τ' ἄλλους ἐν ταῖς πόλεσι πάντας δούλους καὶ ἐλευθέρους ἀμπίσχουσα, συνέχῃ τούτῳ τῷ πλέγματι, καὶ καθ' ὅσον εὐδαίμονι προσήκει γίγνεσθαι πόλει τούτου μηδαμῇ μηδὲν ἐλλείπουσα ἄρχη τε καὶ ἐπιστατῇ, 311b–c.

not at the core of the investigation, are also animated with the same spirit: the goal is to expertly preserve (σῴζειν) the *polis* from destruction, by all means necessary.[10]

Apart from this weaving paradigm and the occasional use of positive adjectives such as φρόνιμος (292d5, 294a8), σοφός, ἀγαθός (296e3), we gain no insight into the royal man's character. We know that he is concerned with the virtues of the chief magistrates of the *polis,* and responsible for weaving courage with moderation within and between them, but unlike what we see in texts by other authors such as Isocrates and Xenophon, Plato's kingly man is not, *himself,* presented as an especially powerful example of virtue. He does not seem to offer a model of virtue that could be emulated by the citizens. Moreover, weaving as a paradigm does not reveal much about his leadership style and abilities either. Why and how are his prescriptions obeyed? How does he interact with those who implement them? Is he in any way especially remarkable or inspiring? Isn't being (or becoming) somehow exemplary the distinctive sign of the kingly man? No matter how counter-intuitive it may be at first glance, the fact that close to nothing concrete is said about his moral virtues, his capacity to inspire by providing an example of virtuous conduct, his charisma, his abilities for leadership suggests that, in reality, the πολιτικός may not be a visible public figure at all. Or even a ruler in the traditional sense of the word. Explicit allusions made by the Stranger allow for that surprising possibility.

Indeed, very early on in the context of the initial division the Stranger asserts that, in fact, nothing prevents the πολιτικός from being a private citizen. In other words, in his view, it is possible to think of the genuine political man as someone who is not serving in a public capacity.[11] This situation does not have to be temporary; the πολιτικός can remain in that position forever and still meet the criterion set by the Stranger to deserve that title. In other words, past, present or future participation in public affairs is not included in the definition of the royal or political man provided by the Stranger.[12] That is perplexing.

---

10 See 297e *sq.,* for instance.
11 τί δ'; ὅστις βασιλεύοντι χώρας ἀνδρὶ παραινεῖν δεινὸς ἰδιώτης ὢν αὐτός, ἆρ᾽ οὐ φήσομεν ἔχειν αὐτὸν τὴν ἐπιστήμην ἣν ἔδει τὸν ἄρχοντα αὐτὸν κεκτῆσθαι; (...) ἀλλὰ μὴν ἥ γε ἀληθινοῦ βασιλέως βασιλική; (...) ταύτην δὲ ὁ κεκτημένος οὐκ, ἄντε ἄρχων ἄντε ἰδιώτης ὢν τυγχάνῃ, πάντως κατά γε τὴν τέχνην αὐτὴν βασιλικὸς ὀρθῶς προσρηθήσεται; 259a–b. This possibility is reiterated at 292b: δεῖ γὰρ δὴ τόν γε τὴν βασιλικὴν ἔχοντα ἐπιστήμην, ἄν τ᾽ ἄρχῃ καὶ ἐὰν μή, κατὰ τὸν ἔμπροσθε λόγον ὅμως βασιλικὸν προσαγορεύεσθαι.
12 We find the same surprising possibility in Aristotle. See Bodéüs (2004) 29 : "La haute idée que se fait Aristote de la politique ne s'accommode visiblement pas du rang volontiers subalterne accordé à la sagacité des politiques-manœuvres qui forment l'exécutif. (...) le vrai politique (...)

For those who don't regard this suggestion as a product of a useless and possibly flawed digression (258e–259d), the most sensible interpretive strategy is to infer that the Stranger wants to keep the possibility open for the genuine πολιτικός to play his role on the margins of public life, as a private advisor of rulers. This is a plausible interpretation, appealing even, in light of Plato's adventures in Syracuse as narrated in the VIIth Letter.[13] In reality, the problem goes deeper and we should not rush for a solution. For nothing in the definition of the πολιτικός as someone who possesses a certain ἐπιστήμη/τέχνη that is essentially theoretical (γνωστική, 258e5, 259c9) seems to require that he be actively practicing his prescriptive expertise, either in a public capacity, as a ruler, or in a private capacity, as an advisor. Through his comparison with the competent physician, the Stranger presents the πολιτικός as *being able* to provide advice (ἱκανὸς συμβουλεύειν, 259a1), not as necessarily providing it. In other words, political expertise allows one to make good political prescriptions. This does not mean that these prescriptions are implemented or even actually provided. They are if the πολιτικός is like an architect currently working on a specific assignment and making sure that his instructions are followed (260a), but it seems that they don't have to be in order for a person to qualify as πολιτικός/βασιλικός. Although it is hard to think of political expertise as disconnected from practice (not only for its enactment but also for its development and acquisition), it is not totally unconceivable. Just as someone could well have studied architecture or medicine without having given prescriptions that actually lead to the construction of a building or the recovery of a patient, perhaps it is possible to imagine a political expert who has never implemented a regime or guided a political community. Most of us would probably not trust arm-chair experts with our house or our health (let alone the state), but this is another question.

To summarize, the elusiveness of the πολιτικός is multifaceted. First, he is portrayed in a way that is in great part indirect, negative. Second, most of the positive elements mentioned are so basic and general that they are only minimally informative. Thirdly, whereas it is not unreasonable to expect him to be the most visible and exemplary individual in the *polis*, some allusions suggest that he acts in the shadow so to speak, at the margins of the public sphere. Fourth, not only is he not necessarily visible, he could also well be inactive (temporarily

---

pourrait n'être pas au gouvernement! (...) [cette conception] ouvre la possibilité au moins théorique d'être politique sans faire la loi, ni être au gouvernement."

13 This possibility is often alluded to but rarely fully explored. For the most comprehensive and detailed version of this interpretation, see Hourcade (2017) 159–74.

or permanently), not performing the prescriptive function corresponding to his science – a capable knower more than an actual doer –and still deserve his title.

Last but not least: does this expert even exist? More precisely, is the Stranger describing a man he thinks *could* even exist? If it is not the case – a possibility he evokes[14] – one should probably not be too surprised by the πολιτικὸς ἀνήρ's intangible presence in the text. Although sophists may be hard to 'capture', this is not a problem that arises in the *Sophist* since sophists do obviously exist, and it is their proliferation that makes the inquiry about their nature so pressing.

b. The *Politikos* as the holder of an elusive science

But maybe the first problem only arises when one holds on to the hope of being able to gain insight concerning the πολιτικός as a type of person, a character or a nature. And perhaps such an expectation is not appropriate?[15] Sure, the inquiry starts with the project of depicting the πολιτικὸς ἀνήρ. But once the idea that what makes a man 'πολιτικός' is the possession of πολιτικὴ ἐπιστήμη is agreed upon (as early as 258b), maybe the definition of that science is really all that matters? Perhaps this is the actual message of the whole dialogue: stop fantasising about a certain type of providential man, and focus, instead on the function such a person is supposed to play and on the knowledge required to do so. One thing is for sure, emphasising the value and necessity of πολιτικὴ ἐπιστήμη/τέχνη is undoubtedly one of the Stranger's clearest and most unyielding commitments.

Thus, perhaps the first problem I identified is only minor after all. Maybe the best way (the only way, really) to get to know the πολιτικὸς ἀνήρ is to focus our attention entirely on the nature of the *expertise* that makes a person worthy of that title.

This approach seems sensible enough, and promising. However, it is probably not an exaggeration to say that the description of that expertise is even more elusive, if possible, than the characterisation of the πολιτικὸς ἀνήρ in the first place. While proclaiming in unequivocal terms that the πολιτικός is defined by the possession of a specific type of expertise, close to nothing concrete is revealed concerning this indispensable ἐπιστήμη/τέχνη. Its highly formal description is

---

14 301e; this passage echoes the general suspicion evoked at 301d. At 300e7 the existence of the corresponding science is regarded as hypothetical: "οὐκοῦν εἰ μὲν ἔστι βασιλική τις τέχνη...".

15 For the idea that there is no such thing as a political nature, see Dixsaut (1995) 254–55: "Personne n'est, par nature, fait pour s'occuper de politique (...) La fonction politique n'est pas liée naturellement à une espèce particulière de nature, possédant sa puissance propre."

almost entirely devoid of concrete content. Isn't this elusiveness even more perplexing than the mystery surrounding the πολιτικὸς ἀνήρ? That indispensable, albeit *missing*, science is quite the elephant in the room.

A way to get around this problem would be to equate this political ἐπιστήμη/τέχνη not with a teachable and learnable set of general principles enabling one to establish and safeguard healthy political communities, but rather with a psychological ability to perceive what particulars situations call for – the kind of sagacity required to make good political decisions that Aristotle will refer to as φρόνησις. It is certainly true that such 'kairotic' ability is attributed to the πολιτικός in the text: he knows when is the right time to make use of the three precious ancillary arts.[16] But is this the very substance of his ἐπιστήμη? Other epimeletic arts where a sense of καιρός is required – medicine, say – would hardly appear to be appropriately described if defined solely in such terms. For does not medicine, as a science, depend first and foremost on what can be discovered, taught and learnt about human bodies, the conditions that favor health and the treatment of illnesses, rather than on the special flair gifted physicians can manifest in the practice of their art? Many general things can and must be learnt first, for a prescriptive expertise like medicine to qualify as science. There is no doubt that kairotic flair and intellectual flexibility are required to become a good practitioner of such arts.[17] But the expertise, as such, is not limited to this 'je ne sais quoi' that seems closer to the divine inspiration alluded to at the end of the *Meno* than it is to science. But perhaps the kairotic ability of the πολιτικός is precisely not just a type of flair, but involves an objective knowledge both of the good and of future events?[18] If it is the case, then we are not talking about a human type of ability, but of divine omniscience. Political ἐπιστήμη/τέχνη would not be attainable by humans, and the best alternative would be a strict adhesion to laws combined with Socratic ignorance.[19] Be that as it may, thinking of political ἐπιστήμη essentially in terms of kairotic ability makes it either uninformative, or turns the whole quest into something inaccessible.

In reality, we do learn a few concrete things about the type of prescriptive treatment provided by political ἐπιστήμη/τέχνη. Here again, the most tangible pieces of information emerge in the context of the discussion of weaving as a paradigm for political expertise. Let us start by recalling that, at first, this paradigm appears to be chosen for its capacity to illustrate a highly formal trait of political

16 305d. This passage is at the heart of Lane's interpretation (1998).
17 To refer to this aspect, Diès (1935) uses the expression "le flair du chef", xiii.
18 This surprising view is expressed by Lane (1998) 6, 145–146.
19 A possibility evoked by Márquez, (2012) 11.

expertise, namely: its architectonic nature (287c). Just as the art of weaving, responsible for the final product that is the fabric, is using the work of subordinate arts (arts involved in the production of the diverse tools and material needed to perform its own function), political expertise finds itself, too, in such an architectonic position. This is a highly formal characterization, but there is also something unique about this formal feature in the case of political expertise: it is *the über*-architectonic art in charge of directing all others within the *polis* (305e). Still, this does not reveal much about the particular content of this expertise. What is it, precisely, that the πολιτικός knows or needs to know in order to be able to play its care-oriented architectonic function?

The only content related information we get concerning political expertise – mainly 'ideological' and eugenic in nature – comes at the very end of the dialogue. We thus learn that: 1) it will select and prepare the proper material required to produce the social fabric (flawed individuals will be eliminated or enslaved and decent ones will be submitted to a form of *paideia* under its direction, 308b–309a); 2) it will weave together two opposite types of virtuous citizens, spirited ones and moderate ones, through conjugal unions (310b–e) and will put both in charge of the ἀρχαί (311a); 3) it will generate a strong political body by ensuring that all citizens share the same beliefs concerning the good, the fine, the just and their opposites (309c). In other words, the πολιτικός's weaving expertise will favor social cohesion by ensuring that all, citizens and slaves, share the same core values, and are protected by a closely knit and well-balanced class of chief magistrates.

This is not nothing, but it is not much. And it is vague.

c. What, if any, is the connection between the philosopher/dialectician and the πολιτικός?

Could these crumbs of information be something like the tip of an iceberg? One thing is for sure, the last measure evoked (with its reference to the good, the fine, the just and their opposites), raises a much debated question, the question of the link between the πολιτικός and the philosopher. Are πολιτικός and philosopher two names that refer to the same person and require the same abilities?[20] Or does the πολιτικός share some of the philosopher's capacities while being a distinct

---

20 "... une même science (...) dans une même tête" as Diès puts it (1935) LIX.

person with a distinct function? Does he benefit from the philosopher's guidance? Do they act like a team, one of them advising, the other receiving advice intelligently?

This enigmatic relationship is undoubtedly one of the most daunting problems posed by the dialogue. In my opinion, however, it is not nearly as baffling as the two previous ones. It is less a perplexing deficiency than a profusion of positive options to pick from. *"Nous avons l'embarras du choix"*, as we say in French. In fact, all possibilities mentioned above are conceivable and all are exemplified in other dialogues. The first one is illustrated by the *Republic* with its philosopher-kings and queens who are scientifically and philosophically trained and who alternate between a life of philosophical training/contemplation and a life of political leadership. The second anticipates the solution favoured in the *Laws*, with its council of elite magistrates, the νυκτερινὸς σύλλογος, whose daily discussions include philosophical questions (such as the distinctiveness and unity of moral virtues) although they are not 'professional' philosophers (*Laws*, 964b–c). And the third is illustrated by the *First Alcibiades*, a dialogue in which Socrates attempts to persuade Alcibiades to let him act as his personal political advisor and educator.[21]

Yet another possibility – implicitly suggested, again, by the paradigm of the weaver – is that the genuine πολιτικός is mostly responsible for the initial 'weaving' of the polis. Just as a weaver creates a product he ultimately relinquishes, it could be the case that the πολιτικός would not be directly involved in the management of the state once his foundational task is complete, or perhaps only occasionally, when legislative 'repairs' are required.[22] We thus have to distinguish the type of 'royal' expertise involved in the foundational process (the constitutional stage), from the virtues required to run the *polis* at a later time by chief magistrates (ἄρχοντες). If the former is what the Stranger has in mind in the *Statesman*, we can think of his πολιτικός as being essentially a philosopher who also happens to work sporadically as a legislator; or, as a philosophically educated legislator; or, as a philosophically educated legislator working in close collaboration with a philosopher-advisor. Be that as it may, it is this foundational process – corresponding to the (fictional) work accomplished by Socrates and by

---

21 *Alc.* 105d–e, 135d. A similar collaboration is also evoked in the *Laws* when the Athenian Stranger suggest that the most effective way for a legislator to better a polis would be to form a team with a young, virtuous, gifted tyrant, 709e–710d.
22 This possibility is evoked in the context of the comparison between the legislator and the physician, 295c–296a. See Lane (1995) 283, who later abandoned this interpretation (1997) 178, n. 76, fully embraced by Márquez (2012).

the Athenian Stranger respectively in the *Republic* and the *Laws* – that would be the object of the πολιτικός's prescriptive attention, not so much the ongoing management of the *polis* that comes in the aftermath, and for which executive officers are responsible.[23]

This surprising possibility appears more plausible (or less implausible depending on one's hermeneutic leanings) if we make the effort to reconnect with the linguistic creativity present in the dialogue. We tend to take for granted that the nominalised adjective πολιτικός refers to what we, nowadays, regard as an actual actor in the field of politics, i.e. a politician, a statesperson, a head of government. In contemporary French, for example, the exact equivalent of the Greek nominalised adjective used by Plato is widely used to refer to a politician or a statesperson – 'un [homme] politique', 'une [femme] politique'. Now, as Skemp observed a long time ago, Plato is apparently the source of the linguistic innovation.[24] However, nothing guarantees that what has since become the common meaning of that nominalised adjective is what Plato had in mind at the time he wrote the dialogue.[25] It is possible that he was intending to use that name to refer to a knowledgeable initiator responsible for establishing the basic legislative structure of a state, something like a 'founding father' rather than an actual ruler. This is also why the commonly used English title '*Statesman*' may be confusing and should probably be avoided; *Statesman* imperceptibly suggests that Plato is talking about a political leader and suppresses other plausible interpretative possibilities.

I have evoked different ways in which the πολιτικός can be tied to the philosopher. At this point, nothing compels us to choose one possibility over another. In my view, the diversity of options is what defines the enigmatic nature of the

---

23 Although this problem calls for a more detailed exposition, here is my basic position on the question of the relationship between the πολιτικός and laws. In my view, 295a makes clear that in the case of collective care, general prescriptions (laws) are necessary. There is no way a πολιτικός can provide personalised prescriptions for each and every citizen individually. Thus, in the constitution established by the genuine (i.e. knowledgeable) πολιτικός, there will be laws. The genuine πολιτικός is a legislator (305b5, 309d1). That said, the only excellent laws (i.e. prescriptions) are those issued by the genuine πολιτικός (not those adopted through a process of deliberation in which non-experts are involved), and like the physician or ship captain, he is not tied by his own past prescriptions. These will be modified by him if necessary. See 295e–297a, 300d.
24 Skemp (1952) 18–20; see also Rowe (1995a) 1–2.
25 Skemp suggests that Plato progressively moved from a use of the word that meant 'so-called politicians' to a dignified use that meant 'statesman'. My suggestion here is a bit different.

connection between the philosopher/dialectician and the πολιτικός in the dialogue. Several possibilities are open; picking even the best interpretative option over the others would involve a mutilation of the text.

d. What is the dialogue's chief objective?

In the wake of these enigmatic features of the dialogue, two formidable questions finally arise. Although they are distinct, they are so closely related that it is hard to treat them separately at times: a) what is the chief purpose of the inquiry conducted by the interlocutors of the dialogue, and, b) what was the targeted audience of the *Statesman* and the objective pursued by its author?

The first question seems easy enough to answer. The discussion's chief aim is announced by the Stranger at the very beginning of the text: to offer a portrait of the πολιτικὸς ἀνήρ. But irrespective of the fact that the results of the inquiry are extremely thin and elusive in that regard, what complicates the question is that the Stranger later denies or, at the very least, qualifies this initial declaration. In a passage that thrills methodologically inclined interpreters, he indeed suggests that defining the πολιτικός is, as such, not the real task of the enterprise. Rather, the genuine goal of the whole exercise is to become a better and more creative dialectician on all possible topics.[26]

Should we take this declaration at face value, or with a grain of salt? And more importantly, how will our decision impact the perspective in which we interpret the whole dialogue? Should we, too, use the dialogue mainly as a dialectical exercise in which the object of the search matters very little, if at all?

One important preliminary remark that can help limit the field of hermeneutic possibilities is to start by considering the targeted audience of the dialogue. We don't need to try to get into Plato's head and evoke spirits in order to come up with a plausible view on this. Indeed, the nature of this audience can be inferred in light of intrinsic features of the dialogue itself. First, we can very reasonably infer that there is a close similarity between the type of participants involved in the discussion led by the Stranger within the dialogue and the targeted audience of the whole dialogue authored by Plato. The discussion involves a small circle of learned men skilled in dialectical discussions (some of them highly experienced, some younger but able to follow the lead of others). At least one of them, namely Socrates, is a skilled dialectician who has dedicated a lot of attention and energy to the examination of politically relevant questions. Now, given the length and

---

26 285d, 286e–287a.

the level of conceptual sophistication of the discussion that takes place between the interlocutors of the dialogue, we can infer that the readership targeted by the dialogue also corresponds to this general profile. The *Statesman* is clearly not a dialogue that is accessible (or likely to appeal) to anyone who is not already used to lengthy, strenuous philosophical investigations. Thus, although we don't have to take the Stranger at face value when he belittles what is supposed to be the main objective of the search (i.e., the definition of the πολιτικὸς ἀνήρ), we can safely infer that skilled philosophers, or at least, intellectually refined readers well-disposed towards philosophy are the targeted audience of the text.

That remains vague but it is nonetheless significant, since it imposes a limitation on the possible objectives pursued *in* and *by* the text. Indeed, whatever these goals are – for why should a text, especially such rich and multi-faceted texts as Plato's, pursue only *one* –, they cannot be objectives that target the public at large. They have to be of special relevance to philosophers and philosophically trained individuals one way or another. If these philosophically trained individuals are also interested in political questions, like Socrates in the dialogue, that's probably even better – although at this point, we can't say if this is a necessary condition.

One thing is for sure: the nature of the targeted audience explains why the *Statesman*, although it shares its starting point with many texts written by other authors around the same period (namely, the portrayal of the truly 'royal' man), offers something drastically different from its contemporary counterparts that can be characterized as a 'mirror for princes'. Indeed, although the (first) declared objective of the discussion is to define the true πολιτικός and "royal man", I do not think that it is safe to postulate that the *Statesman* unequivocally belongs to the 'mirror for princes' genre, despite Pierre Hadot's suggestion in a substantial encyclopedic entry he dedicated to this tradition.[27] I would not go so far as to say that the *Statesman* can in no way be regarded as a 'mirror for princes' – a genre that clearly finds its Greek ancestors in Xenophon's *Cyropaedia* and Isocrates' Letter *To Nicocles*, his *Nicocles* (and possibly his *Evagoras*), for example. But whoever wants to argue that the *Statesman* belongs to this genre must qualify their reading in light of what was just established concerning its possible audience. Plato's *Statesman* can be read as a mirror for princes (i.e., as a text that can be a source of inspiration/edification for current or aspiring political leaders), but not just *any* type of political leader. The type of 'prince' it addresses would have either to be a philosopher himself, to have been philosophically trained, or, at the very

---

27 Hadot (1972) 574, includes both the *Republic* and the *Statesman* in his historical survey of that literary genre since, in his opinion, both works present us with figures of ideal rulers.

least to be well-disposed towards philosophy and capable of following philosophical inquiry while being advised by a philosopher.

Within these limitations, thinking of the *Statesman* as an early representative of the genre of 'mirror for princes' is not impossible. It even makes good sense if we perceive the paradigm of weaving as one of the numerous manifestations that pacifism and the drive towards social cohesion, an orientation that will become more pronounced in the *Laws*, take in Plato's dialogue.[28] In fact, although the utopian intent of the *Statesman* is not as obvious as the *Republic's*, it is probably more ambitious in the sense that the dialogue tries to modify beliefs at a deeper level, by favoring a paradigm shift in the way political leadership is conceived. It is not about waging wars, or being a providential provider for the *polis*, it is about knowing how to weave people together and reinforce the social fabric. The figure of the weaver as an archetype of political leadership can still be of great use today. It sure fits well with the growing awareness of the social significance of relationality and connectedness (as opposed to traditional liberal ideals of independence and autonomy) promoted by feminist thinkers who subscribe to the 'Ethics of Care' in particular.[29] That being said, since this paradigm shift is pretty much the only edifying element present in the text, being a mirror for (philosophically educated) princes cannot constitute the dialogue's *core* objective.

What can this chief objective be, then?

One puzzling option left untouched by these remarks is the possibility that the core objective of the inquiry led by the Stranger (and of dialogue written by Plato) is strictly 'gymnastic' (both as an exemplification of dialectal method and as a training tool for readers), and that the πολιτικός, as the chosen object of inquiry is unimportant, or at least, secondary.[30] We haven't tackled that issue yet. Should we take the Stranger at face value when he claims that the only thing that really matters is the long-term training value of their current dialectical enterprise? And is it plausible to think that the main purpose of the dialogue has little to do with the portrayal of the πολιτικός ἀνήρ as such?

I think that even if we were to take the Stranger at face value, we could not infer that the main goal of *the dialogue* mirrors his own objective. Besides, there

---

28 By pacifism, I don't mean the absolute refusal to engage in war, needless to say; the necessity to be ready for war is clearly evoked at 307e. Rather, I refer to the refusal to put war at the top of the hierarchy of values and to organise the *polis* around it, a tendency strongly condemned by the Athenian Stranger at the beginning of the *Laws* and already perceptible in the *Statesman*. The attention of the πολιτικός is turned inward, toward civic cohesion, protection, not imperialistic ambitions, expansion and military prowess.

29 See, for example, Clement (1996) 2, 11–16.

30 Diès describes the *Statesman* as a "dialogue scolaire", (1935) LXIII, XXVI.

are also good reasons to believe that the Stranger's declaration should be taken with reservations. Here is why.

First, the Stranger's statement makes good sense from the point of view of a dialectician *qua* dialectician. But a dialectician is never *just* that. Given that he is, like the rest of us, an embodied person and citizen, with needs and social responsibilities, the Strangers' assertion should be taken with a grain of salt. As a practicing dialectician, defining angling, weaving, or any other expertise is no less of a useful exercise than defining what the figure of the πολιτικός can be. Any object or activity will do. However, the context in which the inquiry about the πολιτικός ἀνήρ is embedded – the tripartite search for the figures of the sophist, the πολιτικός, and the philosopher (257a, *Sophist* 217a) – suggest that there is a non-dialectical, extra-theoretical reason that motivates the whole dialectical enterprise we are witnessing as readers of this dialogue.

Providing a rigorous exposition on this topic is beyond the scope of my own inquiry, so I will limit myself to what I take to be an uncontroversial observation in light of Socrates' fate, alluded to at 299c. Whereas it is no doubt in the philosopher's interest to *disassociate* himself from the figure of the sophist, from a social point of view, the philosopher will neglect the possibility of an association with the πολιτικός at his own peril. Even if the Stranger's own commitment as a practicing dialectician is essentially towards dialectics, there is little doubt that the objective of Plato's tripartite project is coloured by the hostile climate between philosophy and society evoked in so many of Plato's dialogues, including the *Statesman*.[31]

Moreover, many elements of the Stranger's discourse reveal, albeit implicitly, that he is not as 'pure' and disinterested a dialectician as he might want us to believe. Irony is part of his toolkit.[32] For starters, his declaration that the main purpose of his search can't be to define the πολιτικός is normatively charged (285d–286c, 287a). There is, albeit sneakily, something deprecating about this suggestion. Who could deny that the type of discourse deployed both in the *Sophist* and the *Statesman* is ferociously polemical, despite its apparent cover of dialectical objectivity? One would have to be very naïve not to see that these 'dialectical examinations' ridicule, denigrate and (sometimes) elevate their objects almost as much as they distinguish and define them.[33] Understanding the general

---

31 Rosen's characterization of "the highest form of political existence" as the "transpolitical existence of (...) philosophy" does not contradict that state of affairs, quite the opposite, (1995) 190.

32 See 298a–299e for example. Cf. Diès (1935) LVI, Rosen, 36.

33 The *Statesman* starts with an explicit judgment on the inferior value of the sophist in comparison with the πολιτικός and the philosopher, 257b.

intention behind this type of indirect attack is easy enough in the case of the *Sophist*, but what about the *Statesman*?

Like Socrates in the *Republic* – another powerful war machine on the cultural battlefield – the Stranger seems to be on a mission to put *knowledge* at the top of the social hierarchy in the *Statesman*. That much, as least, is clear. But whereas the *Republic* uses sensational narratives that can affect the beliefs of philosophers and non-philosophers alike (such as the allegory of the Cave), the *Statesman*'s audience is limited to 'intellectuals'. As such, several aspects of this axiological combat are covert in the dialogue. Let me offer one telling example that is hiding in plain sight.

An excellent illustration of this covert tactic that aims at putting knowledge at the top of the social hierarchy is the equivalence established between πολιτικὸς ἀνήρ and βασιλεύς, between πολιτικός and βασιλικός, very early on in the dialogue.[34] These words are used interchangeably from the start and their equivalence is taken for granted throughout the text. That enigmatic feature is rarely discussed by interpreters.[35] Now, in a dialogue that values precise dialectical distinctions, this lexical enmeshment is surprising to say the least. It is especially startling in light of the fact that the Stranger also spends significant time and energy trying to purge the minds of his companions of the idea that the genuine πολιτικός corresponds to the traditional figure of patriarchal power exemplified by the mythological character of the divine, benevolent shepherd, Cronos. The rule of superior royal figures, Aristotle will suggest in his *Politics*, belongs to the past.[36] The message that Aristotle shares in plain terms is close to what the Stranger presents as the lesson of the massive digression on the myth of cosmic reversals (274e, 275c, see also 301e). In light of these declarations, the lexical convergence between βασιλικὸς and πολιτικὸς ἀνήρ cannot be the result of sheer carelessness. It has to be deliberate. What could its purpose be? The easiest way to answer the question is probably to identify the most evident consequences of this enmeshment.

---

34 As early as 258e. The Stranger starts by suggesting that four names are used to refer to individuals who possess the same science, namely πολιτικός, βασιλεύς / βασιλικός, δεσπότης and οἰκόνομος, but since the two last are virtually ignored in the rest of the dialogues, we can safely infer that it is the equivalence established between the two first that really matters for the Stranger's purpose. See Rowe (1995b) 15, n. 11.

35 El Murr is an exception (2015) 11–12, but his account (royalty as a tool to critique democracy) is very different from mine.

36 *Politics*, 1313a3–10.

The main outcome is obvious enough. The merging of terms plays a role close to what Diès has called *"transposition platonicienne"*.[37] The type of transposition I see happening here is mostly axiological. What I mean is that the equivalence established between πολιτικός and βασιλικὸς ἀνήρ is instrumental in *transferring* value from an ancient, prestigious figure (the βασιλεύς) to a new one (the πολιτικὸς ἀνήρ). More precisely, an attempt is made to transpose the prestige held by the eminent, respected, archaic figure of the king, to the emergent figure of the knowledgeable πολιτικός. Whoever the Stranger/Plato wants us to see as the genuine πολιτικός, he also wants us to see as the *kingly* one, the *royal* one, with all the connotations of nobility, authority, superior worth and eminence carried in the words. Needless to say, we are not within the field of 'purely' dialectical consideration here.

Let me be more explicit and try to better emphasise the shock value of such a move. Since one of the very few things we learn about the πολιτικός is that he is the one who possesses the *science* that corresponds to his name, and since βασιλικός and πολιτικός are used interchangeably, we end up with the surprising consequence that the truly *royal* man is the one who possesses πολιτικὴ ἐπιστήμη. Imposing or not, well-born or not, wealthy or not, "ruling or not" (293a), publicly visible or hidden, *he* who possesses that royal/political science is 'king'. In comparison with Socrates, who quips, in the *Gorgias*, that although he has never been actively involved in political affairs, he is the only citizen who took up political expertise (521d6–8), the Stranger's manoeuvre in the *Statesman* brings semantic subversion to another level. That kind of provocative subversion of the language of power was not uncommon in Socratic circles, though. Let us recall the following declarations attributed to Diogenes the Cynic: "At the slave market, Xeniades asked Diogenes: 'What can you do?' Diogenes answered: 'Rule men'."[38] This anecdote suggests that Diogenes considered his own merit as a virtuous, 'private' individual sufficient for leadership, arguably more so than other apparently powerful individuals like 'King' Alexander.[39]

Despite the absence of the outrageous 'in-your-face' style that characterizes the Cynics, I believe that a similar attempt at political subversion is found in the

---

37 Diès (1972) 400–01. "Peut-être y a-t-il eu des génies à s'imaginer inventer à vide et dans le vide, créer de rien leur œuvre et ne dépendre en rien de leur milieu. Pour Platon, création a toujours voulu dire mélange savant de violence et de séduction sur d'aveugle et fatales préexistences : ainsi se crée le monde et se crée la cité, ainsi se fonde une philosophie."
38 Diogenes Laertius, 6.29.
39 On the Cynics as 'kings', see Desmond (2008) 193–99, 207–08.

apparently serene dialectical examination led by the Stranger in Plato's *States-man*. Of course the rationale used to justify that subversion is very different in both cases. Whereas the Cynics provoked kings and argued that *they* were the truly free and powerful ones in light of their virtue, the Stranger/Plato argues that the possession of *political science* is what makes a king kingly.

It would be a mistake, however, to think that Plato was the only one who emphasised the role of intelligence and knowledge as the source of political power. I cannot agree with Skemp when he writes:

> Xenophon's Cyrus (...) is only a specially developed form of the ideal ruler who is a part of the political thought, or perhaps of political longing and desperation, of the Fourth century B.C. Isocrates had much the same hope and he expresses it particularly in his *Address to Nicocles* (...). Plato's criticism is in essence that they hoped for a leader with natural powers and irrational flair for leadership.[40]

A close reading of both Xenophon and Isocrates reveals that although they em-phasize the importance of the ruler's natural gifts and moral exemplarity, they too believed that what political leadership requires, first and foremost, is intelli-gence and knowledge. Thus, in his *Memorabilia*, Xenophon's Socrates declares: "Kings and rulers (...) are not those who hold the sceptre, nor those on whom the lot falls, nor those who owe their power to force or deception; but those who know how to rule (τοὺς ἐπισταμένους ἄρχειν)."[41] That such an expertise exists is pre-cisely what Xenophon is trying to illustrate in his *Cyropedia*. Indeed, Cyrus is pre-sented not so much as a singular, inimitable leader with great 'irrational flair', as he is offered as an example proving that "to rule men might be a task neither impossible nor even difficult, if one should only go about it in a knowledgeable way (ἤν τις ἐπισταμένως τοῦτο πράττῃ)."[42] When it comes to establishing the pri-macy of expertise and intelligence in the ability to rule, intertextuality is espe-cially striking between Plato, Xenophon and Isocrates.[43]

---

40 Skemp 61.
41 βασιλέας δὲ καὶ ἄρχοντας οὐ τοὺς τὰ σκῆπτρα ἔχοντας ἔφη εἶναι οὐδὲ τοὺς ὑπὸ τῶν τυχόντων αἱρεθέντας οὐδὲ τοὺς κλήρῳ λαχόντας οὐδὲ τοὺς βιασαμένους οὐδὲ τοὺς ἐξαπατήσαντας, ἀλλὰ τοὺς ἐπισταμένους ἄρχειν. *Memorabilia*, III, IX, 10–11 (translation by E.C. Marchant).
42 μὴ οὔτε τῶν ἀδυνάτων οὔτε τῶν χαλεπῶν ἔργων ᾖ τὸ ἀνθρώπων ἄρχειν, ἤν τις ἐπισταμένως τοῦτο πράττῃ. *Cyropaedia*, I, I, 3 (translation by W. Miller, slightly modified).
43 Consider the following passages. In Plato's *Statesman*, the Stranger declares: "But this much is clear, that the power of any king to maintain his rule has little to do with the use of his hands or his body in general in comparison with the understanding and force of his mind" (ἀλλὰ μὴν τόδε γε δῆλον, ὡς βασιλεὺς ἅπας χερσὶ καὶ σύμπαντι τῷ σώματι σμίκρ' ἄττα εἰς τὸ κατέχειν τὴν ἀρχὴν δύναται πρὸς τὴν τῆς ψυχῆς σύνεσιν καὶ ῥώμην), 259c. This is very close to a declaration

Still, there is something peculiar about the *Statesman*. In comparison with the ideal figures of rulers found in other texts by contemporaries, the specificity of Plato's *Statesman* resides first, in the idea that knowledge is the *only* thing that defines the πολιτικός, and second, it resides in the fact that close to *nothing* is revealed about the nature and content of this political knowledge. In the *Cyropaedia* and at the end of the *Economics*, Xenophon does provide the reader with concrete advice concerning good management and the ways in which one can establish and maintain leadership.[44] We find there the seeds of something that will take a more sophisticated theoretical form, and a specifically *political* form, in the sixth book of Aristotle's *Politics*. Xenophon's advice may seem rather rudimentary, but it is at least *something*. In comparison, Plato's *Statesman* seems to be a hollow shell, where political knowledge is constantly celebrated while not being concretely shared. Its description remains almost purely formal.

This brings me back to the question of the dialogue's core objective. Before proposing my own solution, the best way to evoke its elusive nature is perhaps to emulate the Stranger and to adopt an indirect approach. So here is a (non-exhaustive) list of what it *is not*. Although a serious political intention animates the *Statesman*:

- it does not offer an art of governance unlike what we find in Xenophon around the same time. It does not present a method to develop or secure political leadership;
- it does not offer a vivid (idealized) portrait of a virtuous leader as a source of inspiration for current or future rulers, unlike Isocrates's *Nicocles*, *Evagoras*, and Xenophon's *Cyropaedia*. Indeed, it says nothing – or so very little – about the character traits of the ideal *politikos*; his status, his origins, his education and so on.

---

found in Xenophon's *Oeconomicus*: "It would be quite right to call men who have many followers who agree with them "high-minded". Indeed, it would be reasonable to describe a man as "advancing with a mighty army" when there are many arms prepared to do what he has in mind. And truly great is the man who can accomplish great deeds by the strength of his mind rather than by muscle." (τούτους δὴ δικαίως ἄν τις καλοίη μεγαλογνώμονας, ᾧ ἂν ταῦτα γιγνώσκοντες πολλοὶ ἕπωνται, καὶ μεγάλῃ χειρὶ εἰκότως οὗτος λέγοιτο πορεύεσθαι οὗ ἂν τῇ γνώμῃ πολλαὶ χεῖρες ὑπηρετεῖν ἐθέλωσι, καὶ μέγας τῷ ὄντι οὗτος ἀνὴρ ὃς ἂν μεγάλα δύνηται γνώμῃ διαπράξασθαι μᾶλλον ἢ ῥώμῃ), *Oeconomicus*, XXI, 8 (trans. Pomeroy). And we find a similar idea expressed in Isocrates as well when he exhorts Nicocles as follows: "Show your authority not by harshness or by severe punishment, but by being superior to all in your intelligence and by convincing all that you can ensure their security better than they can" (ἀρχικὸς εἶναι βούλου μὴ χαλεπότητι μηδὲ τῷ σφόδρα κολάζειν, ἀλλὰ τῷ πάντας ἡττᾶσθαι τῆς σῆς διανοίας καὶ νομίζειν ὑπὲρ τῆς αὐτῶν σωτηρίας ἄμεινον ἑαυτῶν σὲ βουλεύεσθαι), *To Nicocles*, 24 (trans. Usher, modified).
44 For a description of effective leadership, see *Oeconomicus*, XXI, 2–12.

- it is not a 'mirror' offered to a current (or potential 'prince'), unlike Isocrates' *To Nicocles*. In other words, it is not an attempt at influencing a ruler's conduct by offering advice. In fact, it cannot reach or affect politically inclined individuals unless they have already been philosophically trained and remain well-disposed towards philosophy.
- with the possible exception of the Stranger's explanations on the only correct constitution and its best alternative at 291c–303d, it does not offer a demonstration of political expertise. This is unlike the *Laws*, and, arguably, the *Republic*, two works in which concrete political proposals are put forward.

After all these possibilities are discarded, what is left, then? What can the core purpose of the *Statesman* be if we refuse – as I think we should – to take the Stranger at face value when he denies that his main endeavor is to describe the πολιτικός ἀνήρ? In what follows, I want to suggest that the solution to the enigma is to be found *in* the very problems I evoked, especially the second one.

The dire need for this absent science *is* the message of the dialogue.

2 My Proposal: Reading the *Statesman* as a Protreptic Text

The most concise way to summarize the solution I propose would be to say that the *Statesman* belongs to the protreptic genre. Its core purpose is protreptic. But such a characterization is too general to mean much. So many ancient texts can be described as 'protreptic' in one way or another. Protreptic texts can target different audiences and attempt to 'turn' them towards different disciplines, aspirations, or ways of life. Their aim can be *mostly* protreptic, or they can play a protreptic role *somehow*, among other things. Certainly, many (most?) of Plato's texts can be described as playing a protretpic function one way or another. This is not a controversial claim to make. But their protreptic 'concentration levels' vary; the targeted audience of their protreptic effect varies; and the objects towards which they aim at stirring readers also vary.

So let me be more precise. First, my proposal is not to regard the *Statesman* as being animated by a protreptic intent in some vague way. My suggestion is, rather, that the *Statesman* is (or rather *was*) *first and foremost a* protreptic dialogue. Its main purpose at the time it was written was to steer readers in the direction of a search, a pursuit that was still ahead of them once they had read the last line of the text (I use the past tense deliberately – more on this later).

Needless to say, in light of preceding remarks, I don't intend to suggest that the dialogue attempts to turn the general public – youth in particular – towards virtue, or towards philosophy as a form of education, a discipline or a way of life. The *Statesman* is certainly not a protreptic to philosophy in the sense that the early Socratic dialogues are, for instance. For it is addressed to individuals *already* trained in that tradition and well-disposed towards it.

That being said, from the point of view of sociology of knowledge, one could claim that the *Statesman*, like the *Republic*, is a protreptic to philosophy in the more limited sense that it aims at creating a social order in which philosophical knowledge is honored and ranked at the top of the hierarchy of expertise needed in the *polis*.[45] The ironic ferocity with which the Stranger distinguishes the genuine πολιτικός from practitioners of other, highly regarded but "slavish" or merely ancillary arts, for example, and establishes him as the highest prescriptive source in the *polis* suffices to attest that this type of objective animates the text. However, as I have stressed many times before, since the targeted audience of the *Statesman* is already dialectically trained and well-disposed towards philosophy, Plato can't be on a mission to convince the *general public* of the superior value of philosophy.

Thus, it makes little sense to think of this dialogue as a protreptic *to philosophy* in either an individual or social sense. The *Statesman* does not have, I am afraid, the power to 'convert' to philosophy anyone who has not yet been exposed to it in more accessible and pleasant ways before, and its laborious, labyrinthine dialectical progression is not likely to convince the man on the street of the social value of philosophy either. Its protreptic audience can only be philosophers or philosophically trained/philosophically inclined political individuals. Now what is the object of this protreptic attempt directed at philosophers?

In my view, the most plausible hermeneutic approach is to see the *Statesman* as a two-stage protreptic to political science addressed to philosophers. The first stage is negative and polemical. It aims at dissuading intellectually gifted, ambitious individuals who may be tempted to embrace a life dedicated to human affairs to choose prestigious though 'slavish' activities, or politically subordinate functions such as the one depicted by the Stranger as ancillary arts. The second stage is more positive although it requires the soul of a pioneer, so to speak. It encourages them to go for the top position instead of subordinate ones: the kingly position insured by the possession of πολιτικὴ ἐπιστήμη. As such, it aims at triggering a passionate quest for that specific science, and possibly, to stimulate its

---

45 I already made the suggestion that this is the case of the *Philebus*, see Larivée (2009), (2011).

very creation. For where can that science be found? Not in the *Statesman*, assuredly. And, I would add, probably nowhere at the time Plato was writing his dialogue – or if present, still in an early development stage. This is what some powerful passages suggest, such as the one where the Stranger parallels the situation in politics to the vital necessity to engage in a search for expertise in the fields of navigation and medicine (299b–e).

My proposal, thus, is that Plato composed the *Statesman* as a protreptic to a science *that was still to come* at the time he was writing. That science was nowhere to be found, it was badly needed, and Plato believed that it could be developed.[46] In light of our own historical position – a position where political science is a well-established discipline with solid institutional programs and a long academic tradition – being able to sense the urgency of that call requires a special effort of imagination when we read the *Statesman*. And reconnecting with the intense hope that a form of salutary expertise similar to medicine could be developed in that sphere of human life is an even bigger challenge for the modern interpreter. But if we do make the effort to read the text in a perspective close to the original reader's, we come to realize that more than any other political dialogues, perhaps, the *Statesman* represents a powerful attempt to play a crucial role in the birth of that still embryonic field of knowledge. It was meant to stimulate young philosophers to get to work and to do whatever was needed to prepare the advent of this desperately needed and yet still non-existent expertise.

It is tempting to think that the *Statesman*'s protreptic intention was "proleptic", to use the expression coined by Charles Kahn. Plato would trigger the readers' curiosity while knowing that he is in a position to provide, at a later time, elsewhere, material that will offer an answer to the questions he raises in the *Statesman*. However, the *Laws* does not present us with that much desired and needed science (and even less did the *Republic*). For it offers a specific political program, a particular *politeia*. True, the *Laws*, a text in which we see a political expert right in the middle of his prescriptive activity – not only establishing laws for a specific community located in a specific territory, but also teaching the art of lawmaking to his interlocutors – gets closer to depicting such a science (mostly through *example*). But still, the Athenian Stranger's expertise is applied to the materialization of a specific program in the *Laws*. It gives us a 'live' illustration of the application of political expertise to a specific case; it does not teach or present such a science in a general, comprehensive way.

---

46 Does such a science exist? The possibility is evoked in a hypothetical fashion at 300e. One thing is for sure, some think they own it while, in fact, they don't, 302b.

Nothing prevents us from thinking that Plato taught this science, orally, in the context of the Academy. But it is only with Aristotle that we are presented with a comprehensive inquiry on πολιτικὴ ἐπιστήμη, in written form. Aristotle does describe the conceptual work he accomplishes in his *Ethics* and his *Politics* as πολιτικὴ ἐπιστήμη.[47] We find there a general and comprehensive study of politics that can guide legislators in their prescriptive work in a variety of different contexts.

In fact, although this exceeds the scope of the present text, it is interesting to note that both the *Nicomachean Ethics* and the *Politics* present multiple traces of intertextuality with Plato's *Statesman*.[48] In his review of *endoxa*, Aristotle explicitly evokes the *Republic* and the *Laws* as counterpoint to his own reflections on the best possible regime(s). His criticisms of the regimes put forward in these Platonic dialogues are brief and dismissive. However, even if Aristotle does not explicitly refer to the *Statesman*, an attentive reader will be struck by the recurring presence (sometimes obvious, sometimes subtle) of that dialogue in his texts. Could the seeds of what became Aristotle's foundational work on πολιτικὴ ἐπιστήμη have been planted by Plato through his *Statesman*? Be that as it may, the protreptic perspective I propose is the best way, I believe, to do full justice to the historical significance of the *Statesman* despite the frustration we rightly feel as modern interpreters when we read it.[49]

---

47 *NE*, 1094a26–b11. The term ἐπιστήμη is omitted in other occurrences of πολιτικὴ (1094b15, 1095a16, 1099b29, 1102a12, a21, 1180b31, 1181a12, a23) but we can infer its implicit presence in light of the first description. Since the *Nicomachean Ethics* and the *Politics* seem to be part of the same project, I infer that this description applies to both. For explicit mentions in the *Politics*, see 1288b22, 1324b24, 29, 1332a32.

48 Besides the parallel passages between the *Statesman* and Aristotle's *Politics* identified by Bonitz (259b–d: 1252a7, 1255b16; 259e: 1253b18; 293c: 1255b20; 291d: 1279a33; 293c: 1282b2; 294a–97b: 1286a9, 1288a1; 296b: 1287a33; 302e: 1289b5), the definition of moral virtue as mean, as well as the beginning and end of the *Nicomachean Ethics* are clearly reminiscent of the *Statesman*, especially *NE* 1094a26–1094b6, 1180b29–end, and the reference to the "true political expert" at 1102a, also present in the *Eudemian Ethics*, 1216a23–27 and the *Politics*, 1288b27. My suggestion is not that the *Statesman* would be "proto-Aristotelian", to borrow Lane's expression, (1998) 192. Rather, I propose to read the *Statesman* as a programmatic work that aimed at stimulating philosophers to found and develop politics as a science. *NE* 1181b12–16 clearly indicates that Aristotle saw himself as a pioneer in that regard: "Well then, since previous thinkers left the subject of legislation unexamined, it is better, perhaps, if we ourselves start a further investigation of it, and of the constitutions in general, so that as far as possible, that part of philosophy that deals with things human may be brought to completion." (Trans. Rowe).

49 Needless to say, my own position is at odds with Lane's when she declares that it is "not surprising that the *Statesman* has proved so infertile in later political thought", Lane (1998) 6.

Maurizio Migliori
The Multifocal Approach: The *Statesman* as the Key to Plato's Political Philosophy

The present contribution[1] requires a degree of patience from the reader for two reasons: 1) because the thesis I wish to uphold will (possibly) become clear only at the end of the exposition;[2] 2) because I assume an awareness on the reader's part of my texts on "How Plato Writes".[3] Here I can only succinctly mention three points.

I. Plato himself provides some indications on his mode of writing in the *Phaedrus*. Leaving aside the question of the *Agrapha dogmata*, I will mention that the philosopher notes the difficulty of communication, sets out the rules for constructing a good speech, and highlights the additional limits of writing, which requires a considerable degree of caution on the writer's part, since he must never write the *most valuable things*, to avoid possible misunderstandings. Finally, Plato speaks of how one can write in terms of a "game" (παιδιᾶς, 276d2), and of very fine games that are often so important as to become one's life pursuit (276d).[4] The *written game* thus becomes the hallmark of the philosopher, who is:

> He who believes that in a written discourse on any subject there is bound to be *the playing of a game* (παιδιάν), and that no work in verse or prose that deserves to be treated with much seriousness (σπουδῆς) has ever been written (277e5–8).

II. This "game" aspect accounts for one distinguishing feature of the dialogues: the author himself often complicates issues that he could discuss in far more simple terms. In other words, Plato clearly seeks not so much to instruct his readers as to lead them to think, to *philosophise*, by stimulating them with increasingly complex games.[5]

---

1 The English translation of this paper has been done by Sergio Knipe.
2 To prove persuasive, this thesis would require a longer and more complex treatment; to justify many of my claims, which contrast with conventional interpretations, I shall have to refer to Migliori (2013).
3 "Come scrive Platone" is the title of Ch. 1 of Migliori (2013) vol. I, 25–190.
4 At the time of writing the *Phaedrus*, Plato had already "published" a long series of dialogues, including the ten books of the *Republic*. In all likelihood, then, he had his own experience in mind when he wrote the above words.
5 In my works I have offered many examples of very evident 'games': see e.g. Migliori (2013) vol. I, 104–141.

https://doi.org/10.1515/9783110605549-003

III. If we view this particular method of writing in the light of the question of the succession of the dialogues,[6] we soon find that they follow an order of increasingly theoretical depth. Moreover, subsequent texts often solve problems that previous dialogues had left open.[7] On the basis of *substantial textual evidence*, we may hypothesise that Socrates' pupil sought to develop *a written maieutics*, a grand protreptic[8] composed by remaining faithful to what is stated in the *Seventh Letter*:[9]

> But nor do I think that delivering the argument (ἐπιχείρησιν) about these topics would be a good thing for men, except for the few who are capable of finding solutions on their own, based on a few indications. As for the rest, it would fill some of them with a mistaken and absolutely inappropriate feeling of contempt, and others with excessive and vain expectations, as though they had learnt splendid things (341e1–342a1).

As in the *Phaedrus*, Plato fears that his readers might fool themselves into believing that they know a lot of things because they have read and memorised them, whereas in fact they have not discovered – and hence learnt – anything at all. The writer must therefore display a kind of communicative reticence,[10] and address

---

6 With all due caution, we may regard the results of stylometric studies conducted by blocks – rather than on individual dialogues – as generally reliable. See Kahn (2008) 43–55.

7 Many examples of this have been provided by exponents of the Tübingen-Milan school such as K. Gaiser, H. Krämer, G. Reale, and T.A. Szlezák.

8 That is, a call to philosophise by also suggesting philosophical themes, data and problems in a provocative way.

9 I do not doubt the authenticity of the *Seventh Letter* in the least; as I cannot discuss the question here, I will refer to the contribution of two leading scholars. The first, the author of a fine old book (Pasquali, 1967, 42), writes with regard to the authenticity of the text: "proving it once more, if we were forced to do so, would require more time than intellectual effort. Rather than coming up with any new arguments, it would be best to collect those so often put forward over the last years, which are persuasive in their complete negativity, and show the unlikeness of the figure of a forger portraying neither a saint nor a sinner – which is what the heroes of fabrications tend to be – but rather a good man conscious of the great responsibilities he has taken up, often with limited success, and of the errors he somewhat reluctantly confesses. This would be a forger who, with no other aim but to make the whole task more difficult for himself, introduced in a chiefly political and autobiographical letter a philosophical treatise, which even at the time must have been intelligible only to those well acquainted with the evolution of Plato's later thought, while proving unintelligible to most people". The second scholar, Friedländer (2004) mentions Robin, who "maintained there was no conclusive evidence for their authenticity. Conclusive evidence? No. I repeat August Boeckh's methodological principle that only forgery, not authenticity, can be proved conclusively – in the absence of external evidence, to be sure" (236).

10 The most valuable things are not always Principles, nor are they always the same things: the progression from simple to increasingly complex dialogues, alters the whole value framework.

those readers who are capable of *proceeding on their own on the basis of limited indications*. This is precisely what Plato endeavoured to do with his own writing, by *stimulating* the reader with information and problems he must reflect on and work on.

A difficult presentation

In presenting his political philosophy,[11] Plato must not only come to grips with a difficult topic, but set it within the framework of his own dialectical-systemic vision, which he variously illustrates in his last dialogues. In brief, the fundamental concept at play is that of "relation". An object is always understood within the context of a specific relation, which means that reality is a complex relational web. This holds true not just for relatives, but for all entities, which must always be "contextualised". For instance, within a binary model of opposite terms, *doxa* is condemned: *episteme* is the only true knowledge, which concerns stable ideal realities; hence, *doxa* cannot be as true and indisputable – to the extent that this is possible in the human condition – as *episteme* (*Timaeus*, 29b–c). If instead we follow Diotima (*Symposium*, 201e–202a)[12] and adopt a ternary scheme, we get a different situation: just as on the ontological level between being and nothingness there lies the ever-changing reality which both is and is not, *doxa, which stands halfway between knowledge and ignorance,* carries epistemological value, to the point that can be certain or even true. Indeed, on the practical level it is no worse a guide than *phronesis* (*Meno*, 97a–c), while on the epistemological level it can even apply to the Ideas – such as those of beauty, justice, and goodness (*Statesman*, 309c).[13]

For instance, in Plato's early texts one of these things might be *what lies behind the question "What is X?"*, i.e. the Idea, which is only presented in later works; in these latter texts, the question might take the form of *"What is the relation between the Ideas?"* – and so on.

11 I will be focusing exclusively on the major triad comprising the *Republic*, *Statesman* and *Laws*, in order to note some of the key points in Plato's discourse; for a systematic reconstruction, see Migliori (2013) vol. II, 1018–1142; on the *Statesman*, see Migliori (1996).

12 Eros is neither beautiful nor good, yet this does not mean that he is ugly and bad. To make her point, *for no apparent reason* the priestess extends her argument to the epistemological level: there is a mean between knowledge and ignorance, namely *right opinion*.

13 To take another example related to the theme of knowledge and truth, the author constantly switches between two opposite judgements. On the one hand, he stresses human limits: in the *Apology*, the Delphic Apollo pronounces Socrates to be wise because he knows that "human wisdom is worth little or nothing" (23a6–7), which is to say that "in reality <his> wisdom amounts

The reality we are analysing must therefore be viewed in the light of a specific web of interrelations. What this means is that the moment in which he starts to make detailed references to his conception of politics, Plato must face the problem – inevitably raised by his conception of reality – of distinguishing between the ideal level and the empirical one,[14] between the model and its factual expression, while at the same time linking the two and thereby clarifying the difference and relation between the concrete and the abstract.

The *first point* to be noted is that the philosopher places little trust in human interventions. Events such as wars, famines and natural calamities produce effects that make themselves felt for years and show the limits of all rational intervention. Hence, we must acknowledge that

> the deity controls all human affairs, and chance and the favourable occasion (τύχη καὶ καιρός) cooperate with it. Furthermore, it must be admitted that these are followed by a third factor closer to us (ἡμερώτερον), namely art. For I believe that enjoying the help of an expert captain in a storm is more advantageous than not (*Laws*, 709b7–c3).

As everything depends on divine will and chance, human action only comes into play as a secondary factor. Still, in certain dangerous situations, human action is certainly useful, as is shown for instance by the example of the experienced captain. The author stresses *both the opportuneness of this intervention and its limits*, but the background is a pessimistic one: in Book 8 of the *Republic*, Plato describes the process of degeneration from a good state to increasingly worse ones *as an almost natural and/or inevitable process*. The reason for this is to be sought in the nature of the object: *all that is born is destined to undergo corruption* (546a).

This brings up a *second point*: the polis *is already in danger*. Mindful of the terrible events of the Peloponnesian War, Plato is extremely worried, most of all by the lack of unity. No Greek city is worthy of its name, since *it is not one but*

---

to nothing" (23b3–4). This view is confirmed by many dialogues – as one would expect, given that God alone is *sophos* (*Phaedrus*, 278d) – down to Plato's last work, in which he suggests that we "lead our lives according to that nature whereby we are almost complete puppets, who participate in truth to a small degree" (*Laws*, 804b2–4). On the other hand, Plato often argues that truth can and must be attained. In *Phaedrus*, 278c–d, for instance, knowledge of the truth is presented as the precondition for correct communication. In the *Laws* themselves we read: "Truth is the highest of all goods for the gods, and the highest of all goods for human beings; let him who wishes to be blessed and happy, partake of it from his earliest days, in such a way as to *live most of the time in truth*" (730c1–4). Therefore, *in one respect* we do not partake of the truth, but *in another respect* we can live truthfully most of the time.

14 Indeed, the relation between polities and their ideal paradigm mirrors that between concrete entities and the Ideas; in both cases, *Nous* plays a decisive role.

many. In particular, there are always *two* cities at war with one another: the city of the rich and that of the poor – although to these we may add *countless* subdivisions. By levelling these out, it is possible to make a city stronger than others that seem bigger but in fact are not, due to their inner divisions (*Republic*, 422e–423b). The greatest ill of all is that which divides the city and makes it *manifold instead of one*; the greatest good is that which binds the city together and makes it *one* (*Republic*, 462a–b).[15]

Nevertheless, social fragmentation is something irreparable and inevitable. The state springs from the multiplicity of needs: at *Statesman* 274b–c, Plato describes the condition of the "first" human beings, who were weak and an easy prey for wild animals. This condition fostered the development of arts, which were then brought together, giving rise to the political art: the art of ruling everyone, *taking care of the community as a whole* (276c).[16] Complexity, then, is intrinsic to the social dimension: at *Statesman* 287b–289c, the Stranger outlines the interplay of causes[17] that make up the sum of human crafts, the "civil society" which

---

15 Plato's underlying conviction is that "the ideal state is the one which attains *unity* in the most perfect way, while the imperfect state is the one in which *duality, schism and multiplicity* hold sway" (Reale 1997, 29).

16 At *Laws* 676a–681d, Plato provides a more detailed description of the birth of society and of the various forms of political organisation. A series of catastrophes force men to make a fresh start over and over again (Plato here applies to politics the "pendular" model presented in relation to the cosmos in the myth of *Statesman* 268e–274e; on this text, see Migliori (2013) vol. I, 534–537. In this narrative, a sort of deluge spares only mountain shepherds who have very little knowledge. In this context, there is neither social life nor law, but only a peaceful patriarchal society that abides by its traditions (678e–680b). Slowly but steadily, through socio-economic development, which leads to the reintroduction of agriculture, and through the essentially natural tendency for human beings to band together, the model grows more complex; this, in turn, engenders the need for laws and hence lawgivers (681c–d).

17 Plato stresses the circularity of reciprocal relations with the use of a game: he lists seven activities and ranks the *primary good* (τὸ πρωτογενές) sixth, which then 'forces' him to draw up the list again with the correct ranking: 1. *primary good*, the relation with nature necessary in order to obtain raw materials; 2. the crafting of tools, 3. of vessels, 4. of supports, 5. of protections, 6. of ornaments and amusements; 7. the art of the care of the body. Moreover, only for the first activity – almost to justify its place at the head of the list – does Plato state that it requires the action of the others. It is easy to see how this claim, which is certainly true, also applies to all other relations, insofar as every art makes use of tools it does not produce itself. Thus the author forces us to rethink the whole list, which should be viewed not as a linear sequence – with a 'before' and an 'after' – but rather as a series of links, with a circular flow.

manufactures things and/or engages in all the various human activities;[18] without all this there could be neither the *polis* nor the political art (287d3–4). What emerges here is a far more complex picture than the one that is usually attributed to Plato on the basis of the *Republic*.

Yet there is more to it: society is not made up of workers alone, but also – and especially – of *different* subjects. Reality is marked by diversity and hence by inner conflict, which is often framed in ethical terms, as the contrast between the best and the worst (*Laws* 627b5–8). Plato pays much attention to differences – in gender, wealth, and function – which are to be approached through different strategies. Gender differences must be confined to their proper sphere: in those sectors where they carry no weight, the range of action for women is increased. Differences in wealth are held to be of great interest (737b) on account of the contrasts they engender: unless a ban on private property is enforced, it is necessary to contain these differences through restrictions and rules, by avoiding precious metals and easy gains (741e–743e), and by more generally limiting the field of individual ownership. By contrast, in the case of labour Plato emphasises the importance of differences, in view of the principle of functionality,[19] while arguing that such differences must be redefined in the light of the primacy of the whole over the needs of its parts. The gist of the argument is that differences must not be dismissed, but brought together as parts serving a goal that belongs to the whole.

Finally, there is a *third point* that makes Plato's task more complicated, namely the link between politics and ethics: every adult male is at once an individual and a citizen. Plato stresses this unity, which emerges from his very definition of politics, which consists in the care not just of the *polis* but also of the soul:

> knowing the nature and conditions of men's souls, then, is one of the most useful things for that art designed to treat (θεραπεύειν) them; and this, I would argue, is precisely the task of politics (*Laws*, 650b6–9).

It is important to stress the co-presence of these two elements while steering clear of any one-sided perspective – in an attempt, for instance, to reduce Platonic politics to ethics. It is enough here to recall the definition of statesmen, as it emerges

---

18 Other activities are then mentioned, related to animate beings (the raising of animals and the keeping of slaves), then *servants*, understood as intermediaries (merchants, bankers, heralds and messengers), secretaries, priests and soothsayers, and finally the statesman's opponents, such as the sophists. In the closing section of the dialogue, mention is made of the direct collaborators of the statesman: the educator, the general, the judge, and the orator (303d–304d).

19 Each person must have only one occupation, (preferably) that to which he is naturally inclined.

from the first *diaeresis* of the *Statesman* in its final, revised version (258b–267c; 274e–276e): a guiding theoretical scientist who takes care (ἐπιμέλεια) of human society as *a whole* by means of persuasion rather than force. This point had already been made in the *Republic*: the wisdom required of the Guardians is no ordinary knowledge (ἐπιστήμη), but one

> which does not take counsel about some particular activity related to the city but about the city as a whole (ὅλης), to establish how it can best relate to itself[20] and other cities (428c12–d3).

We must accept the multifaceted nature of Plato's discourse and hence the co-presence of different goals, at different levels: Platonic politics simultaneously consists in the care of the soul, of the human being, of society, and of the state.[21] Significantly, Plato stresses that the underlying principle is always the same: "he who wishes to behave rationally in the public and private sphere" (*Republic* 517c4–5) must look to the Idea of the Good.

The contribution of the *Laws*

In addition to the three problems just outlined there is the problem of exposition. In a direct form of communication this might not be a major problem, but in the case of a series of texts that protreptically unfold by means of allusions, the question proves far more complex. Plato's thought can therefore more easily be understood if we set out from the *Laws*: as he has already addressed a number of questions in his two previous works, the *Republic* and the *Statesman*, here the author can be more explicit, for example as regards *the presence of different ideal models*. The Athenian states that he is about to make a surprising move:

---

20 As Plato's dialectical expositions suggest, this is the relation of the whole with its parts, of the parts with their sum, and of the parts with one another.

21 Just as significantly, Plato establishes the parallel between the soul and the city as a key element in the *Republic*. No doubt, this parallel should not be pushed too far, or else it risks oversimplifying what the author himself explicitly presents as an already simplified picture (*Republic* 368c–e; 545b). On the contrary, an effort should be made to pick up all the clues which Plato leaves behind to suggest that the question is a more complex one. For example, the list of the five kinds of state presented in Book 8 – aristocratic, timocratic, oligarchic, democratic, and tyrannical – does not directly fit within a triadic system. Moreover, when discussing the processes of degeneration, Plato brings into play a range of different factors that show just how complex socio-political reality is.

it will be clear to him who reasons it out and has some experience that we are establishing *a state that ranks second compared to the excellent one* (δευτέρως ἂν πόλις οἰκεῖσθαι πρὸς τὸ βέλτιστον). Perhaps one might reject it, owing to unfamiliarity with lawgivers who are not also tyrants. But it is in fact the most correct thing to describe *the excellent polity, and the second and the third* (τὴν ἀρίστην πολιτείαν καὶ δευτέραν καὶ τρίτην), giving then the choice to the individual who is charged with founding the city (739a3–b1).

Therefore: 1) there are various possible models, starting from the excellent one; 2) the *Laws* does not present the first paradigm, evidently because the *Republic* is more than enough; 3) the second paradigm might be opposed by those who believe that in the constitution of a model the lawgiver should be totally free, which is not the case here; 4) it is possible to suggest a third model; 5) all these models are suggested for the statesman, who is to select the one most suited to the situation at hand; 6) we can thus infer that no model is being suggested with the idea that it should be mechanically implemented.

The text also clarifies the relation between the various paradigms:

One should not look elsewhere for a model polity (παράδειγμά γε πολιτείας) but, holding fast to this one, endeavour to establish one that is as like to it as possible. That which we are now engaged upon, if it came into being, would somehow be the closest to that immortal model (ἀθανασίας ἐγγύτατα), and would therefore rank second. After these, we will describe the third, if God so will. For the present, however, let us discuss this one, what it is like and how it can become such (739e1–7).

The idea, then, is that of a progressively worsening series: the first paradigm embodies the highest degree of perfection;[22] the second[23] assumes the existence of some human limits and imitates, as far as possible, the first, the infeasibility of which the Athenian emphasises, almost in mocking terms: stressing the need for the utmost unity, he claims that it must concern not just wives and children, but also *eyes, hands and thought as though these were a single being* (739c–d). Plato thus outlines a *kind of unity that turns out to be excessive and unlikely.* Moreover,

---

22 This is further distinguished (739b8–c3) with reference to the complete sharing of things, by also recalling the ancient proverb that among friends all things are common. Plato ends his argument with a formula – "this holds in the case that in some place either it is thus now, or it will be in the future" – that is reminiscent of the formulas used in the *Republic* (and which I shall shortly be referring to).

23 Even this *second* paradigm is an ideal one, as is confirmed by the aim of the discussion: "let us attempt, then, first of all, to found the city *rationally* (λόγῳ)" (702e1–2). Moreover, in this case too, many will object that the lawgiver seems to operate "as though he were telling dreams or moulding the city and citizens out of wax" (746a7–8); the author instead invokes the right to establish a model (παράδειγμα, *Laws* 746b7) based on what is most beautiful and true.

he claims that a state of this sort will be inhabited by deities or the offspring of gods, who will find genuine happiness within it (739d) – a further indication that it is something *non-human*. In his discussion of equality, Plato sets out from an acknowledgement of the fact that *absolute equality is impossible to attain*. While this statement does not necessarily undermine the *Republic*, it certainly delivers a strong blow against radical interpretations of so-called "Platonic communism".[24] Finally, Plato stresses once more that there is always a gap between a theoretical model and its practical implementation:

> it seems really difficult, my dear guests, to find polities that are unquestionably valid both in practice and in theory (636a4–5);
> however, we must conclude that the arrangements described so far will never find such favourable conditions that they can be fully be carried out as they are in theory (745e7–746a1).

Plato goes so far as to state that a moderate and just power is *unlikely* (711d–e). We must hope *for a sort of miracle*: when a city has a virtuous tyrant and suitable lawgiver, "a deity has done everything it does when it wishes a city to be established" (710d1–3). It is no coincidence, then, that the model in question is placed under the divine aegis of Chronos, so to speak, whom we also find in the myth of the *Statesman*. Seeing that men are incapable of self-government, *like a good shepherd* the god entrusts them to daemons: human beings can therefore avoid all ills. We are to adopt that perfect model "of which the best current governments are an imitation (μίμημα)" (713b3–4).[25] It is not a matter of implementing the model, but rather of accepting it as an inspiring principle, a criterion. Imitation is the only possible path, since it would be an illusion to think that we can implement a divine model,

---

24 Indeed, it is necessary to find a criterion "so that by a rule of symmetrical inequality they may receive offices and honours as equally as possible, and may have no quarrelling" (*Laws* 744c2–4). In order to do so, we must acknowledge that there are two kinds of equality, which produce opposite effects. The first is purely quantitative equality, which assigns the same to everyone; the second is the loftier and almost divine qualitative equality, which is difficult to apply, since it seeks to assign the right measure according to the nature of the subject, so as to give each person what he is due (*Laws* 757c). As the application of this second kind of equality is always met with protest, we cannot forgo the former. "Thus, it is necessary to employ both forms of equality, especially in order to leave as little room as possible for that form which needs good luck" (*Laws* 757e6–758a2).
25 Imitation applies on two levels: the second model imitates the first, the polities imitate the paradigm.

> given that we are not like the ancient lawgivers who – it is now said – issued laws for *heroes who were the sons of gods, being themselves the sons of gods,* and legislated for others who had the same origins; rather, we *are men and the laws we issue now are for the seed of men* (853c3–7).

The second model, which is better suited to human nature, does not overlook "*the inborn weakness of humankind* in all its aspects" (853e10–854a1). However, we should harbour no illusions:

> even today this *logos* tells us that cities governed not by a deity but by a mortal cannot avoid ills and suffering; however, it is necessary to *imitate* (μιμεῖσθαι) by every means the kind of life attributed to the age of Chronos and govern our homes and cities by obeying *in both public and private* the immortal element within us. To the guiding action of *intelligence* (voῦ) we give the name of law (νόμον) (713e3–714a2).

By invoking the truth and *logos*, Plato emphatically states that cities governed by men cannot avoid ills. Furthermore, the philosopher stresses the need to follow the guidelines of *nous*, the immortal part of the human soul, which is to say pure rationality, in both the public and the private sphere, by establishing a close link between intelligence and the law. This point is confirmed by noting the key role played by laws:

> Of all knowledges, those related to the laws, provided they are rightly framed, will prove the most efficacious in making the learner a better man; for were it not so, it would be in vain that the name of the law (νόμος), which is divine and extraordinary for us, is associated with that of intelligence (νῷ) (957c4–7).

This connection is further emphasised on the basis of an ethical reflection: as each person must deal with non-rational emotions, such as pleasure/pain and fear/hope, reasoning (λογισμός) is required in order to determine what is best. "This, having become a shared decree of the city, takes the name of law (νόμος)" (644d2–3). Hence, man must only follow "the leading-string, golden and holy, of reasoning (λογισμοῦ), called the common law (νόμον) of the city" (645a1–2).

Finally, the text clarifies the perspective according to which political issues are to be approached. Given the fundamental relation between the whole and its parts, each individual human being must acknowledge himself for what he is:

> you too, wretched man, being a part (μόριον), always tend towards the whole (τὸ πᾶν) and strive towards it, small though it be. But you fail to perceive that all generation occurs so as to truly ensure happiness for the life of the whole (τοῦ παντός) – which does not exist for you, whereas you exist for it. For every physician and every skilled craftsman always does everything for the whole (παντός) and, by tending towards the greatest common good, produces a part (μέρος) for the whole (ὅλου), and not a whole (ὅλον) for the part (μέρους). You

complain because you ignore that what occurs is the greatest good for the whole (τῷ παντί) but also for yourself, in accordance with the power of common generation (903c1–d3).

This theoretical conception is not a rigid holistic one; rather, the text emphasises once again that the highest good also applies to the individual: there is no contrast between the fate of the city and that of its citizens – obviously so, given the dialectical link between the whole and its parts.

The problem of the *Republic*

Plato's difficulty in writing the *Republic* is perhaps understandable now. The philosopher must present an ideal model in all its abstract perfection. He must adopt a purely theoretical approach, but at the same time 1) he must not overdo things, giving the impression that he is presenting a useless utopia; 2) he cannot make his model too concrete, if he is to remain faithful to its nature. Plato must present the model in all of its perfection, while making it clear that its concrete implementation is a very different thing – in other words, he must present his model as something feasible, without giving the impression that it must be implemented as it is.

Plato's city, therefore, must not be described as an *impossible* one, because *"if it were so, we would deserve to be mocked, as we would be building castles in the sky"* (499c3–5). This *possibility* is repeatedly asserted, at times with a rather 'ambiguous' emphasis.[26] The most significant text is the one stating that this city is both *real and possible*:

> If, then, the best philosophical minds have ever been compelled by some necessity to take charge of the *polis* in infinite time past, or now are in some barbarian country unknown to us, or will be in the future, we are prepared to maintain with reasoning (τῷ λόγῳ) that the polity we have discussed has been, is and will be realised when this philosophical Muse rules the city. *It is not impossible that it exists and we are not speaking of impossible things*; however, we too will admit that these are difficult things (499c7–d6).

What we have here is a *very odd* text, given its references to "some necessity" and a "barbarian country" where the government of the philosophers might become reality, and the unlikely applicability of the model to *all states in any age*. What is particularly striking is the use of a *logos* to affirm a matter of fact. But perhaps

---

26 For example, in his discussion on the role of women, Plato states that his suggestion is *"not only possible but excellent"* (457a3), as it concerns things that are *"possible and useful"* (457c2).

the philosopher is interested in outlining precisely *the necessary and sufficient condition* for implementing the model, at any time, in such a way as to lend plausibility to his suggestion and avoid confining it within the realm of sheer (utopian) dreams.

At the same time, Plato intimates that the real problem is not how to implement this *model*. To do so, he draws a series of comparisons: to defend justice, there is no need to find an absolutely just man, but only one who partakes of justice to a considerable degree (472b–c); and a painter's worth does not depend on the existence of the beautiful man he has painted (472d). The same applies to the *polis*: it is a matter here of finding something that is *"very close"* (ἐγγύτατα, 472c1) to the paradigm (παραδείγματος, 472c4), adopted as a point of reference to determine *which polity is most similar to it* (ὁμοιότατος, 472d1) – *not in order to show that these things are achievable* (472d2).

> Then, you must not force me to show that what we have expounded in the argument (τῷ λόγῳ) is realised exactly in reality. Instead, if we can discover how a city may be governed in a way very close (ἐγγύτατα) to what has been argued, you must say that we have discovered that possibility of realisation which you demanded (473a5–b1).

What it all boils down to, then, is the development of a useful paradigm for human imitation; but Plato in the *Republic* cannot explain the reasons for it, lest this give rise to misunderstandings.

The decisive role of the Statesman

The picture is further clarified by the *Statesman*, a dialogue explicitly devoted to Plato's *political philosophy*. Towards the end of his discussion on the right measure and the art of measurement (*metretikè techne*) (starting at 283b), Plato sets out to clarify his task:

> After this discussion, let us move on to another one concerning the realities we are seeking and the general meaning of arguments of this sort (285c4–6).

This clear break introduces Plato's clarification: the definition of statesman is being sought not for the sake of politics alone, but in an effort to become skilled dialecticians. This claim may seem baffling at first, but it becomes quite clear once we correctly understand "dialectic" as being synonymous with "philosophy". Plato is emphasising that in relation to politics (also) it is necessary to adopt a philosophical, which is to say dialectical, approach. Indeed, the Stranger recalls that while easy demonstrations can be found for sensible entities, things of the highest value – such as incorporeal entities, which are the most beautiful and important of all[27] – can only be approached via reasoning (285d–286a). While politics is no doubt connected to empirical data, in order to adequately discuss it we must bring purely theoretical elements into play,[28] which make this a most difficult science (292d). Indeed, Plato refers to knowledge of the utmost importance and claims that those who ignore such knowledge are terrible politicians, who spoil cities (302a–b).

It is therefore particularly noteworthy that the dialogue on political philosophy makes no significant reference to the theme of absolute equality, but rather – as we have seen – emphasises the fragmented nature of the *polis*, and hence the role of the rational guide who is to govern this complex whole: the statesman. The latter cannot act as a shepherd does: the first *diaeresis*, which leads to the fallacious definition of the statesman as a *shepherd of human beings*, stands in need of correction. Invoking the myth of the reign of Chronos, the Eleatic Stranger points out that only a deity can act as a shepherd of men, since by virtue of its ontological superiority the deity is capable of taking care of *the whole* of society and of *each* of its components in *all* of its aspects. For the same reasons, a human being can be a shepherd of animals[29] but not of human beings (274e–275c). Indeed, the correct *diaeresis* ends (276d5–6) with a clear-cut distinction between the divine *shepherd* (θεῖον νομέα) and the human *caregiver* (ἀνθρώπινον ἐπιμελητήν). A statesman is someone who takes up the task of treating (θεραπεύειν) and taking care of (ἐπιμέλεια) the entire human race, as a whole (275d–276e) – a definition which is never disputed, but is rather confirmed in the closing section (292b–c). Given the connection between the whole and its parts, the statesman may be compared to a weaver: human society, in its complexity, requires a range of crafts to deal with all its various aspects, all its *parts*; a statesman is someone who takes care of *the whole*, of the entire *polis*, and who directs all the various partial activities through laws.

The main contribution of the *Statesman* concerns the nature of the model, as it removes the ideal paradigm from the six classic human polities, which are to be regarded "apart from the seventh: for this must be distinguished from all other forms of government, as a god is from men" (303b3–5). The "divine" model must

---

27 This is clearly a reference to the Ideas. Santa Cruz (1992) 565 n. 81 is not only confident that this is the case, but on the basis of lexical parallels already identified by Gulley (1954) 201, suggests that the whole passage (285d–286b) is possibly to be read as a commentary on *Phaedrus* 250a–d.

28 This emerges most clearly in the presentation of the perfect model in the *Republic*.

29 This is confirmed by the *Laws*: "we wield power over them [i.e. the animals], insofar as we are furnished with a better nature (γένος)" (713d5).

be kept apart from "human" polities; hence, *it does not fall within those that can be concretely implemented*. The paradigm, however, does not represent an abstract *intellectual* operation, but is rather *necessary* as a true form of government, of which *human ones* are only more or less valid (i.e. more or less rational) imitations:

> Of all the other ones we are discussing, it must be said that they are not legitimate; indeed, they are not even genuine forms of government at all, but only *imitations* of the just polity; and those which we regard *as having good laws* imitate it better, while the others imitate it more poorly (293e2–5).

Imitation and law become the fundamental concepts in human politics, as we have seen in the *Laws* – whereas they hardly feature in the *Republic* at all. The point made is an obvious one: as an instrument *imitating* the rules of the perfect ideal model, law cannot be present within it.

However, law poses one serious difficulty. It is to be praised *even though it is not something absolutely just* (οὐκ ὀρθότατον ὁ νόμος, 294d1),[30] since it imitates the system of scientific norms which constitutes the paradigm. This polarised verdict may be understood as a distinction between the *excellent* (the divine ideal state and the application of science) and the *adequate* (the human *polis* which, in a given situation, most approximates that paradigm). Nevertheless, the limits of this weak instrument call for a careful evaluation:

> For the differences of men and action, and the fact that no human thing ever remains static, so to speak, prevent any art, whatever it may be, from establishing in any sector something that is simple and valid in all cases and at all times. ... But we see that the law aims precisely at this, and that it is like an authoritarian and ignorant man, who does not allow anyone to act contrary to his will or to question things, even if this person has found some innovation that constitutes an improvement compared to the logic he has imposed. ... Is it not impossible, then, for what always remains simple to also apply to what is never simple? (294b2–c8).

---

30 Plato here makes skilled use of superlatives: he does so to define the most valuable thing (τὸ δ'ἄριστον, 294a7), which is to say the conscious king; the best, most just and absolutely valid thing (τό τε ἄριστον καὶ τὸ δικαιότατον... τὸ βέλτιστον, 294a10–b1), which cannot be ensured by law; and the "most just" (ἀληθινώτατον, 296e2) criterion to define the kind of rightful government, or "absolute justice" (δικαιότατον, 297b1), which genuine rulers must promote. By contrast, in relation to the factual situation and action of the lawgiver, Plato speaks of what is "better" (βέλτιον, 294c3, 296b6, 300d6), or uses other comparatives that perfectly match the superlatives just listed (δικαιότερα καὶ ἀμείνω καὶ καλλίω, 296c9); the criterion of the laws is described in superlative terms, as something most just and beautiful (ὀρθότατα καὶ κάλλιστα, 297e3), but only in the passage explicitly stating that the first criterion will be put aside.

This text may seem to stand in glaring contrast to the *positive* role that the law is expected to play. Plato does not merely stress the fact that the human condition cannot adequately be dealt with through a static instrument[31] and simple methodology, but presents the law as *an authoritarian and ignorant man*, which hardly suggests that it is something good and necessary. The whole operation is conceived in such a way as to bring out the following problem: "Why, then, is it necessary to pass laws, given that the law is not the most just thing? We must discover the reason for this" (294c10–d1). In keeping with his usual mode of writing, the author does not solve the problem himself, but offers the attentive reader the means to come up with a solution on his own.

One first answer to the problem is based on the aforementioned "common sense" element: it is impossible to govern the state "in a scientific manner" (295a–b), since it is impossible to provide suitable indications to each and every person at all times. We must do with some general guidelines, as a gymnastics teacher might do with a large group of students. Even the unlikely figure of a pure scient-ist cannot constantly follow each individual subject in such a way as to constantly change his indications: he too must limit himself to furnishing general rules, by suggesting what the best course of action is in most cases; in other words, he must resort to the rather inflexible element of the law. Yet this answer is not enough: for it makes the law out to be a "lesser evil", whereas Plato argues that it is a good.

The fact is that Plato's *deliberately* complicated exposition[32] *conceals* the presence of two kinds of law, which are presented in clear terms: "imitative" laws are laid down by an assembly, written by wise men, put to the test of experience, based on knowledge and studied in every detail; the other sort of laws are haphazard, disjointed ones that cannot be verified and which run contrary to art and science. After describing these laws, Plato concludes that their presence increases the irrationality of human choices, to the point of making life, which is already difficult in itself, quite unbearable (298a–299e). It is *this* system of norms that may be described as authoritarian and contrary to all improvement – characteristics that cannot be attributed to legislation designed to imitate the ideal model.

---

31 This static quality is emphasised by the classic image of writing: "in order to save themselves, the others [i.e. the imitative polities] must make use of the laws of this [i.e. science itself], fixing them in writing" (297d5–6).

32 I cannot analytically reconstruct this laboured exposition here: for a more in-depth treatment of the topic, see Migliori (1996) 144–164; 276–282.

> Therefore, in their particular areas these laws written by wise men will be *imitations of the truth* – as far as this is humanly possible (300c5–7).

The value of these laws is so great that Plato expects even the scientist, who is actually above all law, to respect the *nomos*. This last point is justified on the basis of practical considerations (the fact that a true statesman is rarely to be found) and of one underlying reason especially: failure to abide by the law paves the way for a greater ill, the attempt on the part of the tyrant or the sophist to deceitfully pass themselves off as scientists (300b–c), and hence to disregard the *nomos*. Imitative laws are acceptable, because they are a good thing, but an imitator of the scientist is not, since he will *inevitably be subject to error and/or deceit* (300d–e).

The *Laws* too tends to downplay the figure of the philosopher-statesman in favour of the laws:

> If one day a human being, born by divine grace (θείᾳ μοίρᾳ) with a suitable nature, proved capable of assuming such an office, he would need no laws to guide him. For there is no law or ordinance superior to science (ἐπιστήμης), nor is it right for intelligence (νοῦν) to be subject or in thrall to something, when it must have power over all things, if it is true and free by nature. However, *nowhere and in no wise – or only in the smallest degree – is this the case*. Therefore, it is necessary to choose a second path, that of order and the law, which see and discern what is mostly the case, but are unable to see the whole (*Laws*, 875c4–d 5).

The hypothesis is put forward here that – as always, through a sort of "miracle" – a true scientist is born, who has no need of any laws. However, since this would be an exceedingly rare event, it is necessary to choose a different option: the law, which considers only what "usually" and "mostly" happens. It is important to note the expression "only in the smallest degree", which accounts for the impossibility of accepting the exception, confirming the cautiousness of the *Statesman*: the state must be based on laws and not on the rise of outstanding figures.

The laws are designed to bring a modicum of rationality – as far as this is possible – into a vast and disorderly social context: an extrinsic order to be imposed upon a disorderly reality. What we have here is a confirmation of the ethical and political level of what Plato presents as his "cosmic" vision, according to which

> then it would be better to say, as we have often said, that there is in the universe a plentiful infinite and a sufficient limit, and above these a by no means feeble cause which orders and arranges years and seasons and months, and may most justly be called wisdom and intelligence (σοφία καὶ νοῦς) (*Philebus*, 30c3–7).

The disorder is always great, and the limit imposed by a *nous* is just enough to preserve reality and prevent its breakdown. This is also the case with the *polis*, which along with some laws requires, as a constitutive element, a good statesman who also acts as a lawgiver:

> It is certainly clear that law-making somehow belongs to the art of kingship. But what matters the most is not that the laws be in power, but that a man who is endowed with wisdom be king (*Statesman*, 294a6–8).

The problem is not the philosopher-king: implicitly correcting a (one-sided) reading of the *Republic*, Plato goes so far as to argue that:

> when a single man rules according to the laws, imitating him who possesses the science, we call him a king, without distinguishing in name he who rules alone according to the laws by science or by opinion (*Statesman*, 301a10–b3).

What is required is a rational and conscious figure, be it even an ambiguous one like the nightly council, which will keep watch over the city while abiding by those laws that it can and must change, if possible or required.[33] This rational intervention is Plato's sole, tenuous hope, and also explains his many dangerous journeys to Syracuse:

> Neither, my dear Glaucon, can there be any cessation of ills for cities or, I fancy, for mankind, unless the philosophers rule our cities or those whom we now call our kings and rulers take to the pursuit of philosophy seriously and adequately, and there is a conjunction of these two things, political power and philosophy, in the same person (*Republic*, 473c11–d6).

> For these reasons, which we had foreseen and feared, we declared, *under compulsion of the truth*, that neither city nor polity nor man either will ever be perfected until some chance compels this uncorrupted remnant of philosophers, who now bear the stigma of uselessness, to take care (ἐπιμεληθῆναι) of the city, *whether they wish it or not*, and the city submits to them, or else until *by some divine inspiration* (ἔκ τινος θείας ἐπιπνοίας), a genuine passion for true philosophy takes possession either of the sons of the men now in power and sovereignty or of themselves (*Republic*, 499a11–c2).

Once again, the "solution" is a sort of *miracle*. The same point is made, in essentially the same terms, in the *Seventh Letter*:

---

33 This creates a new duality, not without some tensions: from one perspective, primacy must be assigned to the law, which the statesman must respect, but from another perspective it must be assigned to the statesman as lawgiver.

> Mankind, then, will have no cessation from ills until either a generation of genuine philosophers attains political power, or else those who hold power in the cities, *by some divine dispensation* (ἔκ τινος μοίρας θείας), devote themselves to philosophy (326a7–b4).

If a state is entrusted to suitable individuals who abide by good laws, the citizens too will become good. This, however, requires good rulers, who operate in a rational way, are capable of enduring the pressure of the passions, and can be guided by difficult philosophical arguments. There is no "before" and "after" here, only the establishment of a virtuous circle starting from a situation which is *de facto* positive enough to trigger the whole process.[34]

Conclusion

With the help of the *Statesman*, I have sought to reconstruct both the progressive exposition of many elements of Plato's political philosophy and the function of his models, which are not to be applied but rather used as regulating principles. These are graduated models: the *Republic* presents the *first model*, which is developed at a theoretical level in connection to some key philosophical issues; within a dialectical framework, the *Statesman* explains the significance of the "utopian" model, the imitative nature of human polities, and the weight and role of the two pillars of human politics, the law and the statesman; finally, the *Laws* provides the *second model*, which is less bound to theoretical elements and takes account of a range of typically human limits.

Plato undertakes this whole task in a philosophical spirit and in the pursuit of political goals: he hopes that in some Greek city a process will unfold in accordance with the picture he draws in the conclusion of the *Statesman*:

> Let us say, then, that this is the end of the finely woven web of political action: when the art of kingship, taking the behaviour of bold men and that of restrained men, leads them to a common life, in concord and friendship, and creating the most glorious and best of all textures, clothes with it all other men, both slave and free, who live in the states, holds them together by this fabric, and governs and directs them, omitting nothing which ought to belong to a happy city (311b7–c5).

But a vain hope it is: by the time of Plato's death (347 BC), Alexander the Great has already been born (356 BC).

---

34 This is the only real utopian hope harboured by Plato, who calls for this circularity but then describes the opposite process, that of the degeneration of the *polis*, in the *Republic*.

Part II: **What Kind of 'Science' of Government?**

Dimitri El Murr

Theoretical, not practical: the opening arguments of Plato's *Politicus* (*Plt.*, 258e–259d)

Anyone interested in discovering the nature of Plato's conception of political science should take a close look at the first division that opens the *Politicus* (258e–259d). Yet this is seldom done by commentators, probably because the first step of the long *diairesis* that begins to unfold here is usually considered philosophically unconvincing. Indeed, not only does Plato treat as equivalent here *tekhnai* that are obviously very different in nature and scope (i.e., politics, house-holding, slave-management), he also identifies the political leader with the king. Two questionable moves that Aristotle in his *Politics* will significantly reject.

In this paper,* I wish to consider in detail *Plt.*, 258e–259d and Plato's argument (or, as it will turn out, *arguments*) to make statesmanship a 'gnostic' science. This very compressed passage makes several points whose relationship to the issue at stake is not immediately clear but whose individual importance for the political theory of the dialogue should be duly recognized.

1 Why *politikē*?

Before investigating how and why *politikē tekhnē* is situated in the genus of theoretical knowledge, let me first comment on Plato's decision to refer to the direct and constant subject of the dialogue by use of the terms *politikos* and *tekhnē politikē*. This very decision, I take it, illustrates from the start the essentially normative aspect of Plato's project about statesmanship in the *Politicus*.

As the works of Mogens Herman Hansen and others have rightly emphasized, these terms are not part of the Athenian legal lexicon, nor were they used in the speeches made at assemblies. So we must be wary of the retrospective illusion that consists in believing that what we nowadays call a *political leader* or a politician, was considered as such by the Athenians of the 4th century B.C. The fact that the term "politician" is derived from the Greek πολιτικός makes no difference. *Politikos* meant "statesman," and it was philosophers, mainly Plato, Xenophon, and Aristotle, who used this word in the positive sense to refer to a genuine

---

* This paper is an abridged and modified version of Chapter 4 of El Murr (2014).

https://doi.org/10.1515/9783110605549-004

political leader.[1] For an Athenian contemporary of Plato, what we call a politician would be a *rhetōr*, a *politeuomenos*, a *sumboulos* or a *stratēgos*, or could also be referred to by the phrase *rhetōr kai stratēgos*. By devoting a dialogue to the definition of the *politikos anēr* ('the political man'), Plato then makes a terminological choice that reflects a crucial philosophical decision: defining what a political leader ought to be, that is, defining the *true* political leader requires referring to him with a word expressing his proper expertise and the object it applies to.

I am not maintaining that, by itself, the choice of the word *politikos* is indicative of the dialogue's main concern. What is revealing is the central position of this word in a dialogue whose purpose is, *inter alia*, to define the specific science corresponding to this word. Proof of this is how, a bit later in the *Plt.*, when defining the art of clothing, the Visitor makes explicit, and justifies retrospectively, as it were, the inaugural terminological decision of the dialogue:

> V.: It is to these preventives and coverings manufactured from materials that are being bound together with themselves that we give the name 'clothes'; as for the expertise that especially has charge of clothes - just as before we gave the name of 'statesmanship' (πολιτικήν) to the sort of expertise that especially had charge of the state (τὴν τῆς πόλεως), so too now shall we call this sort 'the art of clothes-making', from the thing itself?
>
> (*Plt.*, 279e–280a)[2]

Whence we see that even if the word *politikos* is used in a non-normative manner elsewhere in the Platonic dialogues[3] to refer to the worst politicians in existence, the choice of using this precise term in the masculine takes on a particular importance in the *Politicus*. It also proves to be perfectly consistent with Plato's desire, in this dialogue as well as in the *Sophist*, to signal the actual possession of expertise through the use or creation of words with the suffixes -ικος or -τικος.[4]

It should now be clear that when the Visitor raises the question of whether we must *posit* (258b4: θετέον) the statesman as someone possessing knowledge

---

1 Cf. Hansen (1983) 36: '[...] the meaning of πολιτικός is 'statesman' and not 'politician'. It is used by philosophers in a complimentary sense about a true political leader. It never occurs as a legal term, and in the orators it is a hapax. The neuter τὰ πολιτικά may be used about 'politics', but the masculine πολιτικός occurs only once in some 3000 Teubner pages of Attic rhetoric (Aeschin. 2.184) in a flattering reference to the 'statesman' Euboulos.' See also Hansen (1991) 270: 'our word politician is derived from the Greek *politikos*, but that term is only found in the writings of Xenophon, Plato and Aristotle, never in the language of the law or in the speeches the Athenians listened to.'
2 Translations of the *Politicus* are all borrowed from Rowe (1995).
3 E.g. *Ap.*, 21c4: τις τῶν πολιτικῶν.
4 On the neologisms in the *Sophist* and *Politicus*, see Campbell (1876) xxv–xxvi. On the suffix -ικος in Plato, see Ammann (1953) and Chantraine (1956) 132–152.

(or statesmanship as a science, which, he says, amounts to the same thing), he thereby indicates that the whole point of the dialogue is to justify this initial "thetic" moment of the diairetic process.[5]

The first division then separates all sciences into two distinct classes: the sciences falling under the scope of *gnōstikē*, and those coming under *praktikē*. These two classes are formed on the basis of two distinct illustrative paradigms:[6] arithmetic and carpentry, respectively, two disciplines that are both skills using theoretical knowledge with a defined purpose. But, whereas the skills coming under *gnōstikē* only aim to know their subject, those falling under the class of *praktikē* make use of their expertise in order to produce something.[7] Hence we see that the division criterion here is not the possession of a specific type of expertise, but the use of the expertise *for a specific purpose*. Plato considers that the carpenter's knowledge includes serious theoretical elements, just as the mathematician's knowledge does,[8] but he wants to make clear that this knowledge has a purpose other than knowledge for its own sake, namely *producing something*. Therefore, the first type of knowledge (with arithmetic as its model) does not have any intrinsic relationship with action. As for the second type, it is linked to action, which is here equated with production, on the basis of the model of manual activity.[9]

Let us now consider why Plato claims, perhaps against all expectations, that *politikē tekhnē* falls under *gnōstikē*, and not *praktikē*.

2 Statesmanhip as gnōstikē or praktikē? (*Plt.*, 258e8–259d4)

[1] V.: Then shall we posit the statesman and king and slave-master, and the manager of a household as well, as one thing, when we refer to them by all these names, or are we to say that they are as many sorts of expertise as the names we use to refer to them? Or rather, let me take this way, and you follow me.
Y.S.: What way is that?

---

5 On the successive steps involved in dividing a genus, see El Murr (2016).
6 On the relationship between paradigm and *diairesis*, see El Murr (2006).
7 Cf. *Plt.*, 258e1–2: these practical arts 'complete those material objects they cause to come into being from not having been before' (καὶ συναποτελοῦσι τὰ γιγνόμενα ὑπ' αὐτῶν σώματα πρότερον οὐκ ὄντα).
8 See *Plt.*, 258e4–5: 'Well, divide all cases of knowledge in this way, calling the one sort practical knowledge (τὴν μὲν πρακτικὴν προσειπών), the other *purely* theoretical (τὴν δὲ μόνον γνωστικήν).'
9 Cf. *Plt.*, 258d8–9: αἱ δέ γε περὶ τεκτονικὴν αὖ καὶ σύμπασαν χειρουργίαν.

V.: **[2]** This one. **[a]** If someone who is himself in private practice is capable of advising a doctor in public employment, isn't it necessary for him to be called by the same professional title as the person he advises?

Y.S.: Yes.

V.: Well then, won't we say that the person who is clever at giving advice to a ruler of a country, although he is himself a private individual, himself has the expert knowledge that the ruler himself ought to have possessed?

Y.S.: We will.

V.: But the knowledge that belongs to the true king is the knowledge of kingship?

Y.S.: Yes.

V.: And isn't it the case that the person who possesses this, whether he happens to be a ruler or a private citizen, in all circumstances, in virtue of his possession of the expertise itself, will correctly be addressed as an expert in kingship?

Y.S.: That's fair.

V.: **[b]** Next, a household manager and a slave-master are the same thing.

Y.S.: Of course.

V.: **[c]** Well then, surely there won't be any difference, so far as ruling is concerned, between the character of a large household, on the one hand, and the bulk of a small city on the other?

Y.S.: None.

V.: **[d]** So, in answer to the question we were asking ourselves just now, it's clear that there is one sort of expert knowledge concerned with all these things; whether someone gives this the name of expertise in kingship, or statesmanship, or household management, let's not pick any quarrel with him.

Y.S.: I agree - why should we?

V.: **[3]** But this much is clear, that the power of any king to maintain his rule has little to do with the use of his hands or his body in general in comparison with the understanding and force of his mind.

Y.S.: Clearly.

V.: **[4]** Then do you want us to assert that the king is more closely related to the theoretical sort of knowledge than to the manual or generally practical sort?

Y.S.: Of course.

V.: **[5]** In that case we shall put all these things together - the statesman's knowledge and the statesman, the king's knowledge and the king - as one, and regard them as the same?

Y.S.: Clearly (*Plt.*, 258e8–259d4).

This rather difficult passage raises many problems. But perhaps the main issue concerns the complex structure and overall validity of the Visitor's argument here. At the very least, this page from the *Politicus* did not convince the rare commentators who took an interest in it, notably because, according to them, the argument is 'more persuasive than strict,' or even 'not just invalid, but flagrantly so.'[10] Before moving to the questions this passage raises regarding the nature and status of statesmanship, we should therefore begin with determining as precisely as possible what exactly the Visitor wishes to prove, and how he goes about doing it.

2.1 The structure of the passage

As the last lines of the passage demonstrate, its general purpose is to make it possible to situate the art of statesmanship in one of the two forms of knowledge that have previously been differentiated. I take the structure of the passage to be as follows:[11]

[0] Initial question: is statesmanship a γνωστική or a πρακτική science?

[1] The art of statesmanship, the art of kingship, the art of being a slave-master, and the art of household management are one and the same expertise (258 e8–12)

[2] Proof of [1] (259a1–c5)

    [a] A private citizen can be a genuine king provided he possesses the science of kingship

    [b] The household manager and the slave-master have the same expertise (259b7–8)

    [c] With respect to government, there is no difference between a big *oikos* and a small *polis* (259b9–11)

    [d] Conclusion: statesmanship, kingship, and household management are one and the same expertise (259c1–5)

[3] Kings govern with their intelligence, not through physical force (259c6–9).

[4] The science of kingship is a γνωστική science (259c1–d2).

[5] Answer to the initial question: the science of kingship and statesmanship belong to the class of γνωστική (259d3–4).

---

10 Rowe (1995) 179; 'It may be best to conclude that the argument is more persuasive than strict'; Cooper (1999) 169: 'I think myself that the Visitor's argument here is not just invalid but flagrantly so […].'

11 The order of the text transmitted by the manuscript tradition has been doubted. The last editor of the *Politicus* (D. Robinson, in Duke *et al.*, 1995) followed, with a minute variation, a suggestion made by Sandbach (1977) 50–52 and modified the text edited by Burnet (and Diès) by placing 259d4–6 after 259b6. There is no need for such a modification. Cooper (1999) 168, n. 4 unhesitatingly calls it 'a stunning example of editorial hubris and ignorance.' As Rowe (1995) 180 has convincingly shown, it does not help in clarifying the argument.

I have here summarized the progression of the passage, but I have not yet said anything about its *logical* structure. Unsurprisingly, it is on this very point that the thorniest problems arise. Indeed, although the goal of this page is perfectly clear (determining whether we should place statesmanship in the theoretical or the practical sciences), the means implemented to reach it are distinctly less so.[12]

The Visitor intends to show that political science is a 'theoretical' science (γνωστική), just like arithmetic or geometry. Now, to do this, he begins by asking a question not only about the statesman's expertise, but also about the king's, the slave-master's, and the household manager's, a question whose relationship with the preceding lines is not so clear. The question, which recalls the beginning of the *Sophist*,[13] is: do these names correspond to one and the same form of expertise, or are there as many forms of expertise as there are names?

Hence we see that the Visitor assigns himself two distinct tasks: on the one hand, he wishes to determine whether political science is practical or theoretical (= [0]) and on the other hand, whether the statesman, king, slave-master, and household manager possess the same expertise (= [1]). The question that arises then is: how does the Visitor reach the argument's general conclusion? How does the demonstration of point [1] make it possible to fulfil the first task and reach the conclusion that political science is a "theoretical" science (= [5])?

There is yet another difficulty. Before young Socrates is even able to formulate an answer to the question on the statesman, king, slave-master, and household manager, the Visitor immediately proposes that young Socrates follow him and 'let [him] take this way' (258e11: μᾶλλον δέ μοι δεῦρο ἕπου). Why such an abrupt move? In my view, this is a way of indicating that the arguments that follow aim to justify the initial comparison (= [1]), which appeared to come out of nowhere, and whose utterance may have seemed as abrupt to young Socrates as it does to us. If this is correct, the arguments that span from 259a1 to c5 (=[2]) serve the purpose of setting up the demonstration of point [1], according to which the statesman, king, household manager, and slave-master have the same expertise. If this is indeed the case, then it is a question of understanding how the Visitor proves point [1] with point [2] and, more precisely, what role is played in this demonstration by the argument at 259a1–b6 (= [2][a]), showing that any private individual can be considered a genuine king provided he possesses the science of kingship.

---

12 See Rowe (1995) 179 and the very suggestive analysis of Brown (2009), which has shaped my view of this passage.

13 See *Sph.*, 217a.

So the two questions facing us are: how is the unity of the science of government demonstrated (= [1]), and how do we infer from this that the science of kingship (and political science) is included in the class of *gnōstikē*? Let us consider the two questions and the segments of text corresponding to them in that order.

2.2 Why the statesman, king, household manager, and slave-master have the same expertise (*Plt.*, 259a1–c5 =[2])

At 259a1–b6 (= [2][a]), the Visitor puts forward a conditional line of argument (259a1–2: εἴ..., ἆρ' οὐκ ἀναγκαῖον...) that he will apply by analogy (259a6–8: ὅστις..., ἆρ' οὐ φήσομεν...) to the situation of the statesman. If a private individual has an expertise which allows him to advise a doctor in public employment whose name corresponds to the same expertise, it is then necessary to assign this same name to the private individual. Similarly, the king's advisor ruling over a given territory should be recognized as possessing royal expertise. Whether one actually rules or not thus makes no difference; it is abiding by the knowledge one possesses that determines the legitimacy of the name one has been assigned. Therefore, the person who will legitimately be called king is he who possesses the science of kingship: what makes someone the 'true king' (259b1: ἀληθινοῦ βασιλέως), whether or not he actually rules, is the science of kingship he possesses.

In the next lines, 259b7–c5 (= [2] [b,c,d]), the Visitor ensures that he has young Socrates' agreement on a new point, the equivalence between the household manager and the slave-master: 'next,[14] a household manager and a slave-master are the same thing' (259b7: καὶ μὴν οἰκονόμος γε καὶ δεσπότης ταὐτόν).[15] The connection with the previous point is not immediately obvious, but it appears much more natural as soon as it is observed that household managers, like slave masters, are *private* individuals, simple people exercising their expertise in the sphere of the *oikos*. One could nevertheless ask why young Socrates so readily agrees (cf. 259b8: τί μήν;) to identify these two types of expertise that seem rather far apart. On this point, it should be noted that the translation of *oikos* or *oikēsis* as "house" is an under-translation that does not render the significant economic dimension of the *oikos*, a unit encompassing both the private home, and for rich

---

14 On καὶ μήν in the "progressive" sense, used to introduce a new argument or a new point, see Denniston s.v. καὶ μήν (1).

15 Diès (1934) 4 translates this sentence as follows: 'il en sera de même du chef de la maison et du maître des esclaves.' This translation is perfectly possible but makes less sense. For a good discussion, see Helmer (2010) 213–215.

land-owners, production facilities (including slaves and other workers).[16] If young Socrates agrees, it is doubtlessly because managing the *oikos* and the slaves actually fell to the same person. Indeed, for the master of the *oikos*, managing the *oikos* includes, even if it is not limited to, managing the work of the slaves that are part of it.[17] So at this stage of the argument we can consider as established, on the one hand, that only possession of the expertise of kingship is a criterion for determining who is king, and on the other, that the knowledge of the *oikonomos* and the *despotēs* are one and the same.

The existence of large scale *oikoi* explains, at least in part, why in the following comment (= [2][c]) the Visitor notes that, from the point of view of government (*cf.* 259b10: πρὸς ἀρχήν), there is no difference between a large *oikos* and a small city. If indeed an *oikos* can be so big as to include a large private residence and an entire manufacturing business requiring the work of employees and slaves, its size can only differ from a small city by a small degree.[18] If this is the basis of the Visitor's argument, then it must be recognized that it is quite fragile: the *fact* that some cities and *oikoi* are of comparable size does not prove that the government of *all* cities and *all oikoi* depends on the same science.

In reducing the quantitative difference between the *oikos* and the *polis*, I believe the Visitor seeks to ensure young Socrates' agreement, an agreement he immediately obtains without any hesitation (*cf.* 259b11: οὐδέν). But the basis of his argument lies elsewhere, and has nothing to do with reducing this quantitative difference. Only the large *oikoi* are of course comparable to (small) cities, but what is important is that from the point of view of leadership, Plato thinks that the quantitative criterion is simply not relevant. What the Visitor thus seeks to do here is rid himself of the criterion of the number of people governed, which he does not consider decisive for distinguishing knowledge applied to the *oikos* from knowledge applied to the *polis*. Yet, from there, should one conclude, as the Visitor does, that the science of household management and political science are one and the same?[19] After all, is it not the type, or the nature, of governed individuals

---

16 See Rowe (1995) 179.
17 On the direction of slaves in the *Laws* and its relation to Greek law, see Morrow (1939) 25–46, who shows that, at least in the *Laws*, the manager of an *oikos* and the master of slaves are one and the same.
18 Cephalus, who hosts the conversation we know as the *Republic*, owned a weapon factory which employed more than a hundred slaves, if we are to believe his son Lysias: see *Against Eratosthenes*, 19 (καὶ ἀνδράποδα εἴκοσι καὶ ἑκατόν). On the *oikos* as production and consumption unit, see Netting *et al.* (1984) and Gallant (1991) 12–13.
19 Interestingly, in the descending order of reincarnations in the *Phaedrus*, the πολιτικός and the οἰκονομικός are paired and rank third together with the χρηματιστικός (248d5).

(slaves, freemen, or citizens, for example), not just their number, that is important? I will come back to this issue later, when I consider Aristotle's criticism of this argument.

The Visitor can now draw his conclusion (= [2][d]), and answer the question that he raised a few lines above (*cf.* 259c1: ὃ νυνδὴ διεσκοπούμεθα) when he embarked on the arguments examined in this paper. From the point of view of government, *oikonomikē* and *despotikē* are one and the same science, and the same is true for *oikonomikē* and *politikē*. So it is not difficult to infer, by transitivity, that with respect to governing people, these three sciences are identical.

In the course of the argument, the Visitor eliminated two criteria he considers irrelevant. Whether one is actually a king or not is not a pertinent criterion for determining who has the science of kingship, because anyone is a 'king' (βασιλικός) on the condition that he possesses this science. Similarly, the number of individuals governed cannot help in determining who is a true political expert, because the size of the governed body (a few individuals, an *oikos*, a *polis*...) makes no difference as far as the expertise is concerned.

Why is that important? Because these two arguments make it possible to eliminate the reasonable objection according to which the arts of the 'private' sphere are *essentially* different from the arts of the 'public' sphere. By showing that neither the criterion of public recognition nor the number of people governed is relevant for the definition of the science of governing humans, and by establishing the equivalence between the expertise of the statesman, the household manager, and the slave-master, the Visitor can conclude that only one science deals with governing people, whether one calls it kingship, statesmanship, or household management.[20]

2.3 Statesmanship as *gnōstikē* (*Plt.*, 259c6–d4 = [3,4,5])

How, in the remaining lines of the passage, is the initial question (= [0]) answered? The Visitor continues by maintaining that kings use their intelligence and the force of their minds to rule, not their physical strength (= [3]), an argument he considers as obvious (*cf.* 259c6: ἀλλὰ μὴν τόδε γε δῆλον, echoing 259c1: φανερόν) as the one he has just formulated (the equivalence between the expertise of kingship, statesmanship, and household management). Because the king is alone be-

---

20 Note that the Visitor presupposes the identity of political and kingly science, which he never demonstrates. But I do not see this as a major flaw in the argument. See *infra*.

fore a large number of subjects, whom he therefore does not have sufficient physical strength to dominate, it is obvious that the king rules using something other
than brute force. If he rules, it is through 'the understanding and force of his
mind' (259c8: πρὸς τὴν τῆς ψυχῆς σύνεσιν καὶ ῥώμην), thus with his knowledge.
The obviousness of the case considered here, i.e. the case of the king, actually
explains why the Visitor chose it in the first place: it is indeed a 'pure' case, in
which the theoretical and non-practical aspect of the expertise in government is
clearly visible. The choice of one or the other type of expertise considered previously would have been markedly less clear, since the slave-master may use his
arms to direct the slaves, or the household manager may work alongside other
members of the community. The Visitor then concludes from this that the expertise of kingship does not have much to do with practical knowledge, as previously
defined, and that the science of *kingship*, not *political science*, should therefore
belong to the class of theoretical sciences.[21] Yet, because it has been established
before that the criterion of the number of people governed is not relevant for determining the art of government, and that the science of governing people is
unique, regardless of its name, it is possible to conclude in the end that *political*
science as such is a *gnōstikē* science.

Regardless of how credible this analysis is thought to be, I claim that this
passage is better structured and more philosophically convincing than most commentators maintain. It is true, however, that to demonstrate that political science
is a theoretical science, Plato has used a complex set of arguments, whose details
seem somewhat remote from the local issue addressed in the passage. He did so,
I believe, because these arguments have a great importance for, and a great impact on the rest of the investigation. To the examination of the philosophical issues raised by these arguments I now turn.

3 The unity of the science of government

As we saw previously, the Visitor holds in this passage that there is no difference
between the expertise required for running a large *oikos* and a small city. Indeed,
the Visitor is careful to compare a *big* household (μεγάλης οἰκήσεως) and a *small*

---

21 As Giuseppe Cambiano pointed out to me, the Visitor here uses a comparative (259d1:
οἰκειότερον), which seems to imply that political science has some relationship with *praktikē*. In
my view, Plato is here looking ahead at the next step of the *diairesis*, where the *prescriptive* nature of political science and its indirect relationship with action will become clear. Notice also
that the Visitor refers surprisingly to πολιτικὴ πρᾶξις at the very end of the dialogue (311b8).

city (σμικρᾶς πόλεως). I have already noted that, in some cases, the *oikos* could have impressive dimensions and bring together, in addition to the members of the family, a large number of individuals, which would make it similar, to some extent, to a small city. But it must be noted that the argument claims to be much more general: it is not a question of maintaining that some *oikoi* are *de facto* analogous to small cities; rather, it states that the criterion of the number of people governed is irrelevant in differentiating methods of government.

The argument that there is no difference between governing a city and an *oikos* would appear to be unusual, at best, or even utterly implausible. This, at least, is the opinion of Aristotle, who devotes a large part of the first chapter of his *Politics* (I, 1, 1252a7–23) to criticizing it.[22] Consider Aristotle's main argument against the Visitor's analysis.[23]

> Those,[24] then, who think (ὅσοι μὲν οὖν οἴονται) that the positions of statesman, king, household manager, and master of slaves (πολιτικὸν καὶ βασιλικὸν καὶ οἰκονομικὸν καὶ δεσποτικόν), are the same (εἶναι τὸν αὐτόν), are not correct (οὐ καλῶς λέγουσιν). For they hold that each of these differs not in kind, but only in whether the subjects ruled are few or many: that if, for example, someone rules few people, he is a master; if more, a household manager; if still more, he has the position of statesman or king– the assumption being that there is no difference between a large household and a small city-state.
>
> (*Pol.* I, 1, 1252 a 7–13)[25]

This passage from the *Politics*, like other later ones for the same work, seeks to show that the *oikos* and the city fall under two specifically distinct types of leadership.[26] What differentiates them is that the two forms of community do not have

---

22 The criticism of the thesis claiming that οἰκονομική and πολιτική are one and the same expertise runs through the whole of the first book of Aristotle's *Politics*. For a defence of that view, see Natali (1979–1980). On the polemical unity of *Politics* book 1 and Plato's *Politicus*, see Schofield (1990) 16–20. On the importance of the *Politicus* for Aristotle's *Politics* as a whole, see Ricken (2008) 248–261 who compares the presence of the *Politicus* in the *Politics* to the citation from Augustine's *Confessions* (I, 8) opening Wittgenstein's *Philosophical Investigations*, and writes: 'Beinde sind eine Hommage an den grossen Gegner, mit dem das folgende Werk sich auseinandersetzen wird.' (249)

23 See Natali (1981) who shows the important role played by the opening divisions of the *Politicus* in the elaboration of Aristotle's conception of practical science. On the importance of the *oikos* in Aristotle's conception of the *polis*, see Brendan Nagle (2006).

24 On the plural and Aristotle's Socratic targets in this passage, see El Murr (2014) 104–106.

25 Translation from Reeve (1998).

26 On the direction of slaves and political authority, see *Pol.*, I, 3, 1253b15–20, I, 7, 1255b16–18, and VII, 3, 1325a27–30. On the direction of the *oikos* and political authority, see *Pol.*, I, 7, 1255b19–20.

the same purpose. The family, brought together in the *oikos*, has life and the satisfaction of needs as its purpose, whereas the city, which is composed of families, aims for the good life (*Politics*, I, 2, 1252b10–14 and 27–30). The good of the *oikos* and that of the city are for Aristotle specific goods that cannot be identified. Consequently, the science of the *oikonomos* and that of the *politikos* cannot be the same, since they are intended for individuals of different types, and for different forms of community, each aiming for its own good.

Does Aristotle's criticism invalidate the position Plato defends in our *Politicus* passage? Let us consider the argument based on the analogy with medicine (= [2][a]) which I take to be crucial for the overall argument of the dialogue. Directly in line with the text preceding our passage, where the Visitor recalls that arithmetic and the arts in the same family 'don't involve any practical actions' (258d5: ψιλαὶ τῶν πράξεών εἰσι), the argument from 259a1–b6 shows that the criterion determining who is really king is the possession of the expertise of kingship, or, what the king *knows*, and not what he *does*. Of course, the Visitor says nothing, for the time being, about the content of this expertise, which is conceived independently of all action. But the analogy with medicine, whose Socratic backdrop doubtlessly needs no reminder, shows that just like a doctor must know what is good for the body, the true king must know what is good for those he governs. The end of the dialogue will specify how we must understand the good of the city and of the people it includes. But it is clear here that the Visitor emphasizes the general knowledge the expert must possess in order to do the right thing, and not the particular knowledge specific to his action. Plato would therefore have no trouble conceding to Aristotle that the particular actions of a master toward his slaves differ from the actions of a head of household toward the members of his *oikos*. But this in no way changes the fact that with respect to governing people, all these types of knowledge presuppose knowledge of what is good for people, a form of knowledge that guides each particular action. On this point, the difference separating Plato from Aristotle is obvious: for the latter, what is good for a spouse is essentially different from what is good for a slave, or a citizen; not so for Plato. Hence Plato does not reduce political science to the expertise of a household manager or a slave-master: he shows, on the contrary, what all sciences whose mission is to govern people have in common, regardless of who they are, and regardless of their community. All sciences presuppose knowing (hence their belonging to the genus of *gnōstikē*) what is good for humanity, and consequently, how to govern in a particular manner.[27]

---

27 This last paragraph owes a great deal to the perceptive analysis of Brown (2009).

4 Knowing and Ruling

In keeping with the preceding analysis, let us now return to the argument the Visitor introduces by way of an analogy with medicine. Whether one is in power (*cf.* 259b3: ἄντε ἄρχων) or a private individual (*cf.* b3–4: ἄντε ἰδιώτης), only the possession of the knowledge of kingship justifies one being called a king. As I noted previously, this argument is not only crucial for the Visitor's demonstration in our passage: it is also, and doubtless even more, essential for the political theory defended in the *Politicus*.

First, we should not minimize the paradoxical (in the etymological sense) force of this argument. Indeed, this argument shows that the social or political status of the individual has no relevance with respect to knowing if such and such person is a genuine statesman. A private individual can be a genuine statesman just as well as a public official.

The fact that this argument forms the basis for the Socratic identification of the domestic arts with the art of the statesman clearly indicates that Plato places his investigation on the nature of political science in the same category as the one he assigns Socrates, e.g., in the *Gorgias*, and whose paradoxical (and provocative) force is widely recognized. We know the extent to which, in this dialogue and in others, Socrates calls into question the Athenian ideology devaluing the private individual remaining in the background of public life, in favour of the person devoting his energy to the life of the city.[28] It is indeed the same Socrates, who in the *Gorgias* tells Polus that he is not a statesman (473e6: οὐκ εἰμὶ τῶν πολιτικῶν), and to Callicles, a bit later, that he is one of the rare Athenians 'to take up the true political craft and practice the true politics.' (521d7–8: ἐπιχειρεῖν τῇ ὡς ἀληθῶς πολιτικῇ τέχνῃ καὶ πράττειν τὰ πολιτικά). There is no contradiction between the two statements: by seeking the principles of the art of statesmanship, and by constantly seeking to improve the minds of his fellow citizens, Socrates does not take any part in politics as it is practiced in Athenian assemblies, but as a private individual, he does everything a statesman is supposed to do. In the *Politicus*, Plato therefore continues the Socratic "blurring" of the division between public and private, presupposed by the political practice of his contemporaries. The *Politicus*, for that matter, will go even further, since the choice of weaving as a paradigm for the art of the statesman, that is, the choice of an essentially

---

28 Such an ideology is famously represented in Pericles' Funeral Oration in Thucydides, *Hist.*, II, 40, 2 (trans. Warner): 'we do not say that a man who takes no interest in politics is a man who minds his own business; we say he has no business here at all (οὐκ ἀπράγμονα ἀλλ' ἀχρεῖον).' On ἀπραγμοσύνη, see Demont (1990).

feminine skill representing the work carried out in the *oikos*, positions it as a direct follow-up to this questioning of the public/private division.[29]

There is yet another reason justifying giving great importance to the Visitor's argument at 259a1–b6 (= [2][a]) and it has to with the profound significance of the analogy with medicine. This analogy between the relationship, on the one hand, of a private individual possessing medical expertise to a doctor recognized as such, and, on the other hand, of a private individual adviser to a king, shows first that it is the expertise, and only the expertise, that legitimizes being called king. But that is not all, because it follows from this analogy that, in Plato's eyes, there is no need to actually rule to be a king.[30] Indeed, when a private individual 'giv[es] advice' (259a6: παραινεῖν) to the ruler, he possesses the knowledge that the ruler should possess. The *Politicus* is then considering a more complex case than the one the *Republic* describes. Unlike the *Republic,* where philosophy and statesmanship have a perfectly reciprocal relationship in which the philosopher is king, and the king a philosopher, the *Statesman* considers the possibility of another configuration, where a king actually governs by following a philosopher's advice. The philosopher will consequently be the only statesman, the only true king, but will not hold the title in the eyes of the subjects governed. It is not implausible to think that this argument in the *Politicus* both reflects and justifies the "parenetic" political practices that some sources attribute not only to Plato and his Sicilian experiments, but also to several members of the Academy.[31]

5 King, or Statesman

Let me conclude with one last aspect of the passage we have been examining: the identification of the statesman with the king. Some commentators have judged the general argument proposed at 258e–259d to be profoundly flawed because they have believed (wrongly in my opinion) that it aimed to establish that king and statesman are one and the same.[32] As I have attempted to show, such is not the goal of this argument, which does not prove this identity, but rather accepts

---

29 On this aspect of the weaving paradigm see El Murr (2002).

30 The importance of this argument is highlighted by the rare and thereby noteworthy fact that young Socrates will refer to it by himself later on (292e–293a).

31 See Schuhl (1946–1947). But see also the convincing criticisms put forward by Trempedach (1994) esp. 111–149, of the view that Plato's Academy had a political influence in Athens and beyond.

32 See Cooper (1999) 169–170, n. 7.

it as an indispensable premise to the conclusion it seeks to reach. One may consider, as some have done, that this identity is 'highly questionable' (Cooper, 1999, 168–169) on the grounds that the statesman, who participates in the life of the *polis* like the other free citizens, and the king, who governs territories and expects obedience from his subjects, cannot be identified. Of course, this identification is once again a provocation on Plato's part that would not have failed to shock his contemporaries (as duly noted by Castoriadis, among others).[33] But with the exception of the intent to provoke, the fact that the king and the statesman correspond to different realities in the Greek world of Plato's time sheds no more light on the intention of the *Politicus* than the reality of Persian kingship does on the conception of the philosopher-king in the *Republic*. For Plato, kingship represents a theoretical challenge: it corresponds to a normative project aiming to promote a specific model of government as an alternative to the regime of the *polis* – that goes without saying –, but also a rival to other conceptions of kingship.

We should bear in mind that Plato is not alone in seeing kingship as the best model for political government: over a period of about twenty years, between 380 and 360 B.C., it is likely that Isocrates wrote the speech *To Nicocles* and the *Evagoras*, Xenophon his *Cyropaedia*, and Plato, in all likelihood, his *Politicus*. Despite the differences in the conception each of the three authors has of kingship, all three not only have in common the idea that kingship is a powerful tool with which to criticize democracy and the institutions of the *polis*, but seek, each in their own way, to conceive of a specifically Greek form of kingship. So the interest in kingship in these three authors, who are contemporaries of one another, is not (or perhaps not only) the effect of a reactionary enterprise or an absurd nostalgia for archaic forms of kingship.[34] A normative as well as a critical concern drives these writings and, surely when it comes to Plato, a desire to give new meaning to the main categories of Greek political thought.

6 Conclusion: knowledge, prescription, and the kingly art

By making political science a theoretical science, notably because he sees the genus of *praktikē* as including only manual productive arts, Plato runs the risk of purging political science of effectiveness and any connection to action. Yet the

---

[33] See Castoriadis (2002).
[34] On Mycenian and Homeric kingships, see Carlier (1984).

statesman must take action. Thus the following step of the *diairesis*, i.e. the division of *gnōstikē*, shows that the statesman does indeed act, but in a specific, indirect way.

This division pits the sciences the Visitor describes as involving the making of judgments against those he calls *epitactic* or prescriptive. The paradigm of the sciences involving the making of judgements is the art of calculation (λογιστική), the science of knowing the properties of numbers and judging them as a result. The paradigm of the prescriptive sciences is architecture, because the master-builder draws the plans and then looks after the result of his expertise. It is obvious that the two arts are *theoretical* and not practical. However, we observe that the prescriptive arts are on the border of what we call theory and practice, since the architecture paradigm obviously involves a relationship with action, but it is a relationship mediated by knowledge and the prescriptions it dictates.

We now understand the main point Plato wishes to make with the first two cuts of the *diairesis* in the *Politicus*. Political science is a *theoretical* science, detached from a specific conception of practice equated with manual production: it is a science, analogous to arithmetic (or to dialectic), because its aim is knowledge. Yet, it cannot content itself with knowledge for its own sake, since its role is to direct other arts in what they have to do: Plato therefore connects political science with action through the notion of *prescription* (a distinctive conceptual innovation that we must credit the *Politicus* for in the history of political thought). If it were not a theoretical science, then the statesmanship defined here would obviously not be Platonic, but if it were not *prescriptive*, it would not be statesmanship at all. The efficiency of political science is real, but it is indirect.

Of course, this is not Plato's final word on this issue. By using the weaving paradigm to determine the specific task of political science, the concluding pages of the dialogue (*Plt.*, 305e–311c) define this task in terms of *interweaving*. So, one should ask, is there a fundamental inconsistency between the beginning of the dialogue, where the epistemic, non-practical, status of political science is highlighted, and its conclusion, where the *weaving* done by the statesman is developed at length?[35] Isn't the conclusion of the dialogue in direct contradiction with its beginning, making it seem as if political science directly *produces* something, and consequently, does not content itself with just knowing? This problem may

---

35 This is, e.g., Skemp's view (1952) 122–123, n. 1: 'One can therefore say that, in spite of the classification of πολιτική here as γνωστική rather than χειροτεκτονική, it is a fundamental thesis of this dialogue that statesmanship is an 'applied' science in our sense. The validity of the analogy with weaving rests on this assumption.'

well be one of the key issues in Plato's conception of political science. How indeed can a political science with such a high epistemic requirement take action and transform the social fabric?[36]

---

36 For my tentative solution to this problem, see ch. 9 of El Murr (2014).

Giovanni Casertano
True and Correct in the *Politicus*

In order to provide some reflections on the puzzling relation between 'correct' and 'true' and between 'belief' and 'knowledge' I shall examine lines 277e–279a, as a context for my analysis of the *Politicus*.

A core problem, always prominent in Platonic thought from the early dialogues to the late ones, is that of methods for philosophical inquiry. Briefly, and without providing evidence of this statement here, I can say that in Plato's philosophy three perspectives and three methods coexist:

1. the Parmenidean one, focused on the necessity to reach the truth by means of a correct method, one able to anchor language to reality;
2. the Sophistic one, which is designed to solve the problems that arise in the relationship between true speech and the real world;
3. the Socratic one, which, even though sharing with sophistry the awareness of the inseparability between emotional attitudes and rational procedures, strongly vindicates the necessity to reach, through dialogue, a horizon of truth that goes beyond the individual.

The problem of having a correct method for reaching the truth is also present in the *Politicus*, where the Eleatic Visitor and Young Socrates discuss the definition of the statesman. This research is delineated from the first lines (257b–258b) as the continuation of the one pursued in the *Sophist* (217a–b) where the aim was to define the sophist, the statesman and the philosopher. The continuity between these methods and the recognition of the correctness of the diaeretic method experienced in the previous dialogue, are explicitly affirmed at 266d7–9:

"That such a method of argument (τῇ τοιᾷδε μεθόδῳ τῶν λόγων) as ours is not more concerned with what is more dignified than with what is not, and neither does it at all despise the smaller more than the greater, but always reaches the truest conclusion by itself (ἀεὶ δὲ καθ'αὑτὴν περαίνει τἀληθέστατον)." (All translations of Plato's *Statesman* follow Rowe, 1999, with slight differences in some cases)

This claim is also explicitly connected to what was said at *Soph.* 227a8–11, and it underlies the belief that, whatever the object of the inquiry will be, the most important thing is the method we use in our reasoning, since only correctness of method will lead us to truth. However, a correct (i.e. rationally correct) method is not enough; in order to reach the truth two other hermeneutic instruments have to be combined with it.

https://doi.org/10.1515/9783110605549-005

The first one is myth. In the *Politicus* the myth is presented as the "other route" (268d5: ἑτέραν ὁδόν) to pursue, since the account of the king must be "right and complete" (268b8: ὀρθὸς καὶ ἀκέραιος). As is well known, the myth told by the Eleatic Visitor combines three different myths: 1) The first, on the inversion of the movements of the sun and the stars required by Zeus in order for him to testify for Atreus against his brother Thyestes during the quarrel for the golden fleece; 2) the second, on the kingship exercised by Cronus (identified with the golden age) and 3) the third, on the birth of mankind from earth (269aff.).

The myth is being used here instrumentally, since its goal is to discover what was wrong in the previous argument: after exploring the definitions of the king and the statesman, through dialogue, the speakers had identified the shepherd as the paradigm and, moreover, god had been understood as the one who had power over the city, but without providing any account of the way he does it. The conclusion is that, once the myth has been recounted, it is necessary *to put it to use* (274e2: χρήσιμον) which means *interpreting it* in order to find the mistake.

The crucial point of this part of the dialogue is that the origin of the mistake was not the saying of something *wrong*: "what we said was *true*, but *incomplete* and *unclear*" (275a4–5: ἀληθές, οὐ μὴν ὅλον γε οὐδὲ σαφὲς ἐρρήθη). This claim is confirmed six pages below (281c–d) when, after having said that the account of the art of weaving has been sufficiently (ἱκανῶς) defined, it is added that something *true* has been said, but that it is neither *clear* nor *complete* (τι ἀληθές, οὐ μὴν σαφές γε οὐδὲ τέλον). A quite problematic characteristic of truth emerges here, i.e. its *partiality*: a speech can be true, i.e. well defined (which means procedurally correct) but in the meantime it still could reveal an *unclear* truth, and in particular a *partial* truth, which is not complete and needs something more. This is a problem.

The other instrument used by the philosophical account is the notion of model (*paradeigma*) and it seems that philosophy cannot do without it. At 277c–d, after persuading the Young Socrates that the characterization of the statesman has already been made, the Elean Visitor observes that, nevertheless, the notion of the king has not been given a complete (277a5: τέλεον) shape yet. Moreover, with regard to the use of the myth, the "large-scale illustrations" (277b4: θαυμαστὸν ὄγκον) offered throughout the myth now appear excessive to the Visitor, who thinks that they have been misused, and have made the demostration too long. Finally, it is said that the myth itself was not well defined (277b7: τέλος οὐκ ἐπέθεμεν). However, something can be well defined and fully clear, but only by the employment of language and reasoning (277c4: λέξει καὶ λόγῳ δηλοῦν).

So the myth certainly helps, and it is useful in the search for the truth if we know how *to put it to use,* i.e. how to interpret it, but discourse is the sole and proper way of clarifying and ending any demonstration, especially when it concerns knowledge (277d7: περὶ τῆς ἐπιστήμης). Arguments need models:

"It's a hard thing, my fine friend, to demonstrate any of the more important subjects without using models. It looks as if each of us knows everything in a kind of dreamlike way, and then again is ignorant of everything as it were when awake." (277d1–4)

The model is necessary to *make knowledge stable,* and to transform the partially true, once it is reached, from occasional to everlasting possession of knowledge, and from unclear to clear knowledge.

I should like to examine the puzzling relation between 'correct' and 'true' in the light of 277e–279a. I have divided the passage into five parts in order to make the exposition clearer:

A. 277e6–278a3: The chosen model is one of children who acquire skills in reading and writing: first "they distinguish each of the individual letters well enough (ἱκανῶς) in the shortest and easiest syllables, and come to be capable of indicating what is true (τἀληθῆ φράζειν) in relation to them. [...] But then once again they make mistakes (ψεύδονται) about these very same letters in other syllables, and think and say what is false (δόξῃ τε ψεύδονται καὶ λόγῳ).

B. 278a8–c1: Well then, isn't this the easiest and best way of leading them on to the things they're not yet recognizing (ἐπὶ τὰ μήπω γιγνωσκόμενα)? What way? To take them first back to those cases in which they had a right opinion (ὀρθῶς ἐδόξαζον), and having done that, to put these beside what they're not yet recognizing (τὰ μήπω γιγνωσκόμενα). By comparing them, we demonstrate that there is the same kind of thing with similarity and identity in nature (τὴν αὐτὴν ὁμοιότητα καὶ φύσιν), until the things in which they had a right opinion (τὰ δοξαζόμενα ἀληθῶς) have been shown set beside all the ones that they don't know; once the things in question have been shown like this, and so become models (παραδείγματα οὕτω γιγνόμενα), they bring it about that each of all the individual letters is called both different, on the basis that it is different from the others, and the same, on the basis that it is always the same as and identical to itself, in all syllables.

C. 278c3–6: We come to be using a model when a given thing, which is the same in something different and distinct, has been correctly opined (δοξαζόμενον ὀρθῶς) there, and having been brought together with the original thing, brings about a single true opinion (μίαν ἀληθῆ δόξαν) about each separately and both together?

D. 278c8–d6: Then would be surprised if our minds by their nature experienced this same thing in relation to the individual "elements" of everything (περὶ τὰ τῶν πάντων στοιχεῖα), now, in some cases, holding a settled view with the aid of truth (ὑπ'ἀληθείας) in relation to each separate thing, now, in others, being all at sea (φέρεται) in relation to all of them – somehow or other having a right opinion (ὀρθῶς δοξάζει), but once again not knowing these same elements when they are transferred into the long "syllables" of things and the ones that are not easy (εἰς τὰς τῶν πραγμάτων μακρὰς καὶ μὴ ῥᾳδίους συλλαβάς)?

E. 278d8–279a5: How could anyone begin from false belief and get to even a small part of the truth (ἐπί τι τῆς ἀληθείας καὶ μικρὸν μέρος), and so acquire wisdom (φρόνησιν)? I dare say it's impossible. Well, if that's the way it is, the two of us would not at all be in the wrong in having first attempted to see the nature of models as a whole (ὅλου παραδείγματος ἰδεῖν τὴν φύσιν) in the specific case of a further insignificant model, with the intention then of bringing to the idea of the king (ἐπὶ τὸ τοῦ βασιλέως εἶδος), which is of the greatest importance, something of the same form from less significant things somewhere, in an attempt once more through the use of a model to recognize in an expert, systematic way what looking after people in the city is, so that it may be present to us in our waking state rather than in a dream (ὕπαρ ἀντ'ὀνείρατος)? Absolutely right. Then we must take up once again what we were saying before, to the effect that since tens of thousand of people dispute the role of caring for cities with the kingly class, what we have to do is to separate all these off and leave the king on his own; and it was just for this purpose that we said we needed a model (πρὸς τοῦτο δὴ παραδείγματος δεῖν τινος). As it is well known, the model used for the search of the statesman is that of weaving.

Let me now provide some observations on these passages. First, the *instrumental* character of the model appears clear: as in the paradigm of children who learn how to read, inquiry into the nature of the statesman should be made by identifying sameness and difference, and separating sameness from what is similar to it; regarding the statesman, he should be separated from all types of men that take care of the city in some way, and contend for the title of king or statesman. Separating sameness means individuating the true characteristics of something, and distinguishing them from those that are merely similar, and not the true ones. This is a point in common with the *Sophist*, where similarities are understood as "very slippery things" (231a7, tr. Fowler) i.e more difficult to individuate. In the *Politicus* the role of the model, understood as necessary (δεῖν) in searching for the truth, is also characterised through the image of the dream: individuating sameness by means of a model is like passing from a dream to reality (277d1–4); we could observe that the dream is not false, but precisely the world of the partial and unclear truth mentioned a few pages above. Arguably, this type of truth could become real (i.e. clear, well defined and fixed in the soul) but only through discourse.

I should like to make a second point with regard to A) above. Again, we have to refer to the previous dialogue: opinion and discourse are, fundamentally, the same, and both *doxa* and *logos* can be true or false; in the *Sophist* (264a–b) it has been said that thought, opinion and discourse are the same; thinking and opinion are silent dialogues of the soul with itself, and discourse is thought expressed in sounds. Both opinion and discourse can be true or false, and between truth and falsity there is a clear opposition. Even when B), C) and D) refer only to opinion and not to discourse, arguably we could understand that what is said could also refer to *logos* as well. In B) it seems that 'correct' and 'true' are assimilated: when we have a correct opinion about a group of elements that makes them recognizable in other groups that we do not know yet, we have a *true* opinion about them. In this case having a *correct* opinion is the same as having a *true* opinion. The equivalence between true and correct opinion is enhanced in C) and D), even if these two passages seem to be positioned against regarding the *origin* of opinion as correct or true. In fact C) declares that it is the 'correctness' of the belief that determines the emergence of 'true' opinion, while in D), conversely, it is said that the possession of 'truth' is what allows 'right' belief.

So I should like to emphasize that in the *Politicus* there is an identification, or at least a fluctuation in the use of 'correct' and 'true' which is different from other dialogues, where these two notions are clearly distinguished. For instance, we could read, in the light of the difference between 'correct' and 'true', the two discourses made by Socrates in the *Phaedrus* (the first one veiled and the second one bareheaded) about the question whether it is right or wrong to give ourselves to those who do not love us. We could assume that the first speech made by Socrates, apparently "rectifying" that of Lysias, is a 'right' discourse, but Socrates himself denies it, using adjectives which lead us to think that it is a false discourse: the speech that Phaedrus obliged Socrates to make (242d5: ἠνάγκασας εἰπεῖν) is defined as horrible: δεινόν (242d4), impious, ἀσεβῆ (242d7), and not true, οὐκ ἔτυμος (244a4). Conversely, we should take the bareheaded Socrates' discourse about the necessity to be loved by those who love us, with all the corollaries about divine *mania* and the immortal soul, as a 'right', 'true' discourse.

In the *Politicus* the qualification of "correct" is applied mainly to method, and it is quite common. Nevertheless, it is applied to a state's constitution too. How much of this correctness is in relation to truth is difficult to say. We should start our analysis by saying that the method in question is, as in the *Sophist*, the diairetic one that uses division and separation: in order to have not only a 'correct' discourse but also a 'well defined' one (ὀρθὸς καὶ ἀκέραιος; ἀκέραιος = unmixed, pure, intact, undamaged) it is necessary to separate the statesman from all other men who care for human rearing (268a–d).

In order to be correct, this division should not isolate a small part of them from a big part: at 262b–263d, Plato introduces the very important distinction between part and class, μέρος and εἶδος, that characterises the diairetic method:

it should be noted, however, that even if the meaning of this strategy is very clear, the terms are interchangeable (εἶδος, γένος e ἰδέα), as in the case of correct and true.

The correct way to divide an idea or a genus is to cut it in the middle, since only this way do ideas match (ἰδέαις). Only this way will the part into which an idea or a genus has been divided be of the same class as that class (τὸ μέρος ἅμα εἶδος ἐχέτω). For example, if we have to divide humankind, we should not divide it between Greeks and Barbarians, but between men and female, for only this way will each one of the two sections be both genus and part (γένος ἅμα καὶ μέρος).

Briefly, 'class' and 'part' (εἶδος καὶ μέρος) are different: for example, the class (εἶδος) "female" is also a part of what is said to be the species, but there is no necessity that a part such as, for instance, the "Greeks" be also a class. Nevertheless, there are no rules for the division in order to grant the correctness of the method, while for the inverse procedure, that of the composition or of the weaving of ideas, as for example in the paradigm of the fabric, the true expert turns out to have the capacity of interlacing warp and weft 'correctly' (283a2–9). I shall not dwell on this concept here, though.

We said that 'correctness' is also the essential characteristic of a good constitution. In this characterisation not only is 'correctness' interlaced to 'truth', but knowledge and opinion too play a key role in this peculiar relation, which is not here a relation of opposition, as in other Platonic dialogues. Moreover, the dangerous notion of imitation also plays a part here.

The Eleatic Visitor says that there are many different criteria to judge constitutions: depending on who holds power, it is possible to have the government of one, few or many; regarding citizens' conditions it is possible to speak of riches and poverty; regarding citizens' conditions in respect of leaders, it is possible to speak about consent or coercion. Finally, regarding the structure of a constitution we have government with or without laws. Now, we have to observe that all these criteria are inadequate for the Eleatic Visitor: if royal power, i.e. the power of the true statesman, is a science, as it should be, the criterion (τὸν ὅρον) should not be any one of the above mentioned, but only knowledge itself (292 a–c). The governors' ἐπιστήμη is thus the criterion for determining the correctness of a constitution, or more precisely of the *only* right constitution. At 293a–e it is said that "we must look for the correct rule (ὀρθὴν ἀρχήν) in relation to some one person, or two, or altogether few – when it is correct (ὅταν ὀρθὴ γίγνηται)." Correctness consists in the true possession of expertise, i.e. of real science. The example of the doctor is very clear:

"We believe in them whether they cure us with our consent or without it, by cutting or burning or applying some other painful treatment, and whether they do so according to written rules or apart from written rules, and whether as poor men or rich. In all these cases we are no less inclined at all to say they are doctors, so long as they are in charge of us on the basis of expertise, purging or otherwise reducing us, or else building us up – it is not matter, if only each and every one of those who care for our bodies acts for our bodies' good, making them better than they were, ans so preserves what is in their care. It's in this way, as I think, and in no other that we'll lay down the criterion of medicine and of any other sort of rule whatsoever; it is the only correct criterion (ὅρον ὀρθόν μόνον). Yes, just so. It must then be the case, it seems, that of constitutions too the one that is correct in comparison with the rest, and alone a constitution, is the one in which the rulers would be found truly possessing expert knowledge, and not merely seeming to do so (τοὺς ἄρχοντας ἀληθῶς ἐπιστήμονας καὶ οὐ δοκοῦντας μόνον). [...] this is the constitution that alone we must say is correct (μόνην ὀρθὴν πολιτείαν)."

Here the Eleatic Visitor adds the problematic reference to imitation:

> All the others that we generally say are constitutions we must say are not genuine (οὐ γνησίας), and not really constitutions at all, but imitation of this one (μεμιμημένας ταύτην); those we say are "law-abiding" have imitated it for the better, the others for the worse.

I shall come back later to the problem of imitation; let us consider now the topic of the correctness of a constitution in relation to laws. The achievement of written laws surely constituted an important milestone in the improvement of Greek society from its origins. Plato's treatment of this topic, on the face of it very reactionary, and driven by great esteem for times past, is on the contrary very contemporary nowadays. Plato is well aware of the fact that power exercised without laws is a notion hard to accept. Nevertheless, the issue of correctness (294a4: ὀρθότητος) is not a meaningless one.

According to Plato, the best thing for a city is not that laws rule, but that a wise royal ruler (μετὰ φρονήσεως) do so. This thesis is predicated on the fundamental relationship between law and its applicability, i.e. it takes it to consideration the application of the laws to the concrete lives of the citizens or, to say it in another way, it points to the relationship between law's generality and the particularity of the cases to which law must be applied. The issue turns specifically on the acceptance that law is general, and must govern everyone, but it does not automatically follow that it will be recognized as such by each one and every person:

> For the dissimilarities between human beings and their actions, and the fact that practically nothing in human affairs ever remain stable (ἡσυχίαν), prevent any sort of expertise whatsoever from making any simple (ἁπλοῦν) decision in any sphere that covers all cases and will last for all time (294b).

The same holds for law: it rules without expertise or science (ἀτεχνῶς):

> Then it is impossible for what is perpetually simple (ἁπλοῦν) to be useful in relation to what is never simple (πρὸς τὰ μηδέποτε ἁπλᾶ τὸ διὰ παντὸς γιγνόμενον ἁπλοῦν)»?" (294c). The legislator "will never be capable, in prescribing for everyone together, of assigning accurately to each individual what is appropriate for him." (295a). "For how would anyone ever be capable of sitting beside each individual perpetually throughout his life and accurately prescribing what is appropriate to him? (294e–295b).

That is why written law, which is applied to single cases but has been designed to rule over everybody, cannot prescribe exactly what is best and right for each one. Thus, it can never prescribe the best.

Plato's examples are very clear. By setting rules ἐπὶ τὸ πολύ, a gymnastic trainer does not take care of the needs of each individual (καθ'ἕνα ἕκαστον), and does not prescribe for him what his specific body needs (294d–e). Analogously, if a doctor had to be out of the country for a while, and thought that his patients would not remember the instructions he had given them, he would want to write down reminders for them. But if he came back unexpectedly and found them in different health conditions, he would make the fool of himself if he did not change his former prescriptions. The same is true for a steersman who, "watching out for what is to the benefit of the ship and the sailors, preserves his fellow sailors" (296e–297a) without written laws but using his expertise as law. The expertise, the ἐπιστήμη, is better than the written laws; and so a constitution will be correct only when those in power will use "the strength of their expertise, as [something] more powerful than the laws" (297a). Only in this way will rulers be able to provide the citizens with what is right, accompanied as it is by "the intelligent application of their expertise (τὸ μετὰ νοῦ καὶ τέχνης δικαιότατον, 297b)." The problem is that:

> a mass of any people whatsoever would never be able to acquire this sort of knowledge and so govern a city with intelligence; and that we must look for that one constitution, the *correct* one, in relation to a small element in the population, few in number, or even a single individual, putting down the other constitutions as imitations [...], some of them imitating this one for the better, the other for the worse (297b–c).

Thus, the law is insufficient for determining the correctness of a constitution. Moreover, it could even become an obstacle for the fulfilment of what is best. A paradox could arise if we understand written law as the only thing that can prescribe the good, and if it were established that no individual can give different prescriptions. In fact, if someone knew of better laws, but these happened to run counter to the established ones, Athenian legislation prescribed that these could rule, though only after having persuaded Athens's Assembly. This procedure is described by Demosthenes (*Against Timocrates*) and Aeschines (*Against Ctesiphon*).

How should the act of imposing the law by force be regarded? Again, the example of science, in particular medicine, helps us to understand the issue: if a physician with a correct understanding of his art (ἔχων δὲ ὀρθῶς τὴν τέχνην) prescribes the best for his patient in a way counter to the written laws and heals him, which will be the correct name for this kind of 'violence'? Whatever it is, the Stranger claims, it is not "mistake" (ἁμάρτημα) or "virus" (νοσῶδες).

The 'mistake' that runs counter to the art of politics is the bad and the unjust; someone compelled to do something different, but also finer and better, should not say that he had suffered shameful, unjust treatment at the hands of the one who had compelled him (296a–e).

Moreover, this topic has to do with the relationship between law and truth. It is in fact absurd to consider written laws to be the only depository of the truth, since that would put a stop to the search for truth. Arguably, this thesis would fruitfully provide a lot of issues nowadays. The Stranger asks Young Socrates to suppose that it should be a rule not to permit a steersman or a doctor to work independently if they made errors in their work (for instance, saving someone and ruining others simply by chance). It would be necessary to write in the Assembly rules for navigation and medicine, and compel every steersman and doctor to work according to these regulations. In this way we would have found a remedy for some absurdities, but new and worse ones would arise (298a–e).

> Suppose anyone is found inquiring into steersmanship and seafaring, or health and truth in the doctor's art (ἰατρικῆς ἀλήθειαν), [...] above and beyond the written rules, and making clever speculations of any kind in relation to such things. In the first place one must not call him an expert doctor or an expert steersman, but a star-gazer, some babbling sophist (299b–c).

But the search for truth cannot depend on written rules: if everything was done on the basis of written rules and not on the basis of expertise

> it's clear both that we should see all the various sorts of expertise completely destroyed, and that they would never be restored, either, because of this law prohibiting inquiry; so that life, which even now is difficult, in such a time would be altogether unliveable (ὁ βίος, ὣν καὶ νῦν χαλεπός, εἰς τὸν χρόνον ἐκεῖνον ἀβίωτος γίγνοιτ' ἂν τὸ παράπαν) (299e–300a).

Even if written laws were an obstacle to the search for truth and run *counter to* it, they could still nonetheless perform a positive function. In fact, the real question is not just to determine whether the constitution is correct with or without written or unwritten laws, but whether it is founded on the science of those who govern, i.e. whether power is exercised wisely, and attains the good for the citizens. Should a governor, without paying attention to the written laws, use power for his own benefit (and not for the benefit of the citizens), the harm would be greater than the one he could inflict if he followed written law.

Once we assume that the *correct* constitution (namely, the *true* constitution) is the one which is founded on the governors' science, the question of imitation will arise, since the "second navigation" is the one which is based on the written laws and which refuses to act against them (300c). While the wise man, who is really expert in the art of politics, will act in accordance with his art, without considering written laws when he understands that the best thing to do is something different from what they prescribe, the second-best governor will act in accordance with the laws. The laws, if written by those who know (300c6: τῶν εἰδότων), are 'imitations of the truth': μιμήματα τῆς ἀληθείας (300c5–6:). The genuine expert will act in accordance with his art, without considering the written rules. Thus, anyone who acts differently because it is best, will be doing the same as the true statesman (300d).

Nevertheless, if men without science (300d9: ἀνεπιστέμονες) did so, "they would be undertaking to imitate what is true, but would imitate it altogether badly (παγκάκως), but if they did it on the basis of expertise, this would be *no longer imitation but that very thing that is most truly what it sets out to be* (οὐκ μίμημα ἀλλ'αὐτὸ τὸ ἀληθέστατον)» (300d9–e2).

Since no large collection of people is capable of acquiring any sort of royal expertise, it is necessary that constitutions of this type (if they want to imitate well that true constitution which is the only one which is directed with art) refuse to act against the laws, after having set them up (300e–301a). To sum up: since nowadays there is not a real and true king, it is necessary to write laws, following the traces of the truest constitution (301d8–e4: μεταθέοντας τὰ τῆς ἀληθεστάτης πολιτείας ἴχνη).

The page we have just read raises some issues and, as often, even if the general meaning is clear, the same does not hold for all the arguments. First, it is said that written laws are *always* an imitation of truth (300c), since truth is the science of the true statesman, i.e.of him who leads with science and for the sake of the citizens (and not for his own sake). The constitution of the true statesmen is the *very true one*. What it is not clear here is *why* the politician-king should set up some written laws, since his power is always the best, with or without written laws.

At 301d–e Plato provides a justification for the *second best*, i.e. the law-abiding constitution: since today there is no real true king, it is useful to set in place some written laws which could *imitate* the true constitution. But, again, who will *write* these laws? The true king will not need them; maybe those who do not possess the art of politics should do so? But how can they imitate the true constitution without knowing it?

In fact, at 300 d, it is said that those who have no science, the ἀνεπιστέμονες, would imitate the truth badly, and this presumably means that their constitution will be worse. The question is even more complex: those who possess the true art of politics would imitate 'the truth' by giving some written laws to the city, but the Stranger claims that in this case it is not really 'imitation' that they would be doing, but what is most true (300d9–e2). So the problem is this: if the law is always an imitation of something else, and the true king has no need of it, he does not 'imitate' the truth but rather 'performs' the truth; conversely, if law is not set up by the true king, it is unclear who could 'imitate' the truth, for those who do not know it (namely, those who have no science of it) naturally could not imitate it.

In conclusion, I should say that oscillation has a significant *pendant* in other pages of the *Politicus*. It is a common opinion that in Plato there is always an opposition between δόξα and ἐπιστήμη, and that truth belongs only to the latter; this opposition is often ascribed to the difference between human and divine knowledge. Many pages of Plato's dialogues are used to highlight this difference, but, I should say, many others show how problematic this difference is.

In the *Symposium* (202a) correct opinion is intermediate between science and ignorance: it is an inter-medium because it is not grounded in itself, and cannot provide evidence for its objects. In the *Meno* (97a ff.) true opinion, as well as science, can assure the correctness of an action. In the *Theaetetus* (201a–c) true opinion is analogous to science. Thus, truth also belongs to human opinions, and not only to the divine.

This also happens in our dialogue, the *Politicus:*

> I call *divine*, when it comes to be in souls, that *real and true opinion* (ὄντως οὖσαν ἀληθῆ δόξαν) about what is fine, just, and good, and the opposite of these, which is really true and is guaranteed; that is the divine opinion generated in a daimonic man (θείαν ἐν δαιμονίῳ γίγνεσθαι γένει) (309c5–d4).

Thus, once again, what Plato declares he has thrown away, i.e. the unquestioned predominance of opinion, of Protagorean heritage, comes back here: the science of the king, of the true statesman (who, I have to emphasize, is a man) is opinion. It is the true opinion of a daemonic being who lives in truth, and it is exactly the same thing as divine science, or, I should say, *divine opinion*.

Part III: **Interpreting the Myth**

David White
Paradigm, Form and the Good in Plato's
Statesman: The Myth Revisited

The rubric "collection and division" (CD) appears commonly in secondary literature on later Platonic dialogues. This rubric identifies a process (or processes) ex-
tracted from dialogues such as the *Phaedrus*, *Sophist*, and *Statesman* and then
considered as a subject worth close analytical scrutiny. Two recent studies of collection and division[1] include an array of notions which reflect terminological
practices and speculative tendencies familiar to contemporary students of what
in philosophy is now called "metaphysics": kind, class, form, genus, species, natural kinds, whole, part, typological, mereological, substance, *summum genus*,
formal method, taxonomy, same, different, accidental and essential differences,
intension, extension, intensional mereology, necessary and sufficient conditions, simple, indivisible, units, composite, negative forms. This list, drawn from
the articles, is impressive; it is also not exhaustive.

To gather diverse statements and applications of collection and division and
to assume that their Platonic protagonists are using either the same or significantly similar mechanisms throughout all the dialogues in which these statements and applications appear stand as a reasonable line of interpretation. However, this global approach does not take into account the possibility that aspects
or even broad theoretical dimensions pertaining to the structure and scope of CD –
dimensions embodying a metaphysical pedigree – might be introduced and employed *within the narrative and discursive boundaries of a given dialogue*. The primary interpretive thesis of this article is that the structure of collection and division developed in the *Statesman* must be viewed from the standpoint of the entire
dialogue – including the fact that Socrates makes only a cameo appearance at the
beginning (and, perhaps, at the conclusion) and that the myth of the reversed
cosmos spans six Greek pages, a significant section of the entire work. If we assume as a matter of principle that a Platonic dialogue is an organic narrative
unity, then we may ask what affect the myth has on the various appearances of
collection and division in the *Statesman*, both as stated in general terms and as
applied. The hermeneutical inference is not that the structure of CD is unique for
each dialogue in which it appears. Rather, the point is that a codification for this
phase of Platonic methodology will look different if elements in a given dialogue
that may not appear readily relevant to methodological practice are reexamined

---

1 Henry (2011) and Grams (2012).

https://doi.org/ 10.1515/9783110605549-006

from precisely that standpoint. As we shall see, the myth in the *Statesman* becomes a prominent contributor to metaphysical matters involving and related to collection and division, particularly with reference to paradigms, the complex status of Forms and the good.

1 Statecraft and Paradigm

The primary point of the *Statesman* is to define statecraft, a goal stated at the outset of the dialogue. After a number of what turn out to be preliminary exercises in CD aimed at achieving this end, the Visitor notes (268c – translation Rowe unless otherwise indicated) that the statesman has not yet been sufficiently distinguished from those who "crowd around him;" in short, the previous account has been too broad. In order to avoid bringing disgrace to their investigation, the Visitor insists (268e) that they travel another route – a myth – and then proceed as before, taking away "part from part" until they arrive at their destination. The implication is clear that myth will provide necessary information in order that collection and division will succeed. But if *only* myth can establish this new point of departure, then it is essential to determine what this myth has contributed to such dialectical exercise.

If the *Statesman* exists to provide a finished account of the art of a statesman, then we can move quickly to the conclusion of the dialogue since here the Visitor announces that (311b–c):

> this marks the completion of the fabric that is the product of the art of statesmanship: the weaving together, with regular intertwining, of the dispositions of brave and moderate people–when the expertise belonging to the king brings their life together in agreement and friendship and makes it common between them, completing the most magnificent and best of all fabrics and covering with it all the other inhabitants of cities, both slave and free; and holds them together with this twining and rules and directs without, so far as it belongs to a city to be happy, falling short of that in any respect.

This account exemplifies what the Visitor had earlier specified as a *paradigm*, a mode of demonstration essential for defining any of "the more important subjects" (277d; also 278e), a group of realities within which statesmanship surely falls. The Visitor defined paradigm at 278c3–6 (translation modified): "we come to be using a paradigm when a given thing, which is the same in something different and distinct, is correctly identified there, and having been brought together with the original thing, brings about one true opinion about each separately and both together." In general, a paradigm involves a complex connection between two distinct things (more on the structure of a paradigm below) and at 279b, the Visitor establishes in an apparently offhand manner the initial element of the particular paradigm employed to define statecraft:

> By Zeus, Socrates, what do you think? If there isn't anything else to hand, well, what about weaving? Do you want us to choose that? Not all of it, if you agree, since perhaps the weaving of cloth from wool will suffice; maybe it is this part of it, if we choose it, which would provide the testimony we want.

The Visitor then analyzes weaving by means of collection and division from 279c to 283b, eliciting components of weaving which are presumably the same as those of statecraft (thereby establishing the elements required by the Visitor's definition of a paradigm) and ultimately producing the account of statecraft stated (and cited above) at the conclusion of the dialogue.

The Visitor had announced the need for myth at 268c, with the myth proper running from 268e to 274e. As a prerequisite for recognizing the connections between the myth and CD as well as methodology in general, we may observe that the Visitor reminds Young Socrates (and Plato the reader) of the importance of myth at various junctures throughout its narration:

1. 269c– "...as for the state of affairs that is responsible for all these things [the reversed cosmos], no one has related it, and we should relate it now; for once it has been described, it will be a fitting combination toward our exposition of the king."
2. 273e– "as for what is relevant to our showing the nature of the king, it is sufficient if we take up the account from what went before."
3. 274b– "we are now at the point that our account has all along been designed to reach..."

Then, as soon as the narration of the myth is complete, the Visitor states as a matter of strategy that (274e) "we shall put the myth to work" in order to show the errors they had made in previous instances of CD. Finally, less than a page later, the Visitor notes that he introduced the myth (275b – translation modified) "in order that we might see more plainly that other person himself whom alone, in accordance with the paradigm of shepherds and cowherds, because he has charge of human rearing, it is appropriate to think worthy of this name, and this name alone."

The question becomes: to what extent do these announcements – inserted as second-order observations while the narration of the myth is ongoing and shortly after its completion – affect the structure and application of methodology in the dialogue overall?

The Visitor states at 274e that prior applications of CD had suffered from two errors, one greater in import and the other lesser. First, the myth revealed that the Visitor did not distinguish between a divine and a human ruler; also, that the human beings who are elements in this description belonged to the prior cosmic order, under Cronus, and not the present cosmic order, under Zeus. Humans under Cronus originate from the earth, have every necessity given to them and have no need for political constitutions of any sort; humans under Zeus must work and struggle and procreate by nature.

The first error is rectified by the introduction of a reality more sufficiently collected as a terminus of departure for subsequent division – "care" (two instances of which appear at 274d4 and d5). The second, lesser error, will occupy our attention in this article since its implications are more directly relevant to the complex processes ascribed to division and its applications. In this case, the account given of the king functioning in this position erred by being incomplete, and to address this important gap in definition will require virtually the remainder of the dialogue. How did the Visitor achieve this dual awareness of errant methodology? Only by assuming a standpoint for philosophical inquiry (formulated as both collection and division) coordinated with a view grounded in cosmic totality and established by a myth. This is precisely the same perspective which animates the cosmological accounts advanced in the *Timaeus*, accounts realized in the company of a deity capable of fashioning the cosmos and everything in it (more on which below).

The locus of attention for a revitalized and redirected application of CD was secured and sanctioned by the myth. But the myth also provides the source for additional elements in the *Statesman*'s dialectical exercises. If we allow the Visitor's seemingly incidental interjection "By Zeus" to remind us of how Zeus functions in the myth, then we are borne back to the remarkable account of divine activity with respect to the initial formation and consequent restoration of the cosmos. The Visitor will assert that the relevant paradigmatic aspect for determining the nature of statecraft is the weaving of cloth from wool. And upon examination, we recognize that the final account of statecraft stands as a mirror image of what "the god" driving the action of the myth effected as the intertwining – or weaving into a unity – of the two cosmic epochs.

The Visitor elicited from the mythic account of the deity mediating between the all-encompassing rule of Cronus and the rule of Zeus – effectively the absence of rule – that a ruler caring for human beings as if they were a herd of animals must "weave together" a series of opposites according to the mean, just as the god approximated a mean in preserving the life of human beings within the opposing cycles of the cosmic drama. The god tends to the fate of his human herd by striking a mean between providing for every need of humans (Cronus) and leaving them entirely on their own at the mercy of an unattended, ultimately feral cosmos (Zeus).

The manner in which god and divine emissaries bestowed gifts on human beings in order to stabilize and fortify their existence under the domain of Zeus represents a model, a paradigm, for how to care for human beings. In fact, the Visitor explicitly identifies these elements of the myth as "great paradigms" (μεγάλα παραδείγματα – 277b4), noting their propriety in the matter of defining the king (although at this point the Visitor is concerned that their length within the cosmic sweep of the myth may have been excessive – 277b). Furthermore, I submit that the very notion of a paradigm as a methodological device itself originates within the narrative of the myth and is recognized as such, and as signally important, by the Visitor precisely because the Visitor was, so to speak, attentive to his own myth.[2]

In general then, the myth does precisely what the Visitor says it will do – clarify the nature of the king. The myth has achieved this end through the paradigm of the god caring for humanity by realizing the mean between extremes, "weaving" together the polar opposite worlds characterizing the cosmos as a cyclical whole. A human ruler resembles a divine ruler in that the human ruler combines opposites – e.g., the dispositions of brave and moderate people – whereas the divine ruler oversees a unity of opposites by creating, then withdrawing from the cosmos, returning only to establish cosmic harmony as a mean between extremes. Therefore, the god, close counterpart to the *Timaeus* demiurge, serves as divine pole for the paradigm of shepherd mentioned by the Visitor (275b) as decisive for determining the nature of the ruler, since the god has synthesized the cosmos to require this radical shift in circular motion. The final account of statecraft indeed paradigmatically reflects the process of weaving; but viewed from a more fundamental perspective, this account is a mirror image (albeit drawn to a more human scale befitting a ruler) of the god organizing and stabilizing the cosmos.[3]

---

2 El Murr (2006) 9 observes: "As one can easily observe, consideration of the question of how a paradigm is chosen is totally absent....". El Murr's conclusion regarding the origin of paradigms, at least regarding their use in the *Statesman*, would perhaps take a different approach if due attention had been spent on the myth and implications derivable from its content.
3 For more discussion concerning the role of the paradigmatic in the myth, see White (2007) 37–59 (Hereafter MMD).

2 Paradigm and Schema

The Visitor has used weaving as an element in a paradigm to define statecraft. But we have argued that the Visitor elicited the very notion of paradigm from consideration of cosmic consequences detailed in a mythic narrative. It may be inferred then that the Visitor did not arrive for the day's discussion fully equipped with the notion of paradigms as a self-contained and independent dialectical necessity; rather, the Visitor envisioned the need for paradigms as methodologically relevant by virtue of a cosmological narrative so structured that philosophical recognition and employment of paradigms as they pertain to definition mirrors divine activity at an especially fundamental level, i.e., forming and then restoring a fractured cosmos to a state of animate unity. Furthermore, the cosmic perspective required for the complete dimensions and ramifications of this account obviates the possibility of establishing its cogency by means of reasoning and argument – only myth, with its generous narrative limits of plausibility and relevance, will suffice to deliver the required information.

The notion of paradigm itself and the particular paradigm for the problem at hand – defining statecraft – both arise from the narration of the myth. But it is crucial to observe that a paradigm by definition generates "true opinion" (ἀληθὴ δόξαν) – thus the paradigm introduced in this dialogue does not produce knowledge of statecraft. This inherent limitation in the cognitive penetration of paradigms must be kept in mind throughout the following discussion.

Earlier (268c6), the Visitor said that their labors with collection and division had evoked a kingly "schema" (σχῆμα) but not the statesman in the desired sense. Later, after the myth had been narrated, the Visitor contended (275b8–c4) that the schema "of the divine herdsman is still greater than that of a king, and the statesmen who belong to our present era are much more like their subjects in their natures and have shared in an education and nature closer to theirs," to which young Socrates agrees. However, the Visitor insists that these statesmen remain worth seeking, "whether their natures are of the latter or of the former sort." At this point (275d), the process of CD begins anew, with "caring" as the reality to be divided. However, not long after the completion of this phase of division, the Visitor comments that even from this revised and presumably more correct vantage point, "our discussion does not yet seem to have given a complete schema [σχῆμα] to the king" (277a6 – translation modified). The multiple appearances of "schema" during this phase of the conversation intimate that the term has assumed something akin to technical status; if so, then the specific character of a schema must be interpreted in order to understand the Visitor's methodological hesitation at this juncture.

The Visitor has nonetheless continued to reflect on and then to employ the message of the myth. The statesmen sought through CD may be "closer" either to their subjects or to the divine herdsman, Cronus, the god stated in the myth to be in charge of human beings when they are depicted as indistinguishable from herd animals. But the Visitor does not distinguish between these two objects of inquiry in terms of subsequent analysis. If the statesman finally articulated in light of CD is "closer" to the divine herdsman, the account of this type of rule will be of a king "greater" than that of any earthly counterpart. However, the Visitor denies that this difference matters, at least in terms of the inherent value of the object of their investigations. Whether the ruler in question – a human ruler, of course – turns out to be more like a god or more like a mortal human, we must continue to seek out the schema of the king as the exemplar of statecraft. Worth emphasizing here is the fact that the Visitor focuses attention on *schema* as the metaphysical carrier requisite for apprehending the political nature in question. As we shall see, the cognitive connection between paradigm and true opinion exists in a manner similar to the way in which a schema, taken as a certain kind of reality, is related to a Form understood in the canonic sense.

3 Schema and Form

If a paradigm by definition produces true opinion rather than knowledge and if the account of statecraft at the conclusion of the *Statesman* results from application of a paradigm, then determining as accurately as possible the metaphysical status of a schema becomes crucial given that the Visitor has said more than once that their quest seeks the schema of the king. In sum, given that the *Statesman* yields true opinion rather than knowledge about statecraft, is the dialogue so structured to explain why it accesses only a derivative mode of cognition? The answer is yes, and again the myth provides the substance of the response.

The matter of assessing the metaphysical character of a schema appears to become even more complex if we consider that division is typically taken to involve theoretical inquiry aimed at Forms. L. Grams summarizes the problem: "Plato's frequent references to division 'according to nature' (e.g., *Plt* 259d9) suggest that each cut should be made according to a real and unchanging boundary-line between kinds" (144). However, Grams adds, the "difficulty with this approach is that Platonic forms are supposed to be simple, indivisible units, but forms must be composite in at least some sense if *diairesis* separates them into portions" (145). Thus if Forms are simple and indivisible, how can they be divided into parts without destroying their simplicity and indivisibility? Furthermore, what is the connection between Form and schema if, in fact, the final account of statecraft is based on a schema as presumably a kind of reality existing metaphysically in a mode other than that proper to a Form? For if the Form of statecraft exists and is available for scrutiny by the correct practice of CD, why does the dialogue not pursue its theoretical end with that reality fully in view?

Grams proposes a straightforward way to confront the general difficulty posed above, emerging from the necessary unity of a Form: "I argue that the best and simplest option is to reject the initial assumption that the kinds distinguished by *diairesis* always must be forms" (145). This ploy, duly qualified, has merit. But Grams' recommendation does not strictly speaking preserve the canonic character of the Form as putatively subject to division even if it does alter "the kinds distinguished" so that they exist as something other than Forms. After all, a Form divided into kinds (following Grams, kinds invested with a metaphysical character distinct from Forms) remains a reality divided into parts, regardless how these parts are subsequently identified (i.e., as kinds), thereby at least ostensibly destroying the Form's unity.

At this point, it will be instructive to examine how the Visitor clarifies the elements of Form and kind (taken as a "part" of a Form), an account which he develops, albeit briefly, at a high level of abstraction. After the Visitor had criticized the results of their initial attempts at division, young Socrates asked the Visitor (263a3) how to distinguish between a "class" (γένος) and a "part" (μέρος)? The Visitor asserts (263b7–10) that "whenever there is a class (εἶδος) of something, it is necessarily also a part of whatever thing it is called a class of, but it is not at all necessary that a part is a class."[4]

The following inferences are justified:

(i) one class can be a part of another class. But if so, then the latter class cannot be a Form if it is the case that all Forms are simple and as such cannot be subjected to part-whole considerations;

(ii) if a class is definitely asserted to be of another class, then the former class is "necessarily" a part of the latter class. The difference between (i) and (ii) is that a class can exist as a class without necessarily belonging to another class. Thus a class may exist as a part of another class but it need not do so. However, what

---

4 Rowe translates γένος at 263a3 and εἶδος at 263b7 both as "class," thus reflecting the standard conviction that Plato's technical vocabulary is often flexible. We shall argue that the relevant contrast established in this setting is between part and whole; if so, it is immaterial how the Greek terms themselves are rendered as long as this contrast is preserved. It may be observed that later, the divisions of contributory causes (288a–89a) are seven in number and that these would more intuitively be rendered as kinds (following Grams) rather than classes (as Forms). However, in this context Rowe consistently renders εἶδος as "class" rather than "kind."

properties a class has by itself, aside from its potential to become involved in a relational situation, are not specified;

(iii) but if a class is part of another class, then if part means, e.g., what Aristotle says about parts, i.e., that a part is always part of a whole (see *Physics* 207a10), then there is a part-whole relation between the former and latter classes;

(iv) the number of possible parts which can belong to a whole is not specified; presumably the number is limited but may be very large. (We shall see this consequence become crucial to both the theory and practice of CD in the latter stages of the dialogue.);

(v) this part-whole relation suggests, if not implies, that the whole of which classes constitute parts has the capacity to maintain its existence as a whole, and presumably as *one* whole. (This inference will also be discussed below.)

(vi) classes can be parts of other classes, and thus parts of a whole, but a part in the sense the Visitor wishes it to be understood need not be a class. This inference compels inquiry into the nature of both a class as such as well as a part as such, since a part, if it is by definition not a class, must exhibit certain specifiable characteristics in order to maintain itself as a part. Furthermore, if a part is part of a class but not itself a class, then the metaphysical character of a class (as admitting parts) must be clarified if the relation between part and class involves types of being which differ so basically from one another.

(vii) if a class comprises a set of classes – i.e., as a whole of parts – then this whole is not equivalent to a Form (assuming, again, that a Form is necessarily simple and indivisible). Thus it may also be asserted that the unity of a class is not the same as the unity of a Form since one class can be composed of a plurality of classes (as, again, a whole of parts) but a Form exists as, so to speak, a pure and undifferentiated unity.

This brief excursus into implications of a metaphysical cast has been derived from a very circumscribed passage occurring early in the dialogue.[5] But the justification for laying out these implications now is that they help us understand what the Visitor is seeking by emphasizing the schema of the king as the distinctive theoretical object which the conversants in this dialogue are at this juncture equipped to pursue dialectically.

---

5 M.L. Gill (2010) 192 n. 35 asserts that the Visitor "warns Young Socrates not to think he has ever heard a clear account of the manner [of how parts differ from Forms] from him (263b2–4)..." However, Gill does not mention that immediately after this demurral, the Visitor proclaims, with considerable certainty, the passage discussed here (263b5–9). Indeed, the Visitor concludes: "You must always assert, Socrates, that this is what I say rather than the other way around." My contention is that the Visitor's statement of principle concerning the part-whole relation in this context is sufficiently certain in his own mind to warrant close analysis.

4 Form and the Good

Grams cites the *Timaeus* and the function of the demiurge in the formation of elements relevant to the allied notions of nature and natural kinds as they pertain to CD (149, 151). However, Grams' treatment of CD does not mention the myth in the *Statesman* (nor does Henry). Linking the *Statesman* to the *Timaeus* is interpretively apposite, but affinities generated by this link with respect to methodology in the *Statesman* go considerably further than those Grams cites in her article. The following discussion introduces additional elements in the account of creation offered in the *Timaeus*, then combines these elements with counterpart components in the myth of the reversed cosmos in the *Statesman*.

A. The demiurge and the good

Here is *Timaeus* 29a (translation Cornford, modified): "Now if this world is good and the demiurge [δεμιουργὸς – 29a3] good, clearly he looked to the eternal.... Everyone, then, must see that he looked to the eternal; for the world is the best of things that have become and he is the best of causes. Having come to be, then, in this way, the world has been fashioned on the model of that which is comprehensible by rational discourse and understanding and is always in the same state." And a page later (30a2–3 – modified): "God [ὀ θεὸς – 30a2] desired that all things should be good and, so far as might be, nothing imperfect...."

This passage makes evident the fact that according to the *Timaeus*, the demiurge looked to the eternal and unchangeable, i.e., to the Forms when creating the cosmos and everything in it, and that the cosmos, both as a whole and in terms of all its constituent parts, was fashioned in a way which magnified the dimension of the good as an integral feature of its overall structure.

B. The "god" and the shadows of the good

In the *Statesman* myth, the Visitor refers to the creator of the cosmos as "the god" (ὀ θεὸς – 269a4; also 269c4–5 and 269e9). Now this deity cannot be either Cronus or Zeus, each of whom is explicitly assigned dominion over one of the two cosmic cycles (271c, 272b; 272b – Cronus and Zeus, respectively). I submit then that the god in the *Statesman* myth stands as a divine counterpart to the demiurge in the *Timaeus*. This deity mirrors the demiurge in some respects but, crucially, not in other respects. According to the myth, "god" provided all that was needed for human life as resident within nature (271e). But if these necessities existed as types of things (see 271e, e.g., species and flocks), not merely as particulars, then the ensemble of realities which underlies the possibility and actualization of human life exemplifies classes in the sense discussed at 263b–c and elsewhere in the *Statesman*. In this respect, the god and the demiurge function identically. In the *Timaeus*, the demiurge fashions the elements of the natural order by reflecting on the Forms as models and does so in light of the good; by contrast, the manner in which the god executes a similar result in the *Statesman* is ignored. However, the myth does emphasize that all good things in both cosmic cycles are due to divine agency (273b, 273c); the god produces kinds as a mix of good and evil (but more the former than the latter).

The partial and indeed diminished awareness of the good evidenced by the quality of the formations produced by the *Statesman*'s counterpart-demiurge is reflected in the precarious opposition generated by the pair of cosmic cycles. The reversed cosmos illustrates that the inhabitants of the cosmos were created so that over time they could not sustain their natures. The implication then is that when fashioning elements of the cosmos, the god in the *Statesman* myth did not see the Forms as such and glimpsed only a shadow of the good; presumably what the god did see of the Forms animated the creation of living things endowed with a transitory nature, good in some respects and the opposite of good in others. In the *Statesman*, the good as such is never addressed, as it is in the *Republic* and as it will be in the *Philebus*. All that remains of the good characterized as a formative and directive metaphysical reality in the *Timaeus* are, in the Visitor's mythic yet fundamentally fragmented disquisition, vestiges and shadows. Indeed, to rectify these cosmic aberrations, it becomes incumbent on the god to weave together the disparate epochs into a single, uniform cosmos.

An account depicting such grand ministrations can be evoked most effectively as a narrative endowed with suitable vibrancy of detail only through a myth. Furthermore, the fractured formation of the cosmos and the derivative awareness of fundamental elements of Platonic reality on the part of the formative deity has repercussions with a decided metaphysical cast for paradigms as well as for the practice of collection and division.

i. Paradigm and Truth

When the two distinct components of a paradigm are juxtaposed with one another, samenessess become discernible; however, articulation of these samenesses is surrounded by correlative differences. Since these samenesses produce the content of a paradigm (e.g., the "twisting" of distinct human character traits as explicitly mentioned in the final account of statecraft), we may infer that however extensive in content these samenesses may be, they are not sufficient to elevate the cognitive product of the paradigm to the level of knowledge. As emphasized above, paradigms produce true opinion and only true opinion. If we grant then that true opinion, although derivative as a type of cognition, is nonetheless related to knowledge, then it is reasonable to introduce a resemblance relation between the product of a paradigm and what would constitute knowledge, assuming that the object of knowledge is indeed available for scrutiny. This object is the Form of statecraft. But, as such, paradigms cannot reach Forms. They can, however, access schemas. The problem then is to investigate how the dialogue construes the metaphysical link between a schema and a Form. The *Timaeus* makes the relevant point in finely gnomic fashion (29c): "As reality is to becoming, so is truth to belief."

ii. Schema and Form

When Young Socrates asks for clarification concerning the distinction between a part and a class, the Visitor begs off – he will get to this matter "when we have the time" (263b). But I submit that the Visitor does have at least enough time during this conversation to proclaim a myth with a sufficiently developed metaphysical structure to show where work has to be done in order to fulfill Young Socrates' request.

Early in the myth, when the Visitor begins to describe the necessary backward motion of the cosmos itself, he says: "Remaining permanently in the same state and condition, and being permanently the same, belongs only to the most divine things of all, and by its nature body is not of this order" (269d). Although Forms are entities which remain "permanently in the same state and condition," it is relevant that the Visitor refers to Forms only indirectly, by way of contrast to body, a kind of reality which is by nature "not of this order." Indeed, Forms in anything like a canonic sense never appear in the *Statesman* myth. If we take "the most divine things" to refer to Forms, then a later reference to the schema of the king as invisible (286a – one of the "things without body") must be taken with care. The "schema" of the king is invisible qua schema, but it would not necessarily follow that the schema is equivalent to a fully-fledged Form.

We recall the *Republic* concerning the dependency relation of everything with respect to the good (509b – translation Shorey): "...the objects of knowledge not only receive from the presence of the good their being known, but their very existence and essence is derived to them from it, though the good itself is not essence but still transcends essence in dignity and surpassing power." The dependency relation of all things, including the Forms, on the good, has significant metaphysical consequences. Thus if all Forms depend on the good, then it is reasonable to infer that any subsequent type or class distinction deployed at a level of generality approximate to that of the Forms will also depend on the good. To state the implication in the terminology of the *Statesman*: if classes have parts and classes are related to Forms, then parts will also display the good, if only in a derivative sense. Furthermore, "schema" can stand as a technical term (or, with less second-order rigidity, quasi-technical term) for the kind of reality available when using paradigms, i.e., when the activity of definition is aimed at true opinion rather than at knowledge. Thus a schema can be invisible, lack other properties possessed by Forms, yet still exist in such a way as to convey derivative levels of cognition.

The Visitor illustrates the metaphysical coordinates of a schema. In a passage discussed above, we read (275c–d): "...this schema of the divine herdsman is still greater than that of a king, and the statesmen who belong to our present era are much more like their subjects in their natures and have shared in an education and nurture closer to theirs." The Visitor then adds: "Yet they will be neither less nor more worth looking for, whether their natures are of the latter or the former sort." The concerted appeals to nature in this passage (275c3, c7) suggest that the initial indication of a "schema" of the king refers to a kind of being which has a unity marked by metaphysical diversification. If so, then a schema differs from a Form which, we are assuming here, possesses a fundamental simplicity of structure.

The various appeals to nature and cognates point to the schema with respect to its evoking a distinct unity as an approximation of a Form, i.e., as a reality existing in a sense "less than" the mode of existence established by a Form as such. Schema names a reality characterized by a whole-part relation which reflects the reality of a Form but which is not equivalent to that reality. There is an implied connection between a nature (set of all classes and parts of classes bound together as a unity, the totality identified as a schema) and a Form in the canonic sense. Otherwise stated, the unity of a schema is deployable as a nature which controls the whole-part relationships of elements within that nature. We will recall in this regard (as Henry relevantly does, 243), *Philebus* 16c–17a, where Socrates describes collection and division as a gift from the gods, one which he associates with enquiry aimed at establishing certain unities. What the *Philebus* makes explicit as far as the object of CD is concerned, i.e., generating a kind of unity endowed with a degree of independence, functions at an implicit but crucial level of relevance when CD aims at statecraft in the *Statesman* – it is embodied in the notion of schema and the integral presence of schemas in the paradigms of weaving and statecraft.

This approach to the mode of existence of a schema clarifies a comment by the Visitor in his response to Young Socrates concerning the difference between a part and a class. The Visitor asserts that the exponent of CD should "let the part bring a real class [εἶδος] along with it" (262b1–2). On the reading argued here, when a part does "bring a real class along with it," the class is the Form which serves as the metaphysical foundation for the schema. Schemas invite, as it were, the "real class" to enter the picture even though pursuit of the real class, the Form, reaches only part-way via the schema and through the agency of paradigms to the only possible cognitive destination – true opinion. The Visitor is reminding us of a point made at a purely theoretical level earlier (inference vii above), that if a class comprises a set of classes – i.e., as a whole of parts – then this whole is not equivalent to a Form (assuming, again, that a Form is necessarily simple). The schema (of a king, or of course of anything) functions as a distinct metaphysical reality but since it is derived from a Form yet not equivalent to a Form, it "brings a real class with it" by inviting the investigator to reflect on a paradigmatic approximation of a Form, produced as true opinion, so that, if possible, true opinion can be elevated and then become articulated as knowledge.[6]

5 Methodological Implications

An examination of the methodology of the *Statesman* in light of the cosmic perspectives offered by myth as thematically coordinated with this methodology sanctions the following implications:

1. After the myth, the Visitor realizes that the unity of the class to be analyzed via CD admits of multiple divisions, not just division by dichotomy. This methodological extension reflects the fact that the Visitor has discerned enough of the

---

6 Toward the conclusion of his article, Henry (2011) 248–9 n. 35 claims that the use of class and kind retains "their ordinary, non-technical meanings" since "there is little evidence that Plato's diairetic use of εἶδος in the late dialogues is intended to refer to those entities [canonic Forms]; nothing obviously requires it" (248, n. 34). But if the Visitor seeks knowledge, or even (via paradigms) true opinion, then collection and division cannot be aimed merely at "ordinary meanings" of words used as names. Seekers of knowledge are required to direct their cognitive attention toward realities which can yield such knowledge. Henry's egalitarian (and, I believe, mistaken) approach to division in the late dialogues calls to mind *Cratylus* 440c: "...no man of sense will like to put himself or the education of his mind in the power of names."

good, albeit to a diminished degree, to "see" the manifold structure of the analy-sandum and to incorporate this broadened vision into both the theory and prac-tice of division. Thus at 287c–d, the Visitor asserts that it is difficult to make a division into two elements but that division "limb by limb" is appropriate. The Visitor is recognizing that the nature of something to be defined may have multi-ple parts; if so, then only if division identifies each of these parts, however many there may be, will the subsequent account achieve the status of a definition. In turn, this sense of nature exemplifies a unity of unique cast (anticipated in infer-ences iv and v above as derived from the Visitor's statement of principle concern-ing the relation between part and class). The nature of a schema and the perva-sive and hierarchical structure of the good justify this revised approach to division.

2. The description of the object of analysis by means of CD is beholden to the structure of the nature under scrutiny. Thus a strictly articulated genus-species hierarchy becomes subservient to the individual demands placed on CD by the nature being defined. In discussing the Visitor's practice of division with respect to wool-making, Grams observes (142): "The existence of intertwining as distinct from twisting thus depends on the existence of further *differentiae* of twisting, so that a division made 'higher' in the hierarchy depends on a 'lower' subsequent division. In sum, the Visitor's divisions do not always result in kinds that are de-termined by or contained within the scope of the preceding kinds, or that follow an order of ontological priority from general to increasingly specific sub-kinds." However, the Visitor's procedure should also be examined from the standpoint of the nature of the object under scrutiny; from this perspective, the "ontological priority" recognized during the process of division will be controlled by the na-ture of that object. If attention to this nature necessitates a divergent order of kinds and sub-kinds, then the practice of CD will sanction these variations.

3. The good illuminates structural characteristics of what is to be defined with respect to degrees, specifications in terms of greater or lesser. Distinctions in terms of degree are introduced in the *Statesman* by means of "due measurement" (283c–4e). In fact, the dimension of degree is crucial to the metaphysics underly-ing the exercise of method since, as argued above, a schema has a mode of exist-ence which depends on a Form but which is also both self-sufficient in certain contexts as well as "less" than the full reality of the Form as such. We may note, however, that the express theoretical announcement of a kind of reality which explicitly admits of degrees must wait for the *Philebus* and the introduction of what Socrates there refers to as "new tools" (23c–30c). One of these new tools is identified as the unlimited, an element typically understood to evoke a contin-uum as well as the consequent presence of degrees of more and less. If, as argued

here, distinctions between (a) kinds and Forms (as part to whole) as well as (b) schemas and Forms are proper to the metaphysical foundations underlying the account of CD in the *Statesman*, then the introduction of degrees in the practice of these processes may affect specification of properties belonging to either, perhaps both, of these realities.[7]

4. At 266d, not long before the onset of the myth, the Visitor is reviewing the results of his and Young Socrates' initial efforts at definition and he asserts authoritatively that "...such a method of argument as ours is not more concerned with what is more dignified than with what is not, and neither does it at all despise the smaller more than the greater, but always reaches the truest conclusion by itself." This apparent statement of principle is asserted immediately after the practice of CD has seemingly shown that the king and the pig are indistinguishable from one another. If we take this heavy-handed humor to indicate that something has gone seriously awry when CD has been based on this principle, then the missing factor which presumably would have blocked such inapposite conclusions is precisely the value dimension proper to methodology. This dimension would be established with due force by means of the dependency relation derived from the good insofar as the good provides the foundation for all subsequent metaphysical classification. If the practice of a method results in conclusions lumping together pigs and kings, it is possible that the method itself, not just its practitioners, is at fault. In general then, the aspects of process involved in the realization of a Form through the practice of CD admit greater or lesser degrees of success depending on the extent to which the practitioners of method have control of the good – just as the myth has shown in graphic and dramatic detail what can transpire for the cosmos itself if it has been created without due divine consideration of the full foundational force of the good.

The dimension of degrees with respect to the good has been interpreted by Grams to mean that divisions, properly drawn, will reflect the nature of the good with respect to better and worse "insofar as things may more or less closely resemble the good" (149, n. 21). Another reading concerning the function of the good in this regard is possible and which seems more apposite. If, as is surely the case, many diverse types of things and processes involving things can be "better and worse," then Grams' position locates all these contrasting conditions as resident within the good as such via an apparent resemblance relationship. It is

---

7 The presentation of due measure in the *Statesman* is condensed yet worth close examination from the standpoint of certain foundational elements in metaphysics (e.g., being and becoming). For a more developed discussion of due measure, see MMD, 81–96.

more accurate, I submit, to emphasize how attributes of the good will make elements of a division better or worse as given elements of a certain kind of reality. Thus better and worse weaving results from how aspects of the good as such do and do not pertain to the structure of weaving as a certain type of process executed with certain types of material. It is, after all, entirely possible that different aspects of the good will come into play in order to make the paradigmatic process of weaving (as integral to the structure of statecraft) better and worse. Weaving as a craft in the traditional sense works with cloth material that offers a limited degree of resistance; statecraft operates with elements – human beings – characterized with a generous spectrum of possible responses, both positive and negative. What differentiates better and worse statecraft may therefore be very different from what differentiates better and worse weaving.

5. As far as the explicit application of CD in the *Statesman* is concerned, the final statement of the nature of statecraft should be read as only provisional as well as incomplete, given its derivation from a fundamentally fragmented apprehension of the requisite metaphysical realities for conferring the highest possible level of cognition–the Forms as such and the good. Thus the resemblance-factor built into the notion of a paradigm has its counterpart in the resemblance between the schema of a king and the Form of a king. In fact, the schema of the king presented at the conclusion of the dialogue displays the same degree of oscillating stability as an independent entity as that of the cosmos depicted in the myth. In sum, the schema is a delicately poised approximation of the Form of the king. This Form, as such, is "nearer" to the good than the schema which grounds the sustained inquiry of the conversation and applications of methodology recorded in the *Statesman*. But this conversation revolves around a schema and paradigms; in those regards, its conclusions remain tentative at best.

The Visitor's account of statecraft is animated by a vision of the same kind of totality described in the *Timaeus*. The relation between the schema and the Form of the king reflects, in its derivative description and structure, the relation between (a) the cosmos described in the myth of the *Statesman* and the access of the god to the immutable and invisible realities which underlie, or could underlie, the elements of this cosmos and (b) the cosmos fully formed by the demiurge in the *Timaeus* in accordance with the demiurge's explicitly cited apprehension of canonic Forms and divine vision of the good. To take the account of statecraft delivered by the Visitor at the conclusion of the dialogue as orthodox Platonic teaching is to presume that the fundamentally truncated interplay of metaphysical elements permeating the entire dialogue – an account advanced in its entirety by an Eleatic Visitor, not by Socrates – represents orthodox Platonic metaphysics in its final form. The *Timaeus* and the *Philebus* suggest otherwise.

6. At *Republic* 525a, Socrates asserts as a matter of principle that "the study of unity would be one of those which convert the soul and lead it to the contemplation of reality." And in the *Parmenides* (135d–translation Allen) Socrates as a younger philosopher is urged by the elder Parmenides to "drag yourself through what is generally regarded as useless, and condemned by the multitude as idle talk" in order to be trained to "mark off" certain realities, e.g., goodness. The "dragging" Parmenides refers to pertains to the subsequent hypotheses concerning unity and abstract implications related to unity. We note then that once an appropriate interpretive vantage point has been secured on the *Statesman*, various senses and levels of unity emerge:

i. The unity of the *Statesman* which, if taken as organic, entails examining all its parts to determine how they fit into one narrative whole.

ii. The unity of the cosmos as described in the dialogue, establishing the "mythic" conditions of which will direct the reader to important metaphysical implications pertaining to the dialogue's non-mythical sections.

iii. The unity of natures as they come to exist within the cosmos and the distinct metaphysical aspects of this unity as derived from the practices of "the god" who fashioned it.

iv. The unity of Forms, especially to the extent that entities endowed in the dialogue with modes of existence other than those of Forms appear nonetheless integrally related to Forms.

v. The unity of totality, a name functioning as a place marker for a coherent specification of all levels of modality and existence as these elements are evoked throughout the *Statesman* taken as a narrative whole.

If these distinct and divergent senses of unity are relevant to reading and understanding the *Statesman* in its entirety, then we must acknowledge the wisdom conveyed by the *Republic* passage on the crucial character of unity as a theoretically precise prod to contemplating reality insofar as the *Statesman* has depicted the structure of reality.

6 Conclusion

This study has given reasons to believe that the myth in the *Statesman* directly affects (i) the results of collection and division when subjected to critical evaluation by the participants in the dialogue; (ii) the formulation of the operational structure of theoretical elements comprising collection and division (in particular the difficult relation between part and class); (iii) related components of Platonic methodology, e.g., paradigms; and (iv) the final statement of the nature of state-craft, the immediate definitional destination of the work.

It seems fair to say then that the myth in this dialogue, for all its occasionally dizzying eccentricities, does serious and sustained philosophical labor. And it accomplishes these ends by evoking a vision of the good which, although diminished in intensity and scope compared to counterpart treatments in the *Republic* and *Timaeus*, remains vibrantly alive and effective. It may also be observed that reading the myth when juxtaposed with the good and in concert with other areas of analysis in the *Statesman* accords Plato the minimal interpretive courtesy of assuming that he knew what he was doing as far as the narrative structure of the dialogue as a whole is concerned. Collection and division stands as a locus of critical attention especially among students of later Plato with pronounced interests in metaphysics. However, when read in its entirety, the *Statesman* becomes a dialogue of integrated and comprehensive unity allowing its complex yet accessible interrelations to inform readers concerning the intricacies of methodology when pitched at a level of high abstraction, the importance of the good in matters methodological and, in the end, a way to envision and to approximate – but only approximate – the nature of statecraft.

Dougal Blyth
God and Cosmos in *Politicus* 269c–270a and Aristotle

The Eleatic Visitor's god in the *Politicus* myth deserves close comparison with Aristotle's prime mover, since the latter has more in common with the individuating features of this god in its mythical context than with the demiurge or the world soul in *Timaeus*, or cosmic soul in the *Phaedrus* and *Laws*. The god in *Politicus* (i) seems clearly to be ontologically independent (unlike the world soul in *Timaeus*, while the case regarding the gods moving the celestial bodies at *Laws* 899a–b is unclear),[1] (ii) is explicitly called a god and not a soul (unlike cosmic soul in *Phaedrus*, and *Laws* 899b), and (iii) is, intermittently at least, an ongoing cause of movement (unlike the demiurge in *Timaeus*). In these three respects, complete independence, explicit divinity, and causal effect, if not others, this god is remarkably similar to Aristotle's prime mover.[2] Thus I hope a close comparison will both illuminate further the Eleatic Visitor's underlying theology, and provide evidence for what Aristotle must have still found unsatisfactory about Plato's manner of accounting for the world.

The *proimion* to the Visitor's myth seems like a fragment of apodeictic scientific doctrine;[3] rhetorically it is strikingly similar to the beginning of Socrates' great speech in the *Phaedrus*.[4] In the *Politicus* the content of the preface and its connection to a bizarre mythical story with other purposes present major challenges to serious theological and cosmological interpretation, both in principle and practice.[5] My only justification for persisting is the remarkable interest of the

---

1 Menn (1992) 556 n.18 seems mistaken to take *Laws* X.897b1–2 and XII.966d–e as clear evidence for the independence of intellect (*nous*) from soul there (the former passage merely stating that intellect accompanies soul, the latter referring to two stages in the same proof of gods, that soul is the first mover, and some soul acts with intellect); cf. Hackforth (1936) 7. *Philebus* 30b–d seems to be better evidence, but, as a cause there, intellect is not explictly said to produce movement; cf. T.M. Robinson [1970] [= 1995a] 143 with nn.12–14.

2 These are also points of similarity with intellect in Anaxagoras, but I will restrict myself here to the comparison with Aristotle's god.

3 Cf. the comments on the effect the argumentative preface has on the myth itself by M. Miller, (1980) 36, and Horn (2012) 402–4.

4 See Blyth (1997); cf. for the comparison Skemp (1987) 86, and McCabe (1997) 99 n. 25, who, respectively, also compare *Ti.* 27dff. and Aristotle *Metaphysics* 12.6.

5 See Carone (2005) 147–9 for references to discussions of the implausibility of a literal interpretation of the myth as serious cosmology. Carone (149–152) then gives a very useful condensed

https://doi.org/ 10.1515/9783110605549-007

comparison with Aristotle. I will make no reference here to Kronos or Zeus, since these names seem to be used in the myth merely to identify different epochs in relation to human experience, and certainly have no explicit cosmological significance.[6]

The god in the *Politicus* as cause of movement and Aristotle

I begin with the apparent uniqueness in Plato of the god in the *Politicus* as an explicitly external contemporaneous cause of movement, like Aristotle's prime mover. Admittedly it is disputed whether the latter is a moving or final cause, but I believe that question rests on an improper distinction. The prime mover[7] acts as an end according to *Metaph.* 12.7, 1072a26–b4;[8] nevertheless he is responsible for the first heaven's movement, and is called a mover (since in the later books of both the *Metaphysics* and *Physics* the term τὸ κινοῦν systematically replaces

---

but wide-ranging catalogue of theological topics in *Plt.* and other late dialogues, with textual references.

6 N.b. *Plt.* 270a1–2; cf. similarly Lane (1998) 104–5. Nevertheless, there is evidence that 'Zeus' names the derivative wisdom and life of the cosmos in its independent phase, in his identification at *Phlb.* 30c–d with the royal soul and intellect within the world, and the intra-cosmic role of gods including Zeus at *Phdr.* 246e–247a, and cf. the Orphic fragment identifying Zeus with the whole cosmos, cited by Mason (2013) 227 n. 34. If so, then, since Kronos is traditionally Zeus' father, he would seem to be the demiurge in *Plt.* (cf. 273b1–2), who, I suggest below, is also identifiable with the god who moves the cosmos; on this identification of Kronos see also Verlinsky (2008) at p. 64, similarly Menn, (1995) 6 n.1, and Skemp (1987) 85 and, arguing contra, Ionescu (2014) 38, and similarly Seeck (2012) [online ed.: para. 361 n. 21, although cf. para. 396]. The Orphic association of Kronos with the afterlife in Pindar *Ol.* 2.68–85, noted by Ostenfeld (1993), at p. 99 n. 4, in a context of reincarnation (with *Ol.* 2.68–70 cf. Plato *Phdr.* 249a and *Plt.* 271c2) might suggest that the reversal of human life in the age of Kronos playfully represents the process that returns the dead of our era, soul and body, back to the condition necessary for another ordinary reincarnation in the subsequent age of Zeus, in effect by rewinding time; cf. somewhat similarly Verlinsky (2008) 76–8 and 82–3. Of course that is at best only one possible (and perhaps minor) aspect of its human significance in the myth, about which I make no further claims here.

7 πρῶτον κινοῦν: for the expression referring to this god see esp. e.g., *Metaph.* 12.8, 1073a27, 1074a37; cf. 1073a23–5.

8 For a recent attempt to show that this passage does not mean that the prime mover is a final cause see Berti (2010) 371–6; but Berti does not propose how otherwise an unmoved mover can cause movement, according to Aristotle; cf. Menn (1992) 571–3, with the corrections implied in Blyth (2015) 460–2.

terms like ὅθεν ἡ ἀρχὴ τῆς κινήσεως[9] for the moving cause,[10] and clearly means the same thing).[11]

Two initial differences from Aristotle are that the causality of the god in the *Politicus* myth is only intermittent (which I will discuss later), and that this god, unlike Aristotle's, appears itself to be in motion. He seems to rotate (269c5, e5–6),[12] just as the circle of the same described in the *Timaeus* (36c–37c) does.

For the latter reason, Erik Ostenfeld, for example, has argued that this god in the *Politicus* just is the circle of the same, and is imminent within the cosmos, not transcendent.[13] Since this god must, by contrast with the cosmos, be incorporeal (*Plt.* 269d5–e1), it is presumably just intellect (*nous*). But in considering it as intellect, Ostenfeld has difficulty dealing with the more explicit account of rotation in relation to cosmic intellect at *Laws* X.898a–b.[14] Immediately previously there the Athenian announces he will present an image (εἰκόνα) of that movement which intellect resembles (προσέοικεν, 897e4–6); then he states (898a3–6),

> the movement carried in one place must always be moved about a particular centre, as an imitation (μίμημα) of circles turned on a lathe, and must itself in every respect be as akin and similar (οἰκειοτάτην καὶ ὁμοίαν) as possible to the circuit of intellect (τῇ τοῦ νοῦ περιόδῳ).[15]

For the moment just note that the relation between literal perfect rotation, mentioned first, and the 'circuit of intellect' is only said to be very close kinship and similarity, not identity. Next the Athenian states in explanation (898a8–b3),

> Presumably we could never appear as feeble craftsmen of fine images in speech if we assert that both intellect and the movement carried in one <place>, as likened to the carrying (φοραῖς) of a sphere on a lathe, are moved in the same regard and same way and in the same <place?> and about the same things, and with respect to the same things and to one account and one order.

---

9 E.g. *Metaph* 1.3, 983a30.
10 See esp. *Metaph.* 12.4, 1070b22–35, 12.5, 1071a11–17.
11 Or, more precisely, πρῶτον κινοῦν means exactly ἀρχὴ τῆς κινήσεως: see *GC* 1.7, 324a269, cited by Gourinat (2013) 95 n.16; cf. *Ph.* 8.5, 256a4–13.
12 I discuss these passages below.
13 Ostenfeld (1993) 104.
14 Ostenfeld (1993) 105–6.
15 Cf. *Ti.* 34a1–3, 'He allotted to it [the cosmos' body] the movement akin to body, that of the seven that most particularly involved intellect and wisdom (τὴν περὶ νοῦν καὶ φρόνησιν μάλιστα οὖσαν)'. All translations here are my own.

The image of a circling wooden sphere here again illuminates both the activities of intellect and of rotation, as such. But there is no explicit statement that intellect itself literally rotates, and the listing of it separately alongside 'the movement carried in one <place>', as a distinct item, suggests it does not. The points of comparison (that it too is 'moved in the same regard and same way and in the same <place?> and about the same things, and with respect to the same things and to one account and one order') may have systematically different but analogically parallel references involving cognitive functions, structures, context and objects.

Following older scholars such as Skemp,[16] I suggest tentatively that this passage does not commit Plato's thought to a literal interpretation of intellectual movement as physical rotation, and in fact, in context, suggests rather the opposite. Certainly the expression ἐν τῷ αὐτῷ (898a8, cf. ἐν ἑνί, b1) does not explicitly refer to place, and may more generally imply just a unitary and unchanging circumstance or context. Aristotle (*Ph.* VIII.6, 260a18) uses ἐν τῷ αὐτῷ to refer to the changeless condition of the prime mover. If these considerations could be related to the *Politicus*, the parallelism there with Aristotle's unmoved prime mover would become all the more striking. I will discuss the evidence in the *Politicus* below.

Following a further suggestion by Skemp,[17] we might think that Aristotle's concepts of *energeia* and *entelecheia*, as applied to the prime mover, derive from an analysis of movement and change motivated particularly by frustration with the fact that Plato uses the term *kinêsis* and cognates metaphorically for intellectual activity. Or we might think that the verb κινέω, which literally means 'to incite', or 'excite', is not to be understood for Plato to have a range of meaning limited to causing movement in the sense of change, even of place.

There is evidence for this in the *Politicus* that has not (as far as I know) been commented upon. What the bodily component in the world demands, according to the Eleatic Visitor, is change (μεταβολῆς, 269e1–2), and so there must be an occasional alteration in the movement (κινήσεως παράλλαξιν, e4) of the bodily

---

16 Skemp (1967) 25, 83, 86, cf. 22–3; Skemp (1987) 105, and Hackforth (1936) 8, with Ostenfeld (1993) 99 n. 3 for further refs. Robinson (1995a) 133–4 with n. 8 is sceptical, and cf. Robinson (1995b) 19–20. For the opposite view see, e.g., Ostenfeld (1993) and apparently Lisi (2011) 199, while Lisi, 201–2, then provides an interesting discussion of the problem of incorporeal noetic movement in *Plt.* but seems mistaken to conclude it refers to periodic pulses ('latidos') of creative activity. This merely shifts to a new topic the problem of consistency with other dialogues that he seeks to address. Horn (2012) 404, accepts that the god is self-moved but does not specify whether he thinks literally so.

17 Skemp (1967) 88 n. 1.

cosmos, its reversal of direction. In other words, *kinêsis* (although alluding to rotation) does not literally signify *change* of place (as such) here, or else the bodily requirement would already have been satisfied without a reversal.[18] Non-changing *kinêsis* is presumably restricted to rotation.[19] Nevertheless the Eleatic stranger here overlooks the fact (acknowledged elsewhere in Plato) that the parts do change place during rotation, and focuses only on the whole.[20] This is presumably because the primary case of *kinêsis* in this sense is the god's noetic activity, and in this there are no parts. From our naturally more Aristotelian perspective any movement must involve change, and so we must consider whether the god's activity in *Politicus* is only metaphorical quasi-movement (in our sense of the term) before we come to discussing his mode of causing literal movement in the world.

There does seem to be a problem for this view. The preparatory argument in the *Politicus* myth includes the claim,

> always to turn (στρέφειν) itself is just about (σχεδόν) possible for nothing except, by contrast (δὲ...αὖ), the leader of everything moved (269e5–6).

The latter reference in context is unmistakably to the god,[21] contrasted with the cosmos, and at first blush it seems to imply that he causes himself to rotate physically,[22] since that is what στρέφειν means immediately following (e8) and subsequently (although not at 273e3).[23] But σχεδόν is difficult.[24] Taken closely with immediately following οὐδενὶ δυνατόν it implies, strictly speaking, 'possible for

---

18 Seeck (2012) para. 364, seems clearly mistaken, or at least misleading, when he asserts that this passage restricts all *movement* ('Bewegung' = *kinêsis*) to body; cf. his para. 366 (with 372–3), where the précis of the argument inaccurately represents the claim at 269e3–4 as that *rotation* is the smallest *subdivision* of *self-motion*.
19 Cf. also *Ti.* 34a1–3 (cited above) and *Laws* X.893c–d, the latter analysis explicitly contradicting the Eleatic Visitor's view here. Contrast also Aristotle, e.g. *Ph.* V.1–2, and *Metaph.* XII.7, 1072b5–10.
20 See most explicitly *Resp.* IV 436d.
21 Thus e.g. Robinson (1995a) 133 n. 7.
22 Thus e.g. Miller (1980) 37; Mohr (1985) 150–1, seems clearly mistaken regarding the use of αὖ.
23 By contrast the verbs συμποδηγεῖ and συγκυκλεῖ (269c5) are compounds of primarily transitive verbs, the prefix συν- only necessarily implying that the god provides aid to cause the world to find its way and rotate, with no restrictions on how the god does so.
24 As noted by Scodel (1987) 75 n. 5 although his account of the deduction of reverse rotation is inaccurate (there is no role for his claim that self-motion is the change closest to changelessness, nor the inference he attributes to readers, 76). Lisi (2011) 201 translates σχεδόν as governing (only) οὐδενί, and this together as expanded, rather than modified, by πλὴν κτλ ('casi nadie puede moverse siempre a si mismo, con la unica excepción ...'), but LSJ (*s.v.* σχεδόν) shows use

almost nothing ...', leaving open the remote chance, contrary to the argument's requirement, that something else besides the god, such as the cosmos or its own soul, might always cause its own rotation. Better then to take σχεδόν as modifying the whole predication, with the emphasis on σχεδόν... πλὴν τῷ ... ἡγουμένῳ (to expand, meaning, 'it is almost true to say that self-turning is possible for nothing *except* the leader of everything moved'). The Greek is more awkward with this hyperbaton, but it seems possible, and at least fits the argument. The effect would be to create hesitation about making an exception of the god, in the sense of attributing literal physical rotation to him.[25]

On the other hand, perhaps Plato did think the concept made sense that a completely incorporeal, and therefore physically unextended, being rotates literally in space, but I doubt it, and in any case Aristotle undoubtedly thought this unintelligible, with reference to the world soul in the *Timaeus*,[26] and so rejected the applicability of the terms 'rotation' and 'movement' to his god as he developed his own theory.

The god and the forms

It would in any case be a further parallel with Aristotle's god, which *Metaph.* 12.9 identifies as a self-contemplating intellect, if the Eleatic Visitor's god were meant to contemplate the forms as the principles of reality, insofar as the forms in Plato generally correspond in Aristotle with the prime mover himself, as the equivalent primary principle of reality, *qua* completely actual being.

There might be a reference to the forms in the context of discussion of the *Politicus*' god. At 269d5–6 the statement occurs:

> Always maintaining the same attributes and state and being the same (τὸ κατὰ ταὐτὰ καὶ ὡσαύτως ἔχειν ἀεὶ καὶ ταὐτὸν εἶναι), is appropriate only to the most divine things of all.

While the language used has significant terms in common with that applied both to intellect and to what literally rotates in the second *Laws* passage quoted (esp.

---

closely with the dative limited to poetry in the senses 'near' and 'similar to', and in any case this makes σχεδόν redundant.

25 Cf. similarly Seeck (2012) para. 375.

26 Ar. *On the Soul*, I.3, 407a2–b11; cf. Robinson (1995b) 25 and cf. p. 27.

τὸ κατὰ ταὐτὰ (...) καὶ ὡσαύτως, 898a8),[27] most scholars have compared it rather with language used of the forms, for instance ἅπερ ἀεὶ κατὰ ταὐτὰ καὶ ὡσαύτως ἔχει (*Phd.* 78c6).[28] One problem, nevertheless is that, in context, the *Politicus* claim would be most relevant to the argument that it introduces if a contrast were being drawn between the god, who never changes direction, and the cosmos, which must.[29]

I suggest, very tentatively, a possible solution to this difficulty, based on the comparison with Aristotle. In his case, the knower and the form known are the same in actuality, and in the case of the primary instance, the divine intellect's self-knowledge,[30] literally and essentially so.

The claim, first found later in Philo Judaeus (*De opificio mundi* 20), that the forms are located in the divine intellect, is normally thought to derive from interpretation of Aristotle's doctrine.[31] But Plato's *Sophist* 248e–249a can quite properly be read as making the same claim (as Neoplatonists later did read it), that the forms must essentially be actively contemplated by intellect.[32] The argument here establishes, contrary to the Friends of the Forms, that there must be movement, as well as rest, in 'what completely is' (τῷ παντελῶς ὄντι). While the latter phrase (248e7) is frequently taken to mean 'everything there is', and the argument as effectively recognising that what comes to be and changes also belongs to the whole of being, in addition to the forms (a revision of the 'two worlds' theory), it is philologically preferable to understand *to pantelôs on* as meaning

---

27 See also *Ti.* 34a3–4, διὸ δὴ κατὰ ταὐτὰ ἐν τῷ αὐτῷ καὶ ἐν ἑαυτῷ περιαγαγὼν αὐτό, and 41d7, οὐκέτι κατὰ ταὐτὰ ὡσαύτως (of the ingredients of the human rational soul), and Mohr (1985) 146 with further refs. Robinson (1995b) 18 argues against this interpretation on the grounds (i) that ἐν τῷ αὐτῷ differentiates this usage, referring to place (but see, rather, above), (ii) the fact of rotation changes the meaning of the other predicates (but this presupposes his own interpretation), and (iii) the use for rotation lacks the qualification ἀεὶ καὶ ταὐτὸ εἶναι (but, at least once created, the primary rotation *is* everlastingly the same, *Ti.* 41a–b, while in *Plt.* if the god is subject to either physical or metaphorical rotation, that too would be everlastingly the same, and he, in any case, must be so).
28 Also *Phd.* 79d5, cf. d2; *Resp.* V.479a2, e7, VI.484b4; *Phlb.* 61e2–3; *Sph.* 248a11–12, 249b12. Thus e.g., Robinson (1995a) 132 n. 6, also Robinson (1995b) 17–18, Brisson (1994a) 487, Mohr (1985) 146–7, Ostenfeld (1993) 98, and Ionescu (2014) 35 and 38.
29 Thus Lane (1998) 102 glosses 269d5–6 in her analysis of the deduction of reverse rotation as a claim that only the most divine things have the most perfect movement, circular and changeless.
30 νοήσεως νόησις, *Metaph.* 12.9, 1074b34–5; cf. Blyth (2016) 87–90.
31 Nevertheless, Dillon (2008) 230 n.13 suggests it comes from the 'intelligible living being', *Ti.* 39e.
32 For a defence of this view, with criticism of, and references for, the alternative, see Perl (2014) 64–9; see also Gerson (2005) 215–19, esp. 217; Seeck (2011) paras. 376–87, esp. 382, seems mistaken to restrict this to contingent human thought, since that could not guarantee the universality of the claims the Visitor here makes.

'what *perfectly* is',[33] referring only to the forms, and the argument to be that there must be intelligence of these, and so soul and movement, in relation to the forms themselves. 'What perfectly is', in this case, would be a whole constituted by a cognitive unity of intellect and forms, as the root or source of life and so of soul, owing to the quasi-movement consisting in divine intellect's active contemplation of the forms.[34]

If that were what the Eleatic Visitor means in the *Sophist*, then the phrase 'the most divine things of all' (τοῖς πάντων θειοτάτοις) at *Plt.* 269d6 (quoted above) might refer to this complex unity of forms and intellect, which would be what the god there is. This might then suggest the origin of Aristotle's closely analogous conception of a *self*-contemplating intellect, and ultimately of Philo's and subsequently Plotinus' innovations, synthesising these two ideas.

The god and the cosmos

One objection now might be that the god of the *Politicus* must contemplate not the forms, but the cosmos, at least when he retires to his viewing platform (272e3–5), since he notices its subsequent difficulties before he comes to the rescue (273d4–e4). But it is not inconceivable that he looks both ways, like Janus, just as the demiurge in the *Timaeus* looks both towards the forms and the world in constructing the latter.[35] I will discuss this further below.

I tentatively suggest that the most economical way of explaining the role of the demiurge within the myth itself might be to say that this does not require any first moment of creation or a demiurge separate from the god of movement, by

---

33 Cf. *Resp.* 477a3, where it is used of the forms as separate, and Perl (2014) 66; Menn (1995) 21 n. 1, admits that τὸ παντελῶς ὄν could not mean 'the entirety of being', but claims nevertheless that it does refer to sensibles as well as intelligibles (although it is not at all clear how he can say that it is 'natural' to 'stretch' the expression so), and he justifies rejecting its restriction to the forms on the ground that this would undermine agreement between the giants and gods (not so: the only concession required of the gods is that what is moved <in some sense> *is*, 249d, not that it completely or perfectly is).

34 On divine life, as such, cf. here Aristotle *Metaph.* 12.7, 1072b26–30 with Blyth (2017), and cf. Hackforth (1936) 8. *Metaph.* 12.7 and 9 (see above) are thus plausibly taken as evidence that Aristotle, like later ancient philosophers, understood the *Sophist* passage as I suggest it should be understood.

35 See e.g. *Ti.* 30c–d; cf. Hackforth (1936) 8–9.

contrast with the *Timaeus*;[36] rather, demiurgy might be limited to the repeated activity of the god of movement, 're-creating' the world anew, just in time, on each occasion when it is about to disolve into chaos, by restoring its derived life and immortality (270a3–5, 273e3–4), and so its order as a cosmos.[37] In that case, the cosmos would be everlastingly old. Accordingly, the temporal references in the descriptions of its bodily aspect (273b4–7, b7–c1, cf. c7) as 'that fellow-support of its nature from long ago',[38] then as 'a participant in much disorder before entering the present cosmos' and as deriving 'from its previous state', while still strictly temporal in denoting the existence of this element prior to the *present* cosmic phase, would ultimately and primarily signify that corporeality, as such, is originally ontologically, not temporally, a distinct principle from the demiurge.

On such a textually economical account of demiurgy in the *Politicus* myth,[39] that activity is coincident with the god's causation of movement, and is everlasting (although intermittent). This provides two further possible points of comparison with Aristotle's theory, an everlasting cosmos, and a unique and ongoing (albeit mythically intermittent) cause not only of movement, but also of cosmic order, unlike the myth of the *Timaeus* which separates these causes.

The god's mode of causation

But I wish now to abstract more systematically from the playful motif of alternating epochs that is central to the myth and its contribution to the *Politicus* as a whole.[40] This would produce an even closer parallel with Aristotle's cosmology, where of course there is no such alternation of cosmic epochs.

---

36 Skemp (1987) 106, and Robinson (1995b) 21–2 and cf. 28–9, by contrast assume a moment of creation in *Plt.* and see Nightingale (1996) 77 n. 23 for further refs.; Lisi (2011) 200–1 suggests (on the contrary) that *Tim.* represents a snapshot of one of the repeated re-creations in the *Politicus* myth, but then seems to argue for a doctrinal abstraction from strict alternation of epochs.

37 Rowe (1995) 189 *ad* 270a5, identifies the god moving the world with the demiurge, but says nothing about creation. Rosen (1979) 81–2, while rightly, on this view, identifying the 'god κοσμήσας' (273d4) with the mover god, then seems clearly mistaken to deny this is the demiurge. Others identifying the mover god with the demiurge include Skemp (1987) 85, Robinson (1995b) 19, Menn (1995) 10, Lisi (2011) 199, Seeck (2012) para. 361 n. 21, and Ionescu (2014) 37.

38 Rowe (1995) 73 *ad loc.* translates φύσεως as 'origins'; this is semantically alone quite plausible but involves treating the genitive as one of source, which seems slightly less likely in this context and in prose.

39 Cf. McCabe (1997) 100, on simplicity as a principle of explanation.

40 For the playfulness see *Plt.* 268d8, 268e4–6.

This interpretive step is only a thought experiment, but such an abstraction from a distinctive feature of the myth demands some explanation and justification. The motive is neither to advance an interpretation of the myth in the *Politicus* itself, nor a non-literalist interpretation of creation in the *Timaeus*, for instance, nor at all an overall synthetic account of late Platonic cosmology and theology. Rather, given the number of points of comparability with Aristotle's theory so far established, it is important, in order to complete the comparison, to consider the activity of the god of the *Politicus* more closely in relation to Aristotle's prime mover's mode of causation, since that is a key feature of his theory.

Now the two epochs of the *Politicus* myth attribute to the god two distinct stances in relation to the world. These are, alternately, firstly, directly causing its rotation, and secondly, remaining uninvolved with it, when the cosmos rotates on its own in reverse. But in Aristotle's theory there are close correlates for each of these. Firstly, Aristotle's god is the primary cause of movement in the cosmos, directly causing the everlasting rotation of the first heaven, and derivatively the diurnal rotation of all heavenly bodies including the sun, and thereby all generation and destruction and change in terrestrial nature, thus maintaining natural order.[41] Secondly, nevertheless, as an unmoved mover, a self-contemplating intellect and an independently, intrinsically, completely actual being he remains entirely separate from and uninvolved in the world.[42] Since in Aristotle these are co-incident features, we should ask not only how closely they resemble the two stances the god of the *Politicus* takes to the cosmos, but also whether and how far the latter could also be coincident. In Aristotle's case, these two features can coincide because the prime mover is unmoved and only moves as 'that for the sake of which', as an object of attraction.[43]

---

41 See esp., e.g., *Metaph.* 12.7, 1072a21–3, 1072b3–10, with 12.6, 1072a7–18 (and *Ph.* 8.6, 259b22–260a19), and *Metaph.* 12.10, 1075a11–25.

42 I will not discuss here the disputed question whether or not Aristotle's god has any awareness of dependent being (according to some philosophers, contemplating within his own mind the essences of other things, or even, implicitly at least, the cosmos itself, as a consequence of his own being).

43 In Blyth (2015) I have argued that this means that the prime mover excites movement in the first heaven as a quasi-autonomous psychophysical response in the heavenly body, rather than by being the deliberative object of a rational soul in a self-moving heavenly spherical animal, as it were, which is the Neoplatonist Simplicius' explanation, adopted by many modern commentators.

Now whether or not the suggestion is correct that in the *Politicus* the god is not said to rotate physically himself, there does not seem to me to be any explanation given or suggested in the text for how he causes rotation in the world.[44] We can perhaps accept that the world soul of the *Timaeus* is meant to act in a way similar to a human soul on a human body (not that we really understand that either, strictly speaking). Yet the god in *Politicus* acts only intermittently, unlike a soul, and even if we abstract from the myth it would seem his degree of disengagement from the world, ongoing in that case, would mean he could not ever be integrated into it like a soul.[45] Yet perhaps abstraction from the distinction of epochs helps with this problem. It would seem the god's causation of movement, his demiurgic activity, and his care for the world, might be consistent with his non-involvement in it, in accordance with my suggestions about the *Sophist* passage. Recall the idea that in the *Politicus* the god looks both ways like Janus. Insofar as he looks toward the forms, he would be one with them in *to pantelôs on*, and insofar as he looks towards the world, he would generate what the Eleatic Visitor calls the life and wisdom allotted to the latter by its composer (269d1–2), and the teaching of the demiurge, its father (273b1–2). There is no explicit mention of a world soul in *Politicus*, but we can surely call this derivative life and wisdom, linked with cosmic rotation, a world soul.[46] Rather than attributing any deliberate agency to the god, perhaps this means that, as cognitive quasi-rotation, he has a teleological influence, analogous to that of the forms, eliciting a physical imitation consisting in the world's rotation. This would produce yet another similarity with Aristotle (by which I mean of teleological causation, not imitation).[47]

Thus in one sense the god would be nothing other than the self-understanding of the forms, transcendent and self-sufficient, but this perfect being would then be alive with the quasi-movement of intelligence and so continuously and

---

44 Cf. Menn (1995) 46–54 on *nous* as an efficient cause.

45 In effect we are left with the same puzzle as in *Laws* X.898d9–899a6 over three possible mechanisms by which divine soul moves the heavenly bodies: if, as argued above, the god in *Politicus* is not physically internal to the world (the first suggested mechanism in *Laws*), it would then have to act either by means of an instrumental body (unlikely) or guide the cosmos by 'prodigious and wonderful powers', whatever those might be. What follows in effect adopts an explanation of the latter possibility.

46 Cf. Herter (1958) 109–10; also similarly Skemp (1987) 107 with n. 1, and Robinson (1995b) 21.

47 Cf. Skemp (1987) 105.

spontaneously generate soul, self-movement, as the recipient of a derivative in-telligence.[48] Next, soul would be the moving cause of physical movement, pri-marily as literal cosmic rotation, and of the constitution of a world-order within body. This physical rotation as suggested above would arise in soul engaged with body, as an imitation of the model presented of intelligent quasi-movement, and the order of the world by imitation of the forms. Thus in addition to his transcend-ent independence of the world, the god would function as a demiurgic cause tel-eologically, by the co-operation of rational movement with the paradigms of the forms.

I don't claim that Aristotle was as patient as I have tried to be in finding a coherent theology and ontology underlying the *Politicus* myth, nor that the result is entirely clear, or necessarily implied. But the attempt does suggest how close Plato might have come to many of Aristotle's distinctive positions. In addition to being (i) ontologically independent, (ii) explicitly called a god, and (iii) a cause of movement (as initially noted), I have argued that the god of the myth, like Ar-istotle's god, can be interpreted as (at least possibly) (iv) physically unmoved, (v) contemplating within, and as, itself the first principle(s) of being, and as (vi) a teleological contemporaneous cause (vii) of the order of (viii) an everlasting cos-mos. This study also confirms, and in particular highlights, what Aristotle clearly rejected, any idea of divine intellectual movement, metaphorical or not, while he nevertheless retained the association of life and intellect with his first cause of cosmic rotation and order in *Metaph.* 12.7–10.

---

48 Cf., on the priority of *nous* to soul, Hackforth (1936) and Menn (1995) 22–4, notwithstanding my alternative account above of its nature (the unitary self-understanding of the forms, rather than primarily itself a virtue, i.e. one form), and of *Sph.* 248e–249a, the evidence for this.

José María Zamora Calvo
Plato's Reign of Kronos: Proclus' Interpretation of the Myth in the *Politicus*

In the days of Kronos, when he still reigned in heaven, men lived without care, "as gods", in abundance, without suffering pain or conflict. But this happy life of men in the time of Kronos, as described by Plato in the *Politicus* (271c3–274d7), we only know through the myth and we just have a plain account, as in the dialogue itself, in which the Visitor from Elea regrets the absence of an informant (cf. Monserrat Molas 2014, 96–97, 99–102; Brill 2017, 38–41).[1]

In the 5th century AD, in contrast to the literal readings adopted by the members of Middle Platonism, Proclus Diadochus interprets this myth in a non-literal way, establishing a comparison between *Timaeus' demiourgia* and that of Kronos. Timaeus' narrative dissociates – and places at different times –, two states which in fact coexist in our universe, where the realm of Kronos, considered the supreme dialectic representing the culmination of the intellectual order of the gods, corresponds to the intelligible world; while the realm of Zeus, representative of the reason operative in the physical world, corresponds to the sensible domain. In order to justify the difference between divine Providence and fate, Proclus interprets this myth by connecting his exegesis with the demiurgic making of the world.

Proclus considers that the myth in the *Politicus* is limited to the separation of two states, which it places at different times, but which in fact co-exist in our universe: (1) the reign of Kronos, corresponding to the reign of the *intelligible* and (2) the reign of Zeus, corresponding to the reign of the *sensible*. In so doing Proclus seems to have transposed the cycles of Empedocles (*DK* 31 B 187), when Love and Strife govern a sphere alternately, into a division between two spheres – the sensible and the intelligible.[2] Brisson (1995, 363), when interpreting this myth, on the one hand relates it to Proclus' exegesis, but on the other hand proposes placing this alternation in a historical and temporal context occurring in a three-stage

---

1 This paper is part of the R&D Project (Ref. H2015/HUM–3362) Acis & Galatea, and the activities of the UAM Research Group: "Influences of Greek Ethics on Contemporary Philosophy" (Ref. F–055).
2 Cf. Procl. *in Ti.* II.69.24–27: "And Empedocles says the same thing, for he too makes the Sphere twofold –one sensible one, in which Strife holds power, and another intelligible one which is made continuous by Love. He even calls the one an image of the other, and it is obvious which one is an image of which." (Trans. Baltzly 2007, 126). Cf. *in Alc.* 113.18; *in Prm.* 723.22. Cf. Casas Martínez-Almeida (2011) 94–95.

process: (1) in the reign of Kronos, (2) in an autonomous world and (3) in the reign of Zeus.

The traditional interpretation suggests two types of cyclical movement and two zoogonies (cf. Horn 2012). Rowe, however (2002, 166–167), describes the myth as having three types of movement (from East to West in the reign of Kronos; from West to East in the transition period; from East to West in the reign of Zeus) and three types of reproduction /development of human life: two asexual types – in the reign of Kronos, the result of the 'sowing' of souls 'like seeds/gametes' in the earth with growth in a normal direction (from babyhood to adulthood), and in the transition period, with an inverse movement, where the evolution of human life is also in an inverse direction (from dead bodies to new life on earth); and a sexual reproduction mode, the Zeus phase, which corresponds to our era.[3]

	Time period	Movement	Anthropogenesis
Two-stage model:	1. Kronos	West to East	Out of the Earth (from dead bodies)
	2. Zeus	East to West	ex allelon
Three-stage model:	1. Kronos	East to West	Out of the Earth
	2. Inversion	West to East	Out of the Earth (from dead bodies)
	3. Zeus	East to West	ex allelon

In the myth of the *Politicus* (268d8–274d),[4] Plato presents two types of primitive man: one in the Golden Age in the reign of Kronos and the other at the start of the reign of Zeus. The first Age was ruled directly by the gods, and as in Hesiod, there reigned in it an idyllic peace, with happiness and abundance among men living a life of pure nature (271c8). The second kind of life, by contrast, was the result of the autonomous motion of the world (272d6). The gods had ceased to care for men, who suddenly found themselves in new circumstances: they suffered need and want, brought about by a hostile nature which they had to cultivate and master. The gods took pity on them and imparted the first gifts to men: fire, the arts, seeds and plants.

---

3 Brisson (1995) and Rowe (2002a) opt for three phases, although based on different arguments.
4 Cf. Pl. *Lg.* 713c2 ff. Cf. Hernández de la Fuente (2016) 68.

For Proclus the "reign of Kronos" is simply the *intelligible* reign, while the "cycle of Zeus" is the physical world. However, as Baltes (1976–1978, II.49) points out, the *Politicus* myth is a 'thorn in the side' for those interpreters who attempt to develop a single doctrine of Platonic thought since, although it has many details and terms in common with the *Timaeus*, it also diverges significantly from them.[5] So let us proceed, step by step, to attempt to discover the 'thorns' which may be encountered along the hermeneutic route taken by Proclus, for whom the writings of Plato form a coherent whole. Thus, to explain and elucidate the making of the world in the *Timaeus*, the Platonic Diadochus cites excerpts from other dialogues, including the *Philebus* (23–31)[6] and the *Politicus*.[7] Proclus is aware that the context is a determining factor when clarifying the terminology used.

In the 4th century Iamblichus defined what would be taught in schools of Neoplatonic thought in later centuries. We will not enlarge here on this well-known point,[8] but mention only the main guidelines of this programme, based on the principle that the study of the Platonic thought expressed in Plato's dialogues is divided into two cycles. The first cycle includes ten dialogues, starting with the *First Alcibiades*, an introduction to the whole of philosophy. This is followed by eight dialogues read in an order corresponding to a progression, in order, of virtues and knowledge. The *Politicus* is the seventh of the first set, and is devoted to cultivating the theoretical virtues and the knowledge of beings in the domain of physical realities. It comes immediately after the *Sophist* (6th), and before the reading of the *Symposium* (9th) and of the *Philebus* (10th), with these two latter dialogues devoted to the knowledge of beings in the domain of theological realities. The second cycle consists of two dialogues, and "the whole theory of Plato is comprehended in these two dialogues: the *Timaeus* and the *Parmenides*" (Procl. *in Ti.* I.14–17).

1

For Proclus the Platonic myth has to be interpreted allegorically, i.e. not literally, but with reference to other truths through the medium of narration. In his *Commentary on the Timaeus* (I.102.3–103.7) he deals with the Atlantis myth, and in particular with the warning of the priest of Saïs to the grandfather of Critias: "Ah,

---

5 Baltes (1976–1978: II.83) considers that there is only a juxtaposition of *theory* and *lexis*.
6 Cf. Procl. *in Ti.* I.259.27, 262.30, 315.15, 384.24, 403.18, 423.22.
7 Cf. Procl. *in Ti.* I.253,19, 260,14, 312,18, 315,23. Cf. Runia/Share (2008) 8.
8 Cf. Larsen (1972) chapters 5 and 6; Dunn (1976); Hadot (1979); O'Meara (1989) 97–99.

Solon, Solon, you Greeks are ever children. There isn't an old man among you."[9]
(*Ti.* 22b4–5), Proclus starts from words (22b3–4) which do not appear in the
lemma: "The priest is elderly (Παλαιὸς μὲν ὁ ἱερεύς)" (*in Ti.* I.102.3), as if he had
forgotten about them earlier (*in Ti.* I.10.18–19) and then remembers them and decides to add the commentaries on the identity of the elderly, unnamed priest. The
laws of Saïs were made taking the constitution of the ancient city of Athens as a
model. In the organization of the universe, the oldest element takes priority over
the youngest. To explain that age and youth are considered universal symbols,
Proclus refers to the myth in the *Politicus* (270c–272d), comparing the demiurgy
of the *Timaeus* and that of Kronos:[10]

> That is the relation to each other that things have in the creation-cycle of Zeus: those who
> are said to live under the cycle of Kronos are said to travel from older, as the Eleatic Stranger
> says, to younger, while those under [the cycle of] Zeus go in the opposite direction. Here too
> (34b–c) he will say about the soul that the Demiurge introduced soul to be older than the
> body, and on this account gave it greater seniority.[11]

(in Ti. I.103.22–29; trans. Tarrant 2007, 198)

There is a correspondence with the causes which are the "guardians of the coherence of the protective powers" (*in Ti.* I.103.15–16). Similarly, at another point in
his commentary (*in Ti.* I.288.14–15), where he refers to a passage in the *Timaeus*
(37a1) where the Demiurge is called "best of the intelligibles that always exist",[12]
Proclus also refers to a non-literal interpretation of the *Politicus* myth (272e4): "if
the Demiurge belongs to the beings that always exist, he does not create at one
point in time and release the rudder at another".

The activity of the demiurge cannot be interpreted in terms of time, and the
cosmos must be eternal. In his *Commentary on the Timaeus* (I.289.6–290.3) Proclus opposes the argument of the Middle Platonist Severus (Fr. 6 T Gioè),[13] who
considers that the world is everlasting, but that the actual world, which moves,

---

9 <Ὦ Σόλων, Σόλων, Ἕλληνες ἀεὶ παῖδές ἐστε· γέρων δὲ Ἕλλην οὐκ ἔστι> (trans. Zeyl 1997,
1230). Cf. Procl. *in Ti.* I.102.1–2.
10 Cf. Procl. *in Ti.* III.168.17.
11 ἐν γὰρ τῇ τοῦ Διὸς δημιουργίᾳ ταύτην ἔχει πρὸς ἄλληλα τάξιν, ὥσπερ τοὺς <μὲν> ἐν τῇ Κρονίᾳ
περιόδῳ ζῶντας ἀπὸ τοῦ πρεσβυτέρου πορεύεσθαί φησιν ὁ [25] <Ἐλεάτης ξένος> [*Plt.* 270d–e] εἰς
τὸ νεώτερον, τοὺς δὲ ἐν τῇ τοῦ Διὸς ἀνάπαλιν. καὶ ἐνταῦθα ὁ <Τίμαιος> ἐρεῖ [34 B C] περὶ τῆς
ψυχῆς, ὅτι τὴν ψυχὴν πρεσβυτέραν τοῦ σώματος παρήγαγεν ὁ δημιουργὸς καὶ διὰ τοῦτο
ἀρχηγικωτέραν αὐτὴν ὑπεστήσατο. Cf. Festugière (1966–1968) I.146.
12 Cf. Procl. *in Ti.* I.230.1.
13 Little is known about this Platonist. See Dillon (²1996) 262–264, who places him in the late
second century.

had a beginning. Based on the *Politicus* myth (270d7–8), he states that there are two types of revolution by which the actual rotation and counter-rotation of the universe take place. Therefore, the cosmos, which began at a particular point of origin and revolves in its current revolution, is generated, but in absolute terms is non-generated. In contrast to this interpretation by Severus, which reverts to the *Politicus* myth, Proclus replies: "that you are transferring mythical riddles (τὰ μυθικὰ αἰνίγματα) to natural science in an illegitimate manner." (*in Ti.* I.289.14–15).

After this opinion let us examine Severus, who says that in absolute terms the cosmos is everlasting, but that the present one which moves in the way it does is generated. For, [he claims,] there are two kinds of revolution, as the Eleatic stranger showed (*Plt.* 270d7–8), the one with which the universe now proceeds and its opposite. Therefore the cosmos which began from a particular starting-point[14] and revolves with its current revolution is generated, but in absolute terms it is not generated.

(1) Against this interpretation we shall make a reply by affirming that you are transferring mythical riddles to natural science in an illegitimate manner. How could the soul in motion grow weary and change its ancient revolution? How would the universe be complete and self-sufficient if it desires change? If both parties – the object moved and the mover – preserve their own disposition, how can there be space[15] for the change of (direction in) their revolutions? How can Timaeus say (36c5–d1) that the revolution of the Same moves to the right in accordance with the craftsman's decision, while the revolution of the Different moves to the left?"[16] (*in Ti.* I.289.6–22; trans. Runia & Share 2008, 142).

In parallel to a non-literal interpretation of the *Timaeus*, we also find in Proclus a non-literal interpretation of the *Politicus* myth according to which the

14 Cf. Pl. *Ti.* 28b7.

15 Proclus uses the technical term (χώρα) "space in which", which introduces Plato in the *Timaeus* (52d3), also quoted in *in Ti.* I.284.21.

16 μετὰ δὲ ταύτην τὴν δόξαν ἐπισκεψώμεθα <Σευῆρον>, ὅς φησιν ἁπλῶς μὲν ἀίδιον εἶναι τὸν κόσμον, τοῦτον δὲ τὸν νῦν ὄντα καὶ οὕτως κινούμενον γενητόν· ἀνακυκλήσεις γὰρ εἶναι διττάς, ὡς ἔδειξεν <ὁ Ἐλεάτης ξένος> [*Plt.* 270b], τὴν μὲν ἣν νυνὶ περιπορεύεται τὸ πᾶν, τὴν δὲ ἐναντίαν· γενητὸς οὖν ὁ κόσμος καὶ ἀπ' ἀρχῆς ἤρξατό τινος ὁ ταύτην τὴν ἀνακύκλησιν ἀνακυκλούμενος, ἁπλῶς δὲ οὐ γενητός. πρὸς δὴ ταύτην τὴν ἐξήγησιν ἀπάντησιν ἀπαντησόμεθα λέγοντες, ὅτι τὰ μυθικὰ αἰνίγματα μετάγεις εἰς φυσιολογίαν ὡς οὐκ ἔδει· ποῦ γὰρ ἀποκαμεῖν δυνατὸν τὴν κινοῦσαν ψυχὴν καὶ μεταβάλλειν τὴν ἀρχαίαν περιφοράν; πῶς δὲ τέλειον καὶ αὔταρκες τὸ πᾶν, εἰ μεταβολῆς ἐφίεται; πῶς δὲ ἀμφοτέρων τὴν οἰκείαν ἕξιν διασῳζόντων, τοῦ τε κινουμένου καὶ τοῦ κινοῦντος, ἔχει χώραν ἡ ἀμοιβὴ τῶν ἀνακυκλήσεων; πῶς δὲ ὁ <Τίμαιός> φησι [36c] τὴν μὲν ταὐτοῦ περιφορὰν ἐπὶ δεξιὰ κινεῖσθαι κατὰ τὴν δημιουργι- κὴν βούλησιν, τὴν δὲ θατέρου ἐπὶ ἀριστερά;

"reign of Kronos" relates to the intelligible world, while the "reign of Zeus" represents an operative rationale of the physical world and the "inverse revolution" of 272e ff. describes the irreducible resistance of the material element of the universe, similar to the disorderly motion of the material-spatial, χώρα, in the *Timaeus* (cf. Dillon 1995, 365).

In his exposition of the ordering of the world body by the demiurge, Proclus extends his providential activity to include in it the production of matter in disorder and of matter itself (cf. Lernould 2001, 322–326). At this point he challenges the Middle Platonic arguments which consider the demiurge another principle together with Ideas (models) and Matter. Proclus differentiates and unifies the respective causalities of the demiurge, of the model (and of the One). At the upper extreme of the hierarchical scale there is the demiurge as the divine cause of the universe, and at the lower extreme is the substratum which moves with no order or harmony, on which the demiurge imposes order. Between the two extremes, and in descending order, are found the world intellect, the immanent forms (which Proclus identifies with images of being) and the objects informed by nature.

In the *apokatastasis* all the planets return to the starting point. This is a fundamental concept to explain the theory of the 'Great Year'.

> But what if the universe were moved in a circular fashion, but also had various reversals, as it says in the myth in the *Statesman* (269a)? In order that we should not take it this way, Plato places the word uniformly prior to the other words in this sentence. Therefore the Platonist Severus has just got it wrong – we'll speak freely against him on this point – when he admits these mythical reversals of the motion of the cosmos, thus making the cosmos both generated and also ungenerated.[17]
>
> (*in Ti.* II.95.25–96.1; trans. Baltzly 2007, 158)

The Middle Platonist Severus interprets the *Politicus* myth literally, which leads him to adopt the Stoic theory of the periodic "return" (ἀποκατάστασις) of the cosmic cycle[18] as a way of solving the problem of whether the world was "generated" (γενητός) or "ungenerated" (ἀγένητος). Also, as Proclus himself points out, his

---

17 τί γάρ, εἰ κινοῖτο μὲν τὸ πᾶν κυκλικῶς, μεταβάλλοι δὲ ἄλλοτε ἄλλως ἀνατέλλον ἢ δῦνον, ὥς φησιν ὁ ἐν τῷ <Πολιτικῷ> [269 A] μῦθος; ἵν' οὖν μὴ τοῦτο ὑπολάβωμεν, τὸ <κατὰ ταὐτὰ> πρόκειται τῶν ἄλλων περὶ αὐτῆς ῥημάτων. οὐκ ἄρα ὀρθῶς ὁ Πλατωνικὸς <Σευῆρος> – παρρησιασόμεθα γὰρ ἐντεῦθεν πρὸς αὐτόν – τὰς ἀνακυκλήσεις τὰς μυθικὰς προσέμενος καὶ γενητὸν οὕτω ποιῶν καὶ ἀγένητον τὸν κόσμον·
18 Proclus uses the technical term (χώρα) "space in which", which Plato introduces in *Timaeus* (52d3), also cited in *in Ti.* I.284.21.

master Syrianus (*in Ti.* II.96.5–7),[19] in either a commentary on the *Timaeus* or in another specifically devoted to the *Politicus*, was against the literal interpretation of the myth.

To explain the difference between destiny and providence Proclus refers to the *Politicus* myth. For example, in his *Commentary on the Timaeus*, in a discussion on the true nature of fate, from the exegesis in *Timaeus* 41e ("he showed them the nature of the universe and proclaimed the laws of Fate"), Proclus returns once again to the *Politicus* (272e):

"Plato alone saw the true essence of it, for he calls it nature, but dependent on the demiurge. For indeed, how can the demiurge show the nature [of the Whole to souls] if he does not possess the principle himself? And how can he state the laws of fate after having shown the nature of the Whole/the universe/, or rather the total coherence of these laws after establishing this nature? But, even more clearly, in the *Politicus* (272e5–8) he makes the second life of the universe depend on fate, after the separation of the world from the only daemon which governs it and the many other daemons which follow only one. And thus he sets aside from the universe all providence which comes from the daemons and only leaves the governance of fate to it (although the world always counts on the combined effect of providence and fate or destiny, but only the fable separates the former from the latter). For, as he says, fate and the innate impulse itself influence the revolution of the world, just as the Oracles say that nature governs

...the worlds and works, / that the heaven may run its eternal course / dragging all things in its train [fr. 70 Des Places; 36 Kroll][20]

so that the other revolutions can take place, those of the sun, the moon, the seasons, the night and the day.[21] (Procl. *in Ti.* III.273.19–274.7; our translation)

---

19 It is not clear whether in this case Proclus is referring to a commentary by Syrianus on the *Timaeus*, as suggested by Diehl, or to another on the *Politicus*. According to Dillon, his arguments here are probably taken from Syrianus.

20 "Mundi sunt sidera, opera quaecumque a mentibus creantur". Lewy (2010) 96, and n. 126.

21 μόνος δὲ ὁ <Πλάτων> τὴν οὐσίαν αὐτῆς ἐθεώρησε, φύσιν μὲν αὐτὴν εἰπών, ἐξημμένην δὲ τοῦ δημιουργοῦ· πῶς γὰρ ἄλλως δείκνυσι τὴν φύσιν ὁ δημιουργὸς ἢ ἐν ἑαυτῷ τὴν ἀρχὴν ἔχων αὐτῆς; πῶς δὲ <τοὺς εἱμαρμένους νόμους> λέγει μετὰ τὸ δεῖξαι τὴν τοῦ παντὸς φύσιν ἢ τὴν μίαν συνοχὴν τῶν νόμων τούτων τὴν φύσιν ὑποστησάμενος; ἔτι δὲ σαφέστερον <ἐν τῷ Πολιτικῷ> [272e] τὴν δευτέραν τοῦ παντὸς ζωὴν ἐξάπτει τῆς εἱμαρμένης μετὰ τὸν χωρισμὸν τοῦ τε ἑνὸς δαίμονος ἀπ' αὐτοῦ τοῦ κυβερνῶντος αὐτὸν καὶ τῶν πολλῶν δαιμόνων <τῶν> τῷ ἑνὶ ἐκείνῳ συνεπομένων, δι' ὧν πᾶσαν τὴν περὶ αὐτῶν πρόνοιαν ἀφίστησιν ἀπ' αὐτοῦ καὶ ἀπολείπει μόνην τὴν καθ' εἱμαρμένην διοίκησιν, ἀεὶ τοῦ κόσμου τὴν συναμφοτέραν ἔχοντος, τοῦ δὲ μύθου χωρίσαντος ἀπὸ

For Proclus, in the fable Plato differentiates two main governing principles which operate in the world: divine providence and fate. The latter has immediate control over the natural world, but not supreme control over human life. These are alternate cycles, the reign of Kronos and the reign of Zeus, or of providence and of fate, and of the periodical abandonment of the physical universe by the gods (cf. Dillon 1995, 369–370). It is precisely this passage which describes the period in which the demiurge loses control of the reins and as a result the 'second life of the universe' spins out of control. The separation of the universe from providential governance remains exclusively subject to fate. Proclus states that there is a second world period which is presided over by fate, in contrast to the first, intellectual period which is connected to the invisible providence of the gods. The mortal soul, just like the demiurge, must always strive to regain control, therefore aspiring to return to this period and to intellectual contemplation. Nevertheless, this is not enough to ensure unification, but constitutes one of the conditions required to achieve assimilation (cf. Kutash 2011, 272). The human soul has to take drastic measures to escape the form of mortal life.

The souls possess their own periods of transmigration.[22] Proclus seems to take into account the causal role in the return of things to their starting points. Thus, a city or a tree goes from not having existed, to existing for a time, and then to not existing again. This is the ἀποκατάστασις applied to these individual things. Time is therefore not only limited to acting as a cause in cycles of the heavenly bodies, but also in individual perishable things (cf. Duvick 2007, 35–36).

Without going into textual problems, since Proclus' commentary does not really help to define Plato's exact words, when he describes the dance of the heavenly bodies at *Ti.* 40c3–d4. ἀνακυκλήσεις may refer to 'gyrations' or 'revolutions' (cf. *in Ti.* II.96.3), as in the *Politicus* myth (269e3) when Plato uses ἀνακύκλησις, but more often with the meaning of 'retrogradations' or "rotations" of the planets in their own orbits (cf. *in Ti.* III.145.2–3). Proclus explains that the 'screenings' (ἐπιπροσθήσεις) of the heavenly bodies are the media interposed between the divine souls and us, since not all the souls are united immediately one with another, but through more or less numerous intermediaries depending on the soul (cf. *in Ti.* III.150.12–15).

τῆς δευτέρας τὴν προτέραν· <τὸν> γὰρ <κόσμον>, φησίν, <ἀνέστρεφεν εἱμαρμένη τε καὶ σύμφυτος ἐπιθυμία>, καθάπερ καὶ τὰ <λόγιά> [*Or. chald.* 36] φησιν αὐτὴν προστατεῖν
  <κόσμων τε καὶ ἔργων,
οὐρανὸς ὄφρα θέῃ δρόμον ἀίδιον κατασύρων>,
καὶ ὅπως ἂν αἱ ἄλλαι περίοδοι πληρῶνται, ἡλίου, σελήνης, ὡρῶν, νυκτός, ἡμέρας.
Cf. Festugière (1966–1968) V.150; Dillon (1995) 369.
22 Cf. Iambl. *Myst.* 1.10; Procl. *El.Th.* 199.

> The words at what times they are hidden and appear [refer to] both the starting points of the periods and the points at which the cycle is completed (*apokatastasis*), for it is in relation to these in particular that the things in the cosmos 'turn' and transform, bringing total ruin and great changes, as Plato says in the *Statesman*.[23]
>
> (*in Ti*. III.150.16–20; trans. Baltzly 2013, 255)

Proclus returns to the passage in the *Politicus* (270a) to which the Neoplatonists paid most interest: the history of cosmic reversion. In this precise hermeneutic context, he connects the appearances and disappearances of the planets with the phases of the heavenly bodies which traverse the sky. Proclus links this notion of 'conversion' or 'rotation' in the *Timaeus*,[24] cited in his commentary on this Dialogue (III.147.13–14): "have turnings as they undergo their journeys through the heavens (δι᾽ οὐρανοῦ πορευόμενα τροπὰς ἔχειν)", with the "circular motion" or "reversal" described in the *Politicus* (270b10–c2): "We must suppose that this change is, of the turnings that occur in the heavens, the greatest and the most complete turning of all (Ταύτην τὴν μεταβολὴν ἡγεῖσθαι δεῖ τῶν περὶ τὸν οὐρανὸν γιγνομένων τροπῶν πασῶν εἶναι μεγίστην καὶ τελεωτάτην τροπήν)." (trans. Rowe 1997a, 312). In fact, in astronomy, the Greek term τροπή is specifically ascribed to the solstices, i.e. the points in the year when the Sun ceases to ascend or descend from one or other part of the equator (cf. Zamora Calvo & Brisson, 2010, 391, n. 206). All the planets present analogous motions. It is when this reversal occurs 'that the greatest changes come upon us' (*Plt*. 270c4–5): "We must suppose, then, that at that time the greatest changes also occur for us who live within the universe (Μεγίστας τοίνυν καὶ μεταβολὰς χρὴ νομίζειν γίγνεσθαι τότε τοῖς ἐντὸς ἡμῖν οἰκοῦσιν αὐτοῦ)." (trans. Rowe 1997a, 312)[25]

> The function of the Demiurge is to contribute an element of order to Becoming, because an ordered world will be more 'like himself', that is to say, better, than a disorderly one.
>
> (Cornford 1937, 37)

The demiurge, as Intellect, is the cause of order (*in Ti*. I.386.24–25). In fact, the world is ordered because it is moved by an Intellect and a Soul endowed with

---

23 αἱ δὲ 'κατακαλύψεις καὶ ἐκφάνσεις αἱ κατὰ χρόνους' αἵ τε ἀποκαταστάσεις καὶ αἱ ἀρχαὶ τῶν περιόδων· κατὰ γὰρ ταύτας μάλιστα τρέπουσι τὰ ἐν τῷ κόσμῳ καὶ μεταβάλλουσιν, ἀθρόας ἐπάγουσαι φθορὰς καὶ μεγάλας μεταβολάς, ὥς φησιν αὐτὸς <ἐν τῷ Πολιτικῷ> [270B s].

24 "the heavenly bodies which traverse the skies and have phases (ἄστρων ὅσα δι᾽ οὐρανοῦ πορευόμενα ἔσχεν τροπάς)".

25 "We must believe then, that at the time such changes take place in the Universe we human beings living within that universe have to undergo the most drastic changes also." (trans. Skemp 1952, 147–148). Cf. Procl. *in Ti*. I.106.14, 29; 107.21; 114.27; 116.2. Cf. Festugière (1966–1968) IV.191–192; Baltzly (2013) 255, n. 621.

reason (*in Ti.* I.383.10–14). In his explanation of the *Timaeus* (30a2–6),[26] Proclus approaches the theme of demiurgic providence, i.e. he maintains the thesis of a birth of the cosmos according to providence (γένεσις κατὰ τὴν πρόνοιαν), in opposition to the thesis of Plutarch and Atticus, who maintain the birth is temporal (γένεσις κατὰ τὸν χρόνον). For Proclus the primordial motion is natural, rather than the work of a malevolent soul. For Plutarch and Atticus, by contrast, where there is motion there is a soul, a view which becomes false if the existence of other sources of motion can be proved.[27]

> Not in a state of rest but moving shows that the hypothesis has attributed to [the visible] only the nature from which movement [derives]; for, since [that] nature is irrational and without guidance from God, what order could it maintain in addition [to that]? [Plato] indicates this in the *Politicus* (272e5–6) as well. [There], after he has [10] removed the Demiurge from the cosmos, he says that it moves by itself precisely 'by a kind of destiny and connatural desire'. So it is by here postulating before the creation what he there postulated after the creation that he has introduced into the movement of the visible a disorder [15] which arises without [the involvement of] intellect. So much for this [phrase].[28]
>
> (*in Ti.* I.389.5–16; trans. Runia & Share 2008, 260–261)

"The myth of the *Statesman* (esp. 272e) provides Proclus with the authoritative argument for his view of primordial motion." (Martijn 2010, 71). At first (though not in any temporal sense of the phrase), only something 'of nature' is present in the world, and it is not able to impose order, only unassisted motion. The intervention of the demiurge is needed to impose order, as shown in the *Politicus*

---

26 The god wanted everything to be good and nothing to be bad so far as that was possible, and so he took over all that was visible — not at rest but in discordant and disorderly motion — and brought it from a state of disorder to one of order, because he believed that order was in every way better than disorder. (βουληθεὶς γὰρ ὁ θεὸς ἀγαθὰ μὲν πάντα, φλαῦρον δὲ μηδὲν εἶναι κατὰ δύναμιν, οὕτω δὴ πᾶν ὅσον ἦν ὁρατὸν παραλαβὼν οὐχ ἡσυχίαν ἄγον ἀλλὰ κινούμενον πλημμελῶς [5] καὶ ἀτάκτως, εἰς τάξιν αὐτὸ ἤγαγεν ἐκ τῆς ἀταξίας, ἡγησάμενος ἐκεῖνο τούτου πάντως ἄμεινον)." (Trans. Zeyl 1997, 1236).
27 Cf. Procl. *in Ti.* I. 381.26–382.12.
28 τὸ δὲ <οὐχ ἡσυχίαν ἄγον, ἀλλὰ κινούμενον> ὅτι τὴν φύσιν αὐτῷ δέδωκε μόνην ἡ ὑπόθεσις δείκνυσιν, ἀφ' ἧς ἡ κίνησις· ἄλογος γὰρ ἡ φύσις οὖσα καὶ οὐ θεόθεν ποδηγετουμένη ποίαν ἔτι φυλάττειν τάξιν δύναιτο ἄν; δηλοῖ δὲ τοῦτο [10] καὶ ἐν τῷ <Πολιτικῷ> [272 E 5s.]· τὸν γὰρ δημιουργὸν ἀποστήσας τοῦ κόσμου κινεῖσθαί φησιν αὐτὸν ὑπὸ δή τινος <εἱμαρμένης καὶ συμφύτου> καθ' αὐτὸν <ἐπιθυμίας>· ὅπερ οὖν ἐκεῖ μετὰ τὴν δημιουργίαν, τοῦτο ἐνταῦθα πρὸ τῆς δημιουργίας ὑποθέμενος ἀταξίαν εἰσήγαγεν εἰς τὴν τοῦ [15] ὁρατοῦ κίνησιν ἄνευ νοῦ γιγνομένην. καὶ τοῦτο μὲν τοιοῦτον. Cf. Procl. *in R.* II. 13.2; II. 356.6; *Theol.Plat.* V.119.16; *Prov.* 11.

myth, where the world, abandoned by the demiurge, moves by itself in a disorderly fashion 'by a kind of destiny and connatural desire'.[29] But this argument presents a problem, since it introduces a second type of nature, φύσις ἄλογος, the primordial, irrational essence of the universe, which contrasts with the nature described up to this point in 8.5–9. The two types must be differentiated, since primordial nature is an irregular source of motion, and is not receptive of soul; by contrast, precisely because the other nature is receptive of soul, the demiurge inserts it into nature. Irrational nature does not yet possess the aptitude or inherent capacity (ἐπιτηδειότης) to be ordered (*in Ti.* I.392.9–10; cf. *El.Th.* 79). For the world to possess a soul which can participate in intellect (*in Ti.* I.401.18–32), the demiurge must first give 'what moved in a confused and disorderly manner' an aptitude or inherent capacity to receive rational soul, i.e., soul which is apt for receiving intellect. And this disposition, as Festugière (1966–1968, 273, n. 1) explains, is life (ζωή), since the motion of life is regular, or disposed to become regular.

2

The dialectician is analogous to the Cronian monad

ὁ δὲ διαλεκτικὸς ἀνάλογόν ἐστι τῇ Κρονίᾳ μονάδι
Crat. 63.10–11

In fact, from above the sublime Kronos concedes the principles of the intellections to the demiurge and directs the universal demiurgy.[30] In his *Platonic Theology* (I.4.22.2) Proclus maintains that intellectual thought (*noêsis*) is the medium between the intelligible and the intellectual. Uranus, as the chief god of the intelligible and intellectual sphere, is charged with connecting the upper and lower spheres through intelligence. Kronos, who at one and the same time is linked to and separated from his father, receives knowledge of the intelligible through intelligence, and works downwards as a principle in Zeus.

There are double revolutions in the universe: one upwards, that of Kronos, and the other dependent on Zeus. The two revolutions which Proclus mentions refer to the type of life which each soul chooses when it descends to generation.

---

29 Procl. *in Ti.* I.389.11–12. Runia/Share (2008) 261, n. 304 point out that they would prefer to translate this as 'inborn', but the argument depends to a considerable extent on the word-play between φύσις ('nature') and σύμφυτος ('connatural').
30 Cf. Procl. *in Crat.* 63.11–13.

This theory is based on the description of the cycle of mortal generation put forward by Plato in the *Republic* (X. 617d–619a). In coordinating the psychic life-stages of Kronos and Zeus, Proclus posits two hierarchical cosmic cycles linked analogically according to levels, which allows particular souls to transcend the effects of inferior, particular causes, such as the young gods, and to continue the upward path towards their intellectual source, which leads to reality itself, the truth of being. Or to express this in another way, Proclus declares that the soul should look beyond the immediate, particular causes of a manifest object to its intellectual image, and in the end, should turn its gaze to God and to the object itself.

> Yet Plato himself says that, living happily in the time of Cronus, even the God's 'nurslings' operate by dialectic. They converse with both each other 'and the beasts' (for all things there are intellectual) 'through discussions on philosophy', associate and 'seek to learn from every nature if any know of one possessing a particular power for the common pool of wisdom' (*Plt.* 272b–c). But those who revolve (*anakuklein*) the life that is under the dispensation of Zeus require the art of legislation and the measures derived from it for the organization of their states. This is why there are double revolutions (*anakukleseis*) in the universe as well, the one being uplifting and Cronian, the other being providential and dependent on Zeus. For the king Cronus uses all the products of Zeus according to his transcendent superiority, and, through them as images, extends the upward path to particular souls[31].[32]
>
> (trans. Duvick 2007, 35–36; Cf.
> Álvarez/Gabilondo/García 1999, 97)

In his commentary on a passage in *Cratylus* (390c10–11), Socrates proposes the following definition of the dialectician: "And what would you call someone who knows how to ask and answer questions? Wouldn't you call him a dialectician? (Τὸν δὲ ἐρωτᾶν καὶ ἀποκρίνεσθαι ἐπιστάμενον ἄλλο τι σὺ καλεῖς ἢ διαλεκτικόν;)" (trans. Reeve 1997, 109). Proclus considers Kronos as the supreme dialectician, who grants to Zeus, the demiurge, the 'plan' for making the universe (*in*

---

31 Cf. Procl. *in Crat.* 27 & 61.
32 ἀλλὰ καὶ αὐτὸς ὁ Πλάτων τοὺς ἐπὶ Κρόνου εὐδαιμόνως ζῶντας καὶ τοῦ θεοῦ <τροφίμους> κατὰ τὴν διαλεκτικὴν φησιν (*Polit.* 272b–c) ἐνεργεῖν, ἀλλήλοις τε καὶ τοῖς [30] <θηρίοις> (πάντα γὰρ ἐκεῖ νοερά) <διὰ λόγων> συνόντας <ἐπὶ φιλοσοφίᾳ> καὶ ὁμιλοῦντας καὶ <πυνθανομένους> παρὰ πάσης φύσεως, εἴ τινά τις ἰδίαν δύναμιν ἔχουσαν ᾔσθετο εἰς συναγερμὸν φρονήσεως>· τοὺς δὲ τὸν δῖον βίον ἀνακυκλοῦντας τῆς νομοθετικῆς δεδεῆσθαι καὶ τῶν ἐκ ταύτης [35] μέτρων εἰς διακόσμησιν τῶν πολιτειῶν. διὸ κἂν τῷ παντὶ διτταὶ ἀνακυκλήσεις, ἡ μὲν ἀναγωγὸς καὶ Κρονία, ἡ δὲ προνοητικὴ καὶ τοῦ Διὸς ἐξηρτημένη· καὶ γὰρ ὁ βασιλεὺς Κρόνος τοῖς τοῦ Διὸς γεννήμασι χρῆται πᾶσι κατὰ τὴν ἐξηρημένην ὑπεροχήν, καὶ ταῖς μερισταῖς ψυχαῖς δι' αὐτῶν ὡς εἰκόνων προτείνει [40] τὴν ἀναγωγὸν πορείαν. (Procl. *in Cra.* 63.27–41 Pasquali)

Crat. 27.21–24). "Kronos" is the name of the Intellect insofar as it is the most elevated and most separate, so that the supreme intellectual activity is identified with dialectic. Through a play on words, Proclus links division (διαίρεσις) with cutting (τομή), which represents the castration of Uranus, and on the other hand with the recomposing (συναγωγή) and swallowing (κατάποσις) of food. The first of these connections, the linking of division with the castration of Uranus by Kronos, and of Kronos by Zeus, is related to the fragmentation which intervenes in the world soul: the demiurge mixes the fundamental blend which is used to make the world soul (*Ti.* 35a–b), and then, like a smith, transforms and laminates this mass and makes a certain number of divisions in it. He starts by cutting this mass lengthwise into two portions, paradoxically called the Same and the Other, although these two portions are formed by a blend of Being, the Same and the Other. This operation will account for the difference observed between the fixed stars and the planets. Then he divides the portion of the Other into seven sections, to account for the movement of the seven planets known at the time. The apparently erratic motion of the planets probably explains the name 'Other' given to this portion, in opposition to the portion of the 'Same' which represents the apparently regular movement of the fixed stars.

Similarly, a second connection is established between the recomposing or reuniting and the swallowing of his own offspring by Kronos (*in Crat.* 28.2–4). In this context, Proclus alludes to the *Politicus* myth where, according to his exegesis, the motion of the universe follows two opposing directions, one governed by Kronos and the other by Zeus. But in his citation from the *Politicus* (272c1–4), Proclus' exegesis differs from Plato's proposal. In the reign of Kronos, men did not need to work to guarantee their survival, so that they had plenty of free time, and an ideal opportunity to discuss a particular theme not only among themselves but also with the animals; and that theme was myth, not philosophy. The specific proof that Kronos is truly the supreme dialectic stems from the fact that men held discussions with each other and even with the animals, which Proclus considers to be the identifying trait of true dialectic. However, this Proclean exegesis is debatable, since it contrasts with the definition of dialectic in the earlier dialogues, and it is difficult to establish a link between discussion and dialectic which uses procedures of division and re-composition. Similarly, in his presentation of the *Politicus* myth, Plato himself affirms that the men who lived in the reign of Kronos did not engage in philosophy.

From the dialectic point of view, we act 'as if' we were already in the 'reign of Kronos', as if social matter could be modelled without offering any resistance, following the dictates of the intelligible (cf. Delcomminette 2000, 218). Through the medium of etymological interpretation based on the *Cratylus,* Proclus identifies Kronos with pure intellect, separate from the rest. But the supreme activity of the intellect corresponds to dialectic, which from the *Phaedrus,* and particularly in the *Politicus* and the *Sophist,* connects two moments: the division and the recomposition of the intelligible.

Following Proclus, Olympiodorus in his *Commentary on the Gorgias* differentiates between two types of myth: poetical myths, which are 'simply beautiful, but not to excess, as their apparent content is not beautiful, but only their profound content', and philosophical myths, which are 'exceptionally beautiful, as their apparent content is also beautiful' (*in Grg.* 47.1 = 243.1ss.). Like Proclus, Olympiodorus also classifies the myth of Kronos and his offspring as representative of the poetic type, and considers that Kronos is 'pure intellect', so that the poets 'say that he devours his own children and then vomits them up again, as the intellect turns towards itself and is at the same time subject and object of its search' (*in Grg.* 47.3 =244.16 ss.). The etymology which Olympiodorus follows is the same as that proposed by Plato in the *Cratylus* (396b), and according to Damascius agrees with the fact that Orpheus also identifies the intellect with Kronos, and that thoughts themselves are what feed the intellect (Dam. *Pr.* 67 [I.146.12 ff. Ruelle] = *Orph. fr.* 131 Kern).

3

In his *Platonic Theology* (I.5.23.22–24.3) Proclus declares that the truth about the gods is propagated in all Plato's dialogues, and that venerable, clear and supernatural concepts of prime philosophy have been disseminated in all of them, but in some of them obscurely and in others more clearly. In his commentaries he insists that both Plato and the characters who intervene in his dialogues speak with clarity (ἐναργῶς).[33] According to Proclus, Plato applies this procedure when he translates the narratives of the ancient poets into the language of myth: in the *Politicus,* the Stranger from Elea speaks "clearly" (V.6.25.9 and 21); and even more clearly, the myth of the Gorgias separates the reign of Zeus from the reign of Kronos (V.36.132.16–19).

---

[33] Cf. Procl. *in R.* I.45.7, 62.7, 108.10, 186.15, 191.30, 201.27, 203.27, 233.17, 278.2, 280.11, 15; II.9.14, 90.21, 97.11, 105.14, 128.19; *in Ti.* I.129.18, 229.19, 230.1, 284.20, 287.25; II.50.13, 53.12, 110.9; III.179.20, 214.24, 293.23. Cf. Taormina 2000, 35–37.

Proclus shows the connection between evidence and the common notion (*in Ti.* I.285.25). Nevertheless, while in demonstrative language this link is the starting point for demonstration, in allusive language it represents the end point for a persuasive process which runs from one term to the other. According to Proclus, Plato uses this characteristic procedure of allusive language when he translates the stories told by the ancient poets into the language of myth. The discourse of the poets reveals the divine principles through obscure allusions, it imitates sensible things instead of intelligible beings, and from true beings it makes images and falsifications (*in R.* I.44.14–15; 159.15). Nevertheless, the truth, although it may be hidden, is always present in them. Bouffartigue (1987, 132) remarks that 'it is found on the inner face of the veil'. Through this metaphor we can clarify the double status of the myth which separates the truth and brings it closer at one and the same time, acting as the boundary between the world of appearances and that of the real truth. As Brisson (²2005, 148) explains, it relays it from this side to the beings here below, and from the other side to the realities of the world above. But the myths transmitted by the poets are conceived as symbols and as enigmas (cf. Sheppard 1980, 145–160), so that Plato can carry out a meta-linguistic interpretation which discovers the true sense.

Proclus states that the 'translation' of the myths which Plato engages in seeks out their occult meaning (*Theol.Plat.* V.3.18.15–16), and redirects their fiction to the truth. The elaboration of the myths, which aspire to seek out the unspeakable truth (V.3.17.12–13), implies the transition from obscurity to clarity, as it displays the theories concealed in these fables and redirects them to the conditions of philosophical thought (I.4.21.20–21). But this reconversion is based on the non-demonstrative nature of the mythical *logos*, which allows persuasion and sympathy with the divine. This is how the Platonic myths awaken the sleeping soul to common notions, and allow the truth to become clear (I.6.29.9–17).

Proclus corroborates this interpretation with the help of examples, such as the following: Plato shows that the 'unions' and 'mutilations' of the gods, 'named with disguised words' in the myths, are symbols of communion and division (V.3.18.19–20). In the *Gorgias* (523a3–5) Plato returns to the story of Homer (*Il.* XV.187 ff.) on the reign of Kronos transmitted to his sons; he separates the reign of Zeus clearly from the reign of Kronos (V.4236.132.16–19), and he calls this inferior reign the primary and most recent. Thus, Proclus shows that the primary cause of all division is to be found amongst the gods.

Although there is no explicit commentary on the *Politicus*, in Book V of *Platonic Theology* (ch. 6–10 and 25) Proclus carries out what is equivalent to an exegesis of the myth, in which we can clearly appreciate the hermeneutic proposal. Proclus devotes this Book V to the exposition of the intellective gods. The order of the intellective gods is not organized in an ennead (three triads of three members) but instead as a hebdomad (two triads and one monad). After listing the themes (ch. 1–4), he describes the gods of the first triad, that of the source-gods: Kronos (ch. 5–10), Hecate (ch. 11) and Zeus (ch. 12–32). He then focuses on the second triad, that of the chief gods or immaculates (ch. 33–35) and on the monad which occupies the seventh rank (ch. 36). Finally, he offers a description of the intellective gods in the *Parmenides* (ch. 37–40).

The source-gods (πηγαί) proceed naturally from the one who occupies the highest rank among the intelligible gods, i.e. the Living thing itself; and it is specifically from Kronos, one of the source gods, that all else comes (cf. *Theol.Plat.* VI.3.20.7–8 = F 40 *Chaldean Oracles*). Kronos, Hecate and Zeus, who correspond respectively to the triad of intelligible gods – Father or One, Power or Eternity and Intellect or Living thing itself –, form the triad of the source-gods and the principle-gods. The first of these source-gods is Kronos. In his adaptation of a passage from the *Politicus* myth (272b8), where he calls the men from the previous cycle creatures of Kronos, Proclus cites a fragment of a verse taken from the *Chaldean Oracles* stating that 'the intelligible is nourishment' (F 17, cf. *Theol.Plat.* V.8.29.20 y V.25.93.1–2).[34] Kronos is the required step for souls between the intellectual and the intelligible-intellectual. The high level of Kronos represents the first degree of the first intellectual triad. The celestial triad occupies an intermediate position. In fact, the souls at their summit touch the lowest degree of the intelligible-intellectual gods, the 'subcelestial arch' (cf. *Theol.Plat.* IV.20–24). When the souls rise through these two triads they achieve the contemplation of the first triad of intelligible-intellectual gods, the 'supercelestial place'.

In his *Platonic Theology* (V.37.135.11 = F 5.2), Proclus considers Kronos to be a fecund power, as it is he who makes the 'implacable' (ἀμείλικτος) triad of the intellectual gods exist, which cannot be placated by spells, prayers or sacrifices. For this reason, Kronos is assigned to 'the motion of the heavenly bodies, for on him depends time, generation and corruption of beings (*in Ti.* 187.21–22). The etymology of the name Kronos is based on two identifications: with Time (Χρόνος), or with his family relationship with κόρος. This second etymology appears in Cicero (*N. D.* II.25.64) "*Saturnus autem est appellatus quod saturetur*" and in Plotinus, for whom Kronos symbolizes Intelligence: this Kronos (*En.* V.1 [10] 7), or Intelligence 'filled with the beings he engendered, devours them again, as he retains

---

34 This same quotation from the *Chaldean Oracles* also appears in Proclus (*in Ti.* I.18; *in Crat.* 168.92.12–13) and in Damascius (*Pr.* II.91.23). In order to make this observation Proclus is probably referring to the *Phaedrus*, with the intention of showing that the terminology he uses is not only Chaldean but also Platonic.

them in himself and does not allow them to fall into matter and grow according to Rhea'.[35] According to the etymology used by the Stoics, which Plotinus took from them, Kronos (Κρόνος) is the god of 'satiety' (κόρος) and 'intelligence' (νοῦς) (Plot. *En.* V.1 [10] 4.9–10). We can see that the Latin correspondence between *Saturnus* and *satur* coincides with the Greek relationship of Κρόνος and κόρος, just as Plotinus established. St. Augustine in *Agreement among the Evangelists* also refers to the Stoic etymology, transmitted by Cicero, precisely when he explains this passage from Plotinus. The Latin term *Saturnus*, as shown in the Augustinian interpretation, is a hybrid term, half Latin and half Greek, which corresponds perfectly to Plotinus' 'saturated intelligence' if it is written *Satur*-νοῦς.[36]

In the *Cratylus* (396b6–7) Plato had given an etymology for the name Kronos, breaking it down into κόρος and νοῦς. Proclus re-uses this etymology in his gloss on Hesiod (*Works and Days* 111, p. 50. 7–10 Pertusi), and coins the term κορονοῦς for Kronos in his *Commentary on Cratylus* and in the *Commentary on Parmenides* (107, p. 59.5), as Damascius has shown us (*in Prm.* 134.19–20 and 292.164.9–10). Kronos forms part of the order of the 'insenescible' gods who do not age (ἀγήραος) (*Theol.Plat.* V.10.33.22–23), using a quality related to the Chaldean Oracles (cf. Lewy, 2010, 79, n. 48 and 103, n. 154; and des Places, F 187).

> The reason for this is that King Kronos himself makes the gods exist who do not succumb to spells and to the *implacable* triad. (And thus Kronos is also *coronous*, as Socrates says, since he is an intellect which at one and the same time is the summit of the undefiled order of the gods and surpasses the vigorous gods who govern the universe), and the souls which proceed towards him make surprising progress in intellectual activity and also in strength and inflexible power, and do not tend to the material.[37]
>
> (*Theol.Plat.* V.10.35.3–11; our translation)

---

35 Cf. Ramos Jurado (1981) 148–149.

36 Aug. *De consensu Euangelistarum*, I.23.35: "Their more recent Platonic philosophers, who have lived during Christian times, have been embarrassed by this. They try to interpret Saturn in another way, saying that the name Kronos indicates fullness of understanding. For fullness is called *choros* in Greek, and understanding or mind is *nous*. In a way the Latin name favors this [interpretation], if the first part is from Latin and the latter part from Greek: he is called Saturnus, as though he were 'Satur-*nous*' , 'full-mind.'". (trans. Paffenroth 2014: 155).

37 Τούτου δὲ αἴτιον ὅτι καὶ αὐτὸς ὁ βασιλεὺς Κρόνος ὑποστάτης ἐστὶ τῶν ἀκηλήτων θεῶν καὶ τῆς <ἀμειλίκτου> [35.5] τριάδος (διὸ δὴ καὶ κορόνους ἐστίν, ὡς ὁ Σωκράτης φησί, νοῦς γάρ ἐστιν ὁμοῦ τῆς ἀχράντου τάξεως τὴν ἀκρότητα περὶ αὐτὸν ἔχων καὶ τοῖς τὰ ὅλα κυβερνῶσιν ἀκμαίοις θεοῖς ἐποχούμενος)· καὶ αἱ πρὸς αὐτὸν <στελλόμεναι> ψυχαὶ μετὰ τῆς νοερᾶς ἐνεργείας εἰς ἀκμὴν καὶ δύναμιν [35.10] ἄκαμπῆ καὶ ἀρρεπῆ πρὸς τὴν ὕλην θαυμαστῶς ἐπιδιδόασιν.

Kronos represents the culmination of the intellectual order of the gods, while Zeus, or the demiurge, is below him (cf. *Theol.Plat.* V.15.15–24). Zeus, the demiurge by antonomasia, is the 'source of nature' which Proclus, following the denomination of the gods themselves, identifies with the 'prime destiny' (F 102). In the *Timaeus* (41e2–3) Plato says that the souls, after 'setting them each as it were in a chariot',[38] see the 'nature of the universe' and the 'laws of destiny' i.e. the encosmic destiny and its powers.[39] In the *Politicus* (272e5–6) the Stranger from Elea claims that destiny (fate) is the driving force of the natural circular movement of the earth: "fate and innate desire made the earth turn backwards" (*Theol. Plat.* V.32.119.7–19).

The set of references to nature, identified with fate, come from Book X of the *Republic* (the myth of Er), from the *Politicus*, the *Timaeus* and Book X of the *Laws*. Nature, identified with destiny, is the world soul, but is not considered in itself but rather as the driving force of all the movements which serve to weave fate or destiny.

In Book V of his *Platonic Theology* devoted to the intellectual gods, Proclus takes up again the double correspondence between division and the castration of Uranus, on the one hand, and of Zeus by Kronos on the other, and re-composition with the swallowing by Kronos of his own progeny (cf. *Theol.Plat.* V.36.132.20–25). By devouring his own offspring Kronos provides the intellectual nourishment for the beings who follow him in the procession. In this explanatory context, Proclus returns to the *Politicus* myth, where Plato mentions an ancient tradition by which the men who lived under the reign of Kronos saw their food grow spontaneously, so that they were called 'food of Kronos'.[40]

> Truly therefore, this universe has two types of lives, *periods* and *revolutions;* that of Kronos and that of Zeus, as the *Statesman* myth says. And in one of the two periods, the world produces *all goods spontaneously* and enjoys a life free of sorrow and weariness. In the other period, it is part of the confusion of matter and of nature in constant change. In fact, of these two types of life which there are in the world, one is invisible and more intellectual, while the other is more natural and visible, and one is defined by providence and the other proceeds in a disorderly manner according to fate. This latter one is inferior, multiple and natural, and is dependent on the order of Zeus. The former is simpler, more intellectual and invisible, and depends on the order of Kronos. The Eleatic Stranger shows us this clearly when he calls one of these two circular motions that of Zeus, and the other that of Kronos. And truly, Zeus is also the cause of the invisible life of the Whole, the provider of intellect and leader of intellectual perfection, but he raises all beings to the reign of Kronos and, as

---

38 Cf. the central myth of the *Phaedrus* (246a–250c).
39 Cf. Pl. *Phdr.* 248c and *Leg.* X 904c.
40 Cf. Procl. *Theol.Plat.* V.5.24.10–20 Saffrey/Westerink.

he is the leader with his father, causes the whole pericosmic intellect[41] to continue. And if the truth is to be stated clearly, each one of the two periods, that is the visible and the invisible, takes part in both of these gods, but one is more of the reign of Kronos and the other belongs more to the reign of Zeus.[42]

(*Theol.Plat.* V.6.24.23–25.19; our translation)

In *Platonic Theology* (V.6.24.23–25.19 and V.25.92.1–13), commenting on a passage from the *Politicus* (269e–272e), Proclus makes a clear distinction between two 'revolutions': the first is intelligible, governed by divine providence, and the second is 'visible' or 'apparent' (ἐμφανής), governed by destiny or fate (εἱμαρμένη).[43] In his writing on the myth of Er, on the other hand, Proclus concentrates on divinity and motion: he talks of 'the nature of all' (ἡ φύσις τοῦ παντός), which he identifies with destiny (Fate), and which is inferior to the soul because it is not a god, but superior to the soul since it does not move.[44]

Proclus qualifies both the One, as well as the Intelligence and the Soul as 'primordial/primeval' (πρῶτον/πρῶτη), but nature only as "universal" (ὅλη),[45] because there is no primordial/primeval nature. In the *Commentary on Timaeus* and *Commentary on Parmenides* the sphere of nature is not more elevated than

---

41 Proclus uses the term 'pericosmic' (περικόσμιος) to describe the gods of the cosmos, both hypercosmic and encosmic (cf. *Theol.Plat.* II.7.48.13–14). However, as Saffrey and Westerink (1987, 163–164, n. 2) mention in their complementary notes, it often appears as synonymous with encosmic, as in, e.g., Iam. *Myst.* II 1.67.12–13; Syrian. *in Metaph.* 26.10 y 116.20–21; Procl. *Theol.Plat.* I.4.18.7; Dion.Ar. *DN* I 6 (P.G. 3, col. 596C).

[24.23] Εἰκότως ἄρα καὶ τὸ πᾶν τοῦτο διττὰς ἔχει ζωὰς καὶ περιόδους καὶ συγκυκλήσεις, καὶ τὴν μὲν Κρονίαν, τὴν [24.25] δὲ Δίιαν, ὥς φησιν ὁ ἐν τῷ Πολιτικῷ μῦθος. Καὶ κατὰ μὲν τὴν ἑτέραν τῶν περιόδων <αὐτόματα πάντα> φύει [25.1] τὰ ἀγαθὰ καὶ ἀπήμονα ζωὴν ἔχει καὶ ἄτρυτον· κατὰ δὲ τὴν ἑτέραν μετέχει καὶ τῆς ὑλικῆς πλημμελείας καὶ τῆς πολυμεταβόλου φύσεως. Διττῆς γὰρ οὔσης ἐν τῷ κόσμῳ ζωῆς, τῆς μὲν ἀφανοῦς καὶ νοερωτέρας, τῆς δὲ φυσικωτέρας [25.5] καὶ ἐμφανοῦς, καὶ τῆς μὲν κατὰ τὴν πρόνοιαν ἀφοριζομένης, τῆς δὲ καθ' εἱμαρμένην ἀτάκτως προϊούσης, ἡ μὲν δευτέρα καὶ πολυειδὴς καὶ διὰ τῆς φύσεως ἐπιτελουμένη τῆς Δίιας ἐξήρτηται τάξεως, ἡ δὲ ἁπλουστέρα καὶ νοερὰ καὶ ἀφανὴς τῆς Κρονίας. Καὶ ταῦτα σαφῶς ὁ [25.10] Ἐλεάτης ξένος ἀναδιδάσκει, τὴν μὲν ἑτέραν τῶν ἀνακυκλήσεων Δίιον ἀποκαλῶν, τὴν δὲ ἑτέραν Κρονίαν. Καίτοι καὶ ὁ Ζεὺς τῆς ἀφανοῦς αἴτιός ἐστι ζωῆς τοῦ παντὸς καὶ τοῦ νοῦ χορηγὸς καὶ τῆς νοερᾶς τελειότητος ἡγεμώ[42]ν, ἀλλ' ἐπὶ τὴν Κρόνου βασιλείαν ἀνάγει τὰ πάντα καὶ μετὰ [25.15] τοῦ πατρὸς ὢν ἡγεμὼν ὑφίστησι τὸν ὅλον περικόσμιον νοῦν. Καὶ εἰ δεῖ τἀληθῆ διαρρήδην λέγειν, ἑκάτερα μὲν τῶν περιόδων, ἥ τε ἐμφανὴς λέγω καὶ ἡ ἀφανής, μετέχει τῶν θεῶν τούτων ἀμφοτέρων, ἀλλ' ἡ μὲν Κρονία μᾶλλόν ἐστιν, ἡ δὲ ὑπὸ τὴν τοῦ Διὸς τελεῖ βασιλείαν.

43 Cf. Procl. *Theol.Plat.* V.25.93.24–25; V. 32.119.13–22.

44 Cf. Procl. *in R.* II. 357.11–27; cf. Martijn (2010) 28.

45 Cf. Procl. *in Prm.* 703.18–19.

the 'nature of all' i.e. it does not rise above universal nature (ἡ τοῦ ὅλου/παντὸς φύσις).[46]

For Proclus the Platonic conception of the gods appears in the dialogues in many different forms: dialectic, as in the *Parmenides* and the *Sophist*; symbolic, as in the *Protagoras*, the *Gorgias* and the *Symposium*; and through images, as in *Timaeus* and the *Politicus* (cf. *Theol.Plat.* I.4.20.13–19). In his *Platonic Theology* (V.32.119.9–19) Proclus connects the association of nature with fatality (εἱμαρμαρμένη) with two Platonic passages taken from the *Timaeus* and the *Politicus* (272e5–6).[47] Freed from fate through the medium of initiation, the soul flees from the control of the daemons which intervene in the sublunar regions and incite it to surrender to passions.

If the reign of Kronos is placed under the auspices of science and philosophy, the reign of Zeus, by contrast, which corresponds to our age, is marked by oblivion and ignorance, i.e. by the breakdown in participation when material obligations predominate over the demands of the intelligible. Most of the references to the *Politicus* myth in the work of Proclus appear in relation to the exegesis of the demiurgic making of the world in the *Timaeus*. Though we can also find a connection with the *Phaedrus* myth (247d2), where divine thought in the supercelestial place is fed by intellection and 'intact' knowledge (ἀκήρατος), i.e., as Proclus states in *Platonic Theology* (V.5.23.22–23), by the intellectual being turned towards the higher degree, the intelligible, since, as he declares in proposition 167 of the *Elements of Theology*, the intellectual can only turn towards what is superior to it, i.e. the intelligible.

Kronos symbolizes the transcendent intellect (νοῦς) – or to be more precise, in the metaphysical architecture of Proclus, the "culmination" (ἀκρότης) (*El.Theol.* 147) or "the king of the intellectual gods (ὁ βασιλεὺς τῶν νοερῶν θεῶν" (*Theol.Plat.* V.21.2 – whose objects are "universal and indivisible". Meanwhile, Zeus is either the participated intellect (or else as for Plotinus, a pure soul) whose contents are the forms in their multiplicity and a greater particularity. Proclus differentiates the two external monads of the first intellectual triad: Kronos is for Zeus an 'intelligible intellect', and Zeus is for Kronos an 'intellectual intellect' (*Theol.Plat.* V.5.21.26–22.2). These two, therefore, preside over alternate cycles, and represent two permanent levels of reality.

---

46 Cf. Procl. *E.Th.* 21.30–33; *in Ti.* I.338.23–24; *in Prm.* 1045.32–36.
47 In contrast to the Proclean interpretation, and based on a contemporary hermeneutical approach, El Murr (2014) 152–153 points out that the cyclical view of the central myth of the *Politicus* (268d4–274e1) opposes that of the *Timaeus* (41a7–b6).

In his *Platonic Theology* (I.6) Proclus describes the 'authors of myths' as 'divine men' or 'sons of gods'.[48] For the Diadochus, instead of scientific language, we can find the rich and magical language of inspired poetry and myth, which raises us up above our shortcomings (cf. Trouillard 1974, 243). When, for example, the divine paternity is mentioned, the participation of the lower degree in the higher is concealed (cf. Buffière 1973, 545). The discourse of myth, as expressed in Plato's *Politicus*, goes beyond the merely literal, as "the myths reveal the truth as if under a veil (οἱ μῦθοι τὴν ἀλήθειαν ἐπικρυπτόμενοι λέγουσιν)" (*in R.* I.90.6–7).

---

48 Cf. Pl. *Ti.* 40d8.

Anna Motta
Demiurgy in Heavens. An Ancient Account in Plato's *Statesman*

1 Introduction

While books have been published on different aspects of the *Statesman*, the aim of this paper is to follow the lead not of any old or recent research carried out on such a dialogue, but of some ancient research, that which the Neoplatonists used to encourage their disciples to undertake and which seems very far from modern ways of reading the text. All Platonic dialogues are examples of living beings if we look at them in the right way, namely that suggested by the Neoplatonists.[1] By bearing this fascinating exegetical suggestion in mind, we can try to read the *Statesman* as a piece of that living metaphysical literature regarding «the most beautiful and accurate» of sensible things (Pl. *R.* 7, 529c9–d3),[2] organized by an οὐρανοῦ δημιουργός (Pl. *R.* 7, 530a3–7) with whom Plato – as a divinely inspired intellect and the divine architect of the dialogues – has a lot in common.[3] According to the Neoplatonists, Plato has transmitted some of his ideas in a written form and others in a non-written form, just as the Demiurge has made certain parts of his creation visible and others invisible, as in the case of heavenly bodies and things within the world of generation (Anon. *Proll.* 13.18–25). According to the *Statesman* this God,[4] mythically presented as a Demiurge (δημιουργός, Pl.

The present contribution investigates – albeit in a succinct and partial way – one of the topics of the research project on the relation between literary theory and natural philosophy in Neoplatonism that I have developed with the support of the Freie Universität of Berlin and the Dahlem Research School, within the framework of a post-doctoral programme of the TOPOI Excellence Cluster

1 See Anon. *Proll.* 13.6–12. About the cosmos as a world of art and the dialogues as a world of art, see Coulter 1976, 101–103, Kahn (2013) 179 and Motta (2013).
2 This section of the *Republic* is devoted to astronomy: see Franco Repellini (2003).
3 See Procl. *Theol. Plat.* V 10, 33.25.34.1 and Anon. *Proll.* 13.18–25. On the metaphysical literature, see Motta (2014).
4 According to Greek piety (and despite the Platonic and Neoplatonic interpretation) the Gods are responsible for everything important, whether good or bad. Thus, in Hesiod's story of the Myth of Metals, both Zeus and the Gods generally are said to "make" (ποιεῖν) the successive races of mankind (*Op.* 109–58). But when Hesiod comes to describe the origins of the world in his *Theogony*, he speaks of Earth and Heaven as "being born" (γενέσθαι) rather than being made. On the relationship between Plato and the poets see Boys-Stones (2009). About the *Statesman* myth and that in Hesiod, see Tulli (1991), Boys-Stones (2001) 10–14 and El Murr (2010).

https://doi.org/ 10.1515/9783110605549-009

Plt. 270a5), has harmonized the cosmos (συναρμόσαντος, Pl. *Plt.* 269d1). In his role as a mediator, he appears inferior to the immutable Forms – the most divine of all things (τοῖς πάντων θειοτάτοις, Pl. *Plt.* 269d6) – and superior to the material realm he organizes.[5]

My chief aim here is not to provide an identification between the Platonic Demiurge of the *Statesman* and one of the Demiurges of which the Neoplatonists speak,[6] or to survey all the complexities of the demiurgic function in the Neoplatonist universe, where late-antique commentators operate in different exegetical contexts at various levels of complexity. First of all, my aim is to point out that the legacy of the *Statesman* in Neoplatonism is not linked to the content of the whole dialogue but only to a unitary reading of its cosmological and theological implications.[7] Proclus takes into consideration only the content of the myth – recognized also by modern scholars as «one of the most attractive, but also one of the most puzzling parts of the *Statesman*»[8] – as the key element in the dialogue, not in order to show the clear-cut division between two cycles which is outlined in the dialogue, but to suggest a certain degree of "harmonization". In my opinion the harmony of the cosmos may be inferred from a non-literal reading of the myth, because this kind of myth may also function as an εἰκών, a reminder, of the notion of harmony. Indeed, this is one of the roles of scientific poetry, a genre pertaining not to Homeric myths but philosophical ones:[9] to awaken the recollection of forgotten knowledge. So it is just a modern common opinion of scholars

---

5 See Pl. *Plt.* 273d–e. Then Pl. *Plt.* 269d7 and Procl. *Theol. Plat.* V.6, 26.17–20.
6 The identity between the Platonic Demiurge of the *Statesman* and Proclus' demiurgic Zeus emerges quite clearly from the *Commentary on the Cratylus*, which I will be discussing later.
7 See Schicker (1995), El Murr (2009) 113–116, Robinson (2008) 148–162 and El Murr (2014).
8 Rowe (1995) 11. For the interpretation of the myth, see El Murr (2014) 151–188.
9 A philosophical myth has an ἐπιμύθιον similar to that of a Hesiodic myth, however it differs from a mere tale, insofar as its distinctive feature is verisimilitude. Moreover, it is superior to a mere fable, insofar as the plausible tale immediately (εὐθέως) reveals the purpose of the story, thereby offering – even though it is false – the best possible representation of the truth (Anon. *Proll.* 7.36–42 and Olymp. *in Grg.* 237, 18–19). The paideutic tale, which is false by nature, is regarded as a μῦθος which however is most of all a λόγος, insofar as it is a plausible speech and image that, by reproducing the intelligible within the sensible, ensures that the detection of likeness will trigger the epistrophic process of return to the paradigm. The philosophical myth, therefore, is only relatively false: it is a noble lie that has its usefulness and which serves a purpose of mediation in relation to 'epistemological processes'; a lie which, as an imperfect image of a perfect world, derives its nobility from the fact that it reproduces – by likeness and by proceeding from the many to the One – the ontological path which proceeds by unlikeness from the One to the many.

of Platonism that the main purpose of this myth is to draw attention to two short-comings in our attempted definition of statesmanship.[10]

For late-antique exegetes, the central question that the myth of the *Stateman* contains instead ought to lead us to reflect on how the various elements of the text harmonize with one another so as to create a unity (or even an aspect of Unity). The thematic unity of the dialogue, moreover, is to be connected to the thematic unity of the other texts, so that in the eyes of the reader the *corpus platonicum* will take the form of a harmonious and unitary polyphonic composition intended to represent the unity of the metaphysical cosmos.[11] And it is the Neoplatonist reading of three dialogues that are considered "physical" according to the late-antique canon (*Sophist*, *Statesman* and *Timaeus*) which will guide us in the search for a kind of unity to be inferred from dialogues that are thematically connected even though they have different and unique σκοποί. This reading, moreover, discloses a more complicated world than that envisaged in the *Timaeus*: what we can already state on the basis of the texts we have is that for the Neoplatonists there are ὁ πατὴρ τῶν δημιουργῶν of the *Timaeus*, the Heavenly Demiurge of the *Statesman*, i.e. the creator of the heavenly bodies – as Iamblichus and Proclus suggest[12] –, and the Sublunary Demiurge of the *Sophist*.

---

10 See Taylor (1971) 214–217, Morgan (2004) 242, 253–261 and Ricken (2008) 136–137. Cf. Pl. *Plt.* 274e10–275a6. The Eleatic Stranger says that the myth will be useful by calling attention to two errors: a major error in offering a definition of the divine shepherd of the Age of Cronos instead of the human ruler of our own era; and a minor error in defining the Statesman as the ruler of the city without specifying the form of his rule. On the τέλος, see El Murr (2011).

11 In Neoplatonism each dialogue is a cosmos but, at the same time, part of the whole dialogical cosmos, by virtue of the concepts of vertical μίμησις and analogy useful to satisfy the Platonic desire of becoming like God. See Pl. *Tht.* 176b. Before Coulter (1976) and Motta (2014), see also Martano (1974) 37, according to whom the great Neoplatonist intuition «consiste nell'asserita corrispondenza tra il cosmo e la realtà dell'uomo; e quindi nel ritrovamento dell'Essere nella realtà di tutti gli esseri finiti, in cui esso si è venuto come condensando nella molteplicità inesauribile dei suoi aspetti».

12 We have sparse allusions to the *Statesman* in the Neoplatonic tradition because no commentary has survived: from Proclus' *Commentary on the Timaeus* we learn that Syrianus had written a commentary to this dialogue with a specific interest in the myth that he read allegorically (cf. Procl. *in Ti.* II.96.3–7).

2 The Neoplatonist exegesis of the *Statesman's* Zeus and Cronos

If we focus on the *Statesman* alone, we find that its myth revolves around two deities, Cronos and Zeus, only one of whom – within the complex framework outlined by Proclus – is, strictly speaking, a Demiurge. According to the Neoplatonist Proclus, who with regard to this interpretation was influenced not only by Plato's wording but also by the Orphic tradition, Zeus is the supreme πολιτικός, an intellectual Demiurge[13] (a νοῦς), the creator of the universe exercising providential care[14], whereas Cronos, who is not properly a Demiurge but the leader of the intellectual order,[15] is a deity that might coincide with what Plato calls the «Demiurge and Father» (Pl. *Plt.* 273b1–2). This also seems to be suggested by the reference to his transcendent superiority in the *Platonic Theology* (V. 9, 31.11–12). Furthermore, we find an extended account of a Father of the Demiurges, who is identified with Cronos, and a triad of demiurges, identified with Zeus, Poseidon and Pluto respectively in Proclus' *Commentary on the Cratylus* (esp. 149.84–154.87). On the one hand, the picture which may be inferred from this work of Proclus suggests that Zeus is not properly a father because he partakes of some activity above mortal nature. Proclus writes: «Zeus is the Father, but he merits the entire phrase "a father so-called"» (*in Cra.* 97.47, 24–28). On the other hand, according to Proclus' *Commentary on the Cratylus* and his etymologies of divine names, Cronos is a contemplative God, a pure intellect,[16] who governs the whole

---

13 See Procl. *Theol. Plat.* V 6, 26.5–9, *in Ti.* III 162.1–165.3 and *Orac. Chald.* fr. 8.2. He seems to exercise an intellectual activity: consider, for example, his capability of always revolving (see Pl. *Plt.* 269e5).

14 See Procl. *in Cra.* 40. 62, 6–8.

15 For this exegesis, see Pl. *Plt.* 269c5, 270a3, 271d–e, 272e4, 273c3 and Procl. *Theol. Plat.* V 6, 25.27–26.4. For the standard interpretation of the Demiurge and Zeus, see Herm. *in Phdr.* 136.17–10, Procl. *in Ti.* I 308.17–18, Olymp. *in Phd.* 1 § 5.

16 See Pl. *Cra.* 396b and Procl. *in Cra.* 106. 55, 23–107. 59, 8. According to Proclus – on the basis of the third etymology which celebrates Cronos as purity and immaculate thought – King Cronos «is Intellect and institutor of all intellectual life, but Intellect which transcends any relation to perceptible things and is immaterial and separate. It is turned back upon itself, seeing as it turns even those that have proceeded forth from it back to itself, embraces them and establishes them stably in itself. For the Demiurge of the universe, although himself a divine Intellect, nevertheless organizes perceptible creatures and has forethought for inferior creatures. The supreme Cronus, however, is essentially constituted in intellectual thoughts separate from and superior to the totality of existents» (*in Cra.* 107.57, 4–13, trans. Duvick 2007). His role is to lead forth the intellectual thought into multiplicity, and fill himself within intelligible entities.

demiurgic process (*in Cra.* 63.27, 21–23). More than simple labels for two periods of time, in the *Commentary on the Cratylus* the names of Cronos and Zeus *represent* the theological structure of the harmonized universe[17] and are invoked, within the metaphysical-theological system of late Neoplatonism, as εἰκόνες of divine forces which govern the universe. This approach to the universe and the *Statesman* familiar to the Neoplatonists reveals the importance of particular passages of the dialogue, which are set in relation to other passages – as in the etymological section of the *Cratylus* – and which, in the light of an interesting reflection on Neoplatonic cosmic-literary theory, reveal not so much the differences as the similarities between the macrocosm of the All and the literary microcosm, between μῦθος and λόγος, between Zeus and Cronos.

First of all, it should be noted that in the light of this family bond between Cronos and Zeus – which lies at the heart of the Neoplatonist exegesis of the myth – it is possible to say that the whole universe has two natures and consequently that the encosmic Gods, the higher divine genera which follow Cronos and Zeus (Procl. *Theol. Plat.* V 9, 31.20–26), and physical bodies also have a double nature. But we should note, therefore, that: 1) what is more important is the relationship and not the separation between the two Gods[18] (i.e. the two causes), between the different aspects of such a double nature, between metaphysics and physics, between the intelligible and the sensible; 2) the true nature of the body, thanks to the Demiurge, is the principle of all that is good within it, whereas everything else is the remnant of the "ancient state" that guarantees the endurance of evil in the physical world[11]. Accordingly, as a living being (Pl. *Ti.* 30b5–c1; *Phlb.* 29e–30a), the cosmos has a God-given "mind," or thoughtful judgment (φρόνησιν, Pl. *Plt.* 269d1), but it also has a body, as is likewise the case in the dialogical Platonic universe, which the Neoplatonists envisage as being constituted both by what Plato expressed in words and what he committed to writing

---

17 According to what Proclus says in the *Commentary on Plato's Cratylus*, it is not correct to believe that the so-called children of the more universal Gods are removed from their elders and sever their unity with them. Rather, the processions are produced through similarity, because there is one association of essence and an indivisible connection of the powers and the activities among both the children and their fathers. So – Proclo writes (*in Cra.* 104.53, 28–54, 6) – «let us accept that Zeus is also called 'son of Cronus' (396B). For since he is demiurgic Intellect, Zeus procedes from another higher and more uniform Intellect, which on the one hand increases the number of its proper intellectual thoughts, but on the other turns the multitude back into unity [...]. Having established immediate communion with Cronus, and being filled by him with every sort of intellectual good, Zeus is also properly called 'son of Cronus' [...]».
18 According to Carone (2005) 150, Cronos and Zeus do not have a distinct personality, despite their mythical disguises.

(Anon. *Proll.* 13.22–25). Indeed, the anonymous introduction to Plato's writings in the Neoplatonist school of Alexandria (6th cent. AD) detects a correlation between the elements of the dialogue and those of the cosmos (Anon. *Proll.* 16–17) through an analogy between the visible dialogue/sensible cosmos and the invisible dialogue (oral discourse)/intelligible cosmos. As the written/visible part of Plato's oral/invisible lectures (Anon. *Proll.* 13.15–29), this reflects the twofold constitution of the universe, which has received many divine qualities from its creator, but also the possibility of partaking of a bodily nature (Pl. *Plt.* 269d7–269e3).

3 The appeal of myth and the aspiration to unity

Whereas modern readers of Plato's dialogues are seduced – as Ruby Blondell claims at the beginning of her book – by their dazzling interplay of unity and multiplicity,[19] Neoplatonists, by showing the organic composition of a dialogue as a cosmos that is a unitary living being, go *beyond* this, and say that only the unity of the dialogues is able to charm their readers and thereby lead them to the One. Indeed, after having quoted the passage of the *Phaedrus* stating that «there is one starting-point for anyone who is going to deliberate successfully: he must know what it is he is deliberating about, or he will inevitably miss everything»,[20] the anonymous author of the *Prolegomena to Platonic Philosophy* affirms:

> We must maintain that a dialogue has one theme, not many. How indeed could Plato treat more than one theme in a dialogue, when he praises the deity for the very reason that it is one? Besides, he says himself that the dialogue is like a living being, because every literary work is; any well-written piece of literature can be compared to a living being; if, then, the dialogue is comparable to a living being, and a living being has only one purpose, the Good (for the sake of which it has been created), the dialogue must also have one purpose, that is, one theme.[21]
>
> (Anon. *Proll.* 21.23–32)

Approaching Plato's dialogues according to this rule – the first of ten rules listed by the Anonymous in order to discover the right target[22] (σκοπός) of every dia-

---

19 See Blondell (2002) I. On the different ways to approach the dialogues, see Corlett (2005) 1–18.
20 Pl. *Phdr.* 237b7–c1 (trans. Rowe 1986) and Anon. *Proll.* 21.4–6.
21 Trans. Westerink (1962).
22 For the translation of the Greek term see the discussion in Tarrant (1998) 23.

logue – means not only translating the principle of organic composition (suggested by *Phaedrus* 264c) into an interpretative one, but also accepting to read the dialogues in a theological and teleological fashion that entails envisaging them – and each individual dialogue – as a cosmos, a unitary literary cosmos. And inasmuch as a cosmos is a living being, this literary cosmos is shaped in analogy to the macrocosm, and consequently has a unique τέλος, namely a unique σκοπός.[23] So Plato is regarded both as a Demiurge – or better as the Demiurge of the Proclean exegesis of the *Timaeus* (*in Ti.* I.206.26–207.20) – and also as a poet superior to Homer and to the other poets in the matter of proof and of propriety in using myths,[24] just like the Poet of whom Proclus speaks in the *Commentary of the Republic*. Such a Poet of the cosmos is the συνεργὸς τοῦ μεγάλου πολιτικοῦ,[25] namely Zeus.

After having touched upon the vital matter of the unity of the macrocosm that has its microcosmic equivalent in the σκοπός – not only a literary but also a metaphysical tenet – I should like to take into consideration the fact that for the Neoplatonists a cosmogonic tale – not only that of the *Timaeus* but also that of the *Statesman* (268d–274e) – must be read as an εἰκὼς μῦθος closer to a true account than to a fictional story.[26] As a matter of fact, a cosmogonic tale appears to be similar to that scientific poetry[27] which employs εἰκόνες[28] and not σύμβολα.[29] Indeed, in building their physical and metaphysical cosmos, the Neoplatonists stress a close relationship between philosophy and literature that makes it possible to speak about science (including the natural sciences and theology) in a non-

---

23 See Pl. *Ti.* 27c–30d, 92c4. See also Coulter (1976) and Motta (2013).

24 See Anon. *Proll.* 8.1–2 and Motta (2015). This Demiurge is similar to the superior kind of painter that in the *Republic* is also a craftsman (500d6) who paints in words by keeping an eye on the eidetic side of reality (on the potentiality of sight, see Pl. *Ti.* 47a–b). See also Iambl. *ap.* Stob. *Anth.* 3, 201.17–202.17. About the poet and the Demiurge and the interaction between Plato, his dialogues and the poets, see Regali (2012).

25 See Procl. *in R.* I.68.3–69.1.

26 See Pl. *Ti.* 29d2 and Brisson (2012). For the *Statesman* see Robinson (2003) and Miller (2004) 36–39. On myth as a form of persuasion, see Cerri (2007) 47–58.

27 For the Proclean classification, see Procl. *in R.* II. 177.7–179.32 and 180.3–192.3; see Sheppard (1980) 162–197, Bouffartigue (1987), Lamberton (1992), Van den Berg (2001) 115–117, Zamora (2014). A modern reading of the *Statesman* myth as an epistemic instrument may be found in Horn (2012).

28 *Contra* Sheppard (1980) 200.

29 See Steel (1986) 196 who speaks of a fundamental difference between the likeness of the εἰκών and the unlikeness of the σύμβολον. See also Van Den Berg (2001) 120, n. 38 and 126–136.

scientific way, through the kind of mythical poetry[30] that is not at odds with philosophy because it was created by a philosopher/demiurge of truth. Thus through the interplay between philosophy and poetry, between λόγος and μῦθος, the Neoplatonists develop a sort of theological science that aims to establish literary unity as a reflection of metaphysical unity; a science that, as the case of the *Statesman* shows, makes the search for the σκοπός of the dialogue coincide with the exegesis of the myth, and ensures that the literary discourse is assimilated to the cosmogonic discourse in terms of both form and content.

While not a verifiable discourse, a myth possesses a true content that makes it an object of interpretation and a literary instrument to explain the whole Neoplatonic universe; at the same time, the σκοπός appears to be not only an exegetical instrument to reveal the meaning of a text but *the* exegetical instrument to understand a metaphysical cosmos: for it corresponds to the final cause and hence to the metaphysical One. Proclus explicitly claims that the *Timaeus* and the *Statesman* deliver the divine doctrine through the mathematical disciplines invented by Pythagoreans. He also contends that in order to discuss divine beings starting from ethical or physical arguments, it is necessary to employ *images*:[31] in this fashion he is referring to myths, because even when the mathematical aspect is absent we can find something akin to mathematical objects in Plato's myths, which are projected εἰκόνες of a higher reality.[32]

4 Demiurgy and revolutions

In order to further explore this perspective – aimed at revealing the σκοπός and the unity of the cosmos and of the *Statesman* in Neoplatonism, where σκοπός and unity coincide – I will discuss some passages from the *Prolegomena*, Proclus' *Commentary on the Timaeus* and chapter 6 of book V of the *Platonic Theology*. After having quoted the different ways in which Platonic writings can be read in schools, the Anonymous suggests just twelve dialogues divided into two reading cycles, and he traces this division back to the divine Iamblichus:

> He (*scil.* Iamblichus) reduced them all to twelve dialogues, of which he classed some as physical, some as theological; these twelve he further reduced to two, the *Timaeus* and the

---

30 See Petraki (2011) 58–63.
31 For this interpretation, see Procl. *in R.* I.73.17–22 and Van den Berg (2001) 131–133.
32 See Procl. *Theol. Plat.* I.4, 19.4–6. Proclus adds that political as well as physical realities mirror the powers of the Gods (*Theol. Plat.* I.4, 19.12–13).

Parmenides, the *Timaeus* covering all the physical, the *Parmenides* all the theological dialogues. [...] After these (*scil.* the *Cratylus* and the *Theaetetus*) we come to *** which deal with
natural philosophy.[33]

(Anon. Proll. 26.16–21; 26.40–41)

The integration proposed by Westerink for the damaged text in the Iamblichean
curriculum[34] in ch. 26.40 of the *Prolegomena* labels only the *Sophist* and the *Statesman* (and before them the *Timaeus* among the dialogues from the second cycle)
as "physical". Such a proposal – which is commonly accepted – is based on a
scholium on the *Sophist*, where the figure of the sophist is connected to that of a
Demiurge, a divine sophist, the creator of the sublunary world,[35] and on Proclus'
exegesis of both dialogues, especially that presented in the *Platonic Theology*,[36]
where the Diadochus claims the existence of the following relationship between
the physical dialogues from the first cycle:[37]

From the *Politicus* you may obtain the theory of the fabrication in the heavens, of the uneven periods of the universe, and of the intellectual causes of those periods. But from the
Sophist, the whole sublunary generation, and the peculiarity of the Gods who are allotted
the sublunary region, and preside over its generations and corruptions.[38]

(Procl. Theol. Plat. I.5, 25.14–18)

---

33 Trans. Westerink (1962).

34 On this *curriculum* and the others in the Platonic tradition, see Tarrant (2014).

35 This *scholium* suggests that the target of the dialogue is to explain the activity of the sublunary Demiurge: see Iambl. *in Sph.*, *fr.* 1 Dillon and see Westerink (1962) XXXVII–XXXVIII = West-
erink/Segonds (1990) LXIX–LXX, Larsen (1972) 436–442, Dillon (1973) 90–91 and 245–247,
Charles-Saget (1998).

36 For the different ways in which Proclus presents φυσιολογία see Martijn (2010) 297: «Mirroring Nature itself, philosophy of nature consists in fact in a number of hierarchically and serially
ordered phases of *physiologia*, namely theological *physiologia*, which analyzed the universe into
its transcendent causes, mathematical *physiologia*, which through reasoning by analogia, using
ontological images, leads to insight in body and soul of the universe, empirical *physiologia*,
which concerns the phenomena in the sky, and biological physiologia, treating of the informed
living body».

37 Physical dialogues contrasted with the 'theological' work of the first cycle (*Phaedrus*, *Symposium*, *Philebus*), because the Demiurge of the Heavens, detected in the myth, was seen to stand
at the pinnacle of the physical world. But physical dialogues can also include some reflections
on both physics and theology, since Cronos provides Zeus with the principles of all demiurgy
and providence towards sensibles. Uranus, Cronos and Zeus are deities that are "all in all" (ἐν
πᾶσι): each also shares the activities of the other two, while presenting itself according to a distinctive and emerging activity (Procl. *in Cra.* 110. 62, 24–28).

38 Trans. Taylor (1816).

So Proclus allows us to include the *Sophist* and the *Statesman* in that group of dialogues which περὶ φυσικῶν διδάσκονται (Anon. *Proll.* 26.40–41). Such a group has at its summit the *Timaeus*,[39] the dialogue that gathers together all the theories contained in the Platonic physical writings.[40] According to Proclus, a dialogue is physical when it teaches about the entire cosmic creation[41] and cosmic life; hence, the *Statesman* is supposed to be a physical dialogue because it approaches this issue, although it does not simply deal with natural phenomena *iuxta propria principia*, but rather investigates these phenomena as the outcome of forces that transcend them, and on which they depend. Indeed, the target of Plato's *Statesman* is the demiurgy at work in the heavens – namely the Iamblichean theory of a plurality of demiurges associated with the heavenly movements[42] – whereas that of Plato's *Timaeus* is to adduce further information in support of the view that the whole cosmos is a God, endowed with a soul and an intellect, and having characteristics produced by a demiurgic Intellect, which makes it a copy of the model in the Intelligible Living Being by participation in the Good. So, this universe has a status superior to that of physics, since it deals with the higher principles which are the deities Cronos and Zeus: that is why the topics discussed in physical dialogues are always partly theological, even in the *Statesman*.[43] Accordingly, every account about physics – including ones that employ images, like those based on philosophical myths – is an account about the divinity of the universe, or better – in the case of the *Statesman* – about an aspect of its divinity[44]. What is divine is eternal, and the universe, insofar as it is eternal, cannot undergo revolutions; in other words, according to Proclus (*in Ti.* I.289. 6–22), it does not change through successive revolutions. It is individual souls that, through the change of cyclical periods, grow either younger or older. By contrast, universal souls – which on the one hand are connected to Cronos on the basis of the invisible cyclical period and, on the other, govern the whole together with Zeus on the basis of visible providence – become, as they progress, simultaneously older and younger (Procl. *Theol. Plat.* V.10, 35.11–20).

This is the reason why Olympiodorus speaks of the allegorical interpretation of the *Statesman* myth as a commonplace: because such a narrative hints at other

---

39 See Westerink (1962) XXXVII–XXXIX = Westerink/Segonds (1990) LXXI–LXXII and also Festugière (1969).
40 See Procl. *in Ti.* I.13.12–21; *Theol. Plat.* I.7, 32.1–12; 8, 32.15–18; *in Prm.* I.641.14–643.4; Anon. *Proll.* 26.20.
41 See Procl. *in Ti.* I.12.29–30.
42 See Iambl. *in Sph.*, *fr.* 1 Dillon. See also Tarrant (2000) 195–197.
43 See Hoffmann (2012) and Linguiti (2014).
44 See Halfwassen (2000), Neschke-Hentschke (2000) and Steel (2009).

divine truths by speaking in a puzzling manner.[45] The philosophical myth, there-fore, is a way, or rather – according to the interpretation suggested here – the most appropriate way, to talk about the universe and the deity governing it, a deity that resists the literal application to it of the concepts of generation and change. In the *Statesman*, by using a story about a past that is beyond our reach, and resists any attempt to collect evidence about it – also because no one has ever described the event which is the cause of such a past[46] – Plato makes his account sophisticated enough[47] to leave room for a kind of true opinion about that aspect of the study of nature which concerns celestial phenomena connected to Cronus and Zeus. The account is not simply an example of poetry or μίμησις but a λόγος akin to its object[48] – and indeed the whole dialogue comes across as «una ricerca tesa a scoprire somiglianze»[49] – namely, similarities to the subject matter discussed, i.e. the dimension of what belongs to the cosmic realm, which is *ab origine* a mix (of intelligible and sensible elements, or invisible and visible ones).[50] Thus this kind of λόγος that is also a μῦθος – i.e., literally speaking, a mix – is the only possible image that can potentially have a good effect, as an avenue for philosophical insight.[51] With regard to this aspect, Proclus writes:

---

45 See Olymp. *in Grg.* 240, 27.
46 See Pl. *Plt.* 269b5–c2.
47 Plato's dream of becoming a swan who causes great trouble to fowlers unable to catch him could be interpreted as the many and different ways of answering the results caused by Plato's phil-osophical treasure. The Anonymous says: «All men would endeavor to grasp Plato's meaning, none, however, would succeed, but each would interpret him according to his own views, whether in a metaphysical or a physical or any other sense (Anon. *Proll.* 1.42–46, trans. Westerink 1962)».
48 See Pl. *Ti.* 29b–d.
49 Giorgini (2005) 140 n. 9, who describes the *Statesman* in such terms when discussing the opening section, where Socrates claims that we ought always to be eager to become acquainted with our relatives by debating with them. The issue of συγγένεια belongs to the *Timaeus* (29b) too – as Giorgini accurately notes – because it is in this dialogue that Plato points out that ac-counts are akin to the diverse objects which they serve to explain.
50 See Pl. *Ti.* 41c3.
51 See Pl. *Phd.* 72e–77e. For Gordon (2007) all dialogues are paradigms of image-making as an avenue for philosophical insight, inasmuch as they are images of Plato's art.

Very properly therefore (εἰκότως ἄρα καί) does this universe have two sorts of lives, periods, and revolutions: that of Cronos and that of Zeus, as the myth in the *Politicus* says. And, indeed, according to one of the periods, it [*scil*. the cosmos] produces all goods spontaneously, and possess an innoxious and unwearied life; but according to the other it participates in material error, and a very mutable nature.[52]

(Procl. *Theol. Plat.* V.6, 24.22–25.1–3)

When describing the two cycles, Proclus does not clearly distinguish them, or rather, he does not divide them into temporal terms. It thus seems as though, by emphasizing the twofold nature of the lives, periods and revolutions mentioned in the *Statesman*, he sought to introduce what we might define as the concept of "non-exclusive participation". This concept, which – as we shall see – Proclus further elucidates a few lines later, is connected to the causal inclusiveness of the complex and hierarchical metaphysical levels of the Neoplatonists, to which the deities of Proclus' metaphysical-theological system correspond.[53] We may infer from all this that life in the world is twofold at different levels: if there are different revolutions, namely a period closer to Cronos and one closer to Zeus, then moving further down we will also find an invisible/intelligible life and a physical/visible one. Moreover, to further support this interpretation, one may recall that at the beginning of his *Commentary on the Timaeus* Proclus emphasizes how difficult it is to speak of physics apart from theology:

With the whole of philosophy being divided into the study of intelligible and the study of immanent things – quite rightly too, as the cosmos too is twofold, intelligible cosmos and sensible cosmos as Plato will go on to say [*Ti.* 30c] – the *Parmenides* has embraced the treatment of the intelligibles, and the *Timaeus* that of sensibles. That one, you see, teaches us all the divine orders, and the other all the processions of things in the cosmos. But neither does the former entirely leave aside the study of things within the All, nor does the latter fail to study the intelligibles, because sensibles too are present paradigmatically in the intelligibles, while the intelligibles are present iconically among sensibles.[54]

(Procl. *in Ti.* I.12.30–13.10)

The passage very interestingly highlights how important it is to stress the continuity between the two realms, and to understand that they are always linked. In this context the *Statesman* myth further clarifies the point through the Eleatic Stranger's words, as well as the accounts provided before the myth (σαφῶς, Procl. *Theol. Plat.* V.6, 25.21): if we are to explicitly state the truth (εἰ δεῖ τἀληθῆ διαρρήδην λέγειν, Procl. *Theol. Plat.* V. 6, 25.16), it is not correct to claim that

---

52 Trans. Taylor (1816), with slight changes.
53 See *supra* n. 37.
54 Trans. Tarrant (2007).

one period participates in Cronos and the other one in Zeus. It is more correct to say that each of the periods «participates in both these Gods» (μετέχει τῶν θεῶν τούτων ἀμφοτέρων, Procl. *Theol. Plat.* V.6, 25.17–18):

> Zeus is also the cause of the invisible life of the All, the supplier of intellect, and the leader of intellectual perfection; but he elevates all things to the kingdom of Cronos, and, being *a leader in conjunction with his father*, brings into existence the whole peri-cosmic Intellect.
> (Procl. *Theol. Plat.* V.6, 25.11–16)[55]

The myth of the *Statesman* is obviously an elaborate composition both for Neoplatonists and modern scholars, who try to divide it – as Kahn has shown – into six ingredients useful for the better understanding of it: 1) stories from traditional mythology; 2) Empedoclean themes, in particular ones related to Empedocles' account of cosmic cycles;[56] 3) parallels to the doctrine of reincarnation; 4) items from Plato's own cosmology as more fully expounded in the *Timaeus*; 5) a brief account of the origins of civilization; 6) fantastic examples of Plato's comic imagination.[57] Among these six ingredients the section of the *Platonic Theology* quoted above is devoted only to the second one, in order to demonstrate that it is impossible to think that the cycle which we are currently in is portrayed as lacking any divine guidance, although the Eleatic Stranger does not seem to agree with this view.[58] It is possible – as Kahn writes – that the Empedoclean parallels determine the general form of the myth,[59] and it is also possible that Plato borrows from Empedocles two opposite cosmic movements back and forth between the poles of unity and plurality, with a symmetrical movement between diametrically opposed situations.[60] This parallel is totally obscured in the recent interpretation of the myth in terms of a three-stage cycle,[61] and, to some extent, also in the non-literal Neoplatonic interpretation of the cosmic cycles of Empedocles. What I am

---

55 Trans. Taylor (1816) with slight changes.
56 There are other Empedoclean echoes in the myth, among which we can mention the description of the previous period as one of harmony between humans and beasts, without any kind of discord: see Pl. *Plt.* 272b8–d2 and Emp. DK31B128, B130.
57 See Kahn (2009) and Kahn (2013) 221–222.
58 See Pl. *Plt.* 272b1–4 and 272d6–e6.
59 See Kahn (2013) 222–223.
60 See Emp. DK31B17, vv. 1–5 and Pl. *Plt.* 269c4–5 and 269e7–270a8.
61 The standard modern interpretation is in favour of two stages; see Giorgini (2005) 107–109, White (2007) 37–59, Horn (2009), Kahn (2013) 222 and n. 7, El Murr (2014) 145–151, whereas Rowe 1995 (see also Rowe 2002a) believes in a three-stage cycle. For this latter interpretation, see also Brisson (1974) and Brisson (1995), and see *contra* Erler (1995). But before them see Lovejoy/Boas (1935).

going to suggest – following John Dillon[62] – is that, according to Proclus, the Age of Cronos corresponds to the Empedoclean predominance of Love, and must be read as a representation of the intelligible world, whereas that of Zeus corresponds to the predominance of Strife, and is an image of the physical world. Nevertheless, the deeper meaning of the myth – its non-literal interpretation – informs us that there is *no* sequence of cycles, only a poetic representation of the *eternal tension* between the two antithetical forces which make up the universe.[63] This interpretation is also endorsed by Olympiodorus, who explicitly quotes Empedocles in the section of the *Commentary on the Phaedo*, in which he clarifies that suicide is not allowed for reasons which have to do with the mythic. The passage of the *Phaedo* (62b3–4) says «that we are in a sort of custody», and this claim must be read in the light of Empedocles and the allegorical meaning contained in the myth. According to Olympiodorus, the Presocratic philosopher asserts, in B17, that the intelligible and the sensible world come into existence alternately just because

> Our soul sometimes lives in accordance with intelligible reality, and it is then said that the intelligible world begins, and sometimes in accordance with sensible things, when the sensible world is said to begin.[64]
>
> (Olymp. *in Phd.* 1 § 4.5–7)

We may note how the passage confirms that the myth, i.e. an account in the form of a philosophical λόγος,[65] deals with the truth through a most reasonable image (μάλα εἰκότως, Pl. *Plt.* 270b1), insofar as its goal is to represent the intelligible in a sensible way,[66] by expressing, for instance, what exists eternally in terms of time,[67] and by speaking about a cyclical role of the Gods when all happens simultaneously.

---

62 Dillon (1995).

63 See Emp. DK31B17, vv. 7–9. See also Dillon (1995).

64 Trans. Westerink (2009).

65 In the *Phaedo* (61b3–4) we read that a poet, if he wants to be a poet, is supposed to write μῦθοι and not λόγοι. Proclus adds that the poet has to write them ὁμοίους πλάττειν τοῖς ὑποκειμένοις, which is to say that they have to be likely, and linked to their subject matter (*in R.* I.65.25–30). See also Procl. *in R.* I.284.2–8.

66 See Reydams-Schils (2011).

67 See Plot. III 5 [50], 9.24–26.

5 Conclusions

Whereas, from the modern point of view, the myth seems to be offering a parallel between the macrocosm and the human and political cosmos in order to further explore ethical and political issues, the Neoplatonists employ it for a different purpose: without any exaggeration, and without any ethical or political implication, they use the myth to explain the interaction between the different realms, as well as to describe the way in which one is to understand the demiurgic activity pertaining to celestial phenomena. So it is clear that the issue of the thematic unity of the dialogue and that of its myth are linked in the *Statesman*. That is why, in order to grasp the subject of the dialogue, the Neoplatonists choose to focus their attention on the myth, as a fundamental and completely functional element of the dialogue, brimming with arguments and theories, and embedded within the overall argument. The myth is the literary and philosophical place where Plato has set the only target of the *Statesman*, because it is the only place in the dialogue where it is possible to speak about it. Furthermore, it is quite evident that the Neoplatonists are interested in highlighting Plato's philosophical poetry, and its potential as a means to offer an image of the truth rather than the truth itself, i.e. the only possible truth by virtue of its subject matter.[68] This exegetical line has one significant consequence for the reinterpretation of the *Statesman* myth, which we should view as part of a wider plan to offer a non-literal and harmonizing reading of the myths in all the physical dialogues.[69] After all, this myth must be used as an example (παράδειγμα, Pl. *R*. 7, 529d7) – a visible example and hence something like an εἰκών that, along with its likeness to its paradigm, also reveals its unlikeness to it[70] – for understanding the intelligible proportions that govern the movement of the heavenly bodies,[71] as well as the reflection of this movement in different realms, where lives can be lived ὥσπερ οἱ θεοὶ καὶ τὰ

---

68 See Pl. *Ti.* 29b4–5.

69 Reasons for not taking the *Statesman* myth literally to be found in modern exegesis also are discussed in Carone (2005) 146–161. The tendency to harmonize different philosophical traditions as an aspect of Neoplatonism is stressed by Zambon (2002), Karamanolis (2006) and Hadot (2015). However, I think that the term "harmony" fits well for different features of Neoplatonism, including the tendency to read all dialogues as a unitary and harmonic cosmos.

70 See Procl. *in Prm.* II.743.14–21.

71 Proclus says that the title of this dialogue follows the main issue, although Plato talks in it at length about the revolution of the cosmos: but from Plato's point of view, the revolution of the cosmos is dealt with because of its relationship to the statesman. See Procl. *in R.* I.8.28–9.4.

κρείττονα γένη (Procl. *Theol. Plat.* V.6, 26.14–15). Obviously, such an interpretation is in keeping with Neoplatonic exegetical strategies, including the allegorical one, which envisages each text as the visible side of something invisible, thereby making it possible to describe a reality that cannot easily be disclosed to everyone. In conclusion, the Neoplatonists prefer to steer clear of the idea of any cosmic drama, which could be interpreted as a conflict between good and evil, and hence, in accordance with their harmonic reading of the dialogues, they present Plato's world as a harmonic whole.[72]

---

72 See Pl. *Lg.* 7, 821b6–c7 and *R.* 6, 508a4, in which the heavenly bodies are regarded as Gods, and *R.* 2, 377d–383c, where the idea of a change of the Gods for the worse is viewed as being contradictory to their goodness. On the τύποι θεολογικοί see also Anon. *Proll.* 7.25–35. For the Neoplatonic interpretation of this myth regarding the second of the two periods and related to the problem of evil, see Phillips (2007) 140–150, 162–164.

Part IV: **Measuring, Weaving and Women**

Josep Monserrat-Molas
The avoidance of errors, a sense of «due measure»

The passage in Plato's *Statesman* with which this paper is concerned can be found when the dialogue between the Stranger and young Socrates has travelled its uneven and often rocky way to the very middle of the text. In order to find not only answers to difficult questions but also the skill to express these (Sales 1994, 95–105), the two men have contemplated a variety of trails running parallel to their own, and on one such trail have attempted to draw from myth the means to rectify the error of *diairesis* (Monserrat-Molas 2010). Yet the path towards correction is tortuous, for if myth cannot be stopped from creating more than we intend it to create, how then can it be expected to redress the *diairesis* of statesmanship? To clarify how, we need an example or *paradigm* of what is to be defined – namely, the art of statesmanship. And because the procedure is novel, young Socrates must also be offered an example, in order to understand what an example is. When it comes, that example is the art of weaving, and with it the text performs a *diairesis* or division which will serve both as a model of statesmanship, and as proof itself of the shortcomings of this and other paths, of *diairesis*, myth and paradigm.

The object of discussion introduced in the Stranger's reflective interlude is whether or not everything he and young Socrates have discussed so far can serve in the inquiry. It becomes a reflection on the fact that so many paths have been travelled and, in particular, on the need to mould such multiplicity to the needs of the inquiry that prompted it. In other words, the Stranger ponders the question of whether too much or too little has been done – the question of excess and deficiency. In the event, I would argue, this reflection proves to be the axle on which the discussion turns, and this is precisely why Plato allows it textual pride of place in the very middle of the dialogue. The central passage of the dialogue considers the due measure of deeds and words, of facts and of discourse; it begins after the weaving *diairesis* (283a) and ends by returning to the subject of the statesman (287b).[1]

---

1 The preoccupation with measure is common elsewhere in Plato's work: in the *Laws*, the connection between statesmanship and due measure as the only law that can describe good rule is made particularly clear (690ff, for example); in the *Gorgias*, the quest for the good, which characterises each and every kind of technique, is essentially a quest for an orderly and harmonious measure between excess and defect (503–504); again, in the *Protagoras*, Hippias proposes the

https://doi.org/10.1515/9783110605549-010

Its scholarly interpretation has been particularly varied: in certain quarters, it has been considered as an extemporaneous gloss introduced by Plato in order to respond to what he saw as misguided and excessive criticism of the dialogue's first edition;[2] in others, it has been dismissed as little more than a bridge leading the reader to the question of statesmanship, the subject the dialogue should have addressed but lost sight of along the way;[3] yet other readers have seen the examination of due measure as a simple appendix to the question of excess and deficiency;[4] and finally, there are those who have assigned importance to the passage but for entirely different reasons, adducing its «cultural» significance[5] as an example – albeit a partial one – of Plato's «unwritten doctrines».[6] Currently, the most accepted position certainly leaves out the consistence of the passage with the whole dialogue.

In the following pages, I will consider the role that this central passage plays in the entire dialogue.[7] For practical purposes the central passage is subdivided

---

use of measure and moderation to stop speeches from becoming too long or remaining too short (337–338); and finally, in the *Phaedrus*, Prodicus pokes fun at those who cannot find a fitting length for their speeches (267b). In Plato's work, life itself is considered to require the application of measure (*Protagoras* 356–357, the *Republic* 479), and these are only a few examples.

2 Ritter (1910) 90. Cited by A. Diès (1935) xliv. Subsequently Ryle (1966) 26–27.

3 Diès (1935) xliv–xlv holds that Plato would have introduced this lesson on the *métrion* regardless of whether or not he had felt under literary attack, for he would consider the question as part of his doctrine, and it was a matter of communal style: *Phaedrus* 272d, *Laws* 722a. «Le débat sur la longeur du discours», says the French editor, «ne sert ici que de transition» – a transition towards the dialogue's goal, the discussion of statesmanship.

4 Gomperz (1893/1909) II 502.

5 Guthrie (1978) V 169ff, holds that due measure is given such careful attention because it is being introduced as a principle of great importance, resembling the distinction established in the *Sophist* between negative predication and the negation of existence. To his mind it is not merely a phrase of logic but a reflection of the Hellenic attitude of «moderation in all things», anticipating the Aristotelian doctrine of the mean.

6 For Reale (1991) 380: «qui Platone *scopre le carte, ma solo a metà, ossia i fini della fondazione metafisica del discorso di carattere politico che sta svolgendo*. Per il resto, ossia per la fondazione protologica ultimativa, rimanda, con le solite formule, ad altra sede (o, se si preferisce, ad altro momento), impegnandosi a fondo solamente per ciò che interessa il tema del dialogo. Insomma, anche in questo scritto egli non procede al saldo del "debito", ma, ancora una volta, si limita a pagare gli "interessi"».

7 I take a general interpretation of the dialogue from Monserrat-Molas (1999) and (2007). See also Miller (1980), Rosen (1995), Rowe (1995a), (1995b), Accattino (1997), Castoriadis (1999), Delcomminette (2000), Dratwa (2003) and El Murr (2014). On the dialogue's parts, see the outline by E. Wyller (1970), 76–89, which to my mind adequately intuits the architectural arrangement of the various materials employed in the Platonic dialogues and thus composes a «visible» structure. The Stephanus edition contains that part of the text between the beginning of the dialogue

into two parts.[8] The first addresses the notion of *due measure* and the second examines the application of the question of the inquiry itself – arguably, the dialogue's true Gordian knot. This second part consists of two sections, one that examines the dialogue's paradigmatic value for young Socrates in order to find an interpretive key in one of the dialogue's most hotly debated passages (285c–286b); and another (286b–287b) which attempts to illustrate the meaning of the inquiry itself as suggested in the resonance here of the dialogue's first scene (Monserrat-Molas 2012a, 25–54). This resonance of the first scene is considered first (§1), and I conclude the present paper with a consideration of the relationship between the general aim of the passage (§2 «Dialectic as statesmanship»).

1 The resonance of the first scene and the meaning of the inquiry

Having distinguished between the two classes in the art of measurement, and having reiterated the need to preserve such teaching in memory, the Stranger reasons further (*lógon héteron*) on the substance of the inquiry itself and on all concerns with such discussion. Note that his discursive register changes here, and that his subsequent addition has a particular purpose in mind. The previous section ended with his plea for a special effort of *memory* to retain the idea of the two classes of measurement; his new line of reasoning now addresses *the present question in order to answer this and all other questions* (285d). When asked to explain what he means, the Stranger returns to the example of school children learning the letters of the alphabet (cf. 277e–278b). He asks if they learn in order to recognise the individual letters they are given as examples or in order to acquire knowledge in the more general sense of the word. Young Socrates admits that they learn in order to become better grammarians in all respects, and the Stranger then takes this as a paradigm for the subsequent discussion of statesmanship, using the classroom example to pave the way for the following

---

and the beginning of this section (283b1) in little more than twenty-six pages, and the end of the section (285c3) to the end of the dialogue in the same number again. M. Hoffman (1993) 95 n. 2, gives it special attention but does not comment on the dialogue's particular patchwork of parts. See an examination of the compositional division of the *Statesman* and of its parts as constructed by Plato in Monserrat-Molas (2003).

8 This departs from the customary practice of tripartite interpretation: the division articulated at 283c3, 285c4 and 286b4–5 (283b–285c, 285c–286b and 286b–287b) has been considered, for example, by Capelle (1933), (cited by Miller 1980 131 n. 52, who follows him).

question: «What then about our inquiry now about the statesman? Has it been set before us more for the sake of that very thing, or for the sake of our becoming more able dialecticians in relation to all subjects?». The answer of the young Socrates is very clear «[It's...] for the sake of our being more able in relation to all» (285d⁹).

After the consideration of the purpose of the conversation, the next subsection (286b–287b) begins and ends with moments in which Socrates praises the beauty of the things of which the Stranger speaks: the moment that starts it (286b: *kállist'eîpes*) follows the Stranger's observation that no picture can adequately illustrate certain things, and that only through reasoning can the most important and beautiful things be shown; the moment that finishes it comes before their return to what is strictly a discussion of the statesman (287b: *kalôs eîpes*). But first, at 286b, the fragment is an exercise in reminiscence:

> *ES:* Well then, let's remind ourselves of the reasons [*khárin*] why we have said all these things on these subjects.
> *YS:* What reasons?
> *ES:* Not least because of that disagreeableness we felt there was in the length of our talk about weaving – and of that about the reversal of the universe, and about the being of what is not which is the sphere of the sophist, reflecting that it had a rather great length, and in all these cases we rebuked ourselves, out of fear that what we were saying would turn out to be superfluous as well as long. So, say that the foregoing was said by us for the sake of all these cases, in order that we may not suffer any of this sort of misgiving on any future occasion.
> *YS:* I shall do as you say. Tell me what comes next [*lége hexês mónon*] (286b–c).

The word *chárin* points us back to the beginning of the text and is indeed the same word that started the dialogue, even if it now takes a singular accusative form used adverbially in the sense of «*in* anyone's *favour, for* his *pleasure*, i.e. *for* talking's *sake*» (Liddell & Scott). We could translate this as follows: what will we favour? With the same word we used at the beginning of the dialogue to give thanks, we now ask what it is that has prompted reflection upon due measure.

Once again, we find ourselves at a moment in the dialogue where the speakers attempt to observe their dialogical progress. The Stranger proposes that the discussion has been as tedious and uninspired here as it was in the earlier debate with Theaetetus on the subject of the sophist,[10] and he presents three particular reasons for why this should be so: the undue length of the weaving paradigm, the disorder of the universe and finally the sophist's being of not-being. In other words, the three elements of *diairesis*, myth and, finally, the being of not-

---

9 I adopt Rowe's translation, Rowe (1995a). Cf. Rowe (1995b).
10 Cf. 283b, 277b (on the dimensions of the myth); *Soph.* 217e; *Laws* 722a.

being that, accompanied by due measure, made it possible to understand the sophist. As the Stranger describes these three motives, he speaks of the tedious and superfluous. He wants to correct this mistake so that it will not happen again and the young philosopher mildly lets him. Note that young Socrates had not previously considered that the point of their discussion might be reached more expeditiously, nor that they had in any way strayed from the path of their inquiry. He simply relinquishes all responsibility to the Stranger.[11] This answer shows Socrates' agreement with the justification of the various digressions. Let us consider, therefore, that while by choosing not to take up opportunities for debate the disciple resembles his teacher Theodorus, the Stranger in fact *searches* for what it is we have to thank for what has been done, and this in turn reminds us of Socrates' *giving* of thanks.[12]

How are we to understand the defects of which the Stranger speaks?[13] Certainly, the *diaireses* have been alternately drawn out or shortened (and here the coincidence in the number of divisions or the bifurcation of the *diairesis* on the statesman), myth has given more than was needed, and due measure can also be applied to all important things as well as to the statesman. The blindfold of the common measure thus removed from his eyes, might young Socrates conclude that the Stranger has measured not with a common yardstick but by some other hidden means? Whether or not he can, we the readers have no reason to judge the dialogue's merits using its speakers' criteria: that we should find their text pedestrian, long-winded or lacking does not mean that the text itself is fundamentally flawed. Were its author to have believed this, would he not logically have attempted to correct it? Indeed, might the speakers' awareness of the text's defects not be better explained as an indication of their heartfelt desire to communicate with one other? This, *in general terms*, is the subject of the passage that I shall now examine.

---

11 In a very different way, the fragment that runs from 286a to 287a has sometimes been seen as a retraction by Plato when faced by the criticism that a first «edition» of the dialogue would have received. This is the case of Ryle (1966) 286. For Ryle, «Plato had outlived his earlier genius in composing exoterically» (p. 26).

12 It is important to observe that in Socrates' answer a word appears that Theodorus also uses in the initial scene, in the intervention in which the Stranger is asked to begin the conversation with a subject of his choice, committing himself to his own criteria (cf. 257b8–c1). On Theodorus, see Ibáñez (2007) 177–230. The term is *hexês*, an adverb which indicates serial order, indistinct conjunction, immediate continuation, one after another, in order, in a row. Cf. Miller (1980) 132 n. 66.

13 I am indebted to Rosen (1995) and (2007) on the signification of errors and mistakes in Plato's *Statesman*. Cf. Monserrat (2010).

> *ES*: Well, I say that you and I must be careful to *remember* what we have now said and distribute censure and praise of both shortness and length, whatever subjects we happen to be talking about on each occasion judging lengths not in relation to each other but, in accordance with the part of the art of measurement we previously said we must *remember*, in relation to what is fitting.

The Stranger allows young Socrates external authority and the final word: «Well, I say that you and I must be careful to *remember* what we have now said» (286c). Instead of shrugging off the responsibilities of Socrates' apprenticeship by bowing his head before a barrage of arguments and counter-arguments in the style of Theodorus or of those men in Cronos' era (Monserrat-Molas, 2014), he insists upon the *community* that must exist between the two of them. Such common ground will be achieved by sharing the *memory* responsible for what has been established. The value of things must be measured not by their length but by their propriety. The right length will then depend on the subject in question. At 286b–287a, the text discusses earlier instructions for applying measurement. The pleasure or happiness occasioned by a speech are merely incidental factors which cannot help us decide if the length of that speech is appropriate (*tò prépon*). This rule of convenience cannot be valid in general in all cases. This implies that a knowledge is needed to determine when or when not to apply due measure. In fact the same knowledge should be given in the form of *phronesis*. Either way, in the dialogue the Stranger limits himself to methodological speech: what is most deserving of attention is to honour the method of inquiry that uses the «distinction between forms». The method of division [*diairesis*], which had abstracted value or honour, is now justified precisely because of value and honour (Rosen, 1995, *passim*). It becomes clear that priority will be given to the division «according to *eide*», and not that version of *diairesis* which divided things into equal parts. Describing this principle in practical terms, the Stranger continues thus:

> *ES*: [...] then again, in addition to this, if in relation to such discussions someone finds fault with the length of what is said and will not put up with going round in circles, we must not let such a person go just like that without a backward glance, having just made the simple complaint that what has been said has taken a long time, but we should think it right that he should also demonstrate, in addition, that if it had been shorter it would make the partners in the discussion better dialecticians and better at finding how to display in words the things that are; and our instruction will be to take no notice at all of the other sorts of censure and praise, relating to some other criteria, nor even to seem to hear such things at all when they are said. Now enough of these things, if I have your agreement too; let's go back to the statesman, and bring the model of weaving, which we talked about before, to bear on it (286e–287a).

The self-awareness with which the dialogue is put together as an entire piece is also a model in another sense. The temptation is to consider the *diairesis* of less important things as unnecessary – a fruitless journey down an irrelevant path. In fact, if we do not know what is responsible for the *diairesis* in these cases, that path seems to be a circular one (as indeed it is, but with that circular nature that appears in other ways in the Platonic dialogues and in a particular understanding of knowledge: the process of acquiring knowledge is circular inasmuch as the forms or ideas are already at play from the very moment when intelligible perception is possible, even if they have not yet been identified as such. The task of education is to keep the practitioner on his toes, as it were. This is the notion of «going round in circles» 286e, before 283b). Considerations of greater or lesser length can have nothing to do with pleasure, at least not deliberately. What matters is to become a better dialectician; in other words, to exercise one's skills as is duly required in matters of importance. This is what counts, and if someone believes that they can do a quicker job of educating the listener *to be more resourceful or inventive, or more able to reason*, then they must prove this. Attempting to redress his error, the Stranger gives young Socrates an anticipatory example of how to steer clear of error himself in the future by demanding that Socrates should always prove what he proposes and rely on no other criteria than due measure. When we consider the Stranger's attempt to make the young philosopher a better dialectician from this point of view, we may suspect that his contribution in the dialogue has not been as long-winded, confused and erroneous as he would have us believe.

Here at the end of the section, young Socrates praises once more the *beauty* (*kalós*) of the things the Stranger has spoken of. And once again he immediately puts himself in the older man's hands by raising no objection to what the Stranger proposes. This paves the way towards the discussion of the statesman and closes the gate on measure and oratory («Well said [*kalôs eîpes*] – let's do what you say» 287b). M. Miller has noticed a striking parallel between Socrates' dramatic circumstances here and those of men in the former age of the world. Socrates trusts completely the Stranger's authority (268d, 283b), just as those first men lived in perfect heteronomy (268a–b). When the god let go the helm of the world, men were remanded to their own care, without resources – *aporia* (274c). The danger of losing heteronomy is suggested in the forthcoming departure of the Stranger for Athens: the young philosopher will then be at risk, and what will become of him? He will be hard put to assimilate the philosophy on his own, unless he preserves in memory the teachings of the Stranger. But first, if he simply bears them in mind without understanding their necessity, they will become superfluous; and second, the method taught restricting the objects that the Stranger deals with will also become useless. *And here we see the irony in the learning process between present authority and future freedom*: young Socrates must take heed of the Stranger's advice because it comes on that man's authority, but once it is accepted and applied, the philosopher will be freed from his submission to authority.[14] If young Socrates invokes due measure in defence of the diairetic method, he will be applying to himself the dialectical practice just as the Stranger understands it. When the Stranger opposes the censure of speech for its excessive length what he effectively does is to allow Socrates to oppose his own, self-acknowledged weakness for heedless discourse. If Socrates assimilates the advice, he absorbs a teaching that is taken on higher authority but that will then in practice be freed from it.[15] Thus, the text illustrates one of the fundamental mechanisms of teaching and learning.

Having culminated in this moment, the dialogue hereupon proceeds in yet another direction. The Stranger wants the young Socrates to agree that the subject has been adequately discussed, but the very notion of whether entirety has been achieved can only be understood by one who knows due measure. The dialogue has not clarified everything and could therefore continue; but perhaps it is enough to have identified the questions and to have set out in search of answers, and then the dialogue will have succeeded. This is common Platonic practice: we are directed towards the dialogue that carries the dialogue-text beyond the dialogue-text proper; the depths of the dialogue are reflected even at its surface.

2 Dialectic as Statesmanship

An interpretative key to the *Statesman* can be found in the following idea: children learn letters in order to recognise these wherever they are found, and those who perform exercises to define politics eventually become better dialecticians. The difference in the way the Stranger and young Socrates appreciate this idea is that for the young, one does everything only to become a better dialectician.[16] Dialectical art involves using due measure to compose and

---

14 *Cf.* the imperative «Sapere aude!». See Monserrat-Molas (2011).

15 Miller (1980) 72: «Having become 'shepherd', as it were, to himself, young Socrates will no longer need the stranger's personal guidance». The educational perspective comes from this author: he believes – and rightly so, I would argue – that young Socrates is in fact the academic Socrates who has succeeded in the path of philosophy.

16 *Philebus* 16c–18d, 23c–27c, (cf. 55c–59d) distinguishes between *metretics* and *dialectics*: *dialectics* concerns itself with pure objects of knowledge while *metretics* examines the outcome of

interpret in a manner that is suitable and fitting, appropriate and pertinent; and this art is to be applied as carefully in the design of discourse as it is in the consideration of facts. The dialogue of the *Statesman* works its way towards this crucial point of definition: not to recognise that «due measure» is necessary for statesmanship is to make statesmanship disappear as an impossible or false idea, and to ensure that all subsequent inquiry will fail (284a–b).

Bearing in mind that part and parcel of good statesmanship is this art of due measure in the theoretical knowledge of what must be done, becoming a better dialectician means becoming a better statesman.[17] In the *Sophist* the Stranger makes it clear to Theaetetus that dialectic knowledge is not knowledge of a specific nature but an ability that gradually bears its fruit as it is practised through the *logoi* (*Soph.* 253b10) and in the division according to forms. «Then he who is able to do this has a clear perception of one form (*idéan*) extending entirely through many individuals each of which lies apart, and of many forms differing from one another but included in one greater form» (*Soph.* 253d). It is therefore not strange that the question of learning to make appropriate and timely choices with due measure should occupy the central pages of the *Statesman*. To return to the question at the end of the previous section in this paper, certainly enough has been said in the dialogue for it to do what it sets out to do – namely, to lay down the terms for defining the statesman and to describe, in its various dimensions, the sheer girth of such a venture. The *Statesman* attempts to demonstrate the excesses of rationality when the strict formality of an abstract method *(diairesis)* is applied to a subject such as the determination of things political. The centre of the dialogue shows that calculating the appropriate method requires the same skill as deciding what is due in the practice of discourse and judging the good or

---

genesis. The young philosopher confuses *metretics* with *dialectics* just as elsewhere he confuses *dianoia* with *mathematics*.

17 In the *Laws* statesmanship is clearly linked with due measure, which is the principle of good governance. The kings of Argos and Messene ruined their thrones and violated their kingdoms because they ignored the Hesiodic principle that «the moderate [is] more than the immoderate» (690e). Moderation in the spread of the galley's sails and in the loading and management of provisions, due measure in authority: these are what save the ship, the body, the government. The great legislators can avoid great evils if they apply due measure (691c–d). He who saved Sparta was a god and by bringing the royalty to its knees, «restricted it to moderation» (691e), and finally it is moderation that is also demanded of the board of elders or *gerontia* and the *ephoria*. If, indeed, we do not temper one with the other, monarchy with democracy, the one and the many, neither will acquire due measure. The *Laws* discusses *métrion* in terms of such notions as wealth (666c, 746a, 906d, and 920c), oratory (811d and 885b), moral conduct (811d, 816b, 836a, and 955e) or fitting quantity (842c). The conclusion drawn here is that if it is not to become merely a manifestation of blind force, then statesmanship must be practised with due measure.

the bad in all that is done. Art, oratory and method all share the notion of *due measure*, which must be *preserved in memory* to stop rationality in thought, word or deed from unravelling its own thread.

I propose that this passage in the *Statesman* considers the measure of things and the fact that things allow themselves to be measured, and that by adhering to the text, we can keep this clearly in mind. To take a text that poses a fundamental question about knowledge and to try and make of it an answer to that question hardly does credit to the text's clarifying potential. Due measure on the *reader's* behalf should make his point of departure the dialogue's own textual logic. In this way it becomes easier for us to see the locking together of the various smaller pieces that make of this passage an axle for the dialogue, whether these are the reiterated notion that inquiry is activity of community, the need for memory to hold and defend teaching with unflagging persistence from the disorder and destruction inherent in the act of forgetting, the resonance of the initial scene, or the use of formulae charged with philosophical meaning in an attempt to remedy an over-exacting approach to knowledge.

Dialectics, the art of dialogue, the art of inquiry and of shared thoughts[18] are all to be found at the centre of this dialogue on the statesman in one important point: the activity of *community* is required in order to establish a notion of due measure and so determine what characterises words and deeds as good or bad. It is therefore appropriate that due measure should govern both the theoretical domain of the word and the practical dimension of the deed.

It is for the reader and not for the characters in the dialogue to listen to what is said and done, and to decide if it is said and done well. So far we have observed the many mistakes that have been made. All developments beyond the text will largely depend upon the attention and understanding shown by young Socrates; and as for us, our understanding will depend upon our appreciation that the incomplete pieces here are part of a whole that is yet to be determined. If casting off baroque notions of myth and the darkness of that paradigmatic illustration can make our methodology more limber, then having participated in the notion of *due measure* we will pass to the «return of the statesman». We will see that due measure is not in fact a method, but a new guiding principle for the *lógos* that might clarify our object of study: a fundamental and indispensable principle for the new *lógos* that would have to contemplate the object of the definition. «Due

---

18 Thought is the soul «conversing with itself», cf. *Theaetetus* 189e–190a, *Sophist* 263e.

mesure» plays an evident role in the internal architectonic composition of dialogue,[19] but the *Statesman* demonstrates that the definition of «due measure» in real political life is something that is difficult to calculate.

---

[19] Monserrat-Molas (2003) 2016.

Gislene Vale dos Santos
On the Art of Weaving and the Act of Thinking in Plato's *Statesman*

The purpose of this work is to understand to what extent we can say that the act of thinking is analogous to the art of weaving, based on the arguments in Plato's *Statesman* 277c–281a. As it is well known, the *Statesman* is the second installment of a challenge proposed to the Stranger of Elea, that of distinguishing between the sophist, the politician and the philosopher:

> Socrates: – . . . But I should like to ask our stranger here, if agreeable to him, what people in his country thought about these matters, and what names they used (ὠνόμαζον).
> Theodorus: – What matters do you mean?
> Socrates: – Sophist (σοφιστήν), statesman (πολιτικόν), philosopher (φιλόσοφον).
> Theodorus: – What particular difficulty and what kind of difficulty in regard to them is it about which you had in mind to ask? (τί δὲ μάλιστα καὶ τὸ ποῖόν τι περὶ αὐτῶν διαπορηθεὶς ἐρέσθαι διενοήθης;)
> Socrates: – It is this: Did they consider all these one, or two, or, as there are three names, did they divide them (διαιρούμενοι) into three classes (τρία γένη) and ascribe to each a class, corresponding to a single name?[1]

While Plato has provided us with a work named the *Sophist* and another named the *Statesman*, we should search ourselves for the *Philosopher*.[2] The fact that he has not written such a dialogue does not mean that finding that specific human type is impossible. The philosopher seems to walk freely throughout Plato's work, albeit not expressly named. In order to identify the features of this human type – the philosopher – I will discuss the image of weaving in the *Statesman*.[3] Would it be possible, starting out from this image, to identify at least one of the conditions for being a philosopher? With this in view, the present investigation sets out to understand: 1) whether there is something philosophical in the image of weaving; and 2) whether it would be possible to find out a trait that relates to or identifies to some extent the *philosophical* and the so-called *political*.

---

1 *Sophist* 216d–217a. All translations are from Fowler (1921).
2 I use the italics of Diès (1935) VII to refer to this non written work: "*Le* Politique *est, nous le savons, la troisième d'une pièce tétralogie dont la quatrième ne fut jamais écrite:* Théétète, le Sophiste, le Politique, le Philosophe."
3 At *Theaetetus* 174b, when describing the image of the philosopher, Plato indicates one of the features of this human type: "but what a human being is and what is proper for such a nature to do or bear different from any other, this he inquires and exerts himself to find out. Do you understand, Theodorus, or not?"

https://doi.org/10.1515/9783110605549-011

The first question is: What is it for something to have a political nature?[4]

Stranger: – Where, then, shall we find the statesman's path? (Τὴν οὖν πολιτικὴν ἀτραπὸν πῇ τις ἀνευρήσει;) For we must find it, separate it from the rest, and imprint upon it the seal of a single class; then we must set the mark of another single class upon all the other paths that lead away from this, and make our soul conceive of all sciences as of two classes (πάσας τὰς ἐπιστήμας ὡς οὔσας δύο εἴδη).[5]

We are informed that their examination will be conducted by the process of separation, that is, by distinguishing one thing from another. Such a method requires the isolation of a feature that belongs solely to the object of search. This process takes place in the soul, for to distinguish something from something else requires the soul to separate them.

After this observation, the Stranger goes on to expose a number of divisions in order to reach the defining characteristic of the political man. The first genre he distinguishes is knowledge (ἐπιστήμη). There are two types of knowledge, the practical (πρακτικὴν) and the intellectual (γνωστικήν).[6] One of the last genres he distinguishes is that of the shepherd. This splits into two species, the shepherds of bipedal sheep with horns and the shepherds of bipedal hornless sheep. Among the shepherds of hornless sheep is the man who has a political and a kingly profile at the same time (ἅμα βασιλικὸν ταὐτὸνκληθὲν καὶ πολιτικόν).[7] This, however, is still insufficient to describe his true nature, since anyone who can master an art that serves the community can claim for his job the attribute of 'kingly and political'. If politics is qualified as knowledge concerning the coexistence of men,[8] the farmer and the physician can rightfully claim the same qualification, since both activities watch over human life in a community. So the art of division employed thus far is not capable of reaching a common term that characterizes the political nature properly, and is consequently insufficient to lead to a definition.

---

4 About the relationship between Plato and Socrates, Trabattoni (2010) 29 says that "… Platão inaugura então uma ideia de filosofia na qual o saber que se procura (lembremos que a palavra 'filosofia' significa 'amor pela sabedoria') não é só um saber que se encerra em si mesmo, voltado para o puro conhecer, mas é um saber que pretende identificar aqueles princípios gerais fundamentais, os únicos que podem promover o bem-estar do homem (ou seja, sua felicidade), tanto na vida privada como na pública."
5 *Statesman* 258c.
6 According to Monique Dixsaut (1995) 255 "La différence entre ces deux espèces de sciences réside, et réside seulement, dans cette liaison ou non-liaison à l'action." For a discussion on this topic, see El Murr here.
7 *Statesman* 267c.
8 Plato uses the word κτηνοτροφικός (ἀλλ ἀνθρώπων κοινοτροφικὴν ἐπιστήμην), which concerns the food-supplying aspect of common life.

Being forced to choose a different path to achieve a definition, the Stranger now resorts to a myth[9] as a means to improve on what was lacking in his previous attempts.[10] But he myth lacks the fullness of truth, and it is insufficient to reach the proposed goal. While it proposes an equivalence between the divine shepherd and the human shepherd, it does not explain how they came to achieve such a position.[11]

The Stranger then resumes his old-yet-new investigation, repeating the announcement made at the beginning: "Apparently, then, we must expect a complete description of the statesman only when we have defined the manner of his rule over the state."[12] Once again, he chooses the art of division to reach to a definition of the type of government practiced by the politician, because the concept of *political man* is directly linked to that of *government*. They go back to the definition of politics as that prescriptive art of the herdsman that deals with living beings in common.[13] The art of herding is in turn divided into what is imposed by force – tyranny – and what is accepted voluntarily – politics. The Stranger, far from accepting this definition, objects to it as follows:

> But our talk, just like a picture of a living creature, seems to have a good enough outline, but not yet to have received the clearness that comes from pigments and the blending of colors. And yet it is more fitting to portray any living being by speech and argument than by painting or any handicraft whatsoever to persons who are able to follow argument; but to others it is better to do it by means of works of craftsmanship.[14]

---

9 In one of the chapters of his book (2010) 41 [1941] Mattei says in a poetic tone that "Tensionada entre o diálogo e o mito, a filosofia procede do cruzamento de uma palavra e de uma escrita que são encenadas no teatro platônico"

10 Myth seems to be a kind of speech that does not admit refutation. However, it does not guarantee an accurate truth either, and this allows us to say that it is a kind of *metaxy*. Between ignorance and knowledge a third species appears, a sort of true opinion without causal justification.

11 According to Kato (1995) 167 "The Great Myth seems to give us that kind of true belief about the statesman, but not exact knowledge. It is only a knowledge as in a dream. This is, I think, exactly the stage where we are now in search of the being of the statesman."

12 275a: Δεῖ τοίνυν τὸν τρόπον, ὡς ἔοικε, διορίσαντας τῆς ἀρχῆς τῆς πόλεως οὕτω τελέως τὸν πολιτικὸν ἡμῖν εἰρῆσθαι προσδοκᾶν.

13 276c–d: Πρῶτον μέν, ὃ λέγομεν, τοὔνομα μετασκευωρήσασθαι, πρὸς τὴν ἐπιμέλειαν μᾶλλον προσαγαγόντας ἢ τὴν τροφήν, ἔπειτα ταύτην τέμνειν· οὐ γὰρ σμικρὰς ἂν ἔχοι τμήσεις ἔτι.

14 277b–c: ἀλλ᾽ ἀτεχνῶς ὁ λόγος ἡμῖν ὥσπερ ζῷον τὴν ἔξωθεν μὲν περιγραφὴν ἔοικεν ἱκανῶς ἔχειν, τὴν δὲ οἷον τοῖς φαρμάκοις καὶ τῇ συγκράσει τῶν χρωμάτων ἐνάργειαν οὐκ ἀπειληφέναι πω. γραφῆς δὲ καὶ συμπάσης χειρουργίας λέξει καὶ λόγῳ δηλοῦν πᾶν ζῷον μᾶλλον πρέπει τοῖς δυναμένοις ἕπεσθαι· τοῖς δ᾽ ἄλλοις διὰ χειρουργιῶν.

Even though differentiating these two types of conjecture – one by arguments and the other with images – the Stranger seems to combine the two in what follows. A paradigm to be understood only in thought is also portrayed metaphorically as an aid to be understood. The Stranger first explains and then draws,[15] but explanation and drawing alone do not contain, each in itself, the answer to the question at hand. Their mixture may end up in the suggestion of a concept, but if not, will at least keep us questioning.

After going through the genres and appealing to myth, the Stranger makes use of paradigms, conceiving of them as intellectual dividers which do not permit mistaking one thing for another. "It is difficult, my dear fellow, to set forth any of the greater ideas, except by the use of examples; for it would seem that each of us knows everything that he knows as if in a dream and then again, when he is as it were awake, knows nothing of it all."[16] What is brought into question is the ability to make distinctions. Wakefulness and sleep are states that, despite their differences, portray realities as having the same truth value. Yet, none of them is able to make differentiations at the moment of their apprehension of reality, for they are merely apprehending. Nevertheless, at the moment of apprehension, each of these states is taken to be a true one. Faithful to the Platonic argument for distinguishing degrees of reality,[17] the Stranger makes use of dream imagery to show the difference between the various states of the soul. Misunderstanding seems to be a natural condition of human life. For this reason, we need to establish criteria to help us avoid misunderstandings in the process of definition. Since the soul is open to the possibility of error, it is also open to that of knowledge.

I have set out the circumstances that allow thinking in the *Statesman* in order to understand the movement that leads a man to his intellectual skills. Let me now focus on the following statement of the Stranger: "I seem at present in

---

15 In Plato, we cannot consider this statement as a formula. The dynamic of each dialogue is different. The use of the language of imagery is recurrent in Plato, who employs it according to the dialectical needs of the different contexts of his arguments.

16 277d: Χαλεπόν, ὦ δαιμόνιε, μὴ παραδείγμασι χρώμενον ἱκανῶς ἐνδείκνυσθαί τι τῶν μειζόνων. κινδυνεύει γὰρ ἡμῶν ἕκαστος οἷον ὄναρ εἰδὼς ἅπαντα πάντ' αὖ πάλιν ὥσπερ ὕπαρ ἀγνοεῖν.

17 In a note to their translation of the *Statesman*, and on the subject of dream and wakefulness, L. Brisson and J.-F. Pradeau (2003 in note *ad locum*) confirm this: "On retrouve la locution *oúte ónar oúte húpar* en *Philèbe*, 36e, 65e et en *République*, II, 328e. Déjà dans *l'Odyssée* (XIX, 547; XX, 90), *húpar* s'oppose à *ónar*, quand la comparaison de l'ignorance et du "rêve éveillé" a semble-t-il des antécédents préplatoniciens./.../Par la suite, et notamment chez Platon, *húpar* désigne l'état qui suit le rêve (*ónar*) et qui s'y oppose: *Théétète*, 158b–e; *Phèdre*, 277d; *Timée*, 71e; *République*, V 476c; VII 533c; IX, 574e, 576b."

absurd fashion to have touched upon our (*en hemin*) experience (*pathos*) in regard to knowledge (*episteme*)."[18] The movement that leads to knowledge is an affection that makes the soul fall into a state of *aporia*. This state allows it to move, as it opens up a route for further questions, in particular, the essential question about what constitutes the political man.

In this struggle, one of the things the Stranger seems to indicate is that thought consists of an analogical relationship between paradigms:

> Is this, then, a satisfactory definition, that an example is formed when that which is the same in some second unconnected thing is rightly conceived and compared with the first, so that the two together form one true idea?[19]

Even though it is in the form of a question, this statement indicates an act of thinking, here expressed by the word δοξαζόμενον. The soul will be responsible for identifying points of identity within difference by means of the separation and aggregation of the elements involved. When thinking separates distinct elements and identifies common parts among them, it establishes a paradigm. A paradigm is what remains the same, that is, what retains the same identity within the plurality. It is born of the relationship between two principles, the principle of difference and that of identity.[20] It is thus the principle that enables discernment. To think, in these terms, is to use paradigms to interpret, judge, and form opinions about the relationship between multiplicity and unity. Moreover, thinking is what makes it possible for humans to speak about the world.

Therefore, I suggest, thinking is a sort of movement that constantly formulates analogies. To be able to formulate analogies, as I understand it, it to be able to establish proportional relationships between distinct terms, as in

---

18 277d. Similarly, *Theaetetus* 155d indicates that the affection (*pathos*) proper to the philosopher is to wonder (*to thaumazein*), and that this is the beginning (*arche*) of philosophy. On the characterization of *pathos* in Platonic thought, Pradeau (2008) 28 says that "O πάθος é um gênero, o da afecção, isto é, do conjunto dos efeitos que uma coisa qualquer é suscetível de suportar a partir de uma ou de diversas outras realidades. Essa dupla definição da natureza dinâmica de cada realidade dá a Platão um dos instrumentos maiores de sua epistemologia, assim como de sua ontologia. Ela lhe permite, com efeito, distinguir as realidades segundo sua aptidão para afetar outras, e defini-las todas segundo a forma dessas afecções, dessas modificações mútuas; permite ainda conceber uma hierarquia das realidades, segundo o grau de afecção de que são suscetíveis."
19 278c: Οὐκοῦν τοῦτο μὲν ἱκανῶς συνειλήφαμεν, ὅτι παραδείγματός γ' ἐστὶ τότε γένεσις, ὁπόταν ὂν ταὐτὸν ἐν ἑτέρῳ διεσπασμένῳ δοξαζόμενον ὀρθῶς καὶ συναχθὲν περὶ ἑκάτερον ὡς συνάμφω μίαν ἀληθῆ δόξαν ἀποτελῇ;
20 Cf. *Sophist* 259e.

mathematics. Something similar to this passage of the *Statesman* can be found in the *Sophist*: "The complete separation of each thing from all is the utterly final obliteration of all discourse. For our power of discourse is derived from the interweaving of the classes or ideas with one another."[21]

Plato is talking about the origin of *logos*, conceiving of it as a relationship that brings differences together into a unified form of speech.[22] There is an analogy here as well, a proportion that establishes the measure and the harmony of the relationship between the Forms, so that speech will become something composed of differences and identities. Opinion, insofar as it is a sort of *logos*, comes-to-be out of an encounter with the sensible.[23] It can be formulated by reference to two different aspects, the first one intelligible and the other sensible. *Doxa* is conditioned by a further, compositional rendition, that of *logos*.[24] Nevertheless, when propounded, *logos* expresses a *doxa* about differences, starting out from the semantic unity that is expressed or thought.

It is possible that thinking has an opinion about difference and identity which is true and unique. At 258c, it is with the same and single term (ἰδέαν μίαν) that the Stranger seeks to find what is proper to the political man, in order to separate him from the others. However, this identification can be mistaken. While at *Theaetetus* 187b, after having proposed a second hypothesis in the search for what constitutes knowledge, Socrates talks about the possibility of error, in the

---

21 259e: Τελεωτάτη πάντων λόγων ἐστὶν ἀφάνισις τὸ διαλύειν ἕκασον ἀπὸ πάντων· διὰ γὰρ τὴν ἀλλήλων τῶν εἰδῶν συμπλοκὴν ὁ λόγος γέγονεν ἡμῖν.

22 According to Murr (2002) 95 "La symplokè politikè n'est que l'image, imparfaite, d'un autre entrelacement, èternellement à recommencer celui-là e dont le recommencement n'est rien d'autre que le mouvement propre du lógos: la symplokè tôn eidôn."

23 This formulation is supported by the discussion of the *Theaetetus*, especially the first answer given to the question *Is knowledge perception?*

24 According to Dixsaut (2003) 173-174, commenting on some passages of *Republic*, book VI, "L'intelligence doit en outre être dotée de mesure et de grâce: la grâce naturelle de la pensée est sa capacité d'être affectée par le caractère propre (*idea*) de chaque étant, son aptitude à se laisser conduire vers ce qu'elle cherche. Sa puissance d'agir est un ajustement, sa puissance de pâtir un élan. L'unité de l'agir et du pâtir est l'unité d'un accord spontané, d'un mouvement naturellement réglé par ce vers quoi il tend: on ne conduit pas sa pensée, mais la pensée, de son propre mouvement, se laisse conduire. Elle le fait avec élégance, et l'élégance et son contraire dépendent de la perfection ou de l'imperfection du rythme. Le juste rythme ne s'identifie pas à un juste milieu entre le trop rapide et le trop lent, il est une perpétuelle harmonisation des contraires. Pour cette bonne mesure, il n'y a pas de méthode, pour cette élégance pas de recettes. S'apprendre ce qu'on ne savait pas encore est toujours à nouveau pénible, ce qui n'empêche pas la pensée de prendre plaisir à ce jeu divin qu'elle est."

Statesman the discussion has a somewhat different look. An opinion can be both true at a time and void of truth in a different context:

> Can we wonder, then, that our soul, whose nature involves it in the same uncertainty about the letters or elements of all things, is sometimes in some cases firmly grounded in the truth about every detail, and again in other cases is all at sea about everything, and somehow or other has correct opinions about some combinations, and then again is ignorant of the same things when they are transferred to the long and difficult syllables of life?[25]

The soul can be willing to be affected either by the sensible dimension of the *kosmos* or by the one that enables true discourse. The last is the intelligible one. Regarding the first option, the reference to syllables is a reference to elements[26] responsible for one of the dimensions of the sensible. When in contact with syllables, the soul may ignore them, and commit a mistake in interpretation. "Ignoring" here seems to mean exchanging one element for another during the perceptual act. It does not mean that the soul does not notice the elements, but that the exchange causes it to perceive them mistakenly, and thus to ignore the truth of a phenomenal situation. From this, it can be thought that at least two speech-acts are possible, and can be contrary to one another. When interpreting the sensitive dimension of the *kosmos*, it is natural that some confusion occurs. Hence the need for a criterion that allows a correct orientation towards the truth.

The paradigm in this situation comes to solve an epistemological, but above all, an ontological problem, because knowing reality requires discerning it on the basis of criteria that are not subject to becoming. Such criteria would be, in the Stranger's words, a paradigm, or a model that will serve as a parameter of distinction, and possesses in itself the ability to gather together differences in each thing which constitute a unity.[27] The paradigm does not prevent us from errors, but allows us, rather, to identify them.

---

25 278c–d: Θαυμάζοιμεν ἂν οὖν εἰ ταὐτὸν τοῦτο ἡμῶν ἡ ψυχὴ φύσει περὶ τὰ τῶν πάντων στοιχεῖα πεπονθυῖα τοτὲ μὲν ὑπ' ἀληθείας περὶ ἓν ἕκαστον ἕν τισι συνίσταται, τοτὲ δὲ περὶ ἅπαντα ἐν ἑτέροις αὖ φέρεται, καὶ τὰ μὲν αὑτῶν ἁμῇ γέ πῃ τῶν συγκράσεων ὀρθῶς δοξάζει, μετατιθέμενα δ' εἰς τὰς τῶν πραγμάτων μακρὰς καὶ μὴ ῥᾳδίους συλλαβὰς ταὐτὰ ταῦτα πάλιν ἀγνοεῖ;

26 Τὰ στοιχεῖα.

27 According to Bravo (1995) 78 "El concepto de diferencia será, en todo caso, el concepto fundamental de la definición en este diálogo". In agreement with Bravo, we recollect the passages that define a paradigm. Moreover, the political man is sought among a diversity of others. The possibility of picking out unity is intimately connected to the possibility of bringing forth difference which we find at the center of the discussion of the *Statesman*. The definition would be anchored in the presupposition of difference, understood as an epistemological criterion that guides the research proposed by Plato. My agreement with Bravo's thought as exposed here remains restricted to this small point.

Commenting on the passages of the *Theaetetus* and the *Sophist* touching on the definition of thinking, Jean-François Mattei says: "*dianoeisthai* reverberates through the soul the dialectical tension found in the dialogue; the prefix *dia* implying division, but also a mediation that runs through, in temporal sense, a given set."[28] Mattei's words, albeit not directed to the *Statesman*, can be applied to our passage, I believe, for their topic is the same: the conditions for thinking. The soul in this dialogue is also a center of tensions which are reflected in the dialectical method that moves the *Statesman*. Even though the word *dianoeisthai* is not used in this section of the dialogue, its meaning emerges somehow in the words συνίσταται, τῶν συγκράσεων and δοξάζει.

What I should like to emphasize in the words of Mattei is the tension caused by the complexity involved in the act of thinking. The tension here seems to relate very precisely to the foremost feature of thought, namely that of being a relationship between difference and identities as such. When separation becomes the object of thinking, there is no privileging the occurrence either of something sensible or of something intelligible. It is the same with a fabric that comes-to-be from the tensions within the weft. If the weft is undone, the fabric disappears. This reminds us of the passage of the *Sophist* about speech mentioned above. Speech, as well as weaving, is a *symploke*.

Weaving is the paradigm chosen by the Stranger to distinguish the rule of the political man from all other professions that may claim the same kingly title. The paradigm is not a criterion of order expressed in logical form. Rather, it is a kind of image that emphasizes the character of the composition. This paradigm is thought by the Stranger to be the very image of weaving:

> What example could we apply which is very small, but has the same kind of activity as statesmanship and would enable us satisfactorily to discover that which we seek? What do you say, Socrates, if we have nothing else at hand, to taking at random the art of weaving, and, if you please, not the whole of that? For I fancy the art of weaving wool will be enough; if we choose that part only it will probably furnish us with the illustration we desire.[29]

Accordingly, wool weaving is chosen as a paradigm, a kind of model or example of how the political man should work. Weaving and government have something

---

28 (2010) 59. The translation into English is mine.
29 279a–b: Τί δῆτα παράδειγμά τις ἄν, ἔχον τὴν αὐτὴν πολιτικῇ πραγματείαν, σμικρότατον παραθέμενος ἱκανῶς ἂν εὕροι τὸ ζητούμενον; βούλει πρὸς Διός, ὦ Σώκρατες, εἰ μή τι πρόχειρον ἕτερον ἔχομεν, ἀλλ' οὖν τήν γε ὑφαντικὴν προελώμεθα; καὶ ταύτην, εἰ δοκεῖ, μὴ πᾶσαν; ἀποχρήσει γὰρ ἴσως ἡ περὶ τὰ ἐκ τῶν ἐρίων ὑφάσματα· τάχα γὰρ ἂν ἡμῖν καὶ τοῦτο τὸ μέρος αὐτῆς μαρτυρήσειε προαιρεθὲν ὃ βουλόμεθα.

in common. My hypothesis is that this relationship of similarity includes yet another term: thought.

In the introduction to their translation of the *Statesman*, Luc Brisson and Jean-François Pradeau identify differences and identities between the *Statesman* and the *Republic*, and they claim that Plato is searching, in both dialogues, for the excellence of the city, its unity. However, he adopted different means in each dialogue: "first, both dialogues do not compare the city with the same model (the individual soul in the *Republic* replaces the 'fabric' in the *Statesman*)." In the *Statesman*, government is analogous to weaving.

My hypothesis is that weaving is analogous to the most important activity of the soul, even though this is not explicit. The analogy, however, does not refer to the full complexity of the soul. Weaving, in the *Statesman*, would be an analogy for a particular aspect of the soul, the activity of thinking, even when Plato does not discuss the art of weaving as a whole, but only wool weaving. I do not conceive thinking as something separate from its sensible and intelligible conditions. I emphasize specifically its activity, its ability to establish relations, and to identify, from such relations, identities and differences, which constitutes the capacity of the λογιστικόν, *par excellence.*[30]

At the beginning of the process of distinguishing the parts that constitute weaving, the Stranger starts with a macro-category. Weaving is, at first, a preventative action, since it is a means of defense (ἀμυντήριον). As a defense, it is a kind of barrier (φράγμα), not as a roof, but as garments (ἱμάτια). Among the many different types of garment, there is one that does not involve stitching and is composed of threads, interwoven threads. Interwoven threads are, by the logic of the division of the parts in the dialogue, a means of defense.

I should like to emphasize that *logos* also constitutes a defense for humans, since it allows life in a community, an interwoven life, albeit not stitched. The internal relations of a city do not always remain the same but change. That which is interwoven is unwoven and woven back again. I believe that such interweaving favors unity, but always with differences in view. Two threads form a synthesis that generates a fabric, which, in its turn, is the material necessary for a garment.

---

30 *Republic* IV 439d: "'Not unreasonably,' said I, 'shall we claim that they are two and different from one another, naming that in the soul whereby it reckons and reasons the rational and that with which it loves, hungers, thirsts, and feels the flutter and titillation of other desires, the irrational and appetitive — companion of various repletions and pleasures.'" For the ratiocinative dimension of the soul specifically, what does reasoning mean? Or, in the words of Socrates in the *Theaetetus*, "And *do you define thought as I do?*... As the talk which the soul has *with itself* about any subjects which *it* considers... But the soul, ... when it thinks, is merely conversing *with itself*, asking itself questions and answering, affirming and denying." (189e–190a)

Thus, *logos* is the foundation that organizes a city along the right lines. The wise soul establishes the right relations and for that reason can become the ground of good governance. The argument of the Stranger has its own way of being formulated. The division method not only exposes the contents of the analysis, but is itself the very expression of how thinking articulates itself in its most originating dimension. Division and reunion are natural modes by which thinking is constituted. To adopt the Stranger's metaphor: thinking is a weft that articulates identities and differences expressed as *logos,* which is the foundation of the governance of a political soul, who by taking care of itself, cares at the same time for the whole *polis:*

> And just as we called the art statecraft which was concerned with the state, so we shall call the art concerned with clothes, from the nature of its activity, clothes-making, shall we not? And may we say further that weaving, in so far as the greatest part of it is, as we saw, concerned with the making of clothes, differs in name only from this art of clothes-making, just as in the other case the royal art differed from statecraft?[31]

The art of connecting threads produces garments, just as the art of relating with human beings on the grounds of mutual acceptance produces government. Producing clothing and ruling are *technai* expressed in the social body by the weaving of either the woollen threads, or the characters of certain citizens in the *polis.* The result of such a crossing is, in both cases unity: the fabric and the city. If garments protect men in their private dimension (*idios*), government does so in their public dimension (*polis*).[32] The two social dimensions that constitute human culture – the public and the private – are possible thanks to the condition that qualifies and distinguishes humans.[33]

---

31 280a: τὴν δὲ τῶν ἱματίων μάλιστα ἐπιμελουμένην τέχνην, ὥσπερ τότε τὴν τῆς πόλεως πολιτικὴν εἴπομεν, οὕτω καὶ νῦν ταύτην προσείπωμεν ἀπ' αὐτοῦ τοῦ πράγματος ἱματιουργικήν; φῶμεν δὲ καὶ ὑφαντικήν, ὅσον ἐπὶ τῇ τῶν ἱματίων ἐργασίᾳ μέγιστον ἦν μόριον, μηδὲν διαφέρειν πλὴν ὀνόματι ταύτης τῆς ἱματιουργικῆς, καθάπερ κἀκεῖ τότε τὴν βασιλικὴν τῆς πολιτικῆς;
32 "This makes it clear that clothes stand to the body as the city stands to the citizens. In both cases the name derives not from knowledge but from practical production, and so from manufacture. The extension of the previously derived sense of 'caring' from the statesman to the weaver is quite striking. We knew that *epimeleia* is at the heart of the royal art before we learned that it has the same role with respect to weaving. So the model is itself illuminated by that which it is supposed to explain." Rosen (1995) 104.
33 As Vegetti (2010) 40 comments: "A política, porém, pressupõe uma antropologia e esta funda-se numa psicologia. Mas a psicologia platônica pode, por sua vez, ser de tipo fenomenológico, e, por conseguinte, 'político' – como declaradamente é a psicologia do livro IV da *República* e, em parte também, a psicofisiologia do *Timeu*".

As they take place in accordance with *logos*, weaving and ruling are expressions of *symploke*. However, they are expressed through different *technai* which do not share the same process of production but the same intellectual aspect. In other words, *logos* is a human dimension that assumes the possibility of composing not only from categories within itself, but also from different arrangements. Geometry, government and artifacts are all different modes of composing that *logos* performs, all of them are manifestations of a unity constituted by differences. In this sense, *symploke* may be taken as a paradigm that combines differences and identities throughout the processes that follow different *technai*. All human arts have human artisan, while *logos* sets what is according to nature. When building, the architect decides the particular *techne* he wants to use in order to construct the house. When thinking it is not the same. We do not 'decide' anything by the act of thinking but we simply have the ability to compose or interweave what is there. "The process of weaving is, I take it, a kind of joining together."[34]

---

34 281a: Τὸ μὲν τῆς ὑφῆς συμπλοκή τίς ἐστί που.

Nuria Sánchez Madrid
Weaving the Polis. Reading Plato's *Statesman* (279a–283d)

1

Platonic thought always gave an extraordinary importance to the choice of the images most suitable to guide human argumentation and to display the outcomes of cognition. In this vein I aim in this chapter at giving an account about a paradigm well known for the Platonic scholarship as the weaving simile, which I consider a key point in the development of the *Statesman*. Plato's weaving paradigm in the *Statesman* became one of the most visited *topoi* of the dialogue; enigmatical in many aspects, it is particularly interesting for its puzzling appraisal of the political art compared to more transcendental approaches suggested by dialogues such as the *Republic*. Inspired by a hermeneutical account put forth by Schofield,[1] I shall try to cast light upon the section of the *Statesman* that makes use of the weaving paradigm, which I regard as a key argument of the dialogue. But it is not my purpose to discuss either the flaws or improvements in the structure of the *Statesman* by contrast with the structure of other Plato's dialogues. On the contrary, my main goal in this paper will be to give an account of Plato's view of politics as a kind of knowledge, following the diaeretical steps of the weaving paradigm. As is well known, "the weaving passage" is preceded by a lengthy statement by the Stranger from Elea, in which he claims that the first human social core unit was a herd (261 d), an uncanny provisional label that blurs the limits between human and animal forms of community. Moreover, once the mythical age of Kronos has come about, human beings – lacking all tools and all crafts – are forced to struggle for their survival against both wild and domestic animals, the two main kinds that the Stranger tackles, by means of technical instruments that human culture possesses. In this context, the Stranger defines kingship and statecraft as the «art of feeding the

---

This text belongs to a research granted by the projects: New Trust-cm (H2015-HUM-3466), funded by the Community of Madrid, Pensamiento y representación literaria y artística digital ante la crisis de Europa y el Mediterráneo (PR26/16-6B-3), funded by UCM/Santander, and by the UCM 2017 Innovative Teaching Project n.º 169 Contrapicados y puntos de fuga. Las otras historias de la historia de la filosofía.

---

1 Schofield (2006) 3.

https://doi.org/10.1515/9783110605549-012

biped herd» (276 c), whose main failure derives from the fact that it pays no attention to the importance of education for human existence. Up to this point the argumentational thread of the dialogue gives the impression that the government of humans and beasts does not imply any important difference between them. Yet, technical development is not enough to remove the violence produced by the superfluity or lack of goods and facilities in human relationships. So another device – such as the art of education – should be used to weaken the human tendency to collapse under the weight of its own technical products. The Stranger points out that the most highly thought-of arts soon begin to compete with one another for domination, a function that clearly goes beyond their specific goal. Yet he highlights that there is an art capable of ruling over the other arts, including the practical ones, and a theoretical guide might well take on the appearance of a piece of practical behaviour. Thus, a concluding remark of the dialogue states that:

> The consideration of all these arts which have been mentioned leads to the conclusion that none of them is the art of the statesman. For the art that is truly kingly ought not to act itself, but should rule over the arts that have the power of action; it should decide upon the right or wrong time for the initiation of the most important measures in the state, and the other arts should perform its behests (*Pol.*, 306 c–d).[2]

This passage argues for the existence of a «kingly process of weaving» [τὴν δὴ βασιλικὴν συμπλοκήν] (306a) considered as a synoptic art, which is acquainted with the subsidiary objectives, instruments and goals of the other individual arts, and sets out to organize and coordinate them as a whole. Thus the dialogue points out that the initial disappointment produced by the competition between the arts is replaced by the dialogical appraisal of a wise technique or art, which though largely concealed from human eyes and taken as an oxymoron at first, really is capable of ruling human beings. The dialogue between the Stranger and the young Socrates will focus on this strange art, i.e. statesmanship, which consists in the coordination of heterogeneous but complementary elements of the political community. Moreover, the most accurate expression of this kind of coordination will be the art of weaving, one capable of combining and separating the threads of the *polis* into a shared structure. Thus the key features of the art of political weaving will suggest the melding of the heterogeneous parts of one and the same organism. Many pages before, the Stranger had claimed that a new

---

2 Pol., 305c–d: τὴν γὰρ ὄντως οὖσαν βασιλικὴν οὐκ αὐτὴν δεῖ πράττειν ἀλλ᾽ ἄρχειν τῶν δυναμένων πράττειν, γιγνώσκουσαν τὴν ἀρχήν τε καὶ ὁρμὴν τῶν μεγίστων ἐν ταῖς πόλεσιν ἐγκαιρίας τε πέρι καὶ ἀκαιρίας, τὰς δ᾽ ἄλλας τὰ προσταχθέντα δρᾶν» (Fowler, 1962).

method was required to carry the discussion further forward, one that would demand a deeper approach than the provisional definition of statecraft mentioned at the beginning of the dialogue:

> Younger Socrates
> Well, Stranger, it looks as though our account of the statesman were complete now.
> Stranger
> That would be a fine thing for us, Socrates. But not you alone must think so; I must think so, too, in agreement with you. As a matter of fact, however, in my opinion our figure of the king is not yet perfect, but like statue-makers who sometimes in their misapplied enthusiasm make too numerous and too large additions and thus delay the completion of their several works, we too, at this time, wishing to make quick progress, and also to make clear in a grand style the error of our previous course, and, moreover, fancying that the use of great illustrations was proper in the case of a king, have taken up a marvellous mass of myth and have consequently been obliged to use a greater part of it than we should (277 a–b).[3]

In my view the new required method marks the withdrawal of metaphors of shepherding and the selection of weaving as the operation analogous to the making of the *demos* and the *polis*. The text quoted above clearly conveys the Stranger's disagreement with regard to the attempt to adapt the functions of the herd shepherd to the tasks that the statesman has to fulfil, since the replacement of the divine shepherd by the human caretaker and the consequent division between voluntarily exercised care over free and consensual bipeds and the involuntary one did not yield the expected outcome. Indeed, taking care either of animals or human beings seems to be too external a task compared to the deep knowledge that the statesman needs to have about the organism he rules. By doing so, the Stranger also points out the shortcomings of this second definition, arguing that it fails to depict the main activity to be performed by the statesman.[4] Therefore he suggests that they use a more reliable paradigm for explaining which kind of knowledge requires the royal art. The choice of the paradigm has been often judged to constitute a rather arbitrary shift in the dialogue, driven more by aesthetics than logic. There is no doubt that weaving is mentioned in the

---

3 *Pol*, 277a–b: Νεώτερος Σωκράτης: καὶ κινδυνεύει γε, ὦ ξένε, τελέως ἂν ἡμῖν οὕτως ἔχειν ἡ περὶ τὸν πολιτικὸν ἀπόδειξις. Ξένος: καλῶς ἄν, ὦ Σώκρατες, ἡμῖν ἔχοι. δεῖ δὲ μὴ σοὶ μόνῳ ταῦτα, ἀλλὰ κἀμοὶ μετὰ σοῦ κοινῇ συνδοκεῖν. νῦν δὲ κατά γε τὴν ἐμὴν οὔπω φαίνεται τέλεον ὁ βασιλεὺς ἡμῖν σχῆμα ἔχειν, ἀλλὰ καθάπερ ἀνδριαντοποιοὶ παρὰ καιρὸν ἐνίοτε σπεύδοντες πλείω καὶ μείζω τοῦ δέοντος ἕκαστα τῶν ἔργων ἐπεμβαλλόμενοι βραδύνουσι, καὶ νῦν ἡμεῖς, ἵνα δὴ πρὸς τῷ ταχὺ καὶ μεγαλοπρεπῶς δηλώσαιμεν τὸ τῆς ἔμπροσθεν ἁμάρτημα διεξόδου, τῷ βασιλεῖ νομίσαντες πρέπειν μεγάλα παραδείγματα ποιεῖσθαι, θαυμαστὸν ὄγκον ἀράμενοι τοῦ μύθου, μείζονι τοῦ δέοντος ἠναγκάσθημεν αὐτοῦ μέρει προσχρήσασθαι.
4 C. Castoriadis has focused on the reasons of this rejection (1999) 59 ss.

text as a «small example» (279 a),[5] being apparently not itself of any particular importance. Yet this may be an illusion, since the Stranger insists on the fact that he has chosen the new model with precision, by consciously focusing on a common and quite ordinary social activity. It is true that the humble art of weaving will display a *diaeresis* regarding the science of measuring clothes, which is crucial for clarifying the patterns of measure to be found in politics, a method that confirms the view of order prevalent in the dialogue, where the operations involved in the art of weaving manage to produce a well-framed product all by themselves. Moreover, it is a popular art, not a science, which in this case delivers lessons about how to build the *polis*. In this context, the Stranger claims that there is a self-evident analogy between the activities carried out by both arts. More precisely, most similarities between them would be discovered by taking into account not just the external surface, but the structural action that each carries forward. By pointing this out, the dialogue explicitly portrays the same flaws the Stranger found in the statue-definition of the statesman, where the apparent conceptual proximity between the shepherd and the caretaker has already been outlined.

After making these remarks, it is a key point that the first approach to the weaver's activity highlights that the production of any product involves different stages. So the art of carding, the art of darning, the art of spinning and some other related arts take part in the production of a cloak (281 a–d), and demand a long process previously set in motion by other craftsmen, which is then coordinated by the weaver, who works with the warp and the woof. Furthermore, the art of carding begins the process of discarding those materials unfit for the final product (282 b), which reminds us of the goals assigned to *paideia*, the art that is capable of preventing pathological characters from forcing their voices, in cowardly fashion, on the *polis*. Taking these different steps into account, the reader will easily grasp, as part of an overall account of these passages, that the arts involved in weaving mirror, through a materially embedded action, key ontological and ethical distinctions. Put differently, the process of weaving reflects the rational order that unfolds itself in the *phusis* that humans manufacture.[6]

---

5 See Castoriadis (1999) 85.
6 I consider quite useful in this context the following remark of M. Dixsaut (1995) 271: «C'est [...] dans un contexte 'technique' que l'Étranger énonce à quelle condition la politique est vraiment conforme à la nature. Aucun art, dit-il alors, ne consent à employer de matériaux défectueux, tous commencent par rejeter ceux qui compromettraient la solidité et la beauté de ce qu'ils oeuvrent. En agissant de cette façon, la politique se conforme à la nature de toute *téchne*, donc à la

The basic action of discarding unfit materials aims to ease the paradoxicality of the analogy between the group of arts preparing the same woven product and the ethical action performed by the statesman in the *polis*, since the ruler requires to have at his disposal a systematic overview of the arts performed in the state. At a second stage, he must gather the courageous and moderate characters according to a reasonable measure into the political community. So the statesman is expected to set up the structure which gives the *polis* its shape, confronting the ethical and pedagogical sources of those dreaded thing such as *stasis*, antagonism, and imbalances that could entail the destruction of the political body.

None of the tasks the civil ruler has to fulfil could be carried out without considering that the statesman has to be acquainted with the purposes of the community as a whole, and with the art of *kairos*, which makes the statesman «a master timer» (Lane 1998, 142), especially capable of intervening with prudence and success in periods of crisis. Alonso Tordesillas reminds the reader of the *Statesman* of one of the etymological derivations that the Ionians assigned to the word *kairos*: the one referring to the act of firing an arrow to hit the target with exactness often overlaps another one, which indicates the moment in which the shuttle can be passed through threads on the loom.[7] I consider this meaning a key point for the understanding of this central analogy of *The Statesman*.

Moreover, the ruler of the city is expected to know how to connect human beings together with divine ties (309 b–c) through his mastery of the art of degree, which is actually the best pedagogue of human souls. Marriage and procreation will be organized so as to to balance the presence of every psychological quality and virtue in families, hindering the concentration of any single character in any one of them. Finally, the statesman shall rightly choose the human *ethe* fit for holding charge and power, and able to boost «a true fellowship by mutual concord and by ties of friendship» (311 b). All these goals indicate the need for a sound analogy with the weaving process, and also confirm that the weaving master has to coordinate and check the manufacturing expertise involved in the arts that contribute to the production of a cloak, where the labour performed by

---

sienne propre: toute art doit proceder avec intelligence, discernement et prévoyance, aucun artisan n'agit au hasard (*Gorg.* 503 d–504 e). [...] En se conformant à la nature propre à tout art, la politique témoigne qu'elle possède l'intelligence de la véritable nature de la Nature».
7 See A. Tordesillas (1995) 108.

the single craftsmen ends up with the ultimate union of the material elements of the knitted *polis*.[8]

The directive capacity of human beings falls into two parts, one subordinate and one autonomous [*autepitaktiké*], the last being based on the cooperation offered by the subordinate arts. Furthermore, the wise and good statesman will, at critical moments, add *know-how* to the map of arts involved in weaving the polis, for example in the purging of the *polis* by putting some citizens to death or banishing others, or by sending some of them to the colonies and bringing new ones from other cities, as described at 293 d 4–9. These kinds of measure will be taken with calm and correct judgment by the good ruler, who will be capable of handling conflicts beyond the letter of human constitutions, which are often at odds with the critical decisions that are called for. Some interpreters have viewed the expertise of this ruler of the *polis* – as Rosen observes, (1995, 20) – as a form of knowledge which is too practical, and wholly independent of philosophical wisdom. Yet the weaving passage of the *Statesman* seems to suggest that an effective theoretical knowledge is already implied in the measures that experts in statecraft apply to the polical body, measures which appear to be an essential feature of the cyclical crises that the human species suffer throughout history. Indeed, the myth of the historical Ages of the World argues that the Age of Kronos forces human beings to find by themselves a ruler capable of working out the norms of activity fit for uncertain and gloomy times. Moreover, the kind of leadership that statesmanship requires involves architectonic expertise, which covers both the capacity to give orders to subordinate craftsmen and the faculty to proceed wisely in the overcoming of critical circumstances. Thus the statesman has to coordinate subordinate actions, and does not hesitate to create *nomos* by himself when the written laws seem to be too blurred to grasp historical circumstances. The image of the weaving of warp and woof obviously implies a material referent, i.e. the materials that arts such as carding, darning and spinning respectively yield, but it also possesses a more abstract referent, i.e. the reflective process that the statesman is expected to master for the correct weaving of the parts of the *polis*. This ability to articulate the heteronomous characters and parts of the *polis* moves up from the lowest part of the ruler's soul, and manifests

---

8 I find rather insightful the following remark of Vilius Bartnikas about the content of statecraft knowledge derived from Plato's *Statesman* (2014) 136: «When coordination of arts was discussed, it was argued that statesmen do not perform the activities of arts but organize and oversee them so that they could accomplish political ends. [...] They are not experts of a specific field of knowledge. Statesmen must comprehend the general functions of arts and know which expertise is needed to achieve a political end. The architectonical nature of statesmanship reveals that it is a theoretical knowledge with practical results».

itself as the hidden treasure of political theory,[9] but in reality it matches the discovery process of Poe's purloined letter. If it did not highlight the linkage between human thinking and weaving as one of its material translations, the knowledge of how to rule *poleis* would remain an entangled matter. When the Stranger acknowledges in the presence of young Socrates that the distinctions that led them to discover the intertwining of warp and woof are possibly futile, he chooses a therapeutic device to get rid of this doubt by scrutinizing «the general nature of excess and deficiency» (283c), not only in order to gain wisdom about how to make a right ethical decision, but also to make a correct judgment about the length and brevity of discussions.

The above mentioned analogy between weaving and political action yields decided consequences regarding the scope of laws in the effective rule of the *polis*. Although the Stranger moves from the ideal view that laws should be a universal, stable basis for the *polis*, he points out that they are too rigid for judging particular cases. The spirit of Aristotelian *phronesis* seems to be guiding this part of the dialogue, since it confronts the weakness of general laws, which generally stem from abstraction:

> [L]aw could never, by determining exactly what is noblest and most just for one and all, enjoin upon them that which is best; for the differences of men and of actions and the fact that nothing, I may say, in human life is ever at rest, forbid any science whatsoever to promulgate any simple rule for everything and for all time. We agree to that, I suppose? (*Pol.*, 294 a-b)[10]

The Stranger's last remark attempts to put a value, in the presence of young Socrates, on the convenience of considering practical knowledge as dynamic wisdom, capable of judging general cases without the support of an existing written or commonly accepted norm. This capacity will be compared to the capacity of a webmaster to select the right threads, and to discard the bad ones for the weaving of a cloak, a carpet or clothes. Moreover, the ability to recognize the quality of the materials in a craftwork is presupposed in every craftsman, and stems from the training he has successfully undergone. The Stranger's observation reminds us of the later Aristotelian account, in the fifth book of the

---

9 Dratwa (2003) 31 and Lane (1995) 281–284 have focused on the paternalistic features of this conduct assigned to the statesman.

10 *Pol.*, 294 a–b: Ξένος: ὅτι νόμος οὐκ ἄν ποτε δύναιτο τό τε ἄριστον καὶ τὸ δικαιότατον ἀκριβῶς πᾶσιν ἅμα περιλαβὼν τὸ βέλτιστον ἐπιτάττειν: αἱ γὰρ ἀνομοιότητες τῶν τε ἀνθρώπων καὶ τῶν πράξεων καὶ τὸ μηδέποτε μηδὲν ὡς ἔπος εἰπεῖν ἡσυχίαν ἄγειν τῶν ἀνθρωπίνων οὐδὲν ἐῶσιν ἁπλοῦν ἐν οὐδενὶ περὶ ἁπάντων καὶ ἐπὶ πάντα τὸν χρόνον ἀποφαίνεσθαι τέχνην οὐδ᾽ ἡντινοῦν. ταῦτα δὴ συγχωροῦμέν που;

Nicomachean Ethics, of the requirement of supplementing the laws with decrees that adapt themselves to the particular features of a situation, just as the rule followed by Lesbian architects adapts itself to the shape of the stones on that island. Plato's *Statesman* and Aristotle's appraisal of *equity [epieikeia]* see relationship between the increasing improvement of written laws and the attention that architects have to pay to material restrictions.[11] S. Rosen (1995) has tackled an issue connected with the limits of law, i.e. with the boundaries of *techne,* and the superiority of *phronesis,* claiming that *techne* is not capable of superseding practical virtue. I share in part Rosen's interpretative thesis, but would claim rather that the argumentative thread of the dialogue confirms that both arts and theoretical knowledge need the help of a particular art of measurement that guides each of them successfully. In this sense, I shall argue that the paradigm of Plato's *Statesman* denies the existence of political *techne* to a statesman who does not pay the required attention to the *phronesis* portrayed by women working through the different stages needed to prepare the material to be woven. Rosen asserts that politics deals with the soul, but from the point of view of the body, while philosophy deals with all issues, also involving the body, but taking the soul as the ideal. My view is that the survey of individual common arts offers helpful advice for the survival of the *polis,* allowing the reader of the dialogue to grasp the soul which lies behind each technical action, as it aims to coordinate the outcomes previously yielded by subordinate arts.

2

Once the interconnection between the art of ruling the *polis,* human reflection and the art of weaving have been explored, I wish to tackle one paradoxical point related to the last-mentioned art, i.e. the fact that it is an activity generally

---

11 Some interpreters, such as Berger, have pointed out the social sympathy of Athenian democracy for government by decree, see Berger (2010) 18: «The Athenians, it seems, tended to prefer judgment over laws, and regarded laws more as general guidelines than absolute dictators. This may certainly have influenced what Plato suggests in the *Statesman,* i.e. that the very best thing is to judge without laws. It may also have led him to believe that in the absence of a perfect government – and he certainly did not think of the Athenian government as perfect – the laws should be respected at all costs. As far as Aristotle is concerned, he too seems to be in two minds about the Athenian practice. On the one hand, it is highly likely that this practice suggested to him the concept of equity, but on the other, in *Rhetoric* I.1, 1354b he does criticise the tendency to use the laws as mere guides».

assigned to women, a part of the population usually kept far from the domain of statesmen. My aim in this section will be to highlight the high meaning given in the *Statesman* to an art usually carried out by women or slaves, which does not require any special intellectual skill. In my view the use of this image has a deep impact on the scope of Plato's theory of knowledge, which gains with it new nuances thanks to the attention paid to the craft and expertise showed by the female part of the *polis*, normally considered the most uninteresting population from an epistemological point of view. Francesc Casadesús (2010) has hinted that Aristophanes' *Lysistrata* might have provided a suggestive subject for Plato's dialectical meditation on the practical and logical basis of statesmanship. Plato's description of the statesman's activity for building the citizenship of the *polis* explicitly draws attention to the need to interweave different characters, laying aside the social origins of its members, since they will each be chosen in accordance with their own restraint and courage:

> This, then, is the end, let us declare, of the web of the statesman's activity, the direct interweaving of the characters of restrained and courageous men, when the kingly science has drawn them together by friendship and community of sentiment into a common life, and having perfected the most glorious and the best of all textures, clothes with it all the inhabitants of the state, both slaves and freemen, holds them together by this fabric, and omitting nothing which ought to belong to a happy state, rules and watches over them (311b–c).[12]

A well-known excerpt of *Lysistrata* makes clear the «domestic analogies» coming from the female arts of domestic weaving that deeply shock the magistrate in the comedy. Yet Lysistrata's speech contains insightful remarks about the intelligence that statesmen need to draw from the domestic realm. They seem to have forgotten the art of guidance performed in the house, and Athenian women are forced to remind them of its content.[13] Lysistrata's description draws attention to the fact that before weaving a useful cloak, the weaver has to discard the greasy fellows, the burrs, the parasites and plagues of riff-raff, separating out with direct political images the part that deserves to remain in the *polis* and the one that has

---

12 *Pol.*, 311b.c: Ξένος: τοῦτο δὴ τέλος ὑφάσματος εὐθυπλοκίᾳ συμπλακὲν γίγνεσθαι φῶμεν πολιτικῆς πράξεως τὸ τῶν ἀνδρείων καὶ σωφρόνων ἀνθρώπων ἦθος, ὁπόταν ὁμονοίᾳ καὶ φιλίᾳ κοινὸν συναγαγοῦσα αὐτῶν τὸν βίον ἡ βασιλικὴ τέχνη, πάντων μεγαλοπρεπέστατον ὑφασμάτων καὶ ἄριστον ἀποτελέσασα ὥστ᾽ εἶναι κοινὸν τούς τ᾽ ἄλλους ἐν ταῖς πόλεσι πάντας δούλους καὶ ἐλευθέρους ἀμπίσχουσα, συνέχῃ τούτῳ τῷ πλέγματι, καὶ καθ᾽ ὅσον εὐδαίμονι προσήκει γίγνεσθαι πόλει τούτου μηδαμῇ μηδὲν ἐλλείπουσα ἄρχῃ τε καὶ ἐπιστατῇ.
13 Browning Cole (1991) 196: «Weaving is in the classical world a paradigmatically *feminine* activity, whereas politics is just as exclusively a masculine activity».

to be expelled, identified as "civil rubbish". Aristophanes' passage will help us to identify some overlapping points with one of the main goals of the *Statesman*. I will point first to the fact that the plots of both *Lysistrata* and the *Statesman* tackle the humble and female art of weaving as an expression of reflective wisdom in action involved in every single art:

> Lysistrata
> Open up your sewing basket:
> See the skein of tangled wool?
> Put it to the spindle this way,
> Wind it here, now wind it there.
> Thus the war can be unravelled,
> Making truces here, and there.
> Magistrate
> Skiens and spindles? I don't get it.
> Lysistrata
> Sense and skill is all you need.
> Magistrate
> Show me.
> Lysistrata
> Gladly. First you wash the
> city as we wash the wool,
> cleaning out the bullshit. Then we
> pluck away the parasites;
> break up strands that clump together,
> forming special interest groups;
> Here's a bozo: squeeze his head off.
> Now you're set to card the wool:
> use your basket for the carding,
> the basket of solidarity.
> There we put our migrant workers,
> foreign friends, minorities,
> immigrants and wage-slaves, every
> person useful to the state.
> Don't forget our allies, either,
> languishing like separate strands.
> Bring it all together now, and
> make one giant ball of yarn.
> Now you're ready: weave a brand new
> suit for all citizens.[14]

---

14 *Lysistrata,* verses 568–587, trans. Henderson (1988) 46–47.

Lysistrata claims to count on slaves and citizens, allies and aliens for weaving the citizenry's cloak, offering an enlarged view of the *polis*, whose citizens are required to be truly loyal and where those regarded as parasites are set aside. Yet a similar speech also appears in the reasoning that the Stranger of Elea endorses in the *Statesman*. This overview of the tasks that the ruler of a *polis* should carry out depicts an outline of the capacities of the statesman in a quite Platonic sense. Put differently, according to the Stranger of Elea, statecraft involves the *nous* entailed in every well-performed art, confirming a connection between technical performance and the work of intelligence that even humble women display, though they have not received any particular *paideia*.[15] The reproach of Lysistrata, main character of a comedy composed before the Platonic dialogue we discussed, seems to have left some deep traces in the dialectical appraisal of political knowledge in the *Statesman*. Indeed, the knowledge the Stranger of Elea attempted to seek seems to remain concealed into the most common arts exercised in the *polis*, specifically by women, manual workers and slaves. As the well-known quotation from the dialogue *Parmenides* attests, filth, hair and mud have their right too to be considered as participating in their corresponding ideas. As a variation of this Platonic proposition, statecraft should not direct its gaze towards an intelligible, ideal heaven, but rather scrutinize the intelligible features entailed in the practice of the humblest art, the one that offers human society sheltering cloaks and fancy carpets, the way Descartes, in *Rule Ten for the Direction of Natural Intelligence*, pointed to the tapestries and laces accurately woven by women, something usually dismissed as a vacuous activity, since observing their forms and details might be considered a strain for the human intellect. This example yield by Modernity could also help us consider the wide aftermath of weaving as a metaphor of the art of ruling the *polis*. The reflective roots of weaving draw our attention to the roots of an intelligence which unfolds its figures on the material world. All in all, the weaver shows that her technical skill is inspired by a sound consciousness about virtue and vice, health and pathology, applied to the materials belonging to the woven cloak, but in an analogical sense this sense of discernment is intended to shape the woven political community as well.

---

15 See the appraisal of the male fear before this female art in Blondell (2005) 70: «The weaving model [...] celebrates the huge variety of *technai* that organize and sustain the city. Along with this goes both the granting of some initiative and autonomy to all citizens and the re-inscription of gender as a fundamental category for social organization. But as we have seen, female skill terrified the male Athenian imagination. Autonomy and initiative are not, then, to be encouraged in women. Though they will still (presumably) weave literally, they will not be educated to do so metaphorically by participating in government, and the hierarchical organization of all *technai* allows them to be kept in their place».

3

My central aim in this paper was to make a contribution to highlighting the outstanding role that the weaving simile has in Plato's *Politicus*. The choice of this humble art appears in my view in the dialogue as a reminder of the required intertwinement of different kinds of human beings and professions within the *polis*, which the politician ought to be able to perform as an experienced weaver. The analogy also entails a hint at the issue of «due measure», which the politician should be acquainted with, for the art of weaving has to deal with heterogeneous materials before constructing with them a homogenous and well-balanced whole. I hope that my account of some passages involved in the simile's argumentation has helped us to draw two main conclusions. One outcome could be formulated as the dismissal of the charge that manual crafts were poorly understood in the *Statesman*, given that the wisdom of the artist is considered to be a basic feature of the capacity to run a *polis*. The second conclusion focuses on the fact that some key intellectual operations belong to the development of the art of weaving, which seems to perform tasks in an intuitive way, without the support of an exhaustive analysis. Both conclusions display Kant's attention to the fact that the royal art of government could not be reduced to a list of explicit tasks and objective measures, but rather to a series of subjective operations that exhibit the capacity of the ruler to unify disparate elements, insofar as he knows how to attain the goals and face the needs of a well-governed political community. Thus, an everyday art such as weaving highlights the difficulties involved in establishing good measure as the outcome of abstract reasoning, and establishing experience and the capacity to deal with civil heterogeneity at the centre of the assessment of the royal art. To put it in a nutshell, the *Statesman* deserves the special attention of scholars for its judgment about material and technical skills beyond the intellectual faculties, which the ruler of a state needs to possess to lead his community to ethical and political fulfilment.

Thomas More Robinson
Plato's Stateswomen

In this paper I shall be looking at the two levels at which Plato seems to operate when the role and status of women in society is the topic under discussion. Level one is that of a person I shall call the Revolutionary Plato; the second is that of a person I shall call Plato the Traditionalist. This will involve discussion of parts of the *Republic*, *Timaeus*, *Statesman*, and *Laws*, in order to allow me to present the case I wish to make. I shall be assuming (and I lay my hermeneutical cards on the table at once) that 'what Plato is thinking' in a given dialogue is to be found in the drift of that dialogue, a drift which makes itself manifest for the most part, but not exclusively, in the arguments and un-contested asseverations of its lead-speaker. When these are at issue, I shall talk simply of what I take to be a view which Plato held with enough conviction at the time of the writing of such-and-such a dialogue that he was happy to put it into the mouth of his lead-speaker.

Let us begin with the *Republic*, where the Revolutionary Plato is in full stride. Famously, he argues in this dialogue that, given appropriate genetic background and an appropriate higher education, a (small) number of women are just as likely as an equally small number of men of the same genetic background and higher education to prove competent to rule the paradigmatically just society, and that, just like their male counterparts, they will be given the opportunity to do so. The Revolutionary Plato has much more to say than this, of course, in the dialogue, but let me confine myself to this one famous asseveration, since it brings us quickly to the heart of the issue I wish to discuss in this paper.

One can begin by saying that the revolutionary nature of what Plato is saying, in a world in which the door mat theory of women was prevalent, is not in question, even though the number of women involved (one percent of the whole? two percent?) is very small. But it is still a revolution, if only at the level of paradigm; at the level of day-to-day experience Plato is compelled, third time around (in *Republic* 9), to admit that his society of philosopher rulers, male and female, is unlikely ever to see the light of day. The paradigm is also, for Plato, grounded in a very revolutionary psychology, the theory of the tri-partition of soul, and a very revolutionary piece of metaphysical and epistemological speculation, the theory of transcendental forms, each argued for at such length and with such intensity that it is hard to image that Plato could ever have imagined the paradigm to be viable without them.

But there is another, non-revolutionary Plato also walking abroad in the *Republic*. This is the Plato of tradition, who can be very disconcerting in the popular fantasies and generalizations he appears to support. At 469d7, for

https://doi.org/10.1515/9783110605549-013

example, he talks of how plundering the corpses of bodies after a battle is 'the mark of a womanish, petty (*smikras*) mind', and he goes on to talk of its similarity to the cowardly conduct of dogs who snarl at the stones that hit them but don't touch the thrower of the stones. Just a passing remark? Not really, as remarks in future dialogues on woman's innate cowardliness (among other vices) will attest.

A further passage in the dialogue has been put down as a case of the transparent sexism of the age, and, if true, another case of what I call the Traditionalist Plato talking, but I think we should be cautious before accepting such an interpretation. In the same book of the *Republic* (460b) Plato notoriously says, in the context of a discussion about ways of ensuring an appropriate genetic background for the next generation of the Guardian class, that from those young men who are of greater or lesser potential Guardian-material those who "excel in war and other pursuits" must be given "honours and prizes, and in particular, the opportunity of more frequent intercourse with the women" [that is, with members of a group of women pre-selected as being themselves of greater or lesser potential Guardian-material, TMR].

What is one to make of this? Is the stress on 'women as prizes', or is it on trying to ensure the largest possible number of particularly suitable Guardian offspring for the next generation? From what he says immediately afterwards (in the very next sentence in fact), Plato himself has in mind the latter; men who have shown bravery in war and similar pursuits will be given more frequent opportunity to procreate, to the benefit of the state. If there is a problem here, it is probably (for us) the fact that both the women and the men, who are paired at the copulation festivals by a group of older guardians (male and female), have no say in who their partners will be, and the fact that only those children of such unions who are deemed suitable by Guardians chosen to assess them will be allowed to enter upon the path of potential Guardianship. To which Plato the Revolutionary would reply "Precisely; that is exactly how *Kallipolis* will preserve itself as my Just Society."

But we could spend a long time on this passage; let us move on.

Sometime after writing the *Republic* (though exactly when remains disputed) Plato wrote the *Timaeus*, and the Revolutionary and the Traditionalist are, if anything, even more manifestly in operation than they were in the *Republic*. The Revolutionary now has as his theme not just the polis, but that greatest of all entities, the universe itself, and the theory of forms and the doctrine of tripartite soul are brought into play to produce a remarkable vision of its origin and functioning. Furthermore, the Revolutionary can now argue that his new metaphysic and epistemology can – and do – work perfectly in the case of the visible and tangibly real world, not just in the case of its paradigm, the form

Living Creature; as he is at pains to point out when he is laying out his methodology, the world he is about to describe in minute detail is an object of perception just like all the objects of perception which comprise it, and at the same time itself a percipient living body eternally voicing true statements about its own operations.

This is heady material, and it is followed by equally intense discussion of those features of the universe which Plato thinks follow the dictates of *Ananke* rather than Reason. But when he turns his attention to the place of humans in the world, he offers a picture which, while still in many ways revolutionary, is in its assumptions and implications deeply traditional. As the dialogue draws to a close (90e ff. and 92c1–2), he mentions how, from the beginning and continuing on into the present, the punishment for males who were cowardly (that word again…) and unjust in their previous life is to be re-incarnated in a female body, the implication, not surprising to readers of what Plato the traditionalist had to say about women earlier on in the *Republic*, being that a woman's body is a particularly fitting punishment receptacle, given the tendency of females to moral fault anyway.

All of this raises, for myself at any rate, an interesting speculative question, and that is whether, at the time he wrote the *Timaeus*, Plato might still have believed that a small number of women of appropriate genetic background could, even theoretically, be educated away from their natural propensity to *kakia* in general and cowardice in particular, such that they would have some chance of participating in the ruling of a good society. One cannot be sure, but a passage near the end of the dialogue (86e–87a) is worth looking at. Here he repeats the famous doctrine that *oudeis hekon hamartanei* (86e), this time emphasizing in what look like very deterministic terms that the causes of all bad people (*pantes hoi kakoi*) – presumably all bad men and all bad women – becoming such stem from two specific states of affairs, a faulty habit of body (*ponere hexis tis tou somatos*) and an unenlightened upbringing (*apaideute trophe*). It is Plato re-iterating one of the most dramatic philosophical doctrines he likely drew from Socrates, but this time with the rider that the two states of affairs in question must be fought against by all educational means within one's power (87b6–8). The crucial phrase here is 'within one's power' (*hopei tis dynatai*), where the generic *tis* suggests strongly that *pantes hoi kakoi* is indeed meant to be understood here generically (i.e., as comprising all females as well as all males), as so often.

But it needs to be added that the discussion is of *kakia* within the context of bad societies (87a7–b2); Plato could still, I think, have held to his views about the goodness of the rulers of *Kallipolis*, female and male, while continuing to maintain the views expressed here on the moral dangers, for females and males alike in a less good civic and familial environment.

We must also be careful not to add a possible mistranslation to the already disconcerting account of women as punishment receptacles for men who had lived an immoral life in a previous generation (90e ff). At 42a the Demiurge is described as having fashioned males *kreitton* ('stronger') than females. It is probably true, given what he says elsewhere in the dialogue, that Plato the traditionalist thought that the genos of men was 'better' than the genos of women, but to translate the comparative adjective *kreitton* here as 'better' (rather than 'stronger') is (pace Cornford) to opt for a derivative meaning of the word rather than its focal meaning; see *Rep.* 455e1–2, where we are presented with the very straightforward claim that women are [physically] weaker (*asthenesteron*) than men.

At this point we can turn to the *Statesman*, which I take to have been written later than, but still fairly close in time to the *Timaeus*. And the atmosphere is both familiar and different. We are back to talking about the paradigm of a good society, and specifically the paradigmatic leadership of a good society, but the familiar props are missing. The theory of forms and the notion of a tripartite soul, so basic to the argument of the *Republic* and *Timaeus*, are not to be found; and the ruler/s of our good society is/are now invariably understood and described as male. The possibility of just a single ruler of the paradigmatically good society (297c1), who in societies imitating the paradigm would, he says, be called its 'king' (301b1), along with the more familiar notion of a group of rulers, is a small but critical change from the position adopted in the *Republic*. But what has not changed is the notion that a paradigm is called for; and that this paradigm, like the paradigm for a perfect society talked about in the *Republic*, might also finish up never being instantiated (297e).

Also prominently missing from the dialogue's paradigm of a good society is the idea of a classe politique composed, generation after generation, of men and women of appropriate genetic background and appropriate special education. More specifically, prominently missing from the paradigm is the idea of a possible woman-as-ruler, as propounded in the *Republic*. Replacing this is a state in which the ruler, or possibly group of rulers (all male, cf. 309d1 and *passim*) are qualified to rule by their possession of 'a scientific understanding of the art of government' (293c); only such a state, says Plato, has a 'genuine' (*orthen*) constitution (293e1–2). The intelligent and just application (296b1) of the aforementioned 'scientific understanding' will also be sufficient for the production of good government; there will be no need for written laws (297a, d), which will in fact be a characteristic of second-order societies (297e5).

What has happened here? Why would Plato ever go back upon what most people would agree was one of the most forward-looking of his revolutionary ideas in the *Republic*, that is, a plurality of rulers of both sexes? There is no easy answer to the question, and we are left to speculate as best we can. One uncomplicated answer is that Homer is just nodding here, as he occasionally does in the *Republic*; Plato is talking loosely of 'male' rulers in the *Statesman* the way he talks of 'male' philosopher-rulers in the *Republic*. The difference, however, is that at the end of the discussion in the *Republic* he does get round to saying that everything he has said applies to women philosopher-rulers too (*Rep.* 540c); in the *Statesman* there is no such correction. But this, it could continue to be argued on the 'Homer nodding' theory, is simply a slip-up on Plato's part, which he would have corrected had he adverted to it.

Another possibility could be that Plato is using the 'generic' masculine form throughout the discussion, so that *ho politikos* is meant to be understood as 'the statesperson' each time it occurs. This may be a possibility grammatically, but how likely a possibility is it, given the total absence of reference to women from the discussion, and the use of the word 'king' to describe any possible imitation of the paradigm in respect of single leadership (*to hen*, 297c1)?

A third possibility is that we are meant to assume from his silence, as well as perhaps on grounds of the potentially generic reference of a certain piece of grammatical usage, that Plato has not changed his mind; if in the great paradigmatic society portrayed in the *Republic* women can be philosopher-rulers just as much as men, this can be assumed to be as true in the *Statesman* as it was in the *Republic*, along with several other things also unmentioned in the *Statesman* which are prominent features of the *Republic*, like the theory of forms and the tri-partition of soul, which seemed to be indispensable components of the whole theory. But this too seems very unlikely. Had Plato – in the context of his second major discussion of what is needed for the production of a good society – still adhered strongly to these two ideas, which had proved so pivotal in his first discussion, he could have been expected to at least advert to them, if only to clarify where they fitted (or failed to fit) into his current argument. But on that matter he is silent too, and this time one could just as well claim that the silence suggests – if anything – the beginning of a shift in his thinking.

My own view is that Plato the perpetual thinker is now suggesting, fifteen or twenty years on, that he is starting to imagine a somewhat new paradigm for a good society, one which shares some of the features of his former paradigm but not all. And one of the things he seems willing to allow his readers to think is that women are no longer thought to be potential members of the class of *epistemones politikoi*.

What is behind this change? One can only speculate, but it seems to me very possible that Plato the Traditionalist is making himself felt again. As we have seen in the *Timaeus*, reincarnation in the body of a woman will be the punishment for a man who has lived immorally in a previous life on earth (90e). As in the Mikado, it is a punishment which fits the crime: a man who has lived an immoral life is incarnated in the next life in the body of one who is by nature inclined to immorality (*kakia*), a woman.

This sort of thinking is not new, of course; we saw it with clarity as far back as the *Republic*. And if anything it only increases in force in the *Timaeus*. So it should come as no surprise to find Plato the Traditionalist, never far from the surface in each of those dialogues, breaking surface once again in the *Statesman*, this time with the disconcerting view that, in this second version of what constitutes the paradigm of a good society, its rulers will be, not men and women, but men only, or if there is a single ruler, a man.

If I am right about this, I think it helps us to make better sense of a remarkable feature of Plato's subsequent and final dialogue, the *Laws*. If women really don't feature among the *epistemones politikoi* of the paradigmatically good society of the *Statesman*, we can be sure that the matter was quickly noticed, and some pressure put upon Plato to explain himself. And typically, he set out to do that, and took ten years over the task. Equally typically, he had no fear about changing his mind if he felt he had to. In this case, the Revolutionary Plato still adheres firmly, in talking about the features of his 'second-best' society Magnesia, to the idea that there is such a thing as a paradigmatically good society (739cff.), and he singles out (ibid.) as features of it the fact that it has 'the best constitution and code of law', and 'commonality of womenfolk, children, and all possessions'. But it is a society, he now thinks, in which, were it ever instantiated, 'a number of those who live there are, as it were (*pou*), gods, or children of gods' (739d). The reference here can only be to the philosopher-rulers, but the language used to describe them has an extravagance of tone that surpasses anything said in the *Republic*, where at no point is it ever suggested that his rulers will be anything other than flesh-and-blood humans, differing from any others only (though importantly) in possessing the right biological pedigree and appropriate further education. Is that all it is – a slight extravagance of tone? Or is Plato leaving his readers to understand that a very good reason why he left the readers of *Republic* 9 with the impression that he felt it unlikely that his paradigmatic society would ever be instantiated was that something slightly beyond (or maybe even greatly beyond) human-ness in its rulers would be called for, such that they could reasonably be called 'in some way gods, or children of gods'? The answer is unclear, and the great writer of dialogues not treatises leaves us, as so often, to continue dialoguing on the point amongst ourselves.

Turning to his second-best Society, Magnesia, the Revolutionary Plato then proposes something which must have astonished his readership – equal education for all citizens, male and female (805e), with no further 'special' education for any would-be members, male or female, of a supposed classe politique.[1] The idea is dramatically new, and to the modern mind as forward-looking as the proposal years before, in the *Republic*, that a small number of women, of appropriate genetic background and appropriate further education, have as much chance of accessing positions of rule in *Kallipolis* as a small number of men of similar background and educational preparation.

But does the theory deliver?

It does seem at first glance to offer an answer to a question which I think the writing of the *Statesman* must have raised: if we set aside unrealizable paradigms (such as those found in the *Republic* and *Statesman*), in the best realizable society, Magnesia, says Plato, all female as well as all male citizens will receive equal education, and access to rule will turn on the result of a public vote, not on membership of some supposed political class. A natural inference from this would be that women would finish up in positions of political power in Magnesia in more or less equal numbers to men, and in this second-best society a major goal of the *Republic* will have been achieved, and on a scale covering – astonishingly – the whole of Magnesia's citizen population, not just a small part of it. But at this point Plato the Traditionalist re-emerges to have his say, and the traditionalist proceeds to take away with one hand what the revolutionary has offered with the other.

His commitment to education for all females as well as males would appear to be enough to ensure that there would be a plentiful supply of females as well as males for potential election to all the various offices of state. But in practice, despite Plato's statement that women in Magnesia would be eligible to 'enter office' (*archas*) at age forty (785b), the offices in question do not appear to include any major offices of the state. The Minister of Education, for example, a post which Plato describes as 'the most important of the highest offices of the state' (765e), is by statute a 'father of a family'. The Guardians of the Laws Plato refers to unequivocally as 'men' (*andrasi*, 755b5). The all-important Auditors of those finishing their term of office are all 'men' (*andras*, 946a1). And the members of the Nocturnal Council are clearly men too, being comprised of ten Guardians of

---

1 The text, I should add, is very clear, and not a subject of dispute; among the many who see just what is being proposed, see Christopher Rowe (1997b) 52.

the Laws (all male), a Minister and an unspecified number of ex-Ministers of Education (all male), an unspecified number of (male) priests of distinction,[2] and a number of junior members, who, being by statute aged between 30 and 40, are also clearly each one of them men, women being forbidden access to office before the age of forty.

The only other major public office left to which citizens are elected is the Advisory Council. We cannot be certain whether Plato intended women to form part of it, but the fact that those who, in final conjunction with a use of the lot-system, elect its members are once again 'men' (*andra*, 756e4) offers little reason for thinking it likely. If we add to this the fact that only males in Magnesia are entitled to hold property, and that women continue to have their marriages arranged by male relatives,[3] it looks highly unlikely that, by contrast with con-temporary Athens, females have been granted citizenship (814c4) in Magnesia, as some understand Plato to be saying.[4] If there is any political break-through for women in the second-best society, it is at a level well below that enjoyed by male citizens.[5]

Why this apparent disconnect in the *Laws* between equal education for women and equal access to political office for women? There is no easy answer to this question. But I shall do my best to offer some sort of reason.

The most straightforward reason for the disconnect seems to me to be Plato the Traditionalist's continuance in the commonly held belief that in the real

---

2 At *Meno* 81a10 Plato clearly distinguishes priests and priestesses; the word 'priest' is not a generic term covering both. See also *Laws* 800b1, 828b4, 909d9, *Phdr.* 244b1, *Rep.* 461a7. As far as Magnesia is concerned, priests and priestesses are chosen by lot (759c), must be over sixty years of age, and hold office for one year.

3 Bobonich (2002) 88.

4 In distinguishing '*politides*' and 'citizens' Plato is distinguishing between 'free females dwell-ing in the *polis*' and 'citizens' - who are free, *male*, and have *all the rights of full citizenship*. See Sophocles, *Elektra* 1227, Euripides, *Elektra* 1335, where no one would ever infer from the use of the word *politides* that the women in question enjoy the political privileges of citizenship enjoyed by males (such things as access to Assembly meetings, the power to vote there and access to all the major political posts in Athens), even if, out of camaraderie, they address one another warmly as '*politides*'.

5 While it is possible that the several references to '*andres*' are just slips on Plato's part, this seems very unlikely, given the various other instances of high office where males and only males seem to be involved. A more likely explanation, it seems to me, is that women's 'entering office' (785b5) simply means their 'entering public service,' without specification of what the range of such service might be. An example of it would be membership, if elected, of the board of 'female overseers' of Magnesia's marriages, something mentioned in the immediately antecedent para-graph, at 784a1–2. But this does not compare with the *major* offices open exclusively – appar-ently – to men.

world, women — educated or not — had a role to play which made them unfit for all political office other than, as we saw (see n. 4), the one involving supervision of marriages, and even here, where they are unable to adjudicate a particular problem they encounter, they must defer to the final decision of a group of ten (male) Guardians of the Laws (784b–c).

This could, of course, be put down to the standard belief that a woman's place is in the home, and that the chief objective of even an education identical to what all the men had received was simply, in the end, the running of a good household. But Plato's earlier comment on a good society's needing to use all the talent available to it, including that of the fifty percent of society who are women (805a–b), still suggests that Plato had in mind something more broad-ranging than that. For example, his introduction of public eating tables for women, Spartan-style, to go with the public eating-tables for men, suggests that he wants at least a social (if not a political) life for women in Magnesia that is far broader than anything hitherto tried in his own city of Athens. But the reason for so wishing will come to many as something of a surprise, though less so to anyone who is aware of the ability of Plato the Traditionalist to put in an appearance in the dialogues when least expected.

In the present case, one might reasonably have expected that women's equal education to men now empowered them to a life of equality with men in social life too - if only at the level of eating with one another in public. Unfortunately, Plato the Traditionalist suggests a quite different reason, and one much more in line with contemporary beliefs about women. The reason, he says, is simply one of security. Just as common tables for men served as a security device in controlled societies like Crete and Sparta (780c), so too, he says, common tables for women as well as men will serve as a security device in his own society, Magnesia. As he puts it with distressing bluntness: "The very half of the race which is generally predisposed by its weakness to undue secrecy and craft – the female sex – has been left to its disorders by the mistaken concession of the legislator [in societies such as Athens, TMR]... Women - left without any chastening restraint - are not, as you might fancy, merely half the problem; she is a twofold and more than a twofold problem, as her native disposition (*physis*) is inferior (*cheiron*) to a man's" (781b2). He goes on to talk about how women need to be forced out of the shady corners in which they like to hide "into the daylight" (781c), where they can be kept under observation.

This is very uncomfortable reading. It does not suggest, of course, that Plato the Traditionalist's views on women are worse than those of any other Greek of the day; but it does not suggest that they are any better either. And to be sure we fully understand them, we need to spend a moment looking at the precise import for him of the word 'inferior'. A hint of it we first saw in the *Republic* (469d7), when he talks of the 'womanish, petty minds' of those who wait till the battle is over and then rush onto the battle field to rob the dead of their armour and accoutrements. The clear suggestion is that women have a tendency towards cowardice (perhaps unsurprisingly, the word in Greek for 'brave', as we all know, is 'manly', *andreios*), and this is re-reinforced by a strong passage in the *Timaeus* (90e ff.), where, as we saw, he talks about how reincarnation in a woman's body will be the punishment for a man who in a previous life was characterized by 'cowardice and injustice' (90e7). (A previous life characterized by various levels of ignorance, by contrast – ranging from a simple-minded trust in sense-perception to out-and-out stupidity (*amathia*) – will warrant re-incarnation in the body of an animal, ranging from a bird for the former and a fish or other sea-creature for the latter [91d–92b]).

One might perhaps object that the passage I have just quoted, suggesting so strongly as it does that Plato considers women to be characterized by moral fault, particularly but not exclusively cowardice, and hence appropriate punishment-receptacles for males who have demonstrated moral failings, is 'only a myth'. But unfortunately this argument will not work, since later on, in the *Laws* (944d), in a context of open discussion, where no-one would ever claim that myth is involved, Plato has the following to say:

> Now what shall we call a fitting punishment for the coward who throws away [his] weapons...? A human judge cannot, indeed, invert the transformation which is said to have been wrought on Caeneus of Thessaly; he, we are told, had been a woman, but a god changed him into a man. Were the reverse process, transformation from man to woman, possible, that, in a way, would be of all penalties the most appropriate one for the man who has flung his shield away.

With that, I am now finally in a position to make my argument. The reason, it seems to me, why Plato is unwilling, in the *Laws*, to make a causal connexion between equality in education and equality in access to public office is because, in a real world rather than a paradigmatic world, a world where rulers will be recognizable, flesh-and-blood human beings, not 'in some way gods and children of gods', women have a tendency to moral fault (*kakia*) – like cowardice, and more broadly, injustice – such that they cannot be trusted with such power. It is a conclusion which cannot help but distress, but it seems to me the one which makes the most sense of the evidence available.

I'd like to return now to the *Statesman*, and try to place its thinking about the denotation and connotation of the term *politikos* on the spectrum of Plato's ideas about men and women across the four dialogues that have been the theme of this paper. The *Republic*, it seems to me, is both the highlight of, and the outlier in, the system: the (revolutionary) concept of women philosopher-rulers is a central feature of it, but Plato the Traditionalist might well have had feelings running counter to such a concept, given his overall view of women that emerges in the same dialogue, and might even have experienced a certain relief when, by the time he gets round to a third discussion (in Book Nine) of whether his new society might ever see the light of day, he finds he can now, after two earlier bouts of relative optimism about the prospects (mingled, perhaps, with a certain irony), discard the likelihood of its instantiation as being very low.

Whether, by the time he wrote the *Timaeus*, Plato was starting to have second thoughts about a number of features of what he had proposed in the *Republic*, in particular his idea that a small number of women of appropriate pedigree and further education would be just as fit as a small number of men of appropriate pedigree and further education to serve as its philosopher-rulers, we cannot know, but what Plato the Traditionalist says about women in the dialogue, with no clear indication that there might possibly be exceptions to the general rule, suggests that he might well have been starting to have them.

Whatever the case, in a more overtly political dialogue written at around the same time, the *Statesman,* Plato the Traditionalist seems to be asserting himself somewhat more boldly, and there is now no mention of a role for women in the paradigm of a good society. More generally, Plato seems in the *Statesman* to be on the cusp of great change: along with the apparent demise of a leadership role for women in his paradigm of a good society, the theory of forms and the notion of a tripartite soul are also missing, and missing, one has to say, in a context, where if he had still held those notions, he had a perfect opportunity, had he wished to avail himself of it, to re-emphasize their continuing importance to him as the metaphysical, epistemological, and psychological foundation of a good society.

But in all this, it might be objected, you seem to be assuming, that the *Timaeus* antedates the *Statesman*? In response, I would say that, even were the reverse the case, it would be little evidence that the author of the *Statesman* still adheres (if only tacitly) to a theory of transcendental forms as the basis for a good society, since in the opening pages of the *Timaeus* (17c ff.) what looks a lot like a brief summary of the *Republic* is in fact a brief summary for the most part of the hot-button social topics of *Republic* 5, without reference to their putative metaphysical foundation, on which no comments are passed. While from such silence one might infer that Plato still adheres to the doctrine of transcendental forms as the foundation for such a society, one might equally plausibly infer that it is missing from the account because it is by now starting to fade from his consciousness as the ground-support for a good society, a process which will reach its apogee in the *Laws*.

I hasten to add here that I am talking about a doctrine of transcendental forms. What Plato never seems to have abandoned was essentialism as such; what the 'guardians of the laws' (all of them male) in the *Laws* spend their time studying is the problem of the one (form) and the many (forms) (965c), something which as such carries no implication that such forms must be transcendental. But that is another paper.

More important for purposes of the present paper is the relationship between the *Statesman* and the *Laws*, with their shared concept of a second-best society, and how far up the ladder of rule women will ever rise in such a society. I hope that what I have been saying around this particular topic will encourage further investigation of it.

Lidia Palumbo
Mimesis in the *Politicus*

In Plato's dialogues, which are mimetic,[1] the interlocutors talk to each other, and the style of writing enables readers to *visualise* the scene. The scene that the readers *observe* presents the speakers but, much more significantly, it presents the actual *subject matter*. This ability to use words *to make something visible* was an art that was studied intensively by theoreticians of language during antiquity. Indeed, Plato is mentioned in this context by the ancient sources,[2] and he proved himself a master of the art, in particular when applied to philosophy. This art can be identified as *mimetic ability:* the ability to create images exclusively through the use of words: scene-creating words. Although all poets possess this capacity, Plato the poet manages to add an extra effect. Indeed, he creates mimetic scenes that represent philosophical practice,[3] a discussion that thematises *mimesis* itself, its limits and its possibilities.[4]

The mimetic art of *visual writing* is based on a specific characteristic of the Platonic text which is often referred to as "linking of form and content".[5] In this paper I shall explore certain aspects of this feature of Plato's writing with reference to the text of the *Politicus*.

Firstly, though, I should like to clarify a point concerning Plato's aim as an author to invent a form of writing endowed with verbal imagery. I believe that the aim – the reason why the dialogues are dramatic and mimetic – is to enable the

---

1 See Ausland (1997) 374: "By an ancient account, the classical mime features question and answer within a playful dramatic framework, somehow rendering it 'mimetic' par excellence". See also Kosman (1992) 85–92.
2 Demetr. *Eloc.* 51, 218, 226; D.H. *Dem.,* 23.4.
3 See Ausland (1997) 375: "To explore the mimetic nature of the dialogues involves considering how they combine the opposites of theoretical seriousness and playful mimesis within a dramatic medium, and how this combination produces a properly philosophical effect".
4 See Blondell (2002) 37–52 and Halliwell (2002) 37–71. See Ausland (1997) 375: "The Platonic dialogue is a lifelike drama that conveys its author's meaning through a depiction of the words and deeds of more or less definite personae".
5 I am convinced that the form and content of every reading of Platonic dialogues should be complementary and mutually enlightening. On this *quaestio* see Strauss (1964) 52, Szlezák (1991) 21–31, Ausland (1997) 382, 396, Zuckert (2009) 5–7, Miller (2004) XXIII–IV.

https://doi.org/10.1515/9783110605549-014

reader to *take part*[6] in the *mise-en-scène* that acted as a preface to the philosophical discussion.[7]

The participation of the reader in the *mise-en-scène* of the discussion is a primary goal of Plato's texts due to the idea of philosophy that he practiced. Indeed, according to Plato, philosophy is not the practice of reading and writing but is structurally linked to the nature of oral dialogue:[8] only by *participating* in a discussion can one *do* philosophy, and philosophy can only be *done*; in other words it has to be practiced and carried out directly. It should neither be read nor written, nor should it be listened to *passively* as if it were a story.[9]

Starting from the Platonic conception of philosophy as a form of dialogue, it is possible to understand why the dialogues – made up of rhetorical and visual writing, a dramatic form of writing that sets a scene – are designed to involve the reader[10] in the philosophical discussion.

Participation is ensured by a series of mimetic operations. One of these is the way the reader identifies with the character.[11] The identification is not complete or immediate, nor must it necessarily concern a *dramatis persona*.[12] Indeed, not only are the dialogues full of characters who have a name of their own, but also the *physiognomies of human beings*, in other words of personalities, professions and figures who embody a way of life.[13] They include the sophist, the physician,

---

6 See Frede (1992) 2001: "Plato's dialogues are works of art. They are pieces of powerful dramatic fiction which by their art manage to give us a strong sense of what it would be like to listen to a dialectical debate or even to participate in it".

7 See Ausland (1997) 386, 390 and Palumbo (2013a) 35–46. For a different and interesting discussion of the dialogical form see Long (2009) 45–59.

8 See Rowe (2007) 8: "Philosophy, as an activity, *is* the 'art of dialogue', whether internal or with others: *dialektike techne* in Greek, and hence 'dialectic'".

9 See Nightingale (1995) 10 and Zuckert (2009) 2.

10 See Cotton (2014). See also Michelini (2003) 1–13.

11 But see the considerations of Miller (2004) XXII–XXIII and Cotton (2015) 45.

12 "Most of his *dramatis personae* are ordinary people of various kinds, as distinct both from the elevated figures who take center stage in tragedy or epic, and from the buffoons of comedy (though they share points of contact with both). As Bruns observed, the dialogues give us a portrait not just of a series of individuals, but of a society: the Athens of Plato's formative years: Blondell (2002) 66.

13 See Rowe (2007) 11: "We may presumably begin by dismissing the possibility that the characterization (and the dramatic action: that too we must take into account) in the dialogues is for merely ornamental purposes, just on the grounds that it is so obtrusive. It is part of that 'weirdness' of Plato's texts that they force us to try to see whatever point it is that they are making through the fog of a conversation with *this* individual, or these individuals, now. I also propose to dismiss the possibility that Plato is interested in, say, Ion, or Laches, for Ion's or Laches' sake (if he is writing for us, his readers, or any of our predecessors, why on earth should he expect

the businessman, the statesman, the stranger, the athlete, the poet, the weaver, the hedonist, the mathematician, the speech-maker and so on. What is supposed to happen is that the reader can recognise himself by identifying with a way of conducting himself in the world by performing practical tasks and having an intellectual stance. The reader may also identify with a single aspect of such a stance. He may find himself portrayed in the *mise-en-scène*, although in a past era, or as the character he wishes to become. The process of identification also works the other way around: in the text the reader may encounter a character with whom he would never want to be identified: the person he is afraid of becoming.[14] To ensure that the identification takes place, the text needs somehow to represent *the readers' world*,[15] the network of meanings within the reader's universe, and the role that philosophy plays within this universe.[16] Readers can see their own resistance to persuasion through a character. Representation enables readers to see their own mistakes, and, by participating in the discussion about them, they can understand them and avoid making them. Alternatively, they can see the objectification of their own ability to convey an idea, to give form to thought, or to persuade an interlocutor.[17]

The dialogues are mirrors through which we can look at ourselves and contemplate the inner life of our minds.[18]

In this sense, the readers' identification with the characters in the dialogue, their intellectual and existential stance, is one of the purposes of the text's visual writing: this is what makes it a mimetic dialogue, a way of ensuring the readers'

---

them, let alone *us*, to be interested in such figures, neither of whom left much else by way of an imprint on history?). Rather, his interest in them is because of the types of people they are (a rhapsode and a general), and also because the types they represent are, at least within the fictional context, real and familiar – or would have been to the original audience".

14 See Cotton (2014) 127.

15 This is the reason why "the settings of the dialogues are important, since they convey the milieu (physical, social, temporal) in which these persons and their conversations are embedded": Blondell (2002) 63.

16 See Blondell (2002) 63: "the use of dramatic form also allows Plato to color his speakers' words less directly, through more oblique indications of the kind of persons they are (or are represented as being). A person's name, for example, may convey associations of race and social class, and of course gender".

17 See Blondell (2002) 47, Miller (2004) XXVI–XXXI; discussion in Cotton (2014) 108–116.

18 See Ausland (1997) 406.

involvement in the discussion,[19] their participation, their presence in the dramatised discussion,[20] without which there can be no philosophical practice.

The text of the *Politicus* begins by focusing on the ways in which we can identify with others by recognising similarities between intellectual stances. As Socrates states, these ways are always verbal and based on dialogue.[21] Socrates explicitly states:

δεῖ δὴ τούς γε συγγενεῖς ἡμᾶς ἀεὶ προθύμως διὰ λόγων ἀναγνωρίζειν

we must always be eager to recognize those akin to us by talking to them[22]

Syngeneia is the similarity of intellectual stance which can be recognised through *logoi*. In particular, it refers to the way of taking part in discussions, the way of dealing with issues, which distinguishes a character's style and personality.[23] Socrates says he had engaged in a debate with Theaetetus the previous day, and that he had listened to the way he replied to the Stranger (258a).[24] Participation in a discussion therefore helps one to recognise oneself and to recognise things in general; it helps one to discover what an interlocutor is actually like.[25] Even listening to a discussion, Socrates adds, can have the same effect. This suggests that listening to, and reading, a dialogue[26] can be interpreted as διὰ λόγων ἀναγνωρίζειν, a recognition of oneself through discussion.[27]

---

19 My study – writes Cotton (2014) 28 – has at its heart a concern with the experience of learning – the interlocutor's experience of engaging in Socratic discussion and the reader's experience of moving through the text.

20 See Clay (1992) 117: "The effect of Plato's choice of the dramatic mode of discourse is to transport us in time so that we become the audience of a philosophical drama that took place in another age, yet still immediate".

21 See Blondell (2002) 57: "The strictly intellectual content of a person's mind, as opposed to the appearance of the activity of thinking, can *only* be portrayed through language, whether descriptively or dramatically". Since language also constitutes the medium through which real persons express this aspect of the self, in this limiting case a dramatic representation may be indistinguishable from its original.

22 Pl. *Plt.* 258a2–3 (Burnet 1967). Translation by Rowe (Rowe 1999).

23 See Blondell (2002) 41 and McCoy (2008) 139, 146.

24 See Blondell (2002) 269.

25 See Miller (2004) 6.

26 As Cotton (2015) 32 suggests "Plato's dialogues encourage us to regard reading, in the ideal case, as learning. They also present the activity of interlocutors as a model, of sorts, for our activity in reading; one that both guides the way we respond to the texts and provides a reference point for understanding how the responses evoked in reading can contribute to our own process of learning".

27 See Erler (1992) 147–170.

The question posed in the text, before starting a discussion, aims to verify the existence of a common perspective between the interlocutors: agreement about the topic to be discussed and the way to discuss it (258a–b; 260b). The Stranger presents his investigation strategy: the path of the statesman should be sought and isolated (258c). The image of the path immediately reveals that the investigation of statesmanship will be described using words with a visual style of writing that employs similarities and differences. This style of writing relies on several mimetic devices, in particular ὥσπερ, οἷον, καθάπερ and verbs that mean "*to be similar to*". The following statement is made at 261d:

> But we'll certainly not find the statesman rearing individual creatures, like some ox-driver or groom (ὥσπερ βοηλάτην ἤ τινα), but rather resembling (προσεοικότα) a horse-breeder or cowherd.[28]

In the text the visual devices provide the outlines of each issue that is discussed and each topic that is dealt with. Indeed, the issues in the dialogues are never abstract but, thanks to the mimetic devices, are always included within visual and figurative scenes, since the possibility of visualising what is being said enables participation in the discussion. Taking part in the discussion means sharing this visualisation.

At this point the interlocutors in the dialogue (and the readers) are required to verify the similarity of the figure of the shepherd with that of the statesman. It is at this point that the younger Socrates makes the famous error which, according to Plato's intentions, will help many readers to learn how to avoid making mistakes:[29] having been asked to differentiate the two, the younger Socrates suddenly makes a distinction between the herdsman who rears humans and the herdsman who rears animals:

καί μοι δοκεῖ τῶν μὲν ἀνθρώπων ἑτέρα τις εἶναι, τῶν δ' αὖ θηρίων ἄλλη τροφή.

> It seems to me that there is a different sort of rearing of human beings, and in turn another sort where animals are concerned.[30]

The Stranger makes an exemplary correction to Socrates' mistake. It takes up considerable space in the text, and is constructed using an image that employs sev-

---

28 Pl. *Plt.* 261d 7–9. Trans. Rowe.
29 On the pedagogical matter see Miller (2004) 22–28.
30 Pl. *Plt.* 262a3–4. Trans. Rowe.

eral visual devices. One of these is οἷον. The word οἷον is a visual term that functions in the text as a curtain that opens to reveal figures which would otherwise be invisible.

The distinction that separates herds of beasts from herds of human beings is mistaken. Explaining how it is mistaken is the task of the word οἷον. The division is mistaken: it's as if someone (οἷον εἴ τις) tried to divide the human race in two, dividing the Greeks from the barbarians in the belief that there are two different forms because there are two different words:

> This sort of thing: it's as if someone (οἷον εἴ τις) tried to divide the human race into two and made the cut in the way that (καθάπερ) most people here carve things up, taking the Greek race away as one, separate from all the rest, and all the other races together, which are unlimited in number, which don't mix with one another, and don't share the same language – calling this collection by the single appellation "barbarian". Because of this single appellation, they expect it to be a single family or class too.[31]

In stating this, the text has demonstrated nothing. However, what the text has accomplished, with its mimetic imagery, is the juxtaposition of two erroneous divisions which, once juxtaposed, have proved to be similarly mistaken. Juxtaposing two different things to highlight their similarity is the key feature of *diairesis*, of dialectics.[32] It could also be said that the text has presented a *comparison*, though it is important to emphasise that when something is compared to something else, this something else enters the scene with all the paraphernalia, including visual paraphernalia, of its own semantics. After the juxtaposition with the issue of the barbarians, statesmanship will no longer be simply a Hellenic issue.[33]

Juxtaposition, visual matching and comparison are the features of the procedure used repeatedly in the dialogue, both in regard to the weaving model of statesmanship and to each of the figures we are invited to observe in order to distinguish similarity and difference within them.[34]

---

31 Pl. *Plt.* 262c10–d6. Trans Rowe.
32 In Plato's dialogues, the use of arguments – dialectic – is itself a form of showing or image-making.
33 "Toute définition de l'homme – says El Murr (2014) 125 – parce qu'elle est par essence une auto-définition, est aussi le plus souvent une auto-glorification". See also Joly (1992) 84–89 and Blondell (2002) 362.
34 The Stranger is indirect and mimetic. He prefers examples to discursive accounts: see Miller (2004) 34.

Other figures of mistaken divisions are also used to stigmatise the younger Socrates's mistake: the figure of the crane, or the figure of the number ten thousand and so on. The text explores the difference between *eidos* and *meros*,[35] a difference which might never become clear if it were not visualised, and which might never be visualised if it were not represented with figures which the text presents as digressions, offshoots and side streets. Since research is a path, digressions are the side streets of this path.

The Stranger says that errors, in the case of such divisions, are caused by the heedless use of names (263d1). People sometimes believe that differences in denomination correspond to actual differences.[36] This indication shows us the extent of the awareness of Plato the author when using visual writing. The figures dealt with in the dialogues, the visual representations constructed with words, are structured to ensure that names and the things they refer to are kept together to avoid dangerous distances between language and thought.

An important role in the discussions of the *Politicus* is played by the issue of the relationship between name and figure. In 260e the verb παρεικάζω is used to indicate the visual juxtaposition made between the sellers of their own produce (as distinct from sellers of other people's produce) and true rulers who give their own orders (as distinct from heralds who announce other people's orders). This juxtaposition, used at 260c–d, underlies the name that is proposed to refer to someone who gives their own orders, who, by similarity, is named *autepitaktes*.[37]

The figure of the statesman is that of the person who takes care (ἐπιμέλειαν ἔχειν, 265e7) of terrestrial animals that live in herds, are bipedal and lack horns, but the Stranger judges the enquiry to be inadequate and the final definition to be incomplete (267c). At 267d11 the art of statesmanship is defined as ἀνθρώπων κοινοτροφικὴ ἐπιστήμη, knowledge of the collective rearing of human beings. However, since this definition corresponds not just to one figure but many figures of herdsmen, it is impossible to *isolate* the figure of the king in these conditions

---

35 Kahn (2014) 144–145: "This is a warning against what we might call terminological naiveté: the assumption that any group designated by a familiar term corresponds to a natural kind. The divisions of ordinary language do not always cut nature at the joints. The general lesson is that every kind (*eidos*) is a part (*meros*), but not every part is a kind".

36 See Kahn (2014) 225: "It is in this biological context that an important distinction is drawn between an arbitrary "part" or class (*morion*) marked off by any term and a natural kind or form (*genos, eidos*). It is essential to recognize that not every word in the language serves to cut nature at the joints".

37 "Dans l'ensemble des arts cognitifs – El Murr (2014) 113 suggests – les arts prescriptifs sont à la frontière de ce que nous appelons le pratique et le théorique".

(separating the figure from the others who claim the right to be herdsmen together with him). The mimetic choice of the figure of the competitor to the name is particularly interesting.

To solve the problems created by competitors,[38] the enquiry requires a new starting point, another road (καθ'ἑτέραν ὁδόν, 268d5), which is the narration of a myth.[39] Taken in its entirety, myth is a powerful visual device.[40] Through this powerful visual device, it becomes possible to observe the function played by the terms explicitly linked to the semantic field of *mimesis*. They seem to be used in the text to show the reader how to interpret the role of reader by identifying with the story and its atmosphere, and by performing, from the reader's silent vantage point, the activities implicitly requested by the dialogue.

The first occurrence of the terms explicitly linked to the semantic field of *mimesis* is at 274a1 and involves the term ἀπομιμούμενα. We are at the end of the myth. The story has already finished (273e4), but the Stranger briefly examines a part of it to demonstrate kingly nature. Attention is focused on the crucial moment of the inversion of the cycle when the cosmos is brought back to the route that leads to the current generation (ἐπὶ τὴν νῦν γένεσιν ὁδόν, 273e7), the moment when our own era began. This is the first time, albeit only implicitly, that the reader is asked to empathise: reference is no longer made to remote times but to the beginning of our own era. This is undoubtedly the function of νῦν which appears at 273e7. It is a warning that history concerns the reader. It is rather similar to the situation when, at the beginning of the description of the myth of the cave,[41] Glaucon says that the image that has just been presented is strange just as its

---

38 Kahn (2014) 220: "The problem is that, unlike shepherds and cowherds who are unrivaled in their ability to care for their flocks, the Statesman is surrounded by a horde of competitors – from bakers to doctors – who claim to contribute to the nurture and maintenance of the human herd (267e– 268b). Our definition will not be satisfactory until it separates the Statesman from these competitors. (These turn out to be only the first of a series of rivals who will be progressively eliminated in later stages of the definition)".

39 About the (number of) cosmological and historical epochs in the myth see Brisson (1995), Rowe (1995a) and the discussion in Horn (2012).

40 See Miller (2004) 37. El Murr (2014) 153: "Tout mythe platonicien donne à voir, fait voir ce que voit celui qui le raconte": "It was just for these reasons that we introduced our story – says the Stranger – in order that it might demonstrate, in relation to herd-rearing, not only that as things now stand everyone disputes this function with the person we are looking for, but also in order that we might see more plainly (ἐναργέστερον ἴδοιμεν) that other person himself whom alone, in accordance with the example of shepherds and cowherds, because he has charge of human rearing, it is appropriate to think worthy of this name, and this name alone" (Pl. *Plt.* 275b1–7, trans. Rowe).

41 Pl. *R.* 515a. See Cotton (2014) 32.

prisoners are strange. Socrates replies that prisoners are ὁμοίους ἡμῖν, similar to us. The mimetic words express similarity and create assimilation. In the text they play a similar role to that played by the *verba videndi* in the visualisation.[42]

In the text it is stated that at the beginning of our era new situations emerged that contrasted with those of the preceding cycle. Several examples of these contrasting situations are given. The passage containing the first two specifically mimetic terms occurs at this point in the dialogue.

> And everything else changed (καὶ τἆλλά τε πάντα μετέβαλλε), imitating (ἀπομιμούμενα) and following on the condition of the universe (καὶ συνακολουθοῦντα τῷ τοῦ παντὸς παθήματι), and in particular, there was a change to the mode of conception, birth, and rearing, which necessarily imitated (καὶ δὴ καὶ τὸ τῆς κυήσεως καὶ γεννήσεως καὶ τροφῆς μίμημα, 274a1) and kept pace with the change to everything; for it was no longer possible for a living creature to grow within the earth under the agency of others' putting it together, but just as the world-order had been instructed to be master of its own motion, so too in the same way its parts were instructed themselves to perform the functions of begetting, birth, and rearing so far as possible by themselves, under the agency of a similar impulse (ὑπὸ τῆς ὁμοίας ἀγωγῆς).[43]

The text of the dialogue deals here with the issue of the relationship between the whole and its parts: the behaviour of the part is intricately linked to the behaviour of the whole. The part is not just a part of the whole but is also an image. It is precisely the fact that it is "an image of something", a *mimema*,[44] that makes the part something whose view is linked to the view of the whole; its changes are linked to the changes to the whole, and so on. The part provides a vantage point for observing the whole.[45] Since both the whole and the parts are living creatures, the behaviour of the part that *follows* the behaviour of the whole is portrayed as the behaviour of a pupil who follows his teacher, thus conforming to a model.[46] This pattern of relationships appears in all the passages where there is a term

---

42 See Palumbo (2010) 689–700.

43 Pl. *Plt.* 273e11–274b1. Trans. Rowe.

44 At page 274a2 there is a term related to *mimesis* – μίμημα – which is used in reference to the result of reproduction. At page 274d6, a few lines after the previous passage, there is another term related to *mimesis*: συμμιμούμενοι.

45 On the homology between microcosm and macrocosm: human existence "follows and imitates" the life of the cosmos, see Blondell (2002) 354 and Miller (2004) 39. On the relation between the myths of the cosmos in the *Politicus* and the *Timaeus*, see Robinson (2005) 148–162.

46 The Stranger stresses the analogy of cosmos and man with the words "imitate and follow" (273e–274a). See El Murr (2014) 161: "le mythe du *Politique* nous offre non pas un récit anthropocentré mais une image anthropomorphisèe du monde et un récit des relations que ce monde entretient avec la divinité".

related to *mimesis*; it is geared towards dramatisation, responding to the author's intention of involving the reader in the process of identification.[47]

After stating that "we are now at the point that our account has all along been designed to reach",[48] the Stranger describes other consequences of the change of the course of the universe. Then, rapidly narrowing the field of enquiry, he refers to human beings and says "those that relate to human beings will be shorter to relate and more to the point" (περὶ δὲ ἀνθρώπων βραχύτερα καὶ μᾶλλον προσήκοντα).[49] Human beings, more so than other creatures, are in trouble because they have lost the protection of the deity that had looked after them and they had to direct their own lives and take care of themselves. This is the point that the Stranger focuses on:

> Just like the cosmos as a whole (καθάπερ ὅλος ὁ κόσμος), which we imitate[50] and follow for all time (καὶ συνεπόμενοι τὸν ἀεὶ χρόνον, 274d6–7), now living and growing (ζῶμέν τε καὶ φυόμεθα) in this way.[51]

This passage repeats the previous one, confirming the importance of the discourse that underlines the link between the individual and the universe. It is a necessary link (ὑπ' ἀνάγκης, 274 a3), like the link between the part and the whole, or between the image and the model: by looking at the part that follows the whole we become aware of the movement of the whole. It reproduces it; the only thing that is different is the scale of reproduction: the whole can be read in any one of the parts that reproduces it. The passage from the *Sophist*,[52] on which the entire semantics of images and the mimetic technique that reproduces them is based, explains that preserving the proportions of the model is the key feature of faithful representation. The Stranger in the *Sophist* affirms that a *mimema* is a faithful image only if it maintains these proportions,[53] which means that looking at it is like looking at the model that it follows, reproduces and represents. This is true for all the aspects of this reproduction: we are born and live in the same way as the entire universe is born and lives. But, focusing on human beings under Zeus –

---

47 On this mimetic language see Hirsch (1995) 184–5. The dramatic strategies interact with the discursive treatment of the *mimesis*. Mimesis is an explicit concern of *Politicus* and, as we have already seen, the myth is concerned with "imitation" on a cosmic level. See Blondell (2002) 366.
48 Pl. *Plt.* 274b1–2.
49 Pl. *Plt.* 274b4–5. Trans. Rowe.
50 Because we are an "imitation" of it or a "representation that we make together" (ᾧ συμμιμούμενοι, 274d6).
51 Pl. *Plt.* 274d6–e1. Trans. Rowe.
52 Pl. *Sph.* 235d–236c.
53 Pl. *Sph.* 235d6–8.

says Melissa Lane – we see that it means that humans, insofar as they 'follow and imitate' the cosmos, are also necessarily independent of it.[54]

The Stranger says that we can use myth to see how many mistakes we made when we talked about the nature of the king and the statesman in the previous discussion. He refers to two mistakes in the previous discourse, one more important (confusing divine rule with human rule) and the other less so (failing to define the form of government). It is a reductive declaration. Indeed, the role of myth within the dialogue is much more extensive than what appears from the words of the Stranger.[55] Myth is entrusted with the task of providing a *mise-en-scène* for the topic of the whole dialogue and its extraordinary complexity. It has also the task of illustrating[56] the consequences that ensue when this complexity is not understood and the various parts that make up the whole are perceived as being *disjointed* from each other. Myth itself is presented as a totality of myths which take on their real meaning only when they are *linked* to one another (269b–c).[57]

> Well, all these things together are consequences of the same state of affairs, and besides these thousands of others still more astonishing than they; but through the great lapse of time since then some have been obliterated, while others have been reported in a scattered way, each separate from one another (τὰ δὲ διεσπαρμένα[58] εἴρηται χωρὶς ἕκαστα ἀπ' ἀλλήλων). But as for the state of affairs that is responsible for all of these things, no one has related it, and we should relate it now; for once it has been described, it will be a fitting contribution toward our exposition of the king.[59]

---

54 "As set out in the passage on birth and rearing, the notion of imitation – says Lane (1998) 109 – seems straightforward enough: just as the universe has become responsible for its own course (*autokratora*, 274 a5) so must its elements under the same necessity conceive and bear and nourish themselves. The parallel seems direct: autonomous cosmos, autonomous animals. Yet it is vital to see that the imitation required in the story, imitation of the cosmos's autonomy under Zeus by humans who must therefore be themselves autonomous, is perforce of a distinct kind". See also Rosen (1979) 85 and Blondell (2002) 354.

55 "The *Statesman* myth – says Horn (2012) 401 – has a didactical character, and it plays an important part in the context of the argument. I thus want to call the *Statesman* text a 'doctrinal myth. [...] I appeal to the observation that the mythological narrative is linked with a surprisingly large number of accompanying reflections. In at least five places the origin, content, credibility and the gain of the myth are discussed".

56 About the illustrative function of the text of the myth compare Horn (2012) 399 and El Murr (2014) 153.

57 The myth of the *Statesman* is an elaborate composition. Its ingredients include three stories from traditional mythology (268e8: τῶν πάλαι λεχθέντων).

58 See Pl. *Phdr.* 265d.

59 Pl. *Plt.* 269b5–c2. Trans. Rowe.

I think that the operations performed in the dialogue can be interpreted as an invitation to do likewise.[60] Just as myths only reveal a coherent meaning if they are linked to one another, so likewise the parts of the dialogue only make sense when linked to one another.[61] The text of the *Politicus* is full of invitations to return to the starting point,[62] going backwards[63] and following – as it were – the example of the universe. Only by going back several times can one understand the link between the constituent parts of the whole, in the myth[64] and in the dialogue.[65] The link is a mimetic link.[66]

At 277c the Stranger says:

---

60 See Gill (2012) 13, Horn (2012) 394, El Murr (2014) 153.

61 "The Eleatic stranger – says Horn (2012) 402 – claims about his story that it provides the unifying background for three existing mythical subject matters, i.e. for the topic of the reversal of the cycles of cosmic movement, for the topos of the Golden Age under Cronos and for the motif of the births out of the earth (269b5 ff.). He also contends that he gives the first comprehensive exposition of a connection of these mythical materials (269b9ff.), more specifically, in the sense of a first revelation".

62 See: πάλιν δ' οὖν ἐξ ἀρχῆς (264b); ἐπὶ τὴν ἀρχὴν (267a); πάλιν τοίνυν ἐξ ἄλλης ἀρχῆς (268d). See also πάλιν ἐπανέλθωμεν (275c); νῦν δέ γε πάλιν ἐπανορθούμενοι (276e); πάλιν δὴ τὸν ἔμπροσθε λόγον ἀναληπτέον (279a); πάλιν ἤλθομεν (279c); πάλιν οὖν ἔοικεν ἐπανιτέον ἀρχόμενον ἀπὸ τελευτῆς (280b); ἴωμεν πάλιν (287b).

63 "Some of the suggestions I make – as Cotton (2014) 30 affirms – particularly about the way the dialogues encourage us to pause as we read and to move backwards and forwards through the text, work better if we think of the texts as read. But much of what I say applies equally well to reception via performance". See also Blondell (2002) 367.

64 "Humans – as Horn (2012) 407 writes – imitate the cosmos and follow it in each of the two epochs insofar as at the one time they live and grow in one way and at the other time in the other way. Here too we clearly have a dichotomous juxtaposition and a connection of the cosmological and anthropological situation".

65 In the dialogue, the myth makes issues visible, while other parts deal with them only in abstract terms. The aim of the dialogue – to identify the nature of statesmanship – cannot be achieved if argumentation and representation are not brought together, if light is not shed on the other.

66 The theme of *mimesis* in the myth prefigures themes that will become important in the latter part of the dialogue. As with constitutions, human forms of state too are necessary in the Age of Zeus, and can imitate the regiment of Cronos in better or worse ways.

Our account, just like a portrait (ὥσπερ ζῷον),[67] seems adequate in its superficial outline, but not yet to have received its proper clarity (ἐνάργειαν), as it were with paints (τοῖς φαρμάκοις) and the mixing together of colors (τῇ συγκράσει τῶν χρωμάτων).[68]

This passage is crucial to the argument put forward here. It thematizes the issue of verbal visualisation by means of the most common device of dramatic writing: comparison. The *mise-en-scène* of the discussion in the dialogue deals with statesmanship. The discussion is designed to understand its nature. When we learn what it is by the end of the discussion, when we have his definition, *we can observe it as if it were a picture*. Since the discussion has not yet ended, it is compared to an unfinished painting. There is an outline but the figure is still not clearly visible.[69] The sketched figure is not yet complete and still undefined because the *colours have not yet been blended*. These unblended colours represent the words – which have not yet been found – which will have to be intertwined in order to create the verbal image (the definition) that is being sought. It appears as though tentative efforts were being made, trying out the effect of one specific blend of colours, then another and then yet another until the right mix is found. The verb συμπλέκειν[70] is used to indicate the act of intertwining which, by using the terms ἀμείκτον, νομευτική and ἐπιστήμη, is intended to propose a definition of statesmanship at this point in the enquiry (the rearing of non-interbreeding creatures). The outermost of the three terms is ἐπιστήμη. Indeed, the *diairesis* of the ἐπιστῆμαι is the first *diairesis* to be encountered in the dialogue. The term νομευτική is intermediate, while ἀμείκτον is the last one to be "tested" among the "colours" required to colour statesmanship.

Since the dialogue under examination focuses on statesmanship, the dialogue at this point speaks for itself, stating that it is *at a certain point in its course* precisely when the reader is *at a certain point* in the reading. It is still not completely clear what statesmanship actually entails, and this lack of clarity becomes a condition shared by the readers and the characters alike, due to the image of

---

67 "L'Etranger – as Teisserenc remarks (2010) 169 – joue sur le double registre sémantique du terme, particulièrement sensible dans ce contexte, pour préciser que la réalité dépeinte est un vivant mais aussi pour indiquer que la parole et le discours sont eux-mêmes de vivants portraits".

68 Pl. *Plt.* 277c1–3. Trans. Rowe.

69 The reference to the outline (ἔξωθεν μὲν περιγραφὴν, 277c1) is interesting because it suggests something painted from the outside to the inside, namely the intimacy of a meaning approached from the outside.

70 See 267b5–c1: "Of this in turn the part must be woven together (συμπλέκειν, 267b6) as not less than triple, if one wants to bring it together into a single name, calling it expert knowledge of rearing of non-interbreeding creatures" (Trans. by Rowe.)

the portrait. Readers and characters become spectators of the same scene (the unfinished portrait of the statesman) and interlocutors involved in the same discussion (the dialogue we are reading).

Small revolutions occur every time a text speaks about itself. Reading a passage which deals exactly with what we are reading gives us the perception that we are reading about ourselves, and this perception strengthens our identification with the representation; *we become part of it.* The need to *participate, to become a part of something, to share,* is often emphasised in the dialogue, as an invitation made by the Stranger to share thoughts and therefore to share an opinion.

> But this mustn't be just your view alone; I too have got to share it in common (κοινῇ συνδοκεῖν) with you.[71]

As already mentioned, an enquiry needs to be shared to become a philosophical enquiry which can be experienced at first hand.[72] The intention of Plato the author to invite the reader to follow the Stranger's guidelines to the younger Socrates[73] becomes increasingly clear. He says:

> But it is not painting or any other sort of manual craft, but speech and discourse (λέξει καὶ λόγῳ), that constitute the more fitting medium for exhibiting all living things (δηλοῦν πᾶν ζῷον), for those who are able to follow (τοῖς δυναμένοις ἕπεσθαι); for the rest, it will be through manual crafts (τοῖς δ' ἄλλοις διὰ χειρουργιῶν).[74]

Occasionally the younger Socrates seems to lack the capacity to *follow* the Stranger, so the reader is invited to do this better than he can.[75] The theme of example is put forward to "clarify the painting with discourse" and, at 277d, the Stranger says:

---

71 Pl. *Plt.* 277a3–4. Trans. Rowe.

72 Blondell (2002) 377: Although as readers we are required, like the visitor's young interlocutors, to "follow" in linear fashion if we are to grasp the work as a whole, we are also free to turn aside from this path, to backtrack or reject the visitor's leadership if we wish to make detours or digressions of our own.

73 About the combination of critical detachment and personal involvement required in the reader see Cotton (2015) 43.

74 Pl. *Plt.* 277c3–6. Trans. Rowe.

75 See Blondell (2002) 377. On the ways in which we are encouraged to move beyond the reactions of respondents see Cotton (2015) 45.

It's a hard thing, my fine friend, to demonstrate any of the more important subjects without using models. It looks as if each of us knows everything in a kind of dreamlike way (οἷον ὄναρ), and then again is ignorant of everything as it were when awake (ὥσπερ ὕπαρ).[76]

It is perfectly clear that the Stranger is referring to what he is doing in the dialogue: he is using examples to give a satisfactory explanation of the nature of statesmanship. If we are not aware of this, if we do not grasp the exemplary function of the examples, in other words of the myth we have just read and all the figures that have been, and will be, used to explain statesmanship, then nothing can be understood, just as *we forget a dream as soon as we are awake.*

From this perspective the myth presents a *mise-en-scène* of what happens to human beings at the time of Zeus when they lose the memory of the divine model and risk, due to this lack of memory, drowning "in the boundless sea of unlikeness" (273c–e).

It mirrors what happens to the reader who, after looking at an image that used to have an exemplary role as a model, forgets it because he has not understood it. This is what the Stranger is telling us at 277d with his strange (ἀτόπως, 277d6) statement about the way knowledge originates within us.[77] Thanks to the definition of a model at 278c we learn that a model comes into being[78] when something identical, correctly recognised in a different context, once it has been traced back to it, generates a single opinion which is true for each of the two contexts but also for both together.[79]

This definition explains that the myth we have just read about *is* not a model, but it *becomes* (γένεσις, 278c4) a model if, and only if, we are able to follow its indication, generating a single true opinion (μίαν ἀληθῆ δόξαν),[80] which is valid both in the context of the myth and that of *logos*.[81]

---

76 Pl. *Plt*. 277d1–4. Trans. Rowe.
77 "I do seem rather oddly now to have stirred up the subject of what happens to us in relation to knowledge", 277d7–8. Trans. Rowe.
78 See 278c3–4: ὅτι παραδείγματός γ᾽ ἐστὶ τότε γένεσις, and El Murr (2014) 51–53.
79 "Well then, have we grasped this point adequately, that we come to be using a model when a given thing, which is the same in something different and distinct, is correctly identified there, and having been brought together with the original thing, brings about a single true judgment about each separately and both together?" (Pl. *Plt* 278c3–6. Trans. Rowe).
80 Pl. *Plt*. 278c6.
81 See El Murr (2014) 195.

A model that does not generate true opinions is not a model.[82] If we succeed, then reality will appear instead of a dream (ἵνα ὕπαρ ἀντ' ὀνείρατος ἡμῖν γίγνηται).[83] In the dialogue everything seems to veer towards a meaning that is significant for the younger Socrates, the interlocutor of the Stranger and the readers.

Besides myth, the dialogue contains many other paradigms,[84] such as weaving, which is explicitly presented as a *paradeigma*.[85] It is organised mimetically through a complex operation of distinctions which, taking each phase in turn, first separates that phase from what it is distinct from (279c–280a), and then from what it resembles (280b–e).[86] On several occasions it is emphasised that the paradigmatic figure is not yet complete (280e6) because many other figures compete with weaving for its definition. They try to replace weaving in its representative role as a protective and paradigmatic art of the production of defensive fabrics.[87]

The procedure of constructing a *paradeigma*, which is explained while these distinctions are made, cannot be restricted to expressing something that is true (τι ἀληθές, 281d2). It must express something that is clear (σαφές, 281d2) and complete (τέλεον, 281d2), and this will only be possible by continuing to make divisions.[88] Ultimately, the art of weaving is identified with the art of intertwining the warp and the weft (ἀπεκρινάμεθα πλεκτικὴν εἶναι κρόκης καὶ στήμονος ὑφαντικήν, 283b1–2) and what will be shown, in all its clarity (to be visualised and shared) is *the mimetic art of Plato the writer* who, by distinguishing notions, has portrayed the art of making distinctions, exemplifying the art of exemplification, and discussing the art of measurement through length and brevity.

> Listen to a point that it's appropriate (λόγον ἄκουσόν τινα προσήκοντα, 283b8–9) to make in all cases like this.
> Do make it.

---

82 See Teisserenc (2010) 171: "la distinction entre tableau avec couleurs et tableau sans couleurs (277b8–c3) trouve analogiquement son équivalent dans la distinction entre discours usant ou non du paradigme".
83 Pl. *Plt*. 278e10.
84 The method of example – as Blondell (2002) 372 says – like division and myth, is thus another tool for verbal imaging.
85 Pl. *Plt*. 279a–b.
86 See Gaudin (1987) 121–132, Teisserenc (2010) 180–183 and El Murr (2014)193–205.
87 See El Murr (2014) 196–203.
88 Division – as Blondell (2002) 371 suggests – is also a journey, one that brings us progressively closer to our quarry, until it can be "caught" and we can "see" it more easily.

> First, then, let's look at excess and deficiency in general, so that we may distribute praise
> and censure proportionately on each occasion, when things are said at greater length than
> necessary and when the opposite occurs in discussions like the present one.[89]

As Blondell[90] points out, "the criterion for proper length, the Stranger tells us, is 'appropriateness' (τὸ πρέπον, 286c–d). Elsewhere, he uses this word to mean relevant, 'fitting,' or appropriate to a purpose (286c–d). He also employs the cognate verb πρέπει for the appropriateness of a particular mode of explanation, for example, for the choice of *logoi* over visual images in the right circumstances (277c4); for the use of the myth to 'show forth' the king (269c1–2); and to criticize the assumption that the figure of the king required a 'great' paradigm (277b4). In employing this notion to defend the length of his myth, he explains that the primary criterion for appropriateness is not pleasure (except incidentally), or speed of results (which is secondary), but 'respect' (τιμᾶν) for the participants' competence; whether long or short, a discourse is to be judged by its educational value, a criterion that justifies any length, no matter what critics may say (286d–287a). Τὸ πρέπον has many synonyms denoting various kinds of appropriateness or relevance (cf. 284e). One of these is προσῆκον ('belonging'), used by the visitor in *Sophist* to denote the proper coloring of an *eikon*, as opposed to a *phantasma* (*Soph.* 235e1). In the *Statesman*, he uses the same word to justify spending more time on human beings than other animals (274b5). In other words, he uses it, like τὸ πρέπον, for the appropriate size of a discourse or its parts. It is used to introduce the excursus on due measure, in which the discussion of τὸ πρέπον itself occurs (283b8)".

This is the link between form and content in Plato's dialogues. In his definition of the art of weaving, the warp and weft intertwine with the same verb that intertwines the words in the definition.[91] The verb is πλέκω, which means "join together", "compose", "construct" and "invent". When Plato uses this verb, he is not just referring to the composition of the warp and weft which create a fabric, or to the conjunction of terms that gives rise to the definition (of weaving and of politics), or to the construction of the example of weaving which generates a correct opinion of the politics it exemplifies. He is also referring to the very invention of the dialogue we are reading which is capable of πλέκειν,[92] namely of *keeping*

---

89 Pl. *Plt.* 283b8–c6. Trans. Rowe.

90 Blondell (2002) 368–69.

91 Pl. *Plt.* 267b6, 283b1–2, 306a2, 309b7; *Sph.* 262d4.

92 By following an Aristotelian suggestion (at *Politics* 1456a9), we could claim that a dialogue is similar to a well-organized tragedy, both with regard to the way in which the characters are kept together and with regard to the way in which the readers are able to participate in the 'mise-en-scène.'

together or reconciling not only the interlocutors in the *mise-en-scène* of the debate but also the readers who participate in it. This becomes possible due to the extraordinary mimetic capacity of Plato's text which is so full of *enargeia*.

However, the mimetic operation can only be carried out as long as the discourse is completed and brought to a conclusion. This is a recurrent theme of the dialogues;[93] it seems to allude to the crucial relationship between the whole imbued with meaning and its constituent parts, which resemble the building block of a complex construction that cannot be left unfinished (ἀτελής) because its sense only becomes clear upon completion. The order of the route and memory of its various stages are designed to provide understanding of the whole (285c). The Stranger says that it is always necessary to put the topic they are discussing into images which enable similarities and differences to be seen. At 285d–286a he says:

> But I think the majority of people fail to recognize that for some of the things there are, there are certain perceptible likenesses which are there to be easily understood, and which is it not at all hard to point out when one wants to make an easy demonstration, involving no trouble and without recourse to verbal means, to someone who asks for an account of one of these things. Conversely, for those things that are greatest and most valuable, there is no image at all that has been worked in plain view for the use of mankind, the showing of which will enable the person who wants to satisfy the mind of an inquirer to satisfy it adequately, just by fitting it to one of the senses. That is why one must practice at being able to give and receive an account of each thing; for the things that are without body, which are finest and greatest (τὰ γὰρ ἀσώματα, κάλλιστα ὄντα καὶ μέγιστα, 285a5–6) are shown clearly only by verbal means and by nothing else (λόγῳ μόνον ἄλλῳ δὲ οὐδενὶ σαφῶς δείκνυται, 286a6), and everything that is now being said is for the sake of these things.[94]

To impose order on the figures that might dispute the definition of statesmanship, the Stranger proceeds "just as before" (287c7),[95] as he had done when distinguishing between figures that sought to contend the definition of weaving.[96]

To understand the figure of the *true* statesman, as distinct from *false* statesmen – says the Stranger in 291a:

> We must look both at these king-priests by lot, and their subordinates, and also at a certain other very large crowd of people [...]. It's a class mixed out of all sorts, or so it seems to me

---

93 See Pl. *Plt.* 257c; *Prt.* 314c; *Phdr.* 264c.
94 Pl. *Plt.* 285d9–286a7. Trans. Rowe. On this text see Owen (1973) 340–361 and the discussion in Dixsaut (2001) 267–284. For Teisserenc (2010) 171, "il s'agit donc de rappeler la supériorité générale du langage sans pour autant contester que les oeuvres de la parole soient des images".
95 The text seems to go backwards and is full of expressions such as: ὥσπερ ἔμπροσθεν "just as before".
96 See Pl. *Plt.* 281d.

as I look at it just now. For many of the men resemble lions and centaurs and other such things, and very many resemble satyrs and those animals that are weak but versatile; and they quickly exchange their shapes and capacity for action for each other's [...], the chorus of those concerned with the affairs of cities [...] [the chorus] of greatest magician of all the sophists, and the most versed in their expertise. Although removing him from among those who really are in possession of the art of statesmanship and kingship is a very difficult thing to do, remove him we must if we are going to see plainly what we are looking for.[97]

To understand the figure of the true statesman, as distinct from other statesmen – in the final pages in the dialogue – it is necessary to refer to the possession of art rather than to criteria such as willingness or coercion, respect for the law, poverty or wealth, which had initially[98] all seemed relevant. To *visualise* this truth, the Stranger resorts to the figure of doctors regarding whom this discourse, he argues, "had appeared valid":

> Yes, but these people, whether they rule over willing or unwilling subjects, whether according to written laws or without them, and whether they rule as rich men or poor, we must suppose – as is now our view – to be carrying out whatever sort of rule they do on the basis of expertise. Doctors provide the clearest parallel. We believe in them whether they cure us with our consent or without it, by cutting or burning or applying some other painful treatment, and whether they do so according to written rules or apart from written rules, and whether as poor men or rich. In all these cases we are no less inclined at all to say they are doctors, so long as they are in charge of us on the basis of expertise.[99]

According to the text, the only true statesman is the man who possesses statesmanship. The true statesman is a rare person but the only one who really deserves his name. All the others are reproductions, representations or imitations (*mimemata*) of it, and these imitations – a particularly interesting distinction – include reproductions that are better and others that are worse.[100]

> So long as they (*sc.* statesmen) act to preserve it (*sc.* city) on the basis of expert knowledge and what is just, making it better than it was so far as they can, *this* is the constitution that alone we must say is correct, under these conditions and in accordance with criteria of this sort. All the others that we generally say are constitutions we must say are not genuine, and not really constitutions at all (οὐ γνησίας οὐδ' ὄντως οὔσας λεκτέον), but imitations of this one (ἀλλὰ μεμιμημένας ταύτην); those we say are "law-abiding" have imitated it for the

---

97 Pl. *Plt.* 291a1–c7. Trans. Rowe. See Miller (2004) 86.
98 See Pl. *Plt.* 276d–e; 293c–d. See El Murr (2014) 228–232.
99 Pl. *Plt.* 293a6–b5. Trans. Rowe.
100 As in the myth, under Zeus, correct statesmanship is imitation of divine (and true) statesmanship.

better (ἃς μὲν ὡς εὐνόμους λέγομεν, ἐπὶ τὰ καλλίω), the others for the worse (τὰς δὲ ἄλλας ἐπὶ τὰ αἰσχίονα).[101]

It is stated at 297b–c that no great number of men, whoever they may be, could ever acquire political science and be able to administer a state with wisdom, but our one right form of government must be sought in some small number of persons or in one person, and all other forms are merely, as we said before, more or less successful imitations of that.

As soon as he hears the statement about *mimemata*, the younger Socrates says he has not understood.

> What do you mean by this? What are you saying? For I did not understand the point about imitations (τὸ περὶ τῶν μιμημάτων, 297c6) when it was made just now either.[102]

To explain this point, which is quite an undertaking and something that could not be passed over without examining the issue, the Stranger begins to return to the images (εἰκόνας) intertwined within Plato's mimetic writing to which kingly rulers must be referred (αἷς ἀναγκαῖον ἀπεικάζειν ἀεί). These figures are the noble steersman (τὸν γενναῖον κυβερνήτην, 297e11) and the doctor who "is worth many others" (πολλῶν ἀντάξιον ἰατρόν, 297e11–12).

The Stranger invites Socrates and the readers to observe a scene:

> Let us look at the matter by fashioning a kind of figure, using these as material (κατίδωμεν γὰρ δή τι σχῆμα ἐν τούτοις αὐτοῖς πλασάμενοι).[103]

Rarely does Plato make such explicit reference to his dramatic and mimetic writing. The text presents the dreadful treatment we may receive from a doctor or a steersman if they are given absolute power. To avoid this risk, they are subject to restrictions laid down by law. The law is not the kingdom of knowledge but rather its imitation. In the view of the younger Socrates, this imitation would make life unendurable (ἀβίωτος, 299e8), but the Stranger says there is something worse than this imitation,[104] and the unchangeable principle of the sovereignty of law is designed to protect us from this extreme danger. The figure of the δεύτερος πλοῦς (300c2) presents written laws as the second-best method of proceeding; they are

---

101 Pl. *Plt.* 293d8–e5. Trans. Rowe. See 297b–c.
102 Pl. *Plt* 297c5–6. Trans. Rowe. The reference is to 293e. On the *mimesis* of the truth, in the *Politicus* see Woodruff (2015) 334–335.
103 Pl. *Plt.* 297e12–13. Trans. Rowe.
104 See El Murr (2014) 251.

μιμήματα τῆς ἀληθείας (300c5–6), imitations of truth. The figure of the statesman, who would make many changes in his practice without regard to his written rulings reappears at this point in the enquiry as a yardstick for measuring the deviance of possible human behaviour: if, then, this statesman were to do such a thing without knowledge, however, he would imitate badly in every case. But if he did it on the basis of expertise, then it would no longer be imitation (οὐκ ἔστιν ἔτι μίμημα, 300e1), but "that very thing that is most truly what it sets out to be" (ἀλλ'αὐτὸ τὸ ἀληθέστατον ἐκεῖνο).[105]

In this regard, I believe that a parallel with a passage from Aristotle is interesting. At *Poetics* 1448a Aristotle refers to οἱ μιμούμενοι who reproduce the behaviour of human beings and says that these reproductions may be better than we are (βελτίονας ἢ καθ'ἡμᾶς) or worse (χείρονας), or "just like ourselves" (τοιοῦτος):

> The objects the imitator represents are actions, with agents who are necessarily either good men or bad – the diversities of human character being nearly always derivative from this primary distinction, since the line between virtue and vice is one dividing the whole of mankind. It follows, therefore, that the agents represented must be either above our own level of goodness, or beneath it, or just such as we are in the same way as, with the painters, the personages of Polygnotus are better than we are, those of Pauson worse, and those of Dionysius just like ourselves.[106]

In Aristotle representations are distinguished according to their aptitude to improve, worsen or truly represent, while in Plato's text reproductions are distinguished according to whether they are implemented by competent people (ἔντεχνοι, 300e1) or incompetent people (ἀνεπιστήμονες, 300d9). The reproduction made by incompetent people is detrimental to his model (they are ἐπιχειροῖεν τὸ ἀληθές, 300d10) whereas that of competent people – and here the gap between Plato and Aristotle is enormous – is no longer a reproduction, but "that very thing that is most truly what it sets out to be". It is "the most virtuous behaviour" that occurs rarely in reality but is the only true reference point of statesmanship from which all the aforementioned forms of government should be kept separate.

With the exception of the virtuous form, all forms of government are adulterations (303c), supported by men who are not statesmen who are themselves counterfeits, and since they are the greatest of imitators and cheats, they are the greatest of all sophists (303c).

---

105 Pl. *Plt.* 300d9–e2. Trans. Rowe.
106 Arist. *Poetics* 1448a1–6. Trans. Bywater.

So then we must also remove those who participate in all these constitutions, except for the one based on knowledge, as being, not statesmen (οὐκ ὄντας πολιτικοὺς , 303c1–2), but expert in faction; we must say that, as presiding over insubstantial images, on the largest scale (καὶ εἰδώλων μεγίστων προστάτας ὄντας 303c2–3), they are themselves of the same sort (καὶ αὐτοὺς εἶναι τοιούτους, 303c3), and that as the greatest imitators and magicians (μεγίστους δὲ ὄντας μιμητὰς καὶ γόητας μεγίστους , 303c3–4) they turn out to be the greatest sophists among sophists (γίγνεσθαι τῶν σοφιστῶν σοφιστάς).[107]

Within the context of the discourse on the nature of mimetic art, as soon as the sophists are mentioned, the polemical tone of the argumentation increases and superlatives abound.[108] Besides political incompatibility, this may be because the sophists are the true rivals of platonic art, the mimetic art of imitation or of persuasion built on words, visual words which are enchanting and rousing.

Various distinctions from statesmanship are made. Interestingly, after the separation off of "those things that are different from the expert knowledge of statesmanship, and those that are alien and hostile to it",[109] and between those that are precious and related to it, the distinction that stands out pertains to rhetoric, the art of persuading a multitude or a mob by telling edifying stories (304c10–d2):

Well then: to which sort of expert knowledge shall we assign what is capable of persuading mass and crowd, through the telling of stories, and not through teaching?
This too is clear, I think: it must be given to rhetoric.[110]

Rhetoric is the art of creating persuasive figures, figures made up of words, rhetorical figures that should have a political purpose and be governed by politics.[111]

Plato may have written this dialogue to prevent the sophists, who were generally rivals of the academics, to have political credibility as rhetoricians. The dialogue is inseparable from the *Sophist* of which it is the continuation, and clearly shows that its author was the greatest of the rhetoricians.

---

107 Pl. *Plt.* 303b8–c5. Trans. Rowe.
108 See Pl. *Plt* 291a–c and 303c8-d2. See also El Murr (2014) 221–223.
109 Pl. *Plt.* 303e8. Trans. Rowe.
110 Pl. *Plt.* 304c10–d3. Trans. Rowe.
111 See Rowe (1999) XX; El Murr (2014) 218–219.

Laura Candiotto

The very difficult separation from the chorus of the greatest magician of all the sophists

The puzzling presence of Socrates in the *Statesman* (291a1–c6)

1 Introduction

After the dialogue on the sophist, the Stranger says we should search for the statesman (*Statesman*, 258b). If, in the *Sophist*, Plato had achieved the division between philosopher and sophist, in the *Statesman* he would need one between philosopher and statesman. In doing so, he would also need to distinguish the right and good statesman from the general run of politicians of his age.

Defining the good statesman means distinguishing him from the sophists too. And this separation is still more relevant, not only because the sophists played an important political role in Athens, but also because both statesmen and sophists share the same realm of activity, that of doxastic matters and expertise.

The very difficult separation from the chorus of the sophists is the topic of this paper, and it turns on a passage from the *Statesman*, 291a1–c6. The pages I am going to interpret are located within the final definition of the statesman (287b–300e), where we are required to distinguish the statesman from other subordinate functionaries: primary producers of the physical requirements of the community; personal menial servants, money-changers, merchants; clerks, heralds, priests. At this point the chorus of the sophists appears, and the dialogue goes on to say that we must divide off the true ruler and the true constitution from them. It is after this section of the dialogue that we find the famous claim, that the rhetoricians should be at the service of the statesman, entirely and unquestionably (303b).

The necessity of the separation from sophistry is introduced at *Soph.* 217a–b, where it is said that we should divide (διαιρούμενοι) the sophist from the philosopher and the statesman, and where the Eleatic Stranger says, as on our page of the *Statesman*, that it is no easy matter to define each clearly. Plato needed to take into account the sophist too, at the exact moment when he questioned the separation between philosopher and statesman. The reason is that sophistry, thanks to its power of creating illusions, is at work within politics too. Thus, the reciprocal relationship should be determined among three characters, the philosopher, the statesman, and the sophist, dividing them into three classes (γένη).

https://doi.org/10.1515/9783110605549-015

232 of Laura Candiotto

So the problem connected to the definition of the sophist, which is supposed to have been resolved in the *Sophist*, seems to still be an issue in the *Statesman*. Reopening the question in the *Statesman* does not mean dismissing the theoretical results of the *Sophist* as regards adequately defining the sophist and his art, establishing the ontological status of falsity, and consequently of those tools that give power to the sophist, such as images, resemblances, appearances, deceptions, and misjudgements, but it is rather a recognition that the mimetic power of the sophists remains a practical issue for Plato, especially in the doxastic realm of statesmanship as expertise.

The aim of the paper is to clarify why the separation from the sophists is an issue for Plato in the *Statesman*; to provide three answers that seek to frame the question of the relationship between Socrates and sophistry; and to re-examine the issue after the *Sophist*, and offer a new solution.

2 Socrates in the background

The separation from sophistry was an issue for Plato all his life, not only because it was clear to him how great a danger sophistry posed in the education of the young, but also because this issue had to do with his relationship with Socrates and his death.[1] Plato fought for Socrates all his life long, demonstrating through his literary activity, among other things, that he was not a sophist who corrupted the young, or an expert in politics with the power to influence Critias or Alcibi-

---

1 Rowe (2001) has argued against interpretations whereby Plato, in the *Statesman*, would have accepted Socrates' execution, and more generally in Rowe (2002b), against those arguing for Plato's supposed betrayal in the political dialogues. I agree with Rowe, and, moreover, I argue that Plato, in the late dialogues, is still struggling to build up Socrates' memory, as in the first dialogues. The strategy I am going to use to provide some evidence for my argument proceeds from a literary interpretation of lines 291a1–c6, and, specifically, from the analysis of the unusual and puzzling presence of Socrates in them. The role played by Socrates in the last dialogues also requires us to investigate the motives that might have pushed Plato to write in this way, and more generally, the political force of Plato's writings. I cannot engage with this wide and controversial issue in this paper, and thus, my aim is to state my case simply by reference to the *Statesman*. The literary method looks the best candidate in this context, since the issue I am going to address arises, as I shall be talking about soon, precisely from some specific words employed by Plato.

ades.[2] Moreover, Plato well knew that the relationship between Socrates and sophistry was still a hot question among the Socratics and their opponents at the dates of composition even of the late dialogues, and thus he understood that he needed to include it, in some way, within his analysis of statesmanship and the instrumental use of rhetoric.

This autobiographical reason – which can only be inferred indirectly, by framing Plato's writing in his historical context, and remains hypothetical – may have induced Plato to reopen the question about the separation from sophistry in the *Statesman*. In this paper, I assume this reason at the background of my answers, and argue for a constructive solution of this slippery issue in the *Statesman*, claiming that Plato has individuated by κάθαρσις the mechanism through which a kind of separation with benefits operates, which enables him to profit from what has been set apart. As in the example of the craftsman who separates gold from other elements, the art of rhetoric needed to be purified to become available to the statesman (303d4–304e2). Analogously, the image of Socrates needs to be somehow 'purified' by the apologetic nature of his character's construction by Plato. This means, for Plato, his coming up with a strategy of defending Socrates from the accusation of having influenced Alcibiades, Critias and Charmides in their bad conduct. It also means his working out the rhetorical strategies used by speakers as an educational framework when they engage with the city. This is the only way he can preserve Socrates' memory.

As far as I know, the tricky question of the role played by Socrates in the "very difficult separation" has never been addressed in the most established commentaries to the translations (Skemp 1952, Annas and Waterfield 1995, Migliori 1996, Rowe 1999, Brisson and Pradeau 2003, Giorgini 2005, El Murr 2014).[3] I do not see any valid reason for not providing an explanation of the role played by Socrates in these pages: as I see it, the text seems to point directly to this particular literary analysis and interpretation. I found some references to the differences between

---

2 Plato's strategy is to show that, despite Socrates' undeniable influence on both of them, he could not be himself accused of their faults. To achieve this apologetic goal, Plato masked Socrates's political force, as I claimed in Candiotto (2013). On the matter of Socrates' controversial relationship with politics, the *locus classicus* is the *Gorgias*, where at 473e6 Socrates says to Polus that he is not a politician, and at 521d7–8, where he says to Callicles that he is one of the few Athenians who practice the right politics.
3 El Murr (2014) 20–22, has mentioned the presence in the literature of some works, deriving for the most part from a Straussian interpretation, which take into account the role played by Socrates in the dialogue, but he refers to them simply with regard to the choice made by Plato in favour of the Eleatic Stranger instead of Socrates as his main character, at the same time underlining that, in his opinion, this is not the best way to explain the issue.

the Stranger and Socrates in the works of Zuckert (2000) and McCoy (2008) overseas, and in Europe in the works of Narcy (1995) and Casadesús Bordoy (2013), but in a context of discussing the *Sophist*.[4] My objective is to provide some new insights into this intriguing topic in the *Statesman*.

3 Why separation is required

Why is it necessary to separate the statesman from the sophists, and why is it very difficult to do so?

As a preliminary answer, I would say that Plato presents the philosophers and the sophists as difficult to distinguish, insofar as both use rhetoric as part of their arguments (for a detailed analysis of this thesis, cf. McCoy 2008). Nevertheless, the situation here is even more difficult, because (1) it requires distinguishing the statesman from the sophist, and hence (2) dividing into three classes (not two) the philosopher, the statesman and the sophist, as prescribed in the *Sophist*. It follows that the method of division into two classes now needs to result in a division into three classes. This task does not suffer from inconsistencies, but it is achievable through the employment of a methodological technique of division which operates step by step (first philosopher-sophist; then sophist-statesman; and finally statesman-philosopher), where the second term is the one that is analysed, to the exclusion, as is well known, of the case of the philosopher.

Again, however, why is this division so difficult, and also so exhausting and painful (μόγις ἐχωρίσθη, 303d2)?

3.1 The first reason: Socrates's ἀτοπία

The first reason emerges from the dramatic situation, and, specifically, from the character of Socrates.

Socrates is present throughout the dialogue, and he is the character that opens and ends it.[5] Some crucial words connected with precision to Socrates and having regard to his trial – the dramatic date of the trilogy is, in fact, 399 BC,

---

4 Casadesús Bordoy (2013) 21–22; 26 cites *Pol.* 291a–c and 303d to reinforce what he was arguing for the *Sophist* in connection with the Homeric tradition.
5 I have to say that not all commentators agree with this. The topic is controversial because the last words are ascribed to Socrates, but we do not know if he is the young or the old Socrates.

exactly when the trial is taking place – appear meaningfully in the lines I am discussing.

In particular, some typical descriptions of Socrates are detectable in the lines describing the chorus of sophists. Those characteristics are explicitly ascribed to sophists in their various forms, but they could implicitly recall typical features of Socrates, too, such as his being like a satyr (291b1) or a magician (291c3),[6] his ἀτοπία (291a6, b5, b6), and his ignorance (291b6):

> But who are the people you mean? Some very odd (ἀτόπους) people indeed. How, exactly? It's a class mixed out of all sorts, or so it seems to me as I look at it just now. For many of the men resemble lions and centaurs and other such things, and very many resemble satyrs and those animals that are weak but versatile (πάμπολλοι δὲ Σατύροις καὶ τοῖς ἀσθενέσι καὶ πολυτρόποις θηρίοις); and they quickly exchange their shapes and capacity for action for each other's (ταχὺ δὲ μεταλλάττουσι τάς τε ἰδέας καὶ τὴν δύναμιν εἰς ἀλλήλους). And yet now, Socrates, I think I have identified the men in question. Please explain; you seem to have something odd (ἄτοπόν τι) in view. Yes, it's a universal experience that not recognizing something makes it odd (τὸ γὰρ ἄτοπον ἐξ ἀγνοίας πᾶσι συμβαίνει). And this is exactly what happened to me just now: at the moment when I first saw the chorus of those concerned with the affairs of cities I failed to recognize him (ἐξαίφνης ἠμφεγνόησα κατιδὼν τὸν περὶ τὰ τῶν πόλεων πράγματα χορόν). What chorus? That of the greatest magician of all the sophists, and the most versed in their expertise (τὸν πάντων τῶν σοφιστῶν μέγιστον γόητα καὶ ταύτης τῆς τέχνης ἐμπειρότατον). Although removing him from among those who really are in possession of the art of statesmanship and kingship is a very difficult thing (παγχάλεπον) to do, remove him we must (ἀφαιρεῖν ἀφαιρετέον) if we are going to see plainly what we are looking for (*Statesman*, 291a1–c6, tr. Rowe).

Other words relating to Socrates might also be detected at 299b3–c6, where the accusations that brought him to trial are recalled, such as his corrupting the young (299b8), or his making clever speculations (299b5), or being a star-gazer and a bumbling sophist (299b7–8), as Aristophanes charged in the *Clouds*. The passage ends with a reference to the topic of Socrates's choice not to escape from prison because of his respect for the laws of Athens (as described in the *Crito*):

> Suppose anyone is found inquiring into steersmanship and seafaring, or health and truth in the doctor's art, in relation to winds and heat and cold, above and beyond the written rules, and making clever speculations (σοφιζόμενος) of any kind in relation to such things. In the first place one must not call him an expert doctor or an expert steersman, but a stargazer, some babbling sophist (μετεωρολόγον, ἀδολέσχην τινὰ σοφιστήν). The next provision will be that anyone who wishes from among those permitted to do so shall indict him

---

6 For those, like Alcibiades, who do not understand the true nature of Socrates, Socrates is a satyr, or magician (*Symp*.215a4–d6), who uses magical charms (*Charm*.155e2–157c6) to persuade his interlocutors.

and bring him before some court or other as corrupting other people younger (διαφθείροντα ἄλλους νεωτέρους) than himself and inducing them to engage in the arts of the steersman and the doctor not in accordance with the laws, but instead by taking autonomous control of ships and patients. If he is found guilty of persuading anyone, whether young or old (τὰ γεγραμμένα δόξῃ πείθειν εἴτε νέους εἴτε πρεσβύτας), contrary to the laws and the written rules, the most extreme penalties shall be imposed on him (κολάζειν τοῖς ἐσχάτοις). For (so the law will say) there must be nothing wiser than the laws (οὐδὲν γὰρ δεῖν τῶν νόμων εἶναι σοφώτερον) (*Statesman*, 299b3–c6, tr. Rowe).

Arguably, these pieces of literary evidence could lead one to think – though without sufficient reason – that Plato is once again battling in defence of the memory of Socrates in the *Statesman*. These textual references present us with a picture of Socrates as being a sophist. But it is exactly this picture that Plato wishes to fight against, by purifying the image of Socrates from admixture with sophistry (and hence separating him from the chorus of the sophists), and constructing his memory this way. Moreover, this lexicological analysis, combined with his presence as a character, appears to seek to provide some reasons at least for explaining why Socrates is present in the *Statesman*, and more crucially for detecting what his role in it is supposed to be. As I have already mentioned, my thesis is that his presence and role are related to the issue of separation from the sophists. Moreover, the difficulty in the division among philosopher, statesman, and sophist may also arise from the difficulty of placing Socrates on only one side of the division. It is certain that Plato would want to demonstrate that Socrates belongs to the class of philosophers – Socrates is the model of the philosopher for Plato,[7] and his best testimonial (Rossetti 2015)[8] – but this does not mean that this goal was easy to achieve.

By himself, Socrates stands outside of every clearly-defined class. To see this, one needs simply to recall his ἀτοπία. The word ἄτοπος suggests 'being without a definite place', or 'being out of place'. So it is tautological to say that it is very difficult to find someone without knowing where he is, just as it is difficult to find

---

7 I disagree with Ruby Blondell (2006) 386, regarding the idea that Plato might have made use of the Stranger to attain a new model of philosophy beyond that of his teacher Socrates. It is true that it is meaningful to look into the similarities and differences Plato points out between the Stranger and Socrates in the search for the definition of the philosopher (Zuckert, 2000, 69), but this does not mean, I think, that Plato would have chosen the Stranger as the real model of the philosopher. Another option is to consider the Stranger as a proponent of a different method of doing philosophy, without implying that this method is the best, or preferable to the Socratic one. Nevertheless, to properly evaluate this option, an assessment of the development of Plato's philosophy, from the first Socratic dialogues to the late dialogues, is required. But this task cannot be attempted here.

8 On Plato's self-promotion as the true philosopher, cf. Rosen (1996) 77.

someone that 'is in many ways' (as with the world πολύτροπον), which is a depiction of the sophist. While to be "out of the way" and to be "in many ways" produce the same difficulty of not being able to define the object well, they are arguably about being very different, like Socrates (and the sophists). Nevertheless, this difference is difficult for ignorant people to ascertain, as was admitted by the same Socrates in the *Apology* (20a). Zuckert (2000, 70) has stressed that the attitudes of Socrates and the Stranger towards ατοπία-ατροπία are very different; contrary to Socrates, the Stranger struggles to overcome perplexity with philosophical arguments, and for Zuckert, this is what makes the Stranger a sophist in the eyes of Socrates (95). The Straussian school has depicted Socrates as a silent and elusive character in the *Statesman*. My own claim resides in the recognition of Socrates's presence instead. As Socrates himself stressed in the previous dialogues of the trilogy, he was not set apart from the discussion, but "I myself got together in discussion yesterday" (258d). Moreover, he emphasized, maybe ironically, as in the case of Theaetetus, that he would be participating in the dialogue thanks to his homonymy with the young Socrates (257d–258a).[9] Arguably, the elusive presence of Socrates in the dialogue asks us to question the idea that Socrates has been overtaken by the Stranger as a model of the philosopher. My solution is, as we shall see later, that, as in the case of rhetoric, he too will be subjected to Plato's apologetic construction as a purification of his memory, making his presence more acceptable to the city and to future generations, and establishing, yet again, that he belongs to the class of philosophers.

Thus, this first answer to the question about the reasons why separation is difficult tells us that it is the silent presence of Socrates, something also recalled by a number of words related to his typical characteristics, that perilously disclose a number of similarities with the sophists, which creates the difficulty, but it does not explain why. This explanation will be provided by my second answer.

3.2 The second reason: the sophists' ἀτοπία

The second reason stems from the nature of the objects to be divided, in particular the chameleon-like nature of the sophists. The sophists are described as a mixture of all sorts (πάμφυλόν τι γένος αὐτῶν, 291a8), a class of animals weak but

---

9 This point has been underlined by Migliori (2001) 44–45, though he emphasizes that in the last dialogues, apart from the *Philebus* where the topic is the good, Socrates has nothing more to say. Nevertheless, he is still present to his student, even if only through a kinship of names.

versatile (τοῖς ἀσθενέσι καὶ πολυτρόποις θηρίοις, 291b1–2). They quickly exchange shapes and capacity for action with each other (ταχὺ δὲ μεταλλάττουσι
τάς τε ἰδέας καὶ τὴν δύναμιν εἰς ἀλλήλους, 291b2–3). Their power resides in the
great number of their affiliates, and in their having a leader, recognized as the
greatest magician (μέγιστον γόητα, 291c3). The leader enhances his power through
the speeches of the chorus. These sophists are the politicians (in the derogatory
sense used by Skemp (1952, 191) to qualify them as being in opposition to the
statesman). For Migliori (2001, 33–34) this definition of the sophists as the politicians of democracy, whose acts are deceptive in order to mask errors and not
driven by any real knowledge, represents the eighth definition of the sophist, provided in the *Statesman* after the seven set out in the *Sophist*. Thus, as observed by
Rowe (1999, XVII), all existing "statesmen" are actually illusionists. Rowe (2005,
219), moreover, has proposed that we interpret these animals as images of specific varieties of existing politicians, described in *Republic* VIII–IX, with lions as
timocrats, centaurs as oligarchs, and chameleons and satyrs as democrats. This
point is very meaningful for my reply, since it may point to the struggle pursued
by Plato against the politicians of democracy, understood by him as sophists.
This explains why Plato needs to set apart his statesman from the sophists: setting him apart from the sophists means setting him apart from the politicians.

The sophists are difficult to catch, because they have the capacity to quickly
change shape, and they are chameleon-like: they seem not to have any single or
well-defined εἶδος. The sophists are in fact versatile: the word πολύτροπος is one
of the epithets of Odysseus (*Od*.I.1,10.330) and Hermes. It denotes someone who
is much-travelled, but also one who has turned many ways. According to Liddell-
Scott, it is in this second sense that Plato understands Odysseus (*Hp.Mi*.364e).
Odysseus's versatility of mind might be profitably compared with that of the
sophists and the rhetoricians, who are very well disposed to quickly changing
their minds to be able to present the crowd with what it wants to hear from them.
It is the merit of Casadesús Bordoy (2013, 23) to have pointed out the connection
between the *Sophist* and the *Statesman* regarding the expression πολυτρόποις θηρίοις. In his work, he investigates the expression's proximity to the Homeric gods,
who possessed the faculty of mutating into varied human forms, and to Odysseus
too, as I have already noted.

So the second reason for the difficulty resides in the nature of the objects of
investigation, the sophists, recognized as a class of different, multi-shaped individuals with no well-defined or stable characteristics. The ἀτοπία produced by
the object "sophist" is strictly connected with his versatility and his apparent absence of a well-defined εἶδος, and thus with the difficulty of grasping it through
the method of division.

This answer is connected to the first one, because Socrates's ατοπία makes him difficult to define, like the sophists, but for very different reasons. Contrary to the sophists, Socrates is odd because he looks for the truth. But Socrates and the sophists both share the doxastic realm that is the object of inquiry, and the different reasons for their oddness do not make their nature easier to capture.

This second answer has the explanatory power of depicting the motivations for the necessity for separating the two in the *Statesman*. The statesman shares with the sophists and Socrates the experimental and doxastic realm of expertise, and thus the battlefield of the δόξαι sets up the place where the division must be established. The greatest magicians have the power to create illusions, and this capacity is strictly connected to the investigation pursued in the *Sophist* into the art of image-making (*Soph.* 268c–d). In this paper I cannot pursue this line of investigation into the notion of μίμησις,[10] but I do refer to a page of the *Sophist* (254 a–b) that is useful for my argument: the sophist and the philosopher are each difficult to catch for opposite reasons, the sophist because he is a fugitive in the darkness of what is not, the philosopher because of the brilliance of the place he inhabits. Thus, the sophists are cheats and masters of illusion because they change shape in the darkness.

So Socrates, the sophists, and the statesman are difficult to separate because, sharing the same doxastic realm of expertise, they seem to possess the same features, but in reality these are only resemblances. They can be confused due to ignorance of their real nature, and to the mimetic power of the sophists.

3.2.1 Resemblances

The epistemic notion of resemblance occurs also in the images about the sophists as animals (lions), satyrs or centaurs that appear in the lines I have already referred to. The hypothesis put forward by El Murr (2014, 221–223) to interpret these lines as a satyric drama, used traditionally as the coda to a tragic trilogy, is noteworthy. For El Murr, this literary strategy may have the role of reinforcing the necessity to divide off the real statesman from all the political functionaries of Athenian institutions of the day. So these lines appear very significant for the understanding of Plato's aim in the *Statesman,* and as a consequence, I argue, the division of statesmanship from sophistry is still an urgent matter for him.

---

10 Cf. Palumbo (2013b; 1994) on this topic, and, specifically, on the connections between sophists and the art of image-making through the notion of falsehood elaborated in the *Sophist*.

The sophists are animal-like. This reference may have to do with the art of physiognomy, and so with the idea that some physical traits reveal moral attitudes,[11] but more explicitly it has to do with the method of διαίρεσις as hunting (defined in this way in the *Sophist*), and to the sophist as a complex beast (*Soph.* 226a). In the *Gorgias* (516b5–7), all Athenians are depicted as animals, and also in the *Theaetetus* (174d6) they appear very dangerous.

The idea of the chorus, i.e., of a plural subject, emphasizing and reinforcing what the great magicians declare during public performances (or drama) in the city, is also meaningful in this context, since in the *Theaetetus* (174d8) it is said that kings and tyrants are accompanied by their beasts. The word δράμα also appears at *Statesman*, 303c8, and precisely in reference to the view of the performance of satyrs and centaurs. So the word χορός (291c1) may refer to comedy or to other public artistic events with dancers and musicians, and thus connect separation from the sophists with separation from the poets and other artists. The chorus is a multitude (ὄχλος, 291a3), a term that in Plato always carries negative connotations, as is made clear by the subsequent definition of it as a mass of people (πλῆθος, 292e1) in the city capable of acquiring expertise in statesmanship. It is noteworthy that at *Theaet.* 173c2 we find a reference to a χορός, but this time to the χορός of the philosophers, the one Socrates belongs to. El Murr (2014) conjectures that the reference to the χορός in the *Statesman* might be an explicit reference to the *Theaetetus*. Following his hypothesis, I would stress that Plato, using the same semantic reference to the χορός, might desire to underline the affinity, but at the same time make explicit how different these two kinds of people are. As I have already claimed, they might appear similar, but only to the ignorant, who do not recognise their real nature. Using the same image, Plato wants to emphasize the strong difference between Socrates and the sophists. A further difference should be recognized between the chorus and the good statesman: for Plato, politics should not be a public performance art, as the image of the chorus implied, and as it was practiced in the democratic state. This kind of politics practiced by the sophists should be banished and their art should be purified – as I shall argue in the next section – and placed at the service of the good statesman.

The resemblance to "lions" may also be connected to *Gorgias* 483e–484a, where Callicles speaks about their "lion-hood", and their natural antagonism to law. If this connection has plausibility, and is understood within the context of

---

11 On the ancient conception of animals' moral attitudes, cf. Ps. Aristot. *Physiogn.* 805b–806a, 808b, 809b–810a.

the φύσις-νόμος debate which characterises sophistry, we could find here a further critical pointer to the need for separation from the sophists. i.e., their antagonism to law.

Coming back to the resemblance to animals, Michel Narcy (1995) claims that it is Plato who needs separation from the animals, not Socrates, and so he maintains that "L'Étranger ne peut donner sa propre définition du politique sans réfuter Socrate" (232).[12] For Plato, indeed, the philosopher has to resemble the divine (*Theaet.* 176b1). "Les hommes, des animaux; la cité, un élevage; ses habitants, du bétail: à une telle philosophie politique, la définition de l'art politique par l'*anthroponomikon* est parfaitement conforme. Il est difficile de nier qu'en rejetant au contraire cette définition, c'est la philosophie politique de Socrate que rejette l'Etranger." (233).

Narcy's thesis is important for my argument, because it ascribes to the relation with Socrates a specific role in the development of the Stranger's philosophy. I thus agree that Plato is struggling here for separation – it is notable that the first separation pursued in the *Statesman* (258b–268d) is the one of living creatures into animals and men, followed by that of men into Barbarians and Greeks – but I cannot find in the *Statesman* the idea of a divine statesman, corresponding to a divine philosopher[13] (at *Sophist* 216b the Stranger has been described as a "refuting god") who should replace Socrates. The reason is that the statesman has to do with the experimental and doxastic realm of expertise, and thus he has to find a way to separate himself from the sophists in their same, shared space of activity. This goal is very difficult, precisely because they partake of this same realm.

Recalling the image of the *Sophist*, I might add that the statesman has to build the realm of the *chiaroscuro*: he does not belong either to the darkness characteristic of the sophists, or to the luminosity of the philosophers. Contrary to most established and standard readings,[14] I therefore agree with Crotty (2009) in recognising that the statesman is not the philosopher-king or the philosopher-ruler of the *Republic*, but a figure that deals with the issues of the realm of *doxa*. The δεύτερος πλοῦς (300c2), the "second sailing", inversely from that of the *Phaedo* (99d1), is from the ideal government to the second best.[15] The second sailing requires strength to row against the current, so the impetus is to struggle for sep-

---

12 The idea of a philosophical trial of Socrates in the trilogy has been put forth by Miller (1980).

13 On needs to be aware, however, that the same divine philosopher needs to undertake a political role in the city and, thus, to deal with doxastic matters. An image to clarify the idea is the very famous one of the *Republic*, where the philosopher comes back to the cave.

14 "[...] the ideal statesman or king of the *Statesman* turns out to be virtually indistinguishable from the philosopher-ruler of the *Republic*" Rowe (1999) XIII.

15 Cf. Dorter (2013).

aration in the very realm of expertise. But within that realm of δόξα, the states-man should establish αληθής δόξα. Finally, not only Socrates and the sophists, but the statesman too is difficult to grasp, since all inhabit the same doxastic realm. In this mirroring of Socrates and the sophists as part of the struggle to sep-arate them, the statesman appears, as we shall soon see, as the person who will be able to control rhetoric (304d), after the purification that makes it true rhetoric, as it is called in the *Gorgias* (504 d3–e3).

4 Plato's solution: separation as κάθαρσις

This last point brings us to my main conclusions: rhetoric, the art employed – with very different aims – by Socrates and the sophists, is very precious, but it must be purified by the Stranger to make it available to the statesman. What is unacceptable for Plato is that the sophists should be the rulers of our present states, and that Socrates might be confused with them. My claim is that the sep-aration from them is a κάθαρσις, as in the definition of noble sophistry in the *Sophist*,[16] with a very definite peculiarity, which is the art of separation. This is Plato's solution to the difficulty of division, i.e. attaining the division in another way through the purification of rhetoric. In purifying rhetoric, Plato also purifies the art that many thought to be the art of Socrates, and in so doing dangerously perceived him as being very similar to the sophists.

Plato possesses a method to attain his goal, and it comes from the *Sophist*. As is rightly emphasised by commentators,[17] the method of separation as διαίρεσις

---

16 For many commentators, the sixth definition of the sophist in the *Sophist* is controversial for many reasons, especially – and this aspect is crucial for my topic – over the question whether Socratic method may or may not be detectable in it. For my interpretation of the epistemic role of purification in Socratic method, cf. Candiotto (2018) 576–583, and for a discussion of the issues presented by these lines cf. Rowe (2015a).

17 For Lane (1998) 14, the method of διαίρεσις in the *Statesman* is a method of "example and division", not of "collection and division". The use of examples in this dialogue is prominent, and I think that a good and simple reason for this derives from the context with which Plato is dealing, i.e. the realm of expertise and rival arts. El Murr (2015) has recently underlined that "division" and "use of models" are two different methods used in the *Statesman*, and he under-stands the second as the systematic comparison that is made between model (παράδειγμα) and things, and emphasizes its epistemological role in the recollection of forms. This remark is very important for the understanding of the ontological and epistemological goal of our dialogue, and links it to the investigations pursued in the *Sophist*. The common recognition of the epistemic connection between the *Sophist* and the *Statesman* is denied by Dorter (2013), who claims that

has been consistently employed in the *Statesman*, too. However, the kind of separation employed here is not διαίρεσις, but something more similar to that of the sixth definition of the sophist (*Soph.* 230b4–e5), since it is a κάθαρσις as cleansing (the purifiers are called καθαίροντες, those that make the soul clean, *Soph.* 230c4–5) and they seem to me to be in a situation similar to that of those who 'refine' (καθαίρουσι) gold (*Statesman*, 303 d6–7; tr. Rowe).

Plato's solution to the difficulty resides in that cathartic function of separation which makes it possible that something precious shine forth from what we need to set apart. So this method is different from that of διαίρεσις, because it does not require splitting the two genera into two unrelated extremes. On the contrary, it derives a benefit, as does purified gold, from a separation that does need to be made. This kind of separation recognises that what we should set apart possesses a value that should be maintained throughout the process of purification. Thus, harking back to the example of the craftsman separating gold from the other elements, the art of rhetoric must be purified and made available for the statesman (303d4–e2).[18] In the same way, Socrates should be purified by the apologetic construction of his character by Plato, as in the first Socratic dialogues. This last claim is not explicit in the *Statesman*, but I deduce it by recognising the puzzling presence of Socrates within the dialogue – at many levels, as a character, and, thematically, from the various resemblances with the sophists, and by framing it within a general understanding of the aims of Plato's writing.

Thus, in the *Statesman*, "separation" is not only "separation of" but also "separation from", and it is precisely this subtle difference, in my opinion,

---

the διαίρεσις used in the *Sophist* is unique, and not be found in other dialogues. For Dorter (2013) 98, in fact, there emerges in the *Statesman* an awareness that division by words is not sufficient to give us reasons why the topics in question are under inquiry, since these need always to be contextualized (most notably, justice, *Statesman*, 294b). For Crotty (2009) 180, what is investigated in the *Statesman* is the realm of δόξαι, and not that of the ontological digression of the *Sophist* or of the Καλλίπολις of the *Republic*. The interpretation provided by El Murr (2015), however, is not as extreme as those of Dorter or Crotty. For Lane, who follows Skemp (1951) and Migliori (1996) on this point, with whom I agree, the recognition of δόξα as the realm of inquiry does not mean that the Ideas/Forms are not at work, or that catching the εἶδος is not the goal. The examples, in fact, are παραδείγματα, and should be understood as exemplars (Lane, 1988, 87) or, as underlined by El Murr (2015), as that what permits us to recollect the forms in experience.

18 It is notable that in the *Statesman*, differently from the *Sophist*, Plato did not use the more usual medical image for κάθαρσις, but the one that derives from craftsmanship. Nevertheless, the aim of healing the city is the same, and it is detectable also in the lines in which the Eleatic Stranger questions the correctness of the applicability of laws through a comparison with medical expertise. Cf. *Pol.* 259 ff.

wherein its cathartic character resides. This means that the separation is not saturated, and it is the alchemical surplus which is most precious. In the act of separation something remains and, after the purification, it becomes unalloyed gold for the statesman. What remains is rhetoric at the service of statesmanship, and Socrates at the service of Plato, as I will explain in my third reply to the question in the next section. El Murr (2014, 215–217) stresses how this process does not exclude rhetoric from statesmanship, but allows it to attain its purified and extraordinary role in the persuasion of citizens. In purification, something takes pure form out of another thing that contains it. In the example, and then in the parallel explanation of statesmanship, what is crucial is that the separation attains something "alone by itself" (303e4–5). After the cathartic separation, rhetoric becomes subservient to the statesmanship which persuades the populace through the telling of stories, rather than through teaching (304c10–d2).

Once purification is achieved, the separation from the sophists comes very quickly, since rhetoric is just an instrument in the hands of the statesman. Thus, after having said many times that separation is quite difficult, the statesman now says, "this matter of rhetoric seems to have been separated quickly from statesmanship, as a distinct class, but subordinate to it" (304d11–e1).

5 The third reason: the relevance of rhetoric in Plato's writing

Having recognised that for Plato too the separation between philosopher, sophist and statesman would have been an issue because of the puzzling presence of Socrates, I have provided two reasons for this difficulty, which deal with the inability to clearly define objects such as Socrates and the sophists, who exercise their power within the realm of δόξα. At the same time, I brought up the political urgency of solving the difficulty, which led me to understand Plato's solution as the purification of rhetoric as being something at the service of the statesman. Purifying rhetoric, Plato purifies the image of Socrates too, and thus makes clear – once again – his difference from the sophists.

This political urgency impels me to point out that this conclusion may have been very desirable for Plato himself. In fact, not only does the statesman have to use rhetoric (not personally, but by having rhetoricians at his disposal), but Plato, the philosopher, must also use it to guide his audience to philosophy. Arguably, the purification of the image of Socrates (built up in other dialogues as his apology) should be understood not simply as the heroic act of a devoted disciple, but also as the struggle against sophistry pursued by Plato in order to establish his own philosophy as the new leading science, and as the best method for the training of well-born young for politics. In fact, thanks to the separation, Plato would be able to establish a reliable model of the statesman, too.

If this conjecture be deemed to have force, I would therefore derive from it a third reason for the difficulty of the separation. Separation from the sophists is difficult precisely because Plato needs to achieve it within the framework of a literary device – the dialogue – which, strategically, makes use of a number of rhetorical tools, and presents Socrates, who, even while being radically different from them, manifests a number of traits he shares with the sophists, as the model of the philosopher. And it is precisely this intrinsic difficulty that might have motivated Plato to strive for a solution. In so doing he discovered a method of pursuing separation that led to a very profitable result, i.e., the cathartic surplus of that separation as a purified rhetoric and a purified image of Socrates. Starting from this accomplishment, Plato would have been free to use, I would say "without difficulty", the image of Socrates in conjunction with rhetoric in his dialogues.

Part VI: **Wisdom and Law**

Miriam Peixoto

On the Limits of Law and the Sovereignty of the Wise. Conjectures about the Primacy of Law in Plato's *Statesman*

At *Statesman* 293e6–7, the younger Socrates acknowledges as reasonable (*metriōs*) the Stranger's arguments for the thesis that the art of ruling is a science (*epistēmē*). Yet he hesitates to accept some of its consequences. Bewildered, he says "that government should be carried on without laws is a hard saying" (τὸ δὲ καὶ ἄνευ νόμων δεῖν ἄρχειν χαλεπώτερον ἀκούειν ἐρρήθη). The young interlocutor's hesitation provides the Stranger with the occasion to advance further his inquiry about what it is to be a good ruler, now under a new perspective. He introduces the *phronimos*, the wise ruler, and his supremacy over laws. Such a ruler, who holds the "science of kingship" (292e9–10: *basilikē epistēmē*), is a "man who is wise and of kingly nature" (294a8: ἄνδρα τὸν μετὰ φρονήσεως βασιλικόν). The object of the Stranger's investigation is whether the wise ruler can be above the law or whether he cannot prescind from it. He intends to show that it is possible to have a proper government even without having laws (294a3–4: περὶ τῆς τῶν ἄνευ νόμων ἀρχόντων ὀρθότητος).

The question that perplexed the younger Socrates continues even to this day to puzzle the readers of Plato's *Statesman*. Can the wise man rule without laws? The unusual character of this portion of the dialogue seems to have as its background a debate that, during the 5th century BC, had Democritus and Antiphon as its main antagonists. Epiphanius says that, for Democritus, "the laws are a wicked contrivance", and that "the wise man should not obey the laws, but live as a free man."[1] Antiphon, in his turn, in a fragment of his *On Truth*, establishes

---

1 Epiphanius, *Adversus Haereses* III 2, 9 (DK 68 A 166): ἐπίνοιαν γὰρ κακὴν τοὺς νόμους ἔλεγε καὶ 'οὐ χρὴ νόμοις πειθαρχεῖν τὸν σοφόν, ἀλλὰ ἐλευθερίως ζῆν' (trans. from C. Taylor, 1999). At first, the ideas expressed in this passage seem not to agree with the valuation that law and justice receive in the extant fragments of Democritus. This raises doubts about their pertinence, and the purpose of Epiphanius in transmitting them. Doubts such as these may be the reason why H. Diels considered this allusion to Democritus as a testimony rather than a fragment. In another work (Peixoto, 2009, 175–190) I have examined this problem within the scope of the testimonies and fragments attributed to Democritus by Diels. My interest was to evaluate whether such judgment about the just and the unjust, about laws, and about the attitude of the wise towards the laws could be found in other fragments, and whether they were compatible with the ones that deal with this subject.

https://doi.org/10.1515/9783110605549-016

the difference between what operates according to nature and what operates according to convention, by opposing *physis* and *nomos*. He considers that "many of the things that are just according to law are in conflict with nature."[2] Both Democritus and Antiphon share an interest in the theme, but their views regarding the nature of laws and the attitude of men towards them are antagonistic. While Democritus recommends to the wise independence from laws, and, to men in general, their strict observance, Antiphon establishes the primacy of nature, suggesting that it should have priority whenever possible (e.g., in private life), and that laws should be observed only when in public. It seems that this problem was a commonplace in classical antiquity.[3] We find echoes of this debate in at least four of Plato's dialogues: the *Crito*, the *Gorgias*, the *Republic*, and the *Statesman*, which is the theme of this paper. It is interesting to note that both Democritus and Plato seem to have in mind distinct dispositions of men, according to which one may or may not qualify for wisdom. Consequently, each disposition determines a different attitude towards the laws.

In what follows, I should like to examine some of the questions underlying this thesis as exposed in Plato's *Statesman*, in order to evaluate his position and its singularity within the debate around the observance of laws. I intend to show, taking some specific passages of the dialogue into account, how the primacy of wisdom over laws is established. I shall focus on the following aspects of the problem: (I) the *basilikē epistēmē* as a requirement for good ruling; (II) the necessity and the limits of laws; (III) force versus persuasion as the means for the exercise of power; and (IV) a final word about men, the wise and the laws.

1

At 293c5–d2, the Stranger appeals the Platonic *topos* of the distinction between being and seeming to establish in what way the true ruler distinguishes himself from those that only claim to be so, but in fact are not:

---

2 *Pap. Oxyrh.* XI n. 1364, col. 2 (DK 87 B 44 A): ἁ πολλὰ τῶν κατὰ νόμον δικαίων πολεμίως τῆι φύσει κεῖται· According to Antiphon, a man must act in the way that is most convenient to himself. He should follow the laws in public, but act according to nature when by himself.

3 Beside texts or text fragments like those of Democritus and Antiphon, along with above-mentioned Platonic dialogues, the text of Anonymous Iamblichus deserves attention too. Some passages of this text could well be taken as established positions in the debate.

It is, then, a necessary consequence that among forms of government that one is preeminently right, and is the only real government, in which the rulers are found to be truly possessed of science, not merely to seem to possess it.

There is a contrast here, marked by the difference between being and seeming, a distinction that is fundamental not only to the dialogue as a whole, but for all Plato's philosophy. On the one hand, there are "the rulers [who] are found to be truly possessed of science" (τοὺς ἄρχοντας ἀληθῶς), and on the other, there are those who only seem to possess it (τοὺς ἄρχοντας δοκοῦντας μόνον.). In other words, many of those who desire to be politicians and to possess the science that will qualify them to be so, are far away from actually possessing such a science, no matter how much they try to convince others of their proficiency in it by means of persuasion.[4] Throughout the dialogue, the opposition between being and seeming is employed as a mean of discriminating and specifying the definition of the true ruler.[5] What is at stake in the dynamics of the dialogue is the cutting and polishing of its object of inquiry, that is, the political man, aiming at bringing forth the image of the righteous ruler. Insufficient forms of government are gradually left behind as mere misleading appearances. It is interesting to notice at this point the recourse to analogies with medicine and gymnastics, which also takes place in the *Republic*.[6] At *Statesman* 293a9–c3, the Stranger compares the art of the politician with that of the physician:

And physicians offer a particularly good example of this point of view. Whether they cure us against our will or with our will, by cutting us or burning us or causing us pain in any other way, and whether they do it by written rules or without them, and whether they are rich or poor, we call them physicians just the same, so long as they exercise authority by art or science, purging us or reducing us in some other way, or even adding to our weight, provided only that they who treat patients treat them for the benefit of their health, and preserve them by making them better than they were. In this way and no other, in my opinion, shall we determine this to be the only right definition of the rule of the physician or of any other rule whatsoever.

It is worth noting that in Plato's epoch there was a great effort made within the field of medicine to define the boundaries of what would constitute true medicine. Such an effort is testified in the treatise *On Ancient Medicine*, whose

---

4 292 d: οἳ προσποιοῦνται μὲν εἶναι πολιτικοὶ καὶ πείθουσι πολλούς, εἰσὶ δὲ οὐδαμῶς.

5 This distinction can be found at 300d9–e2, where the Stranger speaks of those who try to imitate what is true, but not being competent to do that, imitate it badly, and at 301c1, where he hints at those who pretend to have the science of kingship.

6 As, for instance, in book III, when dealing with the education of the guardians.

author applies himself to the purging of his art from aspects that he considers extraneous:

> Some practitioners are poor, others very excellent; this would not be the case if an art of medicine did not exist at all, and had not been the subject of any research and discovery, but all would be equally inexperienced and unlearned therein, and the treatment of the sick would be in all respects haphazard. But it is not so; just as in all other arts the workers vary much in skill and in knowledge, so also is it in the case of medicine.[7]

How can we understand the picture offered by the Stranger? How does his picture of *iatrikē technē* fit into the economy of his speech? He seems to suggest that, in the exercise of government, as in the exercise of medicine, the acts of the ruler must not be dictated by the inclinations of his will, but they must stick to the rules that regulate the life of men, no matter their social condition. Those who proceed thus should rule the city and purge (*kathairein*) it. This aligns the politician with the physician, who must have the ability to temper and to save. The exercise of government demands from whoever intends to rule a certain science or *savoir-faire*, without which he would be incapable of acting as the physician of the city.[8]

In both politics and medicine, there is a search for an element capable of establishing the difference between the possession of a science and the possession of an art, and the way they influence the practice of each. What in fact matters here is to identify what distinguishes two types of ruler, those whose authority is determined by the possession of an art or science, and those who do not possess them or only seem to possess them. In the *Statesman*, that which qualifies a certain government to receive the label of a righteous government is primarily the acquisition of a certain science, the "most difficult" and yet "the most important one" (292 d4: σχεδὸν τῆς χαλεπωτάτης καὶ μεγίστης κτήσασθαι).

The true ruler must possess such a science, namely the "kingly science" (292e9–10: βασιλικὴ ἐπιστήμη), as part of his nature. It is the same with the nature of the true philosopher, and few are those who can attain this condition. The Stranger insists on this point on many occasions. His doubts about the very possibility of accessing this condition can be seen at 292e1–2: "Does it seem at all possible that a multitude in a state could acquire this science?" He provides answers to this question at different moments. Take, for instance, the analogy between the possession of political science and expertise in the game of *petteia*. The Stranger insists on the difficulty of finding among men those who possess

---

7 *On Ancient Medicine*, I, L. 571.
8 This picture of the politician recalls a recurring *topos* in antiquity, to which Nietzsche called attention much later: that of the philosopher as the physician of civilization.

this science, just as it happens with finding experts in the game of *petteia*:[9] "in a state of one thousand men could perhaps a hundred or as many as fifty acquire it adequately?" (292e7–8).

The dialogue advances further in its distinction among human types. From the simple distinction between those who possess and those who do not possess the science of kingship, by increasing the complexity of his analysis, the Stranger now distinguishes between different types of ruler. At a first level, there is the opposition between the majority of political men (*politikoi*), and those who are wise (*phronimos basileus*) (262d6). Then, as I have already mentioned, there is the opposition between those who actually possess the science of kingship and those

---

9 Plato employs the example of the game of *petteia* in many different contexts in his dialogues. At *Republic* 333 b, the image of the player of *petteia*, the *petteutikos*, is used to establish the difference between those who know how to dispose the pebbles over the game board, and those who can actually play the game. The image appears again in book VI (487c2), when they discuss the type of man to whom the city should be entrusted. When the natural attributes that such a man must possess are exalted — "good memory, quick apprehension, magnificent, gracious, friendly and akin to truth, justice, bravery and sobriety" (487a3–5) — Adeimantus compares the comings and goings of the elenctic movement with the game of *petteia*: "and that just as by expert draughts (*petteia*)-players the unskilled are finally shut in and cannot make a move, so they are finally blocked and have their mouths stopped by this other game of draughts played not with counters but with words" (487b7–c3). There are other allusions to the game in *Phaedrus* (274d1) and in *Laws* (820c7). These demonstrate how much this game must have appealed to Plato as a means to thinking about both government strategies and the labyrinth of speech or elenchus. In this game of strategy, one player cannot take another player's pebbles unless he also risks losing his own. As in our modern game of checkers, the goal is to become the lord of one's own domain, and no longer suffer the attacks of one's opponents. J. Darriulat (2013), in an article named "Platon et le jeu dialectique", discuss the various uses of this game in analogies by Plato: "C'est ainsi qu'on apprend, dans le *Premier Alcibiade* (110e), qu'il est tout aussi délicat de définir la justice que d'apprendre à jouer à la *petteia* ; dans le *Charmide* (174a–b), que Socrate associe (il est vrai pour les dissocier aussitôt) la science qui serait capable de nous donner le bonheur (*poiei eudaimona*) à celle qui nous rendrait habile dans l'art de calculer (*logistikon*) comme dans celui de jouer à la petteia (*petteutikon*) ; dans le *Gorgias* (450d), que parmi les sciences qui progressent dialogiquement (*dia logou*), on trouve, pêle-mêle, avec la rhétorique, l'arithmétique et le calcul, la géométrie et le jeu de *petteia* (*petteutikê*) ; dans la *République* (I, 133a–b), qu'on peut comparer, à l'homme de loi capable de déterminer les justes conventions, le joueur de *petteia* ; dans la *République* encore (II, 374c–d), que l'excellence au jeu de la *petteia* – si difficile qu'il faut, pour bien jouer, s'y adonner dès l'enfance – démontre par l'exemple qu'il n'y a pas d'expertise sans spécialisation ; dans *Le Politique* (299d–e), qu'il ne faut pas s'en tenir craintivement à la lettre des lois mais qu'il faut oser en réécrire le texte selon le contexte, à l'image du bon joueur de *petteia* qui toujours invente de nouvelles parties ; dans les *Lois* (VII, 820c–d), qu'il n'y a pas grande différence entre le calcul des incommensurables et l'art de bien jouer à la *petteia*."

that merely seem to possess it (293c7). In addition, judging by what the younger Socrates says at 292e10–293a1, it is even possible that there are those who possess the science, but do not possess the power that would allow them to put it into practice. This last distinction is of capital importance for the understanding of the thesis that I intend to examine here.

The search for the science of kingship is already present at the beginning of the dialogue, when the Stranger asks the younger Socrates if the political man (258b3: πολιτικὸν τὸν ἄνδρα) would be among the men of science: "should we rank him also among those who have a science, or not?" (258b3–4: καί μοι λέγε πότερον τῶν ἐπιστημόνων τιν' ἡμῖν καὶ τοῦτον θετέον, ἢ πῶς;).

Given the young man's affirmative answer, the Stranger then proceeds with his inquiry about this science, introducing some of its salient aspects. It should be a cognitive science (259d6–7: τὴν γνωστικὴν), more familiar (259d1: οἰκειότερον) to the ruler than the manual and practical ones (259c10–d1: τῆς δὴ γνωστικῆς μᾶλλον ἢ τῆς χειροτεχνικῆς καὶ ὅλως πρακτικῆς βούλει τὸν βασιλέα). Moreover, it would be the only science to include the whole set of knowledge-skills and functions related to the administration of the city (259c1–2: ἐπιστήμη μία περὶ πάντ' ἐστὶ ταῦτα). By the end of the *diairesis* of this cognitive science, there is a match between the art of kingship and the art of politics. Yet an uncertainty remains. At 292e10–293a1, the younger Socrates says that it is possible for someone to have the science of kingship (ἡ βασιλικὴ ἐπιστήμη) without effectively exercising power, just as it is possible that there be rulers who do not possess that science at all, or, at most, merely imitate those who have it.

The acknowledgment that there are rulers who do not possess this art or science imposes an investigation into "the right kind of rule" (293a3: τὴν μὲν ὀρθὴν ἀρχὴν). At 293c5–d2, the Stranger says that neither the laws, nor the voluntary acceptance of a government by its subjects, nor their economic condition must be taken into account when evaluating the rectitude of a given government; it is the possession of political science by those who rule that is determinant. It is the possession of this science – superior to all forms of law and ordinances – that causes the law to occupy a secondary role in the actions of a wise ruler.

2

If a form of government is to be right and true, it is necessary that those who rule actually possess political science, and not only appear to do so or imitate those who do. If this requirement is satisfied, says the Stranger, it is even possible to do without laws. But why this insistence on mitigating the necessity of laws in his evaluation of what constitutes a right government and a true ruler? Even though nomothetics, the science of producing laws, is part of the curriculum of the science of kingship (ἡ βασιλική), the Stranger considers that it would be the best thing (τὸ ἄριστον) if the foundation of good government was in the wisdom of the wise (ἄνδρα τὸν μετὰ φρονήσεως βασιλικόν), rather than in the strength of laws (294a7–8: οὐ τοὺς νόμους ἐστὶν ἰσχύειν). This is a consequence of the evaluation he makes of the range and limits of laws. Among the factors that hold in check the strength of laws a first set can be found in these lines:

> … for the differences of men and of actions and the fact that nothing, I may say, in human life is ever at rest, forbid any science whatsoever to promulgate any simple rule for everything and for all time (294b2–6).

The dissimilarities (ἀνομοιότητες) perceived between men and their actions, and the unstable character of the universe of human things (τὰ ἀνθρωπίνη) present real obstacles to the establishment of an absolute and universal law. Moreover, their rigid character and the fact that they are disposed as written words make laws even more suspicious regarding their ability to stand up to every type of situation that occurs in space and in time. This temporal aspect appears again in the question that the Stranger asks the younger Socrates: "For how could anyone, Socrates, sit beside each person all his life and tell him exactly what is proper for him to do?"[10] What is behind this question is a concern over the possibility of establishing rules of conduct that would be, at one and the same time, precise and also good for the duration of a life.

The Stranger also calls attention to the relationship between what is simple and what is never simple: "So that which is persistently simple is inapplicable to things which are never simple?" (294c7–8). In other words, how can laws, which are meant to reduce something diverse and varied to a minimal common denominator, be capable of regulating a diversity that is resistant to simplification?

In the *Statesman*, as well as in the *Crito*, the laws are also personified, though in a different sense. In the *Crito*, the personified laws engage in dialogue with Socrates, by remembering how he owed to them his own life, from birth to his further development in the city. The laws must be preserved because they are an institution necessary for the safeguarding of the order of the polis, even if their

---

10 πῶς γὰρ ἄν τις ἱκανὸς γένοιτ' ἄν ποτε, ὦ Σώκρατες, ὥστε διὰ βίου ἀεὶ παρακαθήμενος ἑκάστῳ δι' ἀκριβείας προστάττειν τὸ προσῆκον; (295 a9–b3).

content may sometimes leave room for objection.[11] The *Statesman,* however, presents the law as a stubborn and ignorant man:

> ...like a stubborn and ignorant (αὐθάδη καὶ ἀμαθῆ) man who allows no one to do anything contrary to his command, or even to ask a question, not even if something new occurs to some one, which is better than the rule he has himself ordained (294c1–4).

The law is inflexible, unquestionable, and incapable of being updated to include anything new or better that might show up, remaining locked in a sort of solipsism that blocks her off from the very reality that brought her forth. How, then, can something that "is not the most perfectly right" (294d1: οὐκ ὀρθότατον) possibly *become* the "most perfectly right" in a city? Why is it necessary to establish laws at all?

To clarify this issue, the Stranger proposes an analogy with the work of professional trainers of athletes (294d7–e6). Plato uses this example to denounce the limits of democracy, and the idea of a regulatory principle based on the will of the majority and for the satisfaction of the majority. Given the impossibility of dedicating enough time to give proper attention to the needs of each individual athlete, professional trainers opt for a generic training conceived for the benefit of the majority. The same happens with the legislator, who, in the words of the Stranger, "will never be able by making laws for all collectively, to provide exactly that which is proper for each individual" (295a4–7). Hence, the only thing that remains to him is to establish laws for the majority, generic laws, written or not, which prioritize his legislation over the customs of a given locality.[12]

3

The Stranger introduces another aspect of laws that seems important in his inquiry by means of an analogy with medicine. There is a sort of flexibility needed to obtain the best results both when curing diseases and legislating. The problem

---

11 In the *Crito,* the laws engage in dialogue with Socrates, in order to show his friend what Socrates had tried to convince him about. By means of this dramatic resource, Socrates will present Crito with reasons to support the supremacy of the law, and therefore to justify their obedience to it.
12 For S. Berges, "if the Stranger is not defending the view that the perfect king should govern without laws, then laws may be insufficient as far as justice is concerned, but they are not dispensable." (2010, 5–23). If laws are not a requirement for the ruler himself, they subsist as one for his subjects at least.

has to do with the adequacy of laws and the necessity of reforming them based on different contexts and situations, or even with the maintenance of written laws and the establishment of new ones. For M. Lane,[13] the state in which the laws remain immutable imitates the government of the true king, in which the laws remain unchanged during the absence of the king. Such a state must be ready, upon the return of the king, to accept the modifications he will make in order to improve the existent laws.[14] This presupposes that a government can actually be improved. The Stranger asks himself about the way the legislator should work in such cases, whether he should use force or persuasion. He seems to consider it plausible that he who knows better laws than the current ones should act as a legislator for the city, although not before he has persuaded all citizens about the virtues of the laws he intends to propose (296a7–9).

This same defense of persuasion as opposed to the use of force we find in the fragments of Democritus. In fact, he makes the efficacy and virtue of laws depend on their ability to persuade. He also makes the effective benefit of laws towards men depend on their adhesion to them and their disposition for letting themselves be persuaded by them. In the following fragment, we can see in what terms Democritus establishes this relationship between persuasion and laws:

> One will seem to promote virtue better by using encouragement and persuasion of speech than by law and necessity. For it is likely that he who is held back from wrongdoing by law will err in secret, but that he who is urged to what he should by persuasion will do nothing wrong either in secret or openly. Therefore, he who acts rightly from understanding and knowledge proves to be at the same time courageous and right-minded (DK68B181).

The opposition between persuasion and force is a good framework for thinking about the reasons that make someone adhere to a certain type of behavior and avoid others. This has to do with a sort of inner law that translates itself into conviction, and makes the one who possesses it less prone to be caught transgressing the law. Democritus' position in this fragment marks his clear opposition to the kind of justification that we find in Antiphon. To act publicly or privately are decisive factors in the evaluation of the effects of laws in the regulation of human actions. It is about evaluating what the circumstances are in

---

13 Lane (1998).

14 For Lane, "so long as laws are conceived as memoranda rather than as rigid, they serve the useful function of aggregation and approximation while at the same time protecting the possibility of correction by expertise when needed. Laws have a place within the ideal so long as they are properly understood. If names must be understood as tools rather than as evidence, laws too must be understood as tools rather than as the dead and inalterable hand – the mortmain – of the past." (1998) 155.

which they can be most effective. And this is not when they are imposed, for without a proper comprehension of the reasons why such laws must be enforced, there is no proper adhesion to them. What reveals itself as effective for convincing people which actions are just and which unjust is a clear comprehension of their distinct nature. Moreover, conscious adhesion to just actions is itself a determining factor for the assessment of a man's character or his excellence. It reveals his character.

In the *Statesman*, however, we have a slightly different perspective. The use of force seems to justify itself when it comes from someone who possess the right art (296b5–6 : ἔχων δὲ ὀρθῶς τὴν τέχνην):

> Suppose a physician who has right knowledge of his profession does not persuade, but forces, his patient, whether man, woman, or child, to do the better thing, though it be contrary to the written precepts, what will such violence be called? The last name in the world to call it would be "unscientific and baneful error," as the phrase is, would it not? And the patient so forced might rightly say anything else rather than that he had been treated in a baneful or unscientific way by the physicians who used force upon him (296b5–c2).

So if someone who proceeds with art passes recommendations that lead another to perform better actions, albeit contrary to the written laws, such actions should not be deemed harmful. The image of the captain (κυβερνήτης) serves to illustrate this point. The captain always bears in mind what is useful (συμφέρον) to the ship and its crew, and what can keep them safe. However, he does not write rules (οὐ γράμματα τιθείς); he replaces rules with his own art (296e4–297a5: ἀλλὰ τὴν τέχνην νόμον παρεχόμενος). In the question that follows, I see a tentative justification for the attitude of the wise: "so may not a right government be established in the same way by men who could rule by this principle, making science more powerful than the laws?" The strength of the art itself intervenes in this way to secure the right form of government, one that will be superior to the laws precisely because it is founded upon political science (297a1–5).

The possession of such science provides the person who possesses it the requirements that qualify him to rule, even in the absence of laws, or despite them. However, this depends effectively on the current form of government. In other words, a city's political regime may concur with or compete against the wise in the administration of the city, aiding or spoiling the efficacy of his role. Hence, it is not a matter of rejecting or denying the laws, but of the necessity that they be put under the custody of the *phronimos*, and so remain open to change for the better. For the Stranger, it is impossible for the multitude to be able to administrate a city with intelligence (297b8: μετὰ νοῦ) simply by acquiring political science. There seems to be a gap between the possession of this science and the effective exercise of political power. This gap determines that one seek that which is the only form of government that can be properly considered the right government. At the same time, one must keep in mind the remaining forms of government, which are mere imitations of the only rightful one (297b7–c4). These imitations will make use of written laws that are based on the laws of what would be the best form of government.

4

As we have seen so far, the possession of political science is the essential requirement for the political man. When the Stranger claims that few are those who effectively qualify for the possession of such science, he establishes a dichotomy within the city between two (or three, which would make a trichotomy) classes of men. While a small minority fulfills the necessary requirements for the acquisition of political art or science, this science remains inaccessible for the majority of men. These are, therefore, the first two classes of men: the politically wise, and the unwise. If, for the former, law presents itself as an accessory or even as something disposable, for the latter it imposes itself as a necessity.

We can take these dispositions as two ways of considering the character of laws. It is curious that Plato chooses the Stranger of Elea to carry on this discussion. It occurs to me that the distinction between those two types of conduct regarding the laws – that of the politically wise man, and that of the majority of men, who lack political science – could be an expression of the ways of *aletheia* and of *doxa* from Parmenides' poem, transposed to the realm of political thought. If the first is the way that is actually true, and the one that any man that aspires to be a good ruler should take, it is nonetheless an extraordinary way, which remains outside the paths of mortal men. The second way – that of opinion – is the one in which the majority of men wander, those who do not distinguish between being and seeming. By placing an Eleatic in the role of the charioteer of the dialogue, as he had done in the *Sophist*, Plato could perhaps be indicating a key to understanding what would constitute a true city, one rightly ruled by someone who possesses true political science, and who might even dispense with laws. For all we know, this remains a city at the level of the ideal, given the difficulty of finding men that would satisfy the requirements for being a right ruler. The realizable city, on the other hand, given the lack of *phronimoi*, would have to resort to laws, and to be subject to them as the only possible means of keeping itself in order and subsisting.

At 297e5, the Stranger alludes to a second-best form of city, one in which it is expected that no one will rise up against the laws. In this city, an order prevails that is most beautiful and right, insofar as it is a second-best. In it, no one can oppose the laws, for those who dare to oppose them "shall be punished by death and the most extreme penalties".[15]

This type of opposition between wise and unwise, between right governments and imitations of right governments, may also be seen in the *Laws*:

> Yet if ever there should arise a man competent by nature and by a birthright of divine grace to assume such an office, he *would have no need of rulers over him; for no law or ordinance is mightier than Knowledge,* nor is it right for Reason to be subject or in thrall to anything, but to be lord of all things, if it is really true to its name and *free in its inner nature.* But at present such a nature exists nowhere at all, except in small degree; wherefore *we must choose what is second best, namely, ordinance and law, which see and discern the general principle, but are unable to see every instance in detail.*[16]

Two classes of man; two forms of government; two ways for the exercise of politics. One is perfect, true, and best in itself, in which the wise man is free to act in conformity with what his own science teaches him is the best. The other, doomed to relative imperfection, is the one that most closely resembles the first, its laws inspired by the laws of the first, even though never attaining them. This is why it must always depend on the observance of the laws to secure good order. Two ways, distinct from each other by the presence or absence of a natural ability: following the first way, those who do not depend on laws for good acting and good ruling; following the other, those who depend on the laws and must obey them.[17] These lack the science that could provide them with *phronesis*, the

---

15 τολμῶντα δὲ θανάτῳ ζημιοῦσθαι καὶ πᾶσι τοῖς ἐσχάτοις (297e1–3). Democritus has a similar opinion. Cf. fragment DK68B259: "As it has been written concerning hostile beasts and reptiles, so it seems to me one should do in the case of men. According to the ancestral laws one may kill an enemy in every form of community, provided that the law does not prohibit it; prohibitions are made by the religious enactments of each state, by treaties, and by oaths." (Ὅκωσπερ περὶ κιναδέων τε καὶ ἑρπετέων γεγράφαται τῶν πολεμίων, οὕτω καὶ κατὰ ἀνθρώπων δοκεῖ μοι χρεὼν εἶναι ποιεῖν· κατὰ νόμους τοὺς πατρίους κτείνειν πολέμιον ἐν παντὶ κόσμωι, ἐν ὧι μὴ νόμος ἀπείργει·)

16 ἐπεὶ ταῦτα εἴ ποτέ τις ἀνθρώπων φύσει ἱκανὸς θείᾳ μοίρᾳ γεννηθεὶς παραλαβεῖν δυνατὸς εἴη, νόμων οὐδὲν ἂν δέοιτο τῶν ἀρξόντων ἑαυτοῦ· ἐπιστήμης γὰρ οὔτε νόμος οὔτε τάξις οὐδεμία κρείττων, οὐδὲ θέμις ἐστὶν νοῦν οὐδενὸς ὑπήκοον οὐδὲ δοῦλον ἀλλὰ πάντων ἄρχοντα εἶναι, ἐάνπερ ἀληθινὸς ἐλεύθερός τε ὄντως ᾖ κατὰ φύσιν. νῦν δὲ οὐ γάρ ἐστιν οὐδαμοῦ οὐδαμῶς, ἀλλ᾽ ἢ κατὰ βραχύ· διὸ δὴ τὸ δεύτερον αἱρετέον, τάξιν τε καὶ νόμον, ἃ δὴ τὸ μὲν ὡς ἐπὶ τὸ πολὺ ὁρᾷ καὶ βλέπει (*Laws* IX, 875 c3–d5; the italics are mine).

17 For S. Berges (2010) 9, we are confronted with "two classes and apparently contradictory claims about laws". On the one hand, the Stranger says "that a true king will not rely on

indispensable virtue that would allow them to distinguish between being and seeming, between what is just and what is unjust, and without which men are incapable of self-regulation.[18] The virtue of *phronesis* would be for the politically wise man the equivalent of the laws of the unwise. Democritus also presents *phronesis* as the source of the abilities that the political man should possess: to calculate well, to deliberate soundly, to speak without error, and to do what one should.[19]

Notwithstanding the clear incapacity of such men, and their imperative need to have laws, political conduct grounded upon science remains a *telos* to be pursued and aspired to, and it continues to be an inspiration for the ever precarious and limited power of laws. For, as it is said in the *Laws*, "no law or ordinance is mightier than Knowledge".

True *basilike episteme* does not act by itself, but its effect is felt upon those sciences which are focused on action, over which it exercises control. The other sciences must obey it, and statesmen as well, since men of action need to be guided by one who posssesses this science. I agree with M. Dixsaut when she says that he who possesses this science is able to command, because he knows "when it is and when it is not appropriate to start and guide those most important enterprises regarding the cities".[20] However, if the wise man is not himself a man of action, he can still inspire the action of politicians, contributing considerably to the good order of the city. His contribution comes particularly from the possession of the *metretike techne*, i.e., of the just measure, which supports the notion of the aforementioned appropriate time. *Metron* and *kairos* are therefore the ingredients that give authority to the true science. This makes it the only one able to provide "self-directedness" (*autepitaktikê*). The presence of *autos* here is the key to understanding the autonomy of the wise man in regard to the laws. Their nature may seem ambiguous; after all, he is, at one and the same time, the

---

laws except as convenient short-hand to avoid having to review each individual case, and as a reminder on occasions when he has to go away" (294a–297b). On the other hand, he admits "that in the absence of a true king, states must do their best to imitate the rule of the true king and that, to do so, they must stick to their written laws, whether they are, and not attempt to change them or write new ones" (297b–300c). She believes that both positions are problematic.

18 As noted by S. Rosen (1995) 175, the majority are not even capable of ruling themselves, which makes it even less probable that they would be capable of ruling a city.

19 *Etym. Orion*.153, 5: DK68B2: Τριτογένεια ἡ Ἀθηνᾶ κατὰ Δημόκριτον φρόνησις νομίζεται. γίνεται δὲ ἐκ τοῦ φρονεῖν τρία ταῦτα· βουλεύεσθαι καλῶς, λέγειν ἀναμαρτήτως καὶ πράττειν ἃ δεῖ. *Schol. Genev*. I 111 Nic. Δ. δὲ ἐτυμολογῶν τὸ ὄνομά [sc. Τριτογένεια] φησιν ὅτι ἀπὸ τῆς φρονήσεως τρία ταῦτα συμβαίνει· τὸ εὖ λογίζεσθαι, τὸ εὖ λέγειν καὶ τὸ πράττειν ἃ δεῖ. *Cf. Schol*. BT ad Θ 39.

20 Dixsaut (1995) 257.

one who is to give directions for the drawing up of laws and to provide a model for the man of action, and also the one who can do without them. And precisely because he is autonomous, he is able to exercise the *téchnê epitaktikê*. According to Dixsaut, "royal science directs (*archein*, 305d2) every activity because it is the principle (*archên*, *ibid.*) of all activity, a principle at the same time theoretical and practical because it determines the aim of the action and the right moment to act."[21] It seems that these are the reasons that led Plato to establish, in the *Statesman*, the supremacy of the wise with regard to the laws, thus justifying their self-sufficiency. After all, he himself is the source of all regulation, the principle of justice underpinning the laws, so as to provide, for those who are deprived of it, an efficient tool to regulate their private and public lives.

So the government of the true statesman would be one of virtue and science (μετ'αρετῆς καὶ ἐπιστήμης), which distributes things fairly in accordance with human and divine laws, that does no harm, and does not kill or mistreat. But such government of a ruler seems to remain a remote possibility, so that: "If one day a king were born as we are describing him, he would indeed be loved and administer happily holding the helm of that one way of government that would be absolutely straight" (301d4–7). Until that happens, no other possibilities exist for the political men but to imitate the wise, and for the others, to obey the laws. As for the wise men, they, in turn, should move forward governed by the "law" that emanates from within, as a result of their own wisdom.

---

21 Dixsaut (1995) 257.

Part VII: **Bonds and Virtues**

Giovanni Giorgini
Divine and Human Bonds: The Essence of the Art of Politics

At *Politicus* 306a ff the Eleatic Stranger concludes his examination of the art of politics by tackling a difficult problem: the emerging conclusion against the unity of virtue. This was a pillar of Socrates' doctrine – all virtues are one, or united, *qua* virtues. The conversation and dichotomies in this work, on the other hand, have led to the conclusion that certain virtues are opposed to others. Courage (*andreia*) and moderation (*sophrosyne*), for instance, cannot be present at the same time in the same person. This leads to the statement that the art of politics will consist in the ability to 'weave' together these two virtues in order to have excellent citizens.

In this essay, I shall examine this surprising conclusion against Socratic orthodoxy. More specifically, I intend to investigate whether this was a belief Plato reached at the end of his intellectual trajectory. I also intend to examine the notion of "divine and human bonds", the tools of political art, to show that the idea that their combination enables the statesman to have the best possible citizens was already present in the *Republic* and will reappear in the *Laws*. Finally, I should like to emphasize the connection between the vision of political science as the art of weaving and the notion of just measure.

The place of the *Politicus* among Plato's dialogues

In 1866 John Stuart Mill reviewed for the *Edinburgh Review* the three volumes of the monumental work of his friend and fellow radical philosopher George Grote – *Plato and the Other Companions of Sokrates* (1865). Just before the longest quotation of Grote's work, Mill described what characterizes the *Politicus* as compared to the *Republic*, namely a definition of science as "a philosophical and reasoned knowledge of human affairs – of what is best for mankind".[1] This kind of knowledge is different from the metaphysical knowledge typical of the philosopher-kings of the *Republic*, for it is a knowledge applied to practical matters. Grote and Mill caught an important development in Plato's political theory: the eye of the statesman now gazes at the flux of human things, in contrast with the

---

1 Mill (1866) 297–364; see 356.

https://doi.org/10.1515/9783110605549-017

eternity of the idea of the good in the *Republic*. This new perspective, this pensive attitude towards the ever-changing situation of human affairs, is well captured in a statement of the Eleatic Stranger at *Politicus* 294b:

> For the differences of men and of actions and the fact that nothing, I may say, in human life is ever at rest, forbid any science whatsoever to promulgate any simple rule for everything and for all time.

Plato placed the *Politicus* in a triptych of dialogues devoted to the topic of knowledge together with the *Theaetetus* and the *Sophist*. The *Theaetetus* is an aporetic dialogue, ending without answering the initial question about what knowledge is; the *Sophist* marks the introduction both of a new character -the Stranger from Elea- and of a new method – *diairesis*, or division by dichotomy. The sequence of the dialogues and the appearance of these two new elements signal an impasse in Plato's philosophy: he has realized the presence of some problems in his vision of knowledge based on the theory of ideas and, with his usual intellectual honesty and his taste for showing his method as well as his results, has a new character dissect that theory and allow the issues to appear; once this is done, new ways may be explored. In these three dialogues, however, Plato is far from having a merely critical attitude, for several positive results emerge. In the *Theaetetus*, for instance, he confronts the theory of knowledge of his nemesis Protagoras, and quietly admits that, if we confine ourselves to sense-perception, a relativistic conclusion in the style of the Heracliteans is unavoidable. This conclusion, however, only prompts us to search for a firmer, more objective, grounding for our knowledge. In the *Sophist* the pitfalls and traps stemming from the similarity between the philosopher and the sophist are highlighted by the diairetic method, which enables us to catch the wolf-like nature of the sophist, so similar to the dog-like philosopher (but oh, so different), and to realize the emptiness of his enterprise as compared to the fruitful role of the philosopher. The *Politicus* applies the same method to the identification of the true statesman, and to distance him from other characters who bear an apparently strong similarity with him. The defining element is found in the possession of the art of politics, or political science, which sets the true statesman apart from his helpers and from all other pretenders. The dramatic date of the trilogy is during Socrates' trial (399 BCE), and the Eleatic Stranger is metaphorically described as Socrates' philosophical judge (*Sophist* 216b). The dean of American Platonists – Paul Shorey – captured in one phrase the mood and likely time of composition of the

Politicus: "Its style and its tone of 'mixed *pathos* and satire' in the reluctant abandonment of impracticable ideals mark it as probably late".[2]

A fairly secondary dialogue nowadays,[3] the *Politicus* enjoyed much more consideration, and had a very important place among Plato's dialogues, in ancient times. To find evidence for this statement we need only read the opening lines of Aristotle's *Politics*. There he criticizes "those who think that the natures of the statesman (*politikon*), the royal ruler (*basilikon*), the head of an estate (*oikonomikon*) and the master of a family (*despotikon*) are the same": the reference is quite evidently to this dialogue, where the statesman is described as the possessor of the "royal science", which enables him to rule over a city as well as manage a household.[4] Aristotle maintains that it is a mistake to assimilate forms of dominion which are quite different, and therefore to identify political science with the art of being a king or administrator. Aristotle is unfair here to Plato, for he is not considering that the equivalence of the three sciences is a necessary consequence of Plato's revolutionary view of the household: the family becomes public, and is open to the statesman's art; conversely, politics is retracted from the public sphere, and becomes the prerogative of (very) few experts. Moreover, in Aristotle's view Plato erred in considering political art a theoretical and not a practical science. Plato, who used the words 'art' and 'science' interchangeably in the *Politicus*, described political science as an architectonic art, and the statesman as directing subordinates who act upon his prompting and follow his directives. Aristotle, on the contrary, distinguished between contingent and necessary objects of inquiry, and famously maintained that one should not look for the same degree of precision in the two different domains.[5] Plato's wrong classification of the sciences in the *Politicus* was one of the reasons that prompted Aristotle to elaborate his own classification. Many aspects of this work were thus present to Aristotle's mind when he wrote about the "philosophy of human things".

---

2 Shorey (1902) 186.
3 Although after the III International Symposium Platonicum organized by Christopher Rowe in Bristol (1992), which was devoted to the *Politicus*, there has been a revival of interest for this dialogue. This is attested by the appearance of new translations of the dialogue in different languages, monographs devoted to it, and two collections of the Proceedings of the Symposium edited by Rowe himself: see C. Rowe (ed.), 1995; cf. the issue of the journal *Polis* 12 (1993), devoted entirely to the *Politicus*.
4 See Aristotle, *Politics* I 1, 1252a 7–9.
5 Aristotle, *Nicomachean Ethics* I 1, 1094b24ff: "The same exactness must not be expected in all departments of philosophy alike, any more than in all the products of the arts and crafts". Cf. *Metaphysics* II 3, 995a13–14.

The problem of the unity of virtue

The problem I want to address here is the Socratic notion of the unity of virtue, which Plato upheld in most of his dialogues,[6] and the ways needed to create fully virtuous citizens: the *Politicus* is the only dialogue where Plato not only shows a clear awareness of the issues inherent to this position, but also explicitly states that certain virtues are by nature opposed to others.[7] The creation of virtuous, well-rounded citizens becomes therefore a work of art, the art of politics; it is artificial. If there is difference in the degree of determination with which Plato openly questions the Socratic position, there is continuity in his view of the means that the statesman should use in order to create the best possible citizens: in the *Politicus* they are referred to as "divine and human bonds", and they consist in a wise arrangement of marriages and couplings of the citizens, as well as an education aimed at creating common values and therefore concord in the city.

Towards the end of the *Politicus* (306a ff) the Eleatic Stranger concludes his examination of the art of politics tackling a difficult problem and uttering a statement which he believes will sound shocking (*thaumaston*) to his interlocutors: the emerging conclusion against the unity of virtue. This was a pillar of the Socratic doctrine – all virtues are one, or united, *qua* virtues. The conversation and dichotomies in this dialogue, however, have led to the conclusion that certain virtues are opposite to others, and the Eleatic Stranger is fair to the discourse (*logos*): one must follow it to its logical conclusions even if they are unpalatable

---

6 Being a central topic of such dialogues as the *Protagoras* and *Laches*, the problem of the unity of virtues re-emerges in Plato's last work, and finds another, different solution. At *Laws* XII, 963c–964b the Athenian Visitor maintains that "courage, moderation, justice and practical wisdom" are distinct, but at the same time all united as virtues. He goes on to show that the difference between them consists in the presence of intellect (*nous*), which for some is required and for courage is not.

7 There is a huge literature on the subject. For an introduction to the problem, and a very sensible conclusion, I wish to single out Penner (1992). I agree with Penner in seeing a transition from the earlier to the mature dialogues in the consideration of demotic virtues (those which do not require knowledge or wisdom), and in believing that Plato realized that the unity of virtue is present only in "philosophical virtue": this is the science of good and evil, the art of government. A very good recent restatement of the question and opinion in McCabe (2016). See also the interesting position of Cooper (1999) who maintains that the Eleatic Stranger does not speak of different complete virtues but rather of diverse natural inclinations. For another, different opinion see Dorter (1994) 225–6. Dorter refers to *Politicus* 306b, and argues that virtues collide "in a certain way" only for those who dispute about words.

or apparently absurd; this is what had happened during the search for the sophist, where the interlocutors were forced by their reasoning to admit the existence
of not-being.[8] In the *Politicus* the embarrassing but unavoidable conclusion concerns courage (*andreia*) and moderation (*sophrosyne*), two virtues which cannot
be present at the same time in the same person. Indeed -the Stranger maintains-
these two ideas were destined to be in contrast (*stasin*) and at war (*polemian*) with
each other (307c).

Apparently undeterred by the consequences of this reasoning, the Stranger
concludes that political art will then consist in the ability to "weave together" different virtues in order to have excellent citizens. Politics becomes the "art of weaving", and the fabric to be used is the human material the statesman has at hand;
the devices he has at his disposal are described as "divine and human bonds".

This metaphor marks a change from the vision of philosophical education as
the "art of the conversion of the soul" that we find in the *Republic* (VII, 518d). It
is as if Plato had realized that the unity he considers fundamental for a city is a
balance of opposite qualities rather than a single virtue. The main concern remains the same: avoiding disunion, conflict, and civil strife. Stasis is the deadly
ailment of the body politic, and the true statesman should use his (or her!)
knowledge in order to implement the unity of the city. Plato did not exaggerate
the issue or overstate his point. He witnessed the devastation brought about by
the civil war during and after the regime of the Thirty in Athens (404–399 BCE).
He was familiar with Thucydides' description of the slaughters following the stasis in Corcyra and his pensive conclusion that "War is a harsh teacher".[9] He knew
the oath sworn by oligarchs promising to be hostile (*kakonous*), and damage the
demos as much as they could[10]. He therefore conceived the problem of political
unity as the most fundamental issue for a political community, and in all his
works he tried to devise means to have a city in concord. In the *Republic, sophrosyne* was the common virtue of all citizens because it guaranteed that every person
stayed at his place and did not meddle with different occupations: moderation
makes the citizens realize what their 'natural' inclination is and, consequently,
what their station in society should be. Moreover, in this way they follow their
natural inclinations without meddling with other occupations, and contribute to

---

8 See *Politicus* 284c. It is as if the discourse itself took charge, and led the searchers for truth in
an unequivocal direction. Aristotle will use a similar expression when, in many passages of the
Metaphysics, he speaks of how certain thinkers were forced to revise their ideas, and embark on
a certain direction of study by truth itself: see, e.g., *Met.* I 3, 984a 19–20.
9 Thucydides III, 82.
10 See Aristotle, *Politics* V 7, 1310a7–12; Andocides, *De mysteriis* 98.

the creation of a healthy and just city: justice consists in "not meddling with too many things" (*apolypragmosyne, me polypragmonein*).[11] When citizens have common values justice reigns in the city. This is why the entire educational system of Kallipolis is focussed on developing the virtue of *sophrosyne* in all citizens. This very idea, however, presupposes that citizens are different because they have different, and sometimes conflicting, qualities; they are driven by very diverse objects of desire, such as knowledge, glory, or material pleasure. The realization of human diversity is thus already present in the *Republic*, but Plato does not want to abandon the Socratic idea of the unity of virtues, and still believes that it is possible to forge well-rounded individuals through education. The conclusion of the *Politicus* is thus the only evidence of Plato's awareness of the inevitable conflict of opposing virtues. Or rather, it is the best and most clear evidence. For the division of the soul in three parts, each characterized by a specific virtue, already testified to Plato's awareness of the existence of different virtues which could not easily be matched. Indeed, the conclusion that there exist different parts of the soul resulted precisely from the observation that one part may contradict, or be in tension, with another. This is the lesson we learn from the episode of Leontius in *Republic* IV (439e–440a), where the problem of inner conflict is identified for the first time, together with the notion of weakness of the will (*pace* Aristotle).[12]

The question had emerged quite early in the *Republic* during the search (*zetesis*: II, 368d) for the perfect rulers of the city. Once the "city of pigs", characterized by a "natural" virtue, an original simplicity (*euetheia*), was forsaken for a more 'modern' and realistic city, the issue of war entered the conversation: while the original city ("the healthy city, the true city") is peaceful, the more realistic "swollen" city desires to expand, and therefore wages war on neighbouring cities. Socrates realizes that the guardians should thus possess philosophical meekness (*praotes*) as well as courage (*andreia*) and spiritedness (*thumoeideia*), but that these are contrasting qualities; indeed, they are opposite natures (*enantia physis*). He then arrives at the provisional conclusion that there cannot exist good guardians.[13] This statement embarrasses Socrates and his interlocutors, and leaves them puzzled (*aporoumen*). This stumbling block is overcome by looking at an example in nature: dogs have the natural inclination to be friendly to people known to them and hostile to strangers, thus showing two opposite qualities. Likewise, the perfect guardian should be both a lover of knowledge and spirited,

---

11 See *Republic* IV, 431d–433d.
12 I was persuaded of this by the elegant work of Hampshire (1999).
13 *Republic* II, 375a–d.

courageous as well as wise (*Rep*. II, 376a ff)[14]. It is very interesting that Plato overcomes this theoretical problem -the apparent opposition between certain virtues-by showing that it can be solved in practice, that there is a solution in nature. I am persuaded that Plato was a careful observer of reality: he was evidently well acquainted with the practice of dog- and horse-breeders, and believed that a similar method could be used also for human beings. This 'physical' device should be coupled with a moral device – education – in order to mould the perfect guardian, and indeed "the pure race of guardians" (V, 460c). Socrates goes over this subject again in *Republic* VI, when he speaks of the education of the future philosopher-rulers. He there takes it for granted that they will be few in number, because of the difficulty of finding united in one nature the two opposing qualities which are necessary in a good ruler:

> Note, then, that they will naturally be few, for the different components of the nature which we said their education presupposed rarely consent to grow in one; but for the most part these qualities are found apart. [..] Facility in learning, memory, sagacity, quickness of apprehension and their accompaniments, and youthful spirit and magnificence in soul are qualities, you know, that are rarely combined in human nature with a disposition to live orderly, quiet, and stable lives; but such men, by reason of their quickness, are driven about just as chance directs, and all steadfastness is gone out of them. [..] And on the other hand, the steadfast and stable temperaments, whom one could rather trust in use, and who in war are not easily moved and aroused to fear, are apt to act in the same way when confronted with studies. They are not easily aroused, learn with difficulty, as if benumbed, and are filled with sleep and yawning when an intellectual task is set them. [..] But we affirmed that a man must partake of both temperaments in due and fair combination or else participate in neither the highest education nor in honours nor in rule.[15]

I believe that Plato never relinquished the idea that the best sort of citizen is the result of a double action on the rulers' part: education and a eugenic policy. The necessity of such a policy is so pressing that before elaborating on it Socrates maintains that this is the area where the rulers have to rely most on falsehood and deception, to be conceived as medicines necessary for the well-being of the other citizens (V, 459d). They will spur the best men to cohabit with the best women and the worst men with the worst women; they will use festivals and sacrifices to bring together brides and grooms; they will prompt men to have children between the age of 30 and 55 and women between 20 and 40, when they are

---

14 Cf. the structure of ancient Athens in the *Timaeus-Critias*, a city entirely dominated by guards possessing "a nature that is simultaneously spirited and outstandingly philosophical, in order that they can be appropriately gentle and harsh [to friends and enemies]": *Timaeus* 18a.
15 *Republic* VI, 503c–d; cf. IV, 442a; 485a.

in their prime.[16] The emphasis of this marriage and procreation policy, however, is more on the necessity of separating the excellent citizens from the base, not on uniting opposing virtues in order to have the best citizenry. The all-important difference between the two dialogues is that in the *Republic* the eugenic measures are designed to discriminate and segregate the good citizens, the finer spirits (*kompsoteroi*), who identify pleasure with intelligence (*phronesis*), from the bad, the mass who believes pleasure is the good (VI, 505b). In the *Politicus*, by contrast, the issue is how to combine two good qualities which are divergent. In the former dialogue the differentiation is between good and bad; in the latter between two different kinds of good.

The solution of the *Republic*

Among many other things (a political vision, a moral reform, a theory of aesthetics, a treatise on religion, a theory of knowledge) Plato's *Republic* is a huge educational project. It is built on the assumption that education has a fundamental role in preserving and developing the natural virtues. Looking at Plato's image of the tripartite soul, we could say that this project aims at maintaining the natural arrangement (*taxis*) of the soul. For in the original arrangement of the parts of the soul, spiritedness helps reason "unless it is corrupted by bad education" (IV, 441a). The elaborate project that follows aims at making the citizens "harmonious", within themselves and with one another. Inner strife, *stasis*, is the enemy to fight against both individually and politically; for justice consists in "arranging the elements of the soul in a system of rulers and ruled according to nature", while in the case of injustice these elements are arranged in a manner opposed to nature.[17]

The complete unity of the city remains Plato's main concern for the best regime. It can be achieved through different measures, but two remain a constant theme in all his works: education and matching the citizens in a way to produce the best possible offspring. While the first measure concerns man's moral sphere, the second is directed towards his physical constitution, and aims at changing his very character. Throughout his works Plato shows himself to be an enemy of the traditional *oikos*, for he believes that the private dimension is the realm of

---

16 *Republic* V, 459d–461c.
17 *Republic* IV, 444d; cf. IX, 591b. See also X, 611b–d, where Socrates speaks of a "true nature" (*alethes physis*) and of an "original nature" (*archaia physis*) of the soul which equals its rational part (or an original arrangement in which the rational part rules).

selfishness and lawlessness.[18] In the *Republic* he tackles the problem by abolishing the traditional distinction between public and private, the *agora* and the *oikos*. Perhaps the most conspicuous absence in the perfect city of Kallipolis is that there is no market-place, or rather it is used only for economic transactions. Political decisions are made by the philosophers without public deliberation: politics is privatized, so to speak, in the conviction, on Plato's part, that discussion among ordinary people does not lead to the best decisions. On the other hand, the family becomes a public concern for the ruling class, and ceases to belong to the private sphere. One of the main purposes of the philosopher-king is to arouse in all citizens the sense of belonging to a single family. Indeed, one of the most shocking features of Plato's *Republic*, expected by Socrates to raise a wave of laughter and scorn, is the proposal that the ruling class have property, women, and children in common. This measure is deemed necessary by Socrates in order to establish and maintain the maximum of unity in the perfect city he is "building in discourses" (*en logois*) (X, 592a). By having everything in common, by calling everything "mine" and not distinguishing it from what is "not-mine", the guardians of Kallipolis show that love for truth and honour is stronger than love for wealth and material pleasures, and ensure that everything is done for the common good of the citizens. Such a drastic measure is the result of Plato's conviction that every city is characterized by the diversity of its citizens, who pursue different visions of happiness. What makes human beings different is the preponderance of one element over the others in their soul imagined as tripartite: each part is characterized by some kind of love – love of knowledge, love of honour and glory, and love of wealth and pleasure. At the base of Plato's political project there is thus an image of diversity and potential conflict, which can be overcome only by education and drastic measures, such as the abolition of all kind of private possessions for the ruling class.

The proposal was really shocking, as expected, if we may judge from the reactions of two contemporary authors. The comedian Aristophanes mocked and parodied it in his *Ecclesiazusae* (*The Assemblywomen*), probably performed in 391 BCE.[19] And in the *Politics* Aristotle focused his criticism of Plato's political project mostly on this feature, accusing Plato of an exasperated search for unity by reversing the

---

18 Cf. *Laws* VII, 788a–b, where we read: "In the private life of the family many trivial things are apt to be done which escape general notice – things which are the result of individual feelings of pain, pleasure, or desire, and which contravene the instructions of the lawgiver".

19 See Aristophanes, *Ecclesiazusae*, ed. by Sommerstein (1998) and *Aristofane, Le donne al parlamento*, ed. Vetta (1989). I agree with Canfora (2014) about the dating of the two works and its implications.

polis, which is essentially a plurality, into the condition of a family or even an individual.[20] Both authors had hit on something present in Plato's project. By presenting women who dress up as men, participate in the Assembly, and pass a proposal there, Aristophanes places on stage women coming out of the family dimension and entering that public realm which was men's prerogative. Aristophanes caught perfectly the fact that Plato did not mean to abolish the family; rather, he wanted to take it out of the private dimension. The family is open to the activity, and the operating and scheming, of the philosopher; likewise, in Aristophanes' parody, the city is open to the scheming of 'those who know', in this case, women. Aristotle, on his part, caught both the spirit and the sense of Plato's proposal, meant to forge and maintain the unity of the city. He criticized the abolition of private property and the communality of women, children, and goods because he thought it would not achieve the intended result, and would cause many more problems than it solved. In his view, education to virtue and good legislation are a better solution to the problem of making the city "one and common".

The communality of goods, women, and children is an idea never retracted by Plato, although it appears to be superseded in the political proposals of his subsequent dialogues. It remains, however, the best answer to the question of how to create the best regime, because it creates a community of mind conducive to genuine concord. This is clearly stated in the *Laws*:

> That city and polity come first, and those laws are best, where there is observed as carefully as possible throughout the whole city the old saying that "friends have all things really in common." As to this condition – whether it anywhere exists now, or ever will exist – in which there is community of wives, children and all chattels, and all that is called "private" is everywhere and by every means rooted out of our life, and so far as possible it is contrived that even things naturally "private" have become in a way "communized" – eyes, for instance, and ears and hands seem to see, hear, and act in common – and that all men are, so far as possible, unanimous in the praise and blame they bestow, rejoicing and grieving at the same things, and that they honour with all their heart those laws which render the city as unified as possible – no one will ever lay down another definition that is truer or better than these conditions in point of super-excellence. In such a city – be it gods or sons of gods that dwell in it – they dwell pleasantly, living such a life as this. Wherefore one should not look elsewhere for a model constitution, but hold fast to this one, and with all one's power seek the constitution that is as like to it as possible. That constitution which we are now engaged upon, if it came into being, would be very near to immortality, and would come second for unity.[21]

---

20 See Aristotle, *Politics* II 2, 1261a 15–20; cf. II 5, 1263b 30–33.
21 *Laws* V, 739 b–e. Most translators follow Apelt's amendment of *he mia* into *timia*. I have kept the reading of the Mss.

The art of politics: weaving the fabric of civic character

In the *Politicus* Plato uses two models to describe the art of politics: he assimilates it to the science of the shepherd and then, to the art of weaving. In the former case the statesman must look at the example of the divine shepherd of the universe as a model; in the latter, he must assume weaving as a *paradeigma* for his action. While the former was a traditional simile already found in Homer, the latter was a much less elevated comparison, especially because in Greek culture weaving was, since Homer, considered an activity typical of women.[22] Indeed, if we look at how it was described and put on stage by dramatists and playwrights, we could say that it had acquired a connotation of ruse and deceit which were considered typical of women. For instance, Penelope weaves incessantly in order to deceive the suitors and procrastinate her choice, while Clytemnestra and Medea weave deadly garments to perpetrate their murderous acts.[23] The Eleatic Stranger's comparison is introduced by the exclamation "by Zeus!", as if to signal the increased *pathos* this choice would cause.[24] He feigns stupor, as if the choice was completely haphazard, but what precedes shows that this is not the case (278e).[25] I am inclined to think that the choice serves to mark Plato's new and revolutionary view of man and woman and their respective roles. Comparing the uniquely male activity of politics with the typically female occupation of weaving must surely have surprised or even shocked many readers.[26] But Plato was completely unworried by traditional ideas and social conventions, and was certainly not afraid of the possible ridicule he might incur. The force of his reasoning had led him to realize the intellectual equality existing between man and woman, and he was bold enough not to resist this conclusion.

The analogy between the art of politics and the art of weaving is very significant: weaving together different characters means that differences should not be eliminated; the statesman should not transform the natures of the citizens but

---

22 For Homer weaving is a woman's task while war is a man's task. See *Iliad* VI, 490–3; *Odyssey* I, 356–9. Interestingly enough, this idea is replicated by Socrates in his exchange with Alcibiades in *Alcibiades* I, 126e–127a.

23 Indeed, Penelope confesses: "I weave tricks" to the suitors: *Odyssey* XIX, 137. See also Aeschylus, *Agamemnon* 1383; *Choephoroi* 980; Euripides, *Orestes* 25; *Medea* 1066 ff.

24 See Rosen (1995) 101.

25 In her very sophisticated essay Blondell (2005) 55 argues that "Plato uses the figure of the weaver-king to appropriate the long-standing intellectual associations of weaving"; and adds that "weaving is not merely a metaphor but a homology for the activity of the epistemic statesman" (57). See also Capozzi (1989).

26 E. Browning Cole (1991) speaks of outright "scandal".

rather tie them together with right opinion on the most important things, and among them, a wise matrimonial policy. In book 8 of the *Republic* difference was conceived as always bad: the myth of the different metals in book 3 (the "noble lie") brought about the necessity of segregating unequal citizens, for the union of citizens endowed with dissimilar metals cannot but produce disastrous effects.[27] In the *Politicus* Plato seems to have realized that the unity of virtues is not a natural product, but something, rather, artificially effected by the ability of the ruler-educator, since certain virtues are necessarily in contrast with some others. Different characters, opposing virtues, this is the datum in politics, the human material on which the statesman's action is exercised. With a clarity unparalleled in any previous or subsequent dialogue, Plato's Eleatic Stranger flatly states that the form of courage and that of moderation are in perennial hostility and conflict. What is noteworthy is that neither virtue is deemed superior to the other; both are necessary if one is to have a flourishing city. Then at 307d the Stranger reminds us of the seriousness of the matter: if an excess of some virtue or its inappropriate presence may be ridiculous in certain realms, the excessive presence of a single virtue in the political community is extremely dangerous; many cities were destroyed by the rashness and temerity, or the aversion to risk, of their citizens. This is because, if each nature is allowed to pursue its inclination, the citizens possessing it will look for a partner in life with a similar character; they will then teach their offspring to be like them, and this, in the long run, accentuates the force of the predominant virtue. For instance, moderate people are unfit for war, and by teaching the young to be peaceful, their behaviour contrasts with the reality of life: if attacked, they are at the mercy of the attackers, and the city becomes enslaved to the invaders (308a). The situation is not dissimilar for courageous natures: their desire to fight leads their cities towards perpetual war, with the result that they destroy their homeland or render it a slave to its enemies.

Following a suggestion by J. Frederik and M. Arends, we could suppose that Plato had specific groups of people in mind with whom one should identify these different virtues and natures.[28] More specifically, we might think that the moderate people are those engaged in financial and commercial activities as well as being farmers; there is a long tradition of literature that conceives of these as peaceful activities, those of Hesiod being the most famous example. Conversely,

---

27 *Republic* III, 415a–c; VIII, 546e–547a.
28 J. Frederik-M. Arends (1993) 167 suggest that these different natures could be identified with actual types of citizen: moderate people, for instance, are those engaged in financial and commercial activities, the rich and the oligarchs. I think this is a very interesting suggestion, but I prefer to make it more systematic to fit Plato's political view.

the courageous people are the warriors, the agonistic athletes, and those who were described as "the assistants" (*epikouroi*) to the philosopher-kings in the *Republic*. If this view is correct, we should conclude that in the *Politicus* Plato reworked the functioning of the three classes imagined in the *Republic*: instead of having three separate classes, an uneven citizen body harmonized by the common virtue of *sophrosyne*, he here imagines a citizen body made 'smooth' through the work of political science. Instead of a tripartite division, we find in the *Politicus* a bipartite division of the citizen body: the true statesman, doing his job of weaving citizens' characters and 'architectonically' supervising assistants in charge of various departments, and a homogeneous citizen body. The raw material in the *Politicus* is composed of human beings endowed with some virtue; different, and conflicting virtues have to be harmonized in order to create a homogeneous political body. In the *Republic*, on the contrary, the emphasis was on the difference between human beings having diverse and incompatible objects of love; hence the necessity of segregation in order not to spoil the 'purity' of each class.

The Eleatic Stranger can thus conclude by reiterating that these two kinds of virtue are in a perpetual condition of reciprocal hate (*echthron*) and conflict (*stasin*). In order to avoid a disastrous outcome, the statesman has therefore to harmonize the souls of his fellow-citizens. We must assume that he himself is the living example of virtue, and of a well-balanced human being. For the perfect statesman should be measured and have all the "qualities which are located in the mean rather than the extremes"; he should possess the "expertise which assesses things against due measure, suitability, timeliness, desirability, and so on" (284e). Above all, the true statesman is characterized by the knowledge of the "political art", the discriminating factor which genuinely sets him apart from all pretenders.[29] Political art must include knowledge of the "art of measurement", of the kind that deals with "due measure" (*to metrion*, 284e); for the statesman must know the appropriate measure of courage and of moderation that is required to have a well-balanced citizen body, to weave a smooth fabric of citizenry. Already evoked in the *Protagoras* (156c–157e) without fruitful developments, the "art of measurement" here reveals its importance in guiding the statesman's operation of weaving. The process of creating the true statesman[30] is long because it must take into account all the differences (*diaphoras*) among things (285b), namely the changing nature of political reality and the complexity of human nature.

---

29 The statesman in the *Politicus* possesses only true opinion, not knowledge, according to D.A. White (2007). I cannot agree.

30 On the actual possibility to create such a statesman and the rule of wisdom see P. Neiman (2007) and E. Speliotis (2011).

Knowing similarities and dissimilarities is a truly philosophical task, and in performing his task of weaving the statesman uses both "divine and human bonds".

The tools of the trade: "divine bonds" in the *Politicus*

Let's now turn to examine how the issue of the unity of virtue and of the city is presented in the *Politicus*. The Eleatic Stranger forcefully maintains how important is that of the art of politics be conceived as the science of weaving together different characters. If left free to follow their inclination, even virtuous natures would become dangerously extreme. Courage, for instance, turns into reckless daring, while moderation becomes shyness and cowardice. The practical outcomes of the two extremes are both disastrous: war in one case, slavery in the other; both these conditions are the negation of politics, for there can be no political condition when there is war, or the citizens are not free. What is at stake here – how to create political unity – is therefore of the utmost importance, and Plato shows he has realized that this does not happen by nature nor comes about *automatoi*: the unity of the polis is the result of political action, which makes diverse characters coexist through concord and friendship.

However, a drastic preliminary operation must be performed: the statesman must first get rid of the human material in the city which is of low quality. By this metaphor Plato means all the people who have some incurable disease of the soul, such as "atheism, *hybris*, and injustice": such natures cannot be part of the city, they must be suppressed, exiled, or stripped of civil rights (*atimia*: 309a). Plato confirms here his harsh treatment he plans for these categories of people, already eliminated from the body politic in the *Republic*, and destined to receive a similar treatment in the *Laws*. Plato seems to believe that there is a minimum level of 'politicity' required for the individual to be a citizen, and to live together with his fellow-citizens. It is noteworthy that the three 'great vices' which can afflict the human soul remain the same in Plato's thought; and so does the penalty: death. Atheism, thinking that the gods do not exist, or do not care about human beings, or can be appeased by gifts and sacrifices, is the capital vice. Plato devotes many pages to the demonstration of the immortality of the soul, among them the whole of book 10 of the *Laws*, the myth of Er at the end of the *Republic*, and the myth of the final judgment at the end of the *Gorgias*, to counter atheism and reveal the real nature of the gods. *Hybris*, wanton insolence, is a notion especially dear to the dramatists and the gnomic poets, and is replete with religious overtones. It is an offence both towards men and towards the gods, and it was punished by Athenian laws as well. Injustice is the lack of the capital civic virtue, which enables human beings to live together and flourish.

After this purging operation, the statesman takes the human material of good quality, whether similar or dissimilar, and "reduces them to unity, moulding one capacity (*dynamin*) and one idea (*idean*)". Subsequently, he first unites with a divine bond those who are like-born with respect to the eternal part of their souls, and then, after the divine bond, he unites the mortal part by means of a human bond.[31]

The divine bond – education – comes first, because it is more important. It is divine because it is immaterial, and assimilates human beings to god. In the preceding myth at the centre of the dialogue, immaterial entities were described as "the most divine" (269d) in the universe. We also read that the best form of government, where a statesman who really possesses the political art rules, must be set aside from all other forms of government, as "a god" is from men (303b). The eternal part of the soul is the *logistikon*, and I subscribe to Harald Wydra's idea that "Plato's method is one of soul-craft, in which the ruler is an architect of souls".[32] This "divine bond" consists in a correct opinion concerning the most important things supported by argument, namely correct opinion about "what is beautiful, what is just, what is good, and their opposite" (309c). I take "true opinion with assuredness" to mean correct opinion accompanied by the reasons for adhering to it. The Eleatic Stranger adds that this kind of opinion is "divine" (*theian*), and is generated in a "divine nature" (*daimonioi genei*): knowledge and true opinion assimilate man to god, and the rational part of the soul is considered immortal.

In fact, the infusion of true opinion in a soul inclined to courage makes it meek, and ready to participate in just things; whereas without true opinion this kind of nature will incline towards bestiality (*theriode*). The same happens with the moderate character: with the infusion of true opinion, it becomes temperate (*sophron*) and wise (*phronimon*); otherwise it turns into a naive simplicity (*euetheia*).[33] It seems natural to suppose that the instrument of this operation of char-

---

31 *Politicus* 309c. For *syggenes* I follow the hint of D. Farrell Krell (2015), see 36.
32 Wydra, H. (2015) 28.
33 This word has a clear pejorative meaning in this passage, for it identifies a simplicity that makes someone in fact a simpleton. It is interesting to note that at *Republic* I, 343c and 348c Thrasymachus used the word in its derogatory sense to mean naiveté while at II, 372a–b *euetheia* is the simple, original virtue of the inhabitants of the first city, the "city of pigs", and has a positive connotation; see also III, 400e, where Socrates rectifies the evidently common opinion that *euetheia* means simple-mindedness. Again, in *Laws* III the scarce humanity which survives the periodic catastrophes that ravage the universe is characterized by this virtue of simplicity. This seems to show that Plato thought of *euetheia* as a virtue for a different era and a different society:

acter-moulding is philosophy; for philosophy, with its dialectical arm, accomplishes the task of questioning the presumption of knowledge typical of unsophisticated people while, at the same time, allowing correct opinion to emerge.

The political community thus appears an artificial product, a human artefact, in the way political science is a human device. Plato is here deliberately reversing the conclusions of Protagoras' Great Speech in the *Protagoras*. In the sophist's description, political science is Zeus' gift to the human race so that it can survive: *aidos* and *dike*, the two fundamental political virtues, are possessed by all human beings (potentially).[34] The myth of the reversal of the cosmos in the *Politicus* shows on the contrary that politics, as well as philosophy for that matter, was absent in the age of Cronus: it was not needed because human beings, lacking private property, lived peacefully while nature spontaneously offered them nourishment under the supervision of the gods. Human beings, however, were then in a condition of minority and tutelage, from which they emerge in the age of Zeus through political science.

The unity of the body politic is the first preoccupation of the true statesman. First and foremost, political unity is realized through concord, a consequence of a communality of values: *homonoia* springs from thinking and believing the same things. For this, it is not necessary that all citizens know the truth about the most important matters, but it is imperative that they have a correct belief about them. We have heard the Eleatic Stranger maintaining that the true statesman must be able to instil a "true opinion with assuredness" on the most important things in the soul of the citizens who have received a good education. What is immortal in the soul, its rational part, must be harmonized with the divine. Education brings to completion this work of transformation of the soul. This favourable judgment concerning "true opinion" as a good guide for action for most citizens marks a clear departure from the hard and fast distinction between knowledge (*episteme*) and opinion (*doxa*) of the *Republic*;[35] in this respect this position is closer to such dialogues as the *Meno* and the *Laws*, where true opinion is rehabilitated. In the *Meno* especially we read that true opinion is not inferior to science in directing our actions. In fact, it is in the practical realm that true opinion reveals its value: it makes us act correctly, and be useful to our country:

---

in our time of complexity it is not a virtue anymore. See C. Gaudin (1981); L. Brisson (2000) 123; G. Giorgini (2016) 147–162.

34 See *Protagoras* 320c–328d.

35 *Republic* VII, 534a. Note, however, that at *Rep.* IV, 429c as well opinion can be "safeguarded", i.e., certain, thanks to the educational operation of the lawgiver. This concerns the practical virtue of courage; see also IV, 442c.

So that right opinion will be no whit inferior to knowledge in worth or usefulness as regards our actions, nor will the man who has right opinion be inferior to him who has knowledge. [...] Since then it is not only because of knowledge that men will be good and useful to their country, where such men are to be found, but also on account of right opinion.[36]

The "human bonds"

The other important aspect of the art of the true statesman is his ability to use "human bonds" in the attempt to create good citizens. These "human bonds" consist in a careful matrimonial policy aimed at coupling citizens endowed with the opposite qualities of courage and moderation. As we have noted, Plato obliterates the usual distinction between public and private, and believes that the statesman should intervene in the composition of families in the interest of the city. In the *Politicus* there is not the rigid eugenic policy of the *Republic*: in that project, a sacred number determined the right time for coupling for the ruling class; sexual activity was regulated by lot, but the procedure was rigged for eugenic purposes (*Rep.* V, 459c–461c; VIII, 546d); unauthorized couplings were considered impious and unjust (V, 461a–b). His clearer awareness of the necessity to have citizens endowed with opposing qualities rarely found in the same person prompts Plato to abandon the idea of couplings within the same class (likely characterized by the dominance of the same virtue). Therefore, in the *Politicus* we do not find the communality of women and children, and the recommendations for the choice of a partner concern all classes: like should not look for like, and care should be taken to mix peaceful with audacious natures. The prevalence of the public over the private good in the matrimonial sphere is present also in the *Laws*, and the same ideas recur in this late work. Here Plato maintains that there is a universal rule concerning marriages, according to which every marriage should be made not for personal pleasure but for the interest of the community (*Laws* VI, 773b); it follows that men should marry women of opposite character and vice-versa, going against that "natural tendency for everyone to make for the mate that most resembles himself, whence it results that the whole city becomes ill-balanced both in wealth and in moral habits" (VI, 773b–c). In addition, men should marry when they are between 30 and 35 years old and women when they are between 16 and 20 (V, 721b–d; VI, 774a–c); divorce is compulsory when couples do not have children after ten years of being together (VI, 784b). It is interesting to notice that in the *Laws* too Plato maintains that the rulers should

---

36 See *Meno* 98b–c.

take care of mixing the more impetuous natures with the slower ones, making a match that aims at having well-balanced children rather than enriching one party. Plato's ideal remains that of a wise balance, of wealth as well as of character. He forcefully reiterates his conviction that "in respect of excellence what is evenly balanced and symmetrical is infinitely superior to what is un-tampered with" (VI, 773a). We read, however, that this aspect of the matrimonial sphere should not be regulated by the law: it is left to the "enchanting exhortation" of the rulers rather than to the "violence of the written law" (VI, 773d–e), to moral suasion rather than to legal provision.

The Eleatic Stranger's argument in the *Politicus* is that the continuous search for what is like exasperates the prevalent virtue in a person. So, "if courageous character is reproduced for many generations without any admixture of the moderate type, the natural course of development is that at first it becomes superlatively powerful but in the end it breaks out into sheer fury and madness" (310c). The soul that is too respectful, on the other hand, will become dumb and crippled by continuous coupling with the like. The task of the statesman is thus that of creating a smooth fabric by weaving together characters with opposite virtues: he will accomplish his task by creating unanimity (*homodoxia*) concerning values and common purposes (311a). The "kingly art" will therefore lead all the people in the city towards a "common life" thanks to concord (*homonoia*) and friendship (*philia*).[37] The result will be a "happy city": happiness is possible only in a good form of government. And in the best regime not only some but all people are happy.[38]

Differently from the *Republic*, in the *Politicus* the two opposed virtues do not correspond to different parts of the soul; nor are they possessed by specific strata of the population. Another important difference is that in the *Republic* moderation is a virtue that must be possessed by all citizens, the virtue of the body politic, if we wish to keep Plato's organic metaphor; whereas in the *Politicus* moderation is at first a characteristic of only some members of the community and not of the entire citizen body. This virtue has to be integrated into the entire body politic in order to have a well-balanced community. Finally, in this dialogue education is common to all citizens, not reserved for the guardians, but it is preceded by the same sifting operation by the statesman which eliminates the unfit

---

37 In the *Republic* Socrates describes moderation as a kind of order (*kosmos*) and continence (*enkrateia*) of pleasures and appetites (IV, 430e), and maintains that it is a kind of harmony and natural agreement about who is entitled to rule a city or an individual (IV, 432a).
38 Note that in this city there are other people of free condition, and also slaves: the former are probably women, children and metics; the latter are people unfit for citizenship (311c).

elements of the population. The fact that a city is composed of 'appropriate' citizens is therefore a work of art, an artificial product, the result of the statesman's activity in a world devoid of divine guidance. I subscribe to Stanley Rosen's suggestion that "it is not the human being but the citizen who is a work of art".[39]

Courage and moderation: The influence of Thucydides

We may wonder why Plato chose courage and moderation as an example of opposed virtues which cannot coexist in their 'pure' form in a human being. It is important to remember that these are positive qualities, virtues, and become negative only when they are excessive and pressed to the extreme; this is the source of the importance of the art of measure for the true statesman, which plays such a conspicuous role in this dialogue. We may speculate that Plato thought of two living examples of those qualities: Sparta and Athens. Thucydides had already made this comparison, and shown the contrast between Athenian daring and Spartan tardiness in the discourse of the Corinthians in the assembly that preceded the Spartan decision to wage war on Athens.[40] Thucydides is a silent but constant presence in Plato's thought, sometimes evoked in clear allusions to passages of his work.[41] The dramatization of the differences in character between the old-fashioned Spartans and the 'modern' Athenians in the Corinthians' discourse is rhetorically very effective: the two political entities seem to be almost destined to be enemies because their very natures are so different and set them apart. It is worthwhile examining in detail this passage, which describes the difference in "character and constitution" (Thuc. I, 70) of the two peoples. The confidence in the goodness of their constitution (*politeia*) prompts the Spartans to be moderate (*sophrosyne*) but also ignorant (*amathia*) in foreign policy and blunt in the perception of the coming danger: prone to avoiding difficulties, they alone prefer to defend themselves by waiting rather than by using force, unmoved even when

---

39 S. Rosen (1995a) 5. In an evocative way Rosen adds that "the citizen is the simulacrum of the philosopher: the false image of the rational human being" (70).
40 See Thucydides I, 68–71.
41 I am thinking of the definition of justice in the *Republic* (IV, 433a–434c) as *apolypragmosyne*, the exact opposite of that *polypragmosyne* which is the glory of Athens in Pericles' eulogy (see the Funeral Speech in II, 35–43). An almost literal paraphrase of the famous passage on the 'revolution in words' caused by *stasis* (III, 82) can be found at *Rep.* VIII, 540d (see infra). And *Critias* 109e–110a, on the ignorance of the deeds of the past, is a possible reference to Thucydides' praise of the true historian's *akribeia* at I, 20.

the situation requires action. In a word, they have old-fashioned (*archaiotropa*) habits (I, 71). The Athenians, on the contrary, are fast in devising plans and in implementing their decision, valuing more their expectations for the future than what is at hand; they are bold beyond their means, "addicted to innovation" (*ne-oteropoioi*) and, so to speak, "born into the world to take no rest themselves and to give none to others" (I, 70). From the choice of words, it appears evident that in this passage Thucydides was using the *topos* of the different ages, identifying innovation with youth and conservation with old age. The same *topos* is at play in the famous exchange between Nicias and Alcibiades in book 6 of *The History of the Peloponnesian War*. There the young Alcibiades, spoilt by his talent and his success, and knowing his audience well, reminds his fellow-countrymen that "by sinking into inaction, the city, like everything else, will wear itself out, and its skill in everything decay; while each fresh struggle will give it fresh experience, and make it more used to defend itself not in word but in deed" (VI, 18). The experienced statesman Nicias, on the other hand, extols the merits of conserving one's possessions without overstretching in search of more and more: he advises the Athenians to "keep what you have got and not risk what is actually yours for advantages which are dubious in themselves (*ton aphanon kai mellonton*)" (VI, 9). Here too the choice of words seems appropriate to depict the mentality of an elderly and therefore conservative man: being old, preferring what is present, Nicias cannot but see as obscure, vague, and dubious the things in store for the future. This dramatic use of pairs of opposite qualities in Thucydides may have played a role in Plato's realization of the opposedness of certain virtues.

We ought also to take into account that Plato was profoundly impressed by Thucydides' depiction of the 'relativity' of words -the fact that words do not seem to have a fixed meaning in describing human behaviour. Certain actions which have a positive connotation in peace become negative in a situation of war, for instance. It is the famous 'revolution in words' which is the dramatic counterpart of political upheavals, and especially of civil strife:

> Words had to change their ordinary meaning and to take that which was now given them. Reckless audacity came to be considered the courage of a loyal ally; prudent hesitation, specious cowardice; moderation was held to be a cloak for unmanliness; ability to see all sides of a question inaptness to act on any. Frantic violence became the attribute of manliness; cautious plotting, a justifiable means of self-defence (III, 82).

Plato paraphrased this passage in *Republic* VIII while speaking of the decline of political regimes and describing the birth of the democratic man, thus showing his indebtedness to the great historian. Depicting the soul of the son of oligarchic parents, torn between the family values and the bad counsellors, Socrates observes:

> They call a sense of shame silliness, deny it its rights, push it out into exile; moderation they label as unmanliness, trample it into the mud, then throw it out too. As for reasonable behaviour and orderly expenditure, these they persuade him to regard as boorish and illiberal, joining with a crowd of useless desires to drum them out of town.[42]

The problem raised by Thucydides' observation is that of measurement and evaluation, of the right time (*kairos*) and the correct action (*orthotes*), a typically sophistic topic. The sophists, and especially Protagoras and Gorgias, had questioned the objectivity of measurement, and insisted on the importance of context for defining the appropriateness and correctness of an action. Plato tackled this problem throughout his intellectual career. In the *Protagoras* (356d), for instance, Socrates maintained that in the *metretike techne*, the art of measurement, lay the salvation of human life, because "it reveals the truth"; while in the *Republic* (VI, 504c) we read that nothing imperfect can ever be the measure of anything. In the *Politicus* Plato's solution consists in maintaining that quantitative measurement and qualitative evaluation always go together (284d–e). The just measure, moreover, is generated within the entities, not imposed from outside. The statesman must thus be able to make eternal truths and changing human things coexist; in order to do so he must know how to identify the *kairos*, the right time for action.

The statesman as artist

The Eleatic Stranger emphasizes how politics is a science, "probably the most difficult and the most important to acquire" (294d). This statement flies in the face of that typical democratic position which sees all human beings as possessing the necessary qualities to be good politicians – a position we find exemplified in Thucydides' Funeral Speech and in Protagoras' Great Myth. In this perspective, the Myth of the Reversed Cosmos in the *Politicus* may be considered Plato's response to Protagoras: in rivalry with the great sophist in the art of telling myths, Plato shows that political science is not for everyone, but for a very few selected specialists. At the end of the dialogue political expertise emerges as "the knowledge of the relation between other forms of knowledge and the temporal

---

42 *Republic* VIII, 560d.

demands of the moment of action, of *kairos*".[43] This is a recurrent problem in Plato's thought. The origin of the degeneration of the perfect city in the *Republic* is the philosophers' misjudgement of the *kairos*: their mistake in choosing the right time for coupling (*para kairon*: *Rep.* VIII, 546d) produces an ill-balanced offspring who will transform the perfect arrangement into an ordinary aristocracy eager for *time*, a timocracy. We may attribute this mistake to their inability to apply mathematics to practical circumstances, to make what is certain and stable coexist with what is always changeable. In the *Politicus* Plato offers a solution: since knowing how to do something (*techne*) is different from knowing when to do it (*kairos*), the real statesman must possess both arts, which are reunited in political expertise: *politike techne*, which is both the science of weaving different characters and the art of mastering time. Political science also includes the art of measurement, which in the realm of practice does not use only the categories of 'more' and 'less', 'bigger' and 'smaller': non-arithmetical measurement works with excess, deficiency, and suitability, and every measure of this sort is relative to a frame of reference.[44] Plato, however, never came close to the Aristotelian position, which attributes a different, and superior, degree of precision to the theoretical sciences. Plato believed that the superiority of the political over other arts lay precisely in the fact that it could unite theoretical truth and practice, the idea of the good with its historical implementation.

---

43 M. Lane (1998) 3–4.
44 See S. Rosen (1995a) 120–121.

Beatriz Bossi
On Virtue and Wisdom in the *Protagoras*, the *Phaedo* and the *Politicus*: One Thesis or Several?

1 Setting the Problem

In this paper I should like to explore the following questions:

1) whether the thesis of the involvement of all the virtues in wisdom, which I formulate as 'if and only if a person has wisdom, she has all the other virtues',[1] defended by Socrates in the *Protagoras*, and re-iterated with more precision in the *Phaedo* with the formula 'virtue is united to wisdom', still holds in the *Politicus*, and

2) if so, how it can be reconciled with the thesis of non-involvement in wisdom, which could be formulated as 'a person who has one virtue may lack the other ones', a thesis defended by Protagoras in the dialogue named after him, and also supported by the Eleatic Stranger in the *Politicus*.

The issue is *prima facie* controversial. Bobonich[2] defends the view that the Stranger's claims about moderation and courage are *inconsistent* with what he has called 'the thesis of the reciprocity of the virtues', interpreted as 'a person has one virtue if and only if he has all the virtues'.[3] Taken this way, it seems there is no possibility of reconciling the perspectives of the *Protagoras* and the *Politicus*. For if having one virtue entails having them all, one cannot be either just moderate or just brave, as the Stranger seems to suggest in the *Politicus*, if the meaning

---

1 I mean that if a man has wisdom, by implication he must have all the other virtues as well. This does not necessarily mean that 'if a man has one virtue, he has them all' in general terms.

2 Bobonich (1995) 313 defends 'the thesis of the Reciprocity of the virtues'. In my view, reciprocity is a misleading characterization of Socrates' thesis in the *Protagoras*, since it is not the case that if a subject has one virtue in the sense of 'any' virtue he must have them all, but that if a man is wise then and only then, necessarily, he has them all. All the genuine virtues are implied or implicit in wisdom, because all of them are, *stricto sensu*, instantiations of wisdom. See below, section 2.

3 Bobonich (1995) 313–329. Bobonich claims that a person 'might have the virtue of wisdom and thus know what is best for himself all things considered but still do something else because of pleasure or fear and thus lack the virtue of courage or moderation, as Plato understands them in the middle dialogues' (314). Bobonich quotes no passage in support of his view. However, it is evident that Plato believes that if a person is really wise, he cannot help but act virtuously. In what follows I shall consider passages from the *Protagoras*, the *Phaedo* and the *Symposium* to support my interpretation.

https://doi.org/10.1515/9783110605549-018

288 —— Beatriz Bossi

of 'virtue' remains the same. However, the meaning of the word 'virtue' in fact changes in the context of the latter dialogue. More importantly, this interpretation does not give the *reason* why this is so for Socrates, namely, that a person has virtue *stricto sensu* if and only if she has wisdom. When wisdom is present all the other virtues come along with it. And when it is not present, there are other alternatives contemplated in Plato's dialogues. A person can, in a sense, be called 'moderate' (for instance) because a) she has acquired the habit of acting in a moderate way (in the 'popular' sense of the word moderate) through education, without using her intelligence to prescribe action that needs to be taken wisely (as is claimed in the *Phaedo*) or b) she has a natural disposition towards this virtue (but without possessing the *genuine* virtue of moderation), as is claimed in the *Politicus*.

Other scholars, like Mishima, claim that the Stranger's view 'is actually much closer to the position ascribed to Protagoras and is 'plainly un-Socratic'.[4] In my view, it is not the case that Plato adopted Protagoras' perspective in the *Republic* or the *Politicus*, but that he managed to reconcile *his* Socrates and *his* Protagoras in the various perspectives on virtue that he developed in the *Phaedo*, the *Republic* and the *Politicus*.

In this paper, I shall defend the view that the thesis of the necessary involvement of virtue and wisdom is Socratic and Platonic, for it is proposed in the *Protagoras* (in a strong claim that virtue and wisdom are identical), stated with more precision in the *Phaedo* (where wisdom is presented as an essential condition for virtue), and not abandoned in the *Politicus* (where it turns out to be compatible with the thesis of non-involvement). And this is so for a simple reason: the majority will never attain the 'philosophical' level of virtue (297b–c) that involves wisdom, but are likely to remain at the level of so-called 'virtues' that are simply dispositional, and depend on a person's nature; they have nothing to do with wisdom, and begin to operate before education and bonding have taken place. This stage of 'virtue' instantiates the thesis of non-involvement in wisdom.

However, if the city is to become a harmonious piece of fabric, there must be at least one wise agent, namely, the ideal politician/king (292d6) who by implication must have all the virtues as well[5]. Certainly, the genuine politician is assumed to have attained philosophical knowledge of 'the finest greatest things without body' (286a), which apparently means he should have knowledge of the forms. If this is so, his wisdom will also make him genuinely virtuous, in order to be in a position to prescribe education and birth control for those endowed with one of those 'opposing virtues' which I take to be just 'good natural dispositions

4 Mishima (1995) 310–311.
5 Both Mishima (1995) 312 and Bobonich (1995) 313 n. 2, acknowledge this point.

towards virtue'.[6] Thus, the wise politician is an instance of the involvement of all the virtues in wisdom, while those who have good natural dispositions, before moral education and bonding, instantiate no involvement in wisdom. In this way, in my view, Protagoras' and Socrates' opposing views combine in the Stranger's perspective. Both theses are true for different agents at different stages.

Our analysis requires us to precise about a) the meaning of the word 'virtue' in different contexts and dialogues; b) the peculiar kind of unity of the virtues that Socrates defends in the *Protagoras*; and c) how different meanings of virtue make the thesis of involvement compatible with the thesis of non-involvement in the *Politicus*.

I can find at least four different meanings related to the word 'virtue' that co-habit in the dialogues I am considering here. Firstly, 1) there is the highest *'philo-sophical'* type of virtue, which is identified with wisdom in the *Protagoras;* while it is in itself just a single virtue, it receives the names of all the other virtues. Then we have two *'popular'* species described in the *Phaedo*: 2) the 'slavish imitation of genuine virtue', which consists in a certain calculative skill at producing *apparently* virtuous actions, out of the 'lack' of the real virtue it 'pretends' to be (for instance, apparently brave actions out of fear; apparently temperate actions out of lust, etc.: 68d–69c) which should be disregarded, and 3) those popular social virtues which are developed through habit, but without the implication of philosophy and reason (82a–b). Finally, there is the description of 'virtues' in the *Politicus*, which correspond, in my view, to natural dispositions that a person is presumably born with.

As we have argued above, the problem of the compatibility of the thesis of involvement and the thesis of non-involvement can be easily solved if we split the agents into different categories, and consider the clues that Plato offers us in different contexts. At the topmost level (1) there is the one who possesses the philosophical type of virtue, i.e. wisdom, who will also have all the other virtues at the same time (*Protagoras*). Below him, we may distinguish a second level (2), where we find those who have reached 'genuine' virtue through 'divine' true opinion 'with guarantees' (*Politicus*), and are ready to become the *political class* (as it happens they turn out to be quite similar to the class of the guardians in the *Republic*). Below them there is a third class (3) that is constituted by those who have developed good habits, and exhibit *popular* virtue without intellection or wisdom (*Phaedo*). Finally, at the ground level (4) there are those who only have natural inclinations or predispositions (even though they are called 'virtues' in

---

6 In line with El Murr (2014) 268; 271, who follows Dixsaut.

the *Politicus*), and need to go through a process of education and bonding to have access to levels (2) or (3).

If this reading is right, it seems to me that Plato does not change his views on virtue in any major regard throughout these dialogues, but keeps some theses on virtue for the length of his life. The peculiar contribution of the *Politicus* is, I suggest, the dynamic perspective for Plato starts to imagine the path from 'good temperament' to 'good character', and from good character to 'genuine virtue' based on 'divine true opinion with guarantees', instead of regarding these stages as statically stuck in a hierarchical pyramid.

The question whether the second stage of 'genuine virtue' is the same as or different from the one the wise politician/philosopher enjoys in the context of the *Politicus* (as I have suggested here) is rather difficult, because the Stranger does not offer much evidence on the matter. On the one hand, one might be inclined to argue for the view that both stages coincide, as there seems to be explicit evidence for this. Certainly, those who have an orderly nature are said to become 'genuinely moderate and *wise*' (309e), and the courageous are said to become just. These claims could be taken as a signal of the involvement of all the virtues in wisdom, which somehow seems to echo the thesis defended by Socrates in the *Protagoras*. In addition, those born with noble dispositions and raised accordingly are said to be able to 'protect' and unite the rest of the city, freemen and slaves included. They are also said to be the ones to be 'entrusted with offices in common', which is likely to mean that they should be ready to govern and rule the city (311a).

When depicting his ideal city here, Plato never claims that the 'ideal wise king/ politician' is likely to arise out of these officers, or could possibly be 'generated' that way; but, one can assume that they, if any, are likely to be the best source-material. At least Plato seems to indicate that they must be *wise* '*in a political sense*'.

It is well acknowledged that in the *Republic,* the philosopher should be ready to become the wise politician of the city. Has this perspective changed in the *Politicus*?[7] The common element is the grasping of truth, for without truth nobody can

---

7 One can assume that Plato is joking when he makes Theodorus introduce the subject to be considered in this dialogue as an *alternative* between the philosopher and the politician. Naturally, we expect the Stranger to pick one of them, but instead he just claims that 'we must not stop until we have finished with them' (οὐκ ἀποστατέον πρὶν ἂν αὐτῶν πρὸς τὸ τέλος ἔλθωμεν: 257c4–5). When he says that they must search for the statesman on the next page, he starts by assuming that 'he is one of those who possesses knowledge' (τῶν ἐπιστημόνων: 258b4). There are many other clues at various places in the dialogue that may induce one to think that both profiles belong to one and the same person.

become a wise politician. However, the main objection to this view continues to be that those who are educated and bonded are said to have 'true opinion', while the wise politician/king is said to have τέχνη καὶ ἐπιστήμη and φρόνησις.[8]

But can we trust Plato's verbal distinctions denoting different qualities? It does not seem so. Perhaps this question has to remain open. To deal with it we need to get deeper into the meanings involved in the other dialogues we have chosen to analyze.

2 The *Protagoras*: virtues are pieces of different size made of the same gold

To start the project let us go back to the *Protagoras*. Both Protagoras and Socrates agree that virtue is 'one', but they disagree about the type of unity it has[9]. On the one hand, according to Protagoras, virtue is one thing with different parts that have different functions, like the sense-organs on a face. On the other hand, Socrates claims that all virtues are the same thing but carrying different names, like parts of gold that are distinguishable in greatness and smallness (τὰ τοῦ χρυσοῦ μόρια οὐδὲν διαφέρει τὰ ἕτερα τῶν ἑτέρων, ἀλλήλων καὶ τοῦ ὅλου, ἀλλ'ἢ μεγέθει καὶ σμικρότητι: 329d6–8). But this view seems problematic. For two reasons: firstly, what is the import of difference in quantity in the case of the virtues, which are supposed to be qualities? Let us leave this question open for a moment. And secondly, Socrates himself regards the virtues as parts of a whole, and uses different names to denote 'different virtues' at various points in the dialogue, which apparently means that when he uses ordinary language he shares the ordinary view. When Socrates proposes his provocative thesis that all virtues are one and the same because they are like 'parts made of the same gold' he attempts, I sug-

---

8 Monserrat (1999) 248 observes: 'cap teixidor no ha estat mai un element del seu propi tissage'. In my view this is neither denied nor affirmed.

9 " (…) whether virtue is a single thing (Ἕν μέν τί ἐστιν ἡ ἀρετή) of which justice and temperance and holiness are parts or whether the qualities I have just mentioned are all names of the same single being (ἑνὸς ὄντος). This is what I am still hankering after. -Why, the answer to that is easy, Socrates, he replied: it is that virtue is a single being (ἑνὸς ὄντος) and the qualities in question are parts of it. -Do you mean parts, I asked, in the sense of the parts of a face, as mouth, nose, eyes, and ears; or, as in the parts of gold, there is no difference among the pieces, either between the parts, or between a part and the whole, except in greatness and smallness? -In the former sense, I think, Socrates: as the parts of the face, to the whole face" (*Prot.* 329c6–e 2).

gest, to reveal the intimate nature of the virtues, beyond their assumed differences in name and function. If virtue is conceived by Socrates to be basically wisdom, understood as 'knowledge' or 'the art of measurement' (357a3; b4), to say that the virtues are made of the same 'gold' could mean that all of them are just different expressions of wisdom.

Protagoras speaks in terms of parts that *do not resemble* each other,[10] and rejects identity:[11] 'many are brave but unjust, and many again are just but not wise' (329e5–6). However, he regards wisdom as 'the greatest' part of virtue (330a2).

On the other hand, Socrates maintains the thesis that virtue is one thing, essentially wisdom, and yet different virtues characterized by different names are distinguishable 'in size'. The quantitative aspect of the comparison Socrates proposes should give us a clue to understanding in which sense virtues can in *his* view be distinguished. I should like to suggest that they are likely to work as *units of measure* (like the weights that were placed on one of the cymbals of a balance to measure the weight of the goods placed on the other cymbal). At the end of the dialogue wisdom is defined as 'the art of calculating' that establishes the correct value for various pleasures. Let us imagine what Plato might have had in mind when he made use of this strange metaphor suggesting quantitive differences among virtues. Wisdom calculates whether, say, 'eating this piece of cake' is the

---

10 (...) when men partake of these portions of virtue, do some have one, and some another, or if you get one, must you have them all? -By no means, he replied, since many are brave but unjust, and many again are just but not wise. -Then are these also parts of virtue, I asked — wisdom and courage? -Most certainly, I should say, he replied, and of the parts, wisdom is the greatest. -Each of them, I proceeded, is distinct from any other? -Yes. -Does each also have its particular function? Just as, in the parts of the face, the eye is not like the ears, nor is its function the same; nor is any of the other parts like another, in its function or in any other respect: in the same way, are the parts of virtue unlike each other, both in themselves and in their functions? Are they not evidently so, if the analogy holds? -Yes, they are so, Socrates, he said. -So then, I went on, among the parts of virtue, no other part is like knowledge, or like justice, or like courage, or like temperance, or like holiness. He agreed.' (329 e2–330b6).

11 Protagoras complains that 'similar' and 'identical' are not the same. Socrates does not explain in which sense justice and piety are identical to him. We could conjecture that every act of piety is, in a sense, also an act of justice if it is true that the gods are superior to us and deserve our devotion, and conversely, that every act of justice could be somehow regarded as an act of piety, since being just could be understood as one of the duties the gods demand from mortals. If humans are a property of the gods, treating ourselves and others with justice could be regarded as an act of piety. But we might wonder whether these accounts support the view that all virtues are simply different names for 'wisdom'. Plato seems aware of the difficulty, since he appears to offer a more precise version of the identity-thesis ('wisdom and virtue are the same') of the *Protagoras* with the formula μετὰ φρονήσεως at *Phaedo* 69a–c, where genuine virtue is said to be acquired *with* wisdom.

right action to be done by placing this possibility on one cymbal of the balance, and placing the part 'moderation' on the other cymbal. (Be that as it may, I shall return to this interpretation in the light of a parallel obscure passage in the *Phaedo* we shall consider in the next section).

In the final analysis, Socrates will not agree with Protagoras that wisdom is 'the greatest part of virtue', but he suggests that it is the whole of it, like the gold in his analogy. However, the difference in size is never rejected at any place in the dialogue, as if Plato wanted to retain a criterion for distinguishing different virtues, for Socrates remains unwilling to concede to Protagoras that virtues differ in their respective functions, like the organs on a face, which is the obvious way to understand the analogy.

Socrates attempts to persuade his interlocutor that if there is a vice for each virtue but two virtues share the same vice, they must be the same. He picks as his examples moderation (σωφροσύνη) and wisdom (σοφία), and claims that they have the same opposing vice, namely, folly (ἀφροσύνη) (333a–b). One might support Socrates' view by observing that every act of moderation implies an act of wisdom, for moderation follows the due measure which wisdom establishes with regard to pleasure, and conversely, every act of wisdom is moderate, for it cannot be either excessive or defective, but must necessarily achieve the just measure. On the other hand, when due measure is not set, the action cannot be either wise or moderate, but must necessarily imply lack of calculation, and lack of sense or reasonability, i.e. folly.

This argument proves that all genuine virtues are related to wisdom, but it does not prove that all of them are exactly the same.[12] Let me say that I do not believe that Socrates means it either, for he acknowledges difference in 'size' among the virtues. As he unfortunately does not explain the meaning of this metaphor, we are left to conjecture (though the passage in the *Phaedo* we shall consider in the next section may help confirm the idea that different virtues are different *units of measure*).

---

12 Socrates' third argument attempts to defend the unity of wisdom and justice. Apparently Socrates believes that if a man is wise, he must be just, for a man who acts unjustly cannot either think well (εὖ φρονεῖν) or deliberate well (εὖ βουλεύεσθαι). Obviously, Socrates believes that when a man commits an injustice he cannot be said to deliberate 'well', for he understands this adverb in a moral sense, connected to the good, while the many take the adverb as meaning 'fruitfully' (*Prot.* 333b–e). If 'well' means 'right' or 'correctly' in the sense of having the good in view, it would be a contradiction to say that a man thinks 'right' when he has it in mind to do what is wrong. But it would not be a contradiction in terms to say that a man calculates his *profit* 'well' when he is ready to commit an injustice.

It seems to us particularly interesting that the two 'naturally opposing virtues' of the *Politicus*, moderation and courage, are taken here to be one and the same with σοφία, for the lack of them is defined as just one thing, namely, ἀμαθία (incapacity to learn or ignorance). Thus self-control is defined as nothing other than wisdom (οὐδὲ τὸ ἥττω εἶναι αὑτοῦ ἄλλο τι τοῦτ᾽ ἐστὶν ἢ ἀμαθία, οὐδὲ κρείττω ἑαυτοῦ ἄλλο τι ἢ σοφία: 358c2–3) and courage is defined as wisdom about what is and is not to be feared (ἡ σοφία ἄρα τῶν δεινῶν καὶ μὴ δεινῶν ἀνδρεία ἐστίν, ἐναντία οὖσα τῇ τούτων ἀμαθίᾳ: 360d4–5). Though this view seems to run counter the claims in the *Politicus*, it is not necessarily so, once these so called 'virtues' are defined as merely natural dispositions (before education and bonding take place).

Socrates also seems to suggest that the exercise of justice implies the operation of wisdom. Wisdom deliberates well about the appropriate just action to be performed. We can assume that Socrates would extend this view to all the virtues: wisdom tells the wise man that now he should be, say, courageous in the face of certain danger, and prescribes which specific brave action he should perform, all things considered. Analogously, on a different occasion wisdom prescribes moderation, and 'calculates' the limits to be set to certain pleasures, in order to attain the right measure to be enjoyed. Therefore, all the virtues are just one, in the sense that they involve wisdom to calculate the good to be done, but they can be distinguished with different names in ordinary life, because they are different parts of it 'in size'.

At the end of the dialogue, Socrates leaves the description of wisdom as 'the art of measuring' for another occasion: 'What exactly this art and science is, we can inquire into later (ἥτις μὲν τοίνυν τέχνη καὶ ἐπιστήμη ἐστὶν αὕτη, εἰς αὖθις σκεψόμεθα: 357b5–6). This exploration certainly happens to come in the *Politicus*, including the same ambiguity with regard to calling it 'art' or 'science' (ἐπεὶ δὲ μετρητική, ἀνάγκη δήπου τέχνη καὶ ἐπιστήμη: 357b4), as if they were synonyms. Analogously, in the *Protagoras* the art of measuring is said to deal with 'the greater and the lesser'; it is regarded as 'arithmetic in a way' (357a), and it is also described as the study of 'relative' 'excess and deficiency and equality' (357b). Though 'relative', the mention of 'excess and deficiency' seems to point to an assumed 'due measure'. What the art of measure accomplishes in the *Protagoras* is 'the truth'; when this happens, 'appearances lose their power', and we reach that 'peace of mind firmly rooted in the truth' that 'would save our life' (356d–e).[13]

---

13 Also: εἶναι ἡ ἐπιστήμη καὶ οἷον ἄρχειν τοῦ ἀνθρώπου, καὶ ἐάνπερ γιγνώσκῃ τις τἀγαθὰ καὶ τὰ κακά, μὴ ἂν κρατηθῆναι ὑπὸ μηδενὸς ὥστε ἄλλ᾽ ἄττα πράττειν ἢ ἂν ἐπιστήμη κελεύῃ, ἀλλ᾽ ἱκανὴν εἶναι τὴν φρόνησιν βοηθεῖν τῷ ἀνθρώπῳ (*Prot.* 352c3–7).

On the other hand, when Protagoras claims that 'courage comes from nature and the proper nurture of the soul' (ἀνδρεία δὲ ἀπὸ φύσεως καὶ εὐτροφίας τῶν ψυχῶν γίγνεται: 351b1–2) he seems to be adumbrating the Stranger's view that the harmonious city requires the education of naturally opposing dispositions, as is said in the *Politicus*. I will attempt to defend the view that these contrary theses, raised in the *Protagoras*, on the unity of virtue and its possibility of being taught, will turn out to be compatible in the Eleatic dialogue.

3 The *Phaedo*: Genuine Virtue is 'United to Wisdom'

In this dialogue Socrates maintains that the philosopher is the only one who is really brave and moderate. On the one hand, courage is said to be a especial characteristic of philosophers, for they face death without anger, in the hope of attaining that beloved wisdom they had pursued for all their lives (68a–c). There is a strong connection between courage and the belief that death as such is not to be feared.[14] On the contrary, anyone who resents death is not a lover of wisdom but a lover of the body, of wealth or of honors. Analogously, with regard to temperance Socrates wonders:

> And moderation — *what ordinary people call by that name*,[15] which consists in not being excited by the appetites but treating them with disdain and orderliness — is not that the characteristic of those alone who despise the body and spend their lives loving wisdom? (68c8–12).[16]

The philosopher cannot devote himself to the bodily pleasures of drink, food and sex (64d), for he does not find (the highest) pleasure in this type of thing (65a)

---

14 This claim fits with the concept of courage defined in the *Republic* as the preservation of the right belief about what things are to be feared, not abandoning it because of pains, pleasures, desires or fears (429c–d).

15 Socrates has a deeper view of moderation that he develops in the *Charmides,* which could be summarized as the 'awareness of our own limits' in a general sense, all things considered, soul and body. In my view, he seems to suggest that this is the root of the popular concept of moderation as self-restraint with regard to bodily pleasures.

16 καὶ ἡ σωφροσύνη, ἣν καὶ οἱ πολλοὶ ὀνομάζουσι σωφροσύνην, τὸ περὶ τὰς ἐπιθυμίας μὴ ἐπτοῆσθαι ἀλλ' ὀλιγώρως ἔχειν καὶ κοσμίως, ἆρ' οὐ τούτοις μόνοις προσήκει, τοῖς μάλιστα τοῦ σώματος ὀλιγωροῦσίν τε καὶ ἐν φιλοσοφίᾳ ζῶσιν; (*Phaedo*, 68c8–12).

but in the search of wisdom. On the other hand, setting limits to the body is essential for the preservation of the intellectual life he seeks. Moderation preserves thinking.[17]

Let us move now to the difficult passage on the role of wisdom with regard to the exchanges to be performed in life to 'acquire' virtue *stricto sensu*:

"I suspect that this is not the right way to purchase virtue, by exchanging pleasures for pleasures, and pains for pains, and fear for fear, and greater for less, as if they were coins, but the only right coinage, against which all those things must be exchanged is wisdom (ἀντὶ οὗ δεῖ πάντα ταῦτα καταλλάττεσθαι, φρόνησις). And all these things are to be bought and sold against it and with it (καὶ τούτου μὲν πάντα καὶ μετὰ τούτου ὠνούμενά τε καὶ πιπρασκόμενα); and courage and moderation and justice and, in short, true virtue exists only with wisdom, whether pleasures and fears and other things of that sort are added or taken away (τῷ ὄντι ᾖ καὶ ἀνδρεία καὶ σωφροσύνη καὶ δικαιοσύνη καὶ συλλήβδην ἀληθὴς ἀρετή, μετὰ φρονήσεως, καὶ προσγιγνομένων καὶ ἀπογιγνομένων καὶ ἡδονῶν καὶ φόβων καὶ τῶν ἄλλων πάντων τῶν τοιούτων). And separated from wisdom, such virtue which consists in the exchange of such things for each other is but an illusory imitation of virtue, and is really slavish and has nothing healthy or true in it; but the true one really is a kind of purification of all such things, and moderation and justice and courage, and wisdom itself is nothing but a kind of cleansing" (69a 6–c3).

Wisdom (φρόνησις) is said to be 'the only right coin' (μόνον τὸ νόμισμα ὀρθόν) *'against'* which all the other passions, namely, pleasures, pains, and fears, should be exchanged (ἀντὶ οὗ δεῖ πάντα ταῦτα καταλλάττεσθαι). In a second step, Plato makes the metaphor more precise when he makes Socrates add that all these things are to be bought and sold *for what they really are*, 'with' wisdom: καὶ μετὰ τούτου ὠνούμενά τε καὶ πιπρασκόμενα τῷ ὄντι ᾖ (69b1–2). That the transactions should be done μετὰ φρονήσεως (*with* wisdom) excludes the possibility that wisdom is the coin to give away. Calculating 'with wisdom' means

---

17 The awareness of our limits is the key to moderation taken as the maintenance of good relations, both internally and with others (*Republic*, 428d). Moderation depends on the exercise of the best part, namely, reason, for it is reason which sets the right measure. In this sense, this virtue can be called 'good sense' or 'sagacity'. Socrates claims that moderation is surely a kind of order, the mastery of certain kinds of pleasures and desires, which people call 'being master of oneself' and other similar phrases (430e). Then he says: 'I do not know just what they mean by them, but they are, so to speak, like tracks or clues that moderation has left behind in language' (430e7–9). At first, he finds the expression strange, because in a person master and subject are the same, but then he finds that the expression is apparently trying to indicate that 'the naturally better part is in control of the worse' (431a5–6).

calculating wisely. How are we to understand that wisdom is the 'only right coinage'? Socrates takes it, I suggest, as 'the unit of measure' or 'the pattern' by comparison to which one should measure the value of the goods to be bought and sold, namely, pleasures, pains, fears and the like. In a word, wisdom is not the coin to give away to purchase passion, but the unit of measure, the reference, to be used to buy and sell passions in life. Wisdom *knows* 'how much to pay' for them, and prescribes the right price because it can detect, so to speak, their *real nature* and value.

Let us collect our results together. According to the *Phaedo*, every genuine virtue, be it courage, moderation or justice, is claimed to be 'united to wisdom': καὶ ἀνδρεία καὶ σωφροσύνη καὶ δικαιοσύνη καὶ συλλήβδην ἀληθὴς ἀρετή, μετὰ φρονήσεως (69b2–4), while in the *Protagoras* Socrates claims that 'wisdom, temperance, courage, justice and piety are five names for the same thing' (σοφία καὶ σωφροσύνη καὶ ἀνδρεία καὶ δικαιοσύνη καὶ ὁσιότης, πότερον ταῦτα, πέντε ὄντα ὀνόματα, ἐπὶ ἑνὶ πράγματί ἐστιν: 349b1–3); that 'all of them are wisdom, namely, justice, moderation, courage' (ὡς πάντα χρήματά ἐστιν ἐπιστήμη, καὶ ἡ δικαιοσύνη καὶ σωφροσύνη καὶ ἡ ἀνδρεία: 361b1–2) and that virtue is 'entirely wisdom' (ἐπιστήμη ὅλον: b 6).

I deliberately translate σοφία, ἐπιστήμη and φρόνησις as 'wisdom' because in my view they mean the same in the context of the *Protagoras*, namely, 'practical infallible prescriptive knowledge' that measures particular pleasures, pains, fears, loves, etc., and in this way saves a person from wandering and repentance.[18]

It is worth noticing that the formula of the *Phaedo* that 'all the virtues are *united* to wisdom': μετὰ φρονήσεως (69b4) was regarded by Aristotle as the right one, while the conception of virtue as wisdom as it is presented in the *Protagoras* was taken as Socrates' mistake: καὶ Σωκράτης τῇ μὲν ὀρθῶς ἐζήτει τῇ δ' ἡμάρτανεν: ὅτι μὲν γὰρ φρονήσεις ᾤετο εἶναι πάσας τὰς ἀρετάς, ἡμάρτανεν, ὅτι δ' οὐκ ἄνευ φρονήσεως, καλῶς ἔλεγεν (*Nicomachean Ethics* 1144b18–21). Indeed, Aristotle adopted precisely the same preposition (μετὰ) that Plato uses in the *Phaedo*, to describe the relation between ethical virtue and φρόνησις.

In my view, both formulations, though different in expression, point to the same goal. The identity-thesis 'virtue is wisdom' does not mean that Socrates is picking the part for the whole, but that all the other virtues are *essentially* wisdom. Courage, moderation and justice are wisdom exercised on different occasions and in differing circumstances. When one is in danger wisdom is called

---

18 For a full justification of this translation, and an explanation of the misunderstanding caused by Plato's use of these different words as synonyms, see Bossi (2003) (2008) and (2017).

'courage'; when one is attracted by the prospect of pleasure wisdom is called 'moderation'; in our relations with others wisdom is called 'justice'. The 'identity' thesis of the *Protagoras* does not nullify difference. Virtues are analogous to 'parts of gold with different sizes'.

What the *Protagoras* and the *Phaedo* passages have in common is: a) that wisdom measures; b) that it measures properly or correctly; c) that it measures pleasures (and passions in general). What they differ about is that while in the *Protagoras* virtues are parts of wisdom with different names and sizes (as reference-points, I have suggested, or units of measure for calculating properly), in the *Phaedo* virtues are to be acquired as a result of the correct exercise for measuring passions, and for the setting of the correct 'price' to pay when 'buying and selling' them. The emphasis, it should be added, is on the selling, for every virtue is re-garded as a kind of purification from (wrong) passions. And wisdom is the valu-ation-coin that stands as the reference-mark for the exchanges, the way the gold coin is the reference-mark which sets the value of all the other coins used in buy-ing and selling.

The thesis of the *Phaedo* also indicates an essential relation between any vir-tue and wisdom,[19] for only the wise philosopher is regarded as being genuinely virtuous. It is no coincidence that Socrates, who has spent his life as a philoso-pher, is introduced in the dramatic action as the courageous man who faces death with serenity and care for his friends. His courage is the result of his being a phi-losopher, of his getting ready to die by gradually separating his soul from his body as much as possible. His courage is not just a virtue he happens to have by nature, but is due to his philosophical practice; thus, he cannot be conceived as deprived of any virtue, be it courage or moderation.[20]

---

19 On a different front, in the *Phaedo* different virtues are also understood as being the same thing, namely, purification: 'but truth is in fact a purification from all these things, and moder-ation and justice and courage and wisdom itself are a kind of purification: τὸ δ' ἀληθὲς τῷ ὄντι ἦ κάθαρσίς τις τῶν τοιούτων πάντων καὶ ἡ σωφροσύνη καὶ ἡ δικαιοσύνη καὶ ἀνδρεία, καὶ αὐτὴ ἡ φρόνησις μὴ καθαρμός τις ᾖ (69b8–c3). We can conjecture that courage is purification from wrong fear, moderation is purification from excessive pleasure, justice is purification from arro-gance, and wisdom from deceit.
20 When Crito proposes that he delay the end, and enjoy his last moments, as other prisoners do, by having a big meal or having sexual intercourse, Socrates realizes that his poor friend does not really seem to know him after all, for in his view, no gain can be derived from these things (116e).

4 The Vision of Truth Produces Genuine Virtues (*Symposium*)

In my view, the thesis of the involvement of the virtues in wisdom introduced in the *Protagoras* is also supported in some measure in the *Symposium*. Diotima teaches Socrates that only the person who has enjoyed the vision of the Form of Beauty from the topmost rung of the *scala amoris* can become really virtuous, in the sense of possessing all the *genuine* virtues, not just mere imitations, because he would have seen the truth (212a). However, Plato does not explain *how* the vision of truth can change a person, not only in his intellectual convictions, but also in his emotional reactions and character. But he is persuaded that this vision does produce a change. As soon as a certain stage of beauty is reached, the person who has seen it cannot help but immediately love it, and find his ranking of beautiful items changed. What is seen on each step reveals itself as much more beautiful and desirable than preceding items of beauty. It is no coincidence that, after Diotima's teaching, Socrates is described by Alcibiades as having all the genuine virtues implied in her persuasive story about the steps towards beauty. Socrates is introduced as brave in battle and peacetime, moderate in face of pleasures, resilient when confronted with cold or the need for sleep, just with regard to his fellow citizens threatened by tyrants, pious towards the gods and his daemon, etc. and he is said to have 'divine visions' within his soul. However, other signals in the dialogue offer evidence that Socrates might not have reached the top of the *scala*.[21] Plato leaves his case open.

5 On the Implications of a Unitarian Picture

I take the expression μετὰ φρονήσεως in the *Phaedo* and μετὰ νοῦ in the *Republic* (431c5–7) to be either synonymous or quite close to this, and in tune with the view of the *Protagoras* that virtue is basically wisdom, since every virtuous action involves the art of calculation. If this is so, we could conclude our analysis by saying that there is enough evidence in the dialogues we have considered to claim that wisdom turns out to be the necessary and sufficient condition for becoming genuinely virtuous. The 'identity' thesis 'virtue equals wisdom' of the *Protagoras*,

---

21 See Bossi (2016).

if understood as denoting 'essentially the same', and not taken literally as 'absolute identity' (without admitting any difference among virtues), is in tune with the thesis that 'genuine virtue is virtue with wisdom' of the *Phaedo* and with the conditional claim that 'virtue *stricto sensu* should be virtue with intellect' of the *Republic*. So the 'identity' thesis cannot be taken as if wisdom had no correlative virtues distinguishable by different names; the 'identity thesis' is compatible with the distinction of other correlative virtues called after different names according to difference 'in size'. Naturally, I do not mean that *any* action stemming from any virtue, say justice, *qua* wise, is also an example of, e.g., courage. Justice differs from courage; different names denote different virtues in ordinary language, and Socrates does not expect us to change the ordinary meaning of these virtues, but simply sets out to show that all the virtues are 'essentially' wisdom or involve wisdom.

I am aware of the fact that this unitarian interpretation runs against the traditional assumption of a break between the so-called 'intellectualistic' approach of the *Protagoras* and the 'non-intellectualistic' approach of the *Republic* and the *Phaedo*. In my view there is no break because there is no need to assume any 'intellectualism'.[22]

All that must be assumed are different levels of 'virtue': the philosophical, the popular and the natural. At the philosophical level the wise man necessarily has all the virtues, while at the popular and natural levels, one may have one virtue without having the others, because popular virtue depends on habit and education rather than on self-determination and genuine calculus, and natural 'virtue' is merely a pre-disposition towards certain genuine virtues rather than towards others.

6 The *Politicus:* The Wise Virtuous Politician

The purpose of the dialogue is to determine which kind of knowledge, science or art the statesman possesses (and with that 'excuse' to make interlocutors better dialecticians). His γνωστικὴ ἐπιστήμη (259e), which is also described as κριτικὴ καὶ ἐπιστατικὴ (292b), is said to be the greatest and the most difficult state to attain (292d). The ideal king is wise (φρόνιμος: 292d6; 294a8), and capable of prescribing what is precisely the best and the most just thing for everybody (294a10–b1). In addition, it is claimed that whatever wise rulers (τοῖς ἔμφροσιν ἄρχουσιν) do,

---

22 See Bossi (2003), (2008) and (2017).

they can make no mistakes, since they invariably dispense absolute justice to their citizens with understanding and art (μετὰ νοῦ καὶ τέχνης), with the goal of preserving them and make them better than they were, so far as that is possible (297a–b). The Stranger also claims that the ideal statesman would govern with virtue and science: μετ' ἀρετῆς καὶ ἐπιστήμης ἄρχοντα (301d1). The connection between good sense and infallibility reminds us of Socrates' 'powerful governing wisdom that knows the good and prescribes it' of the *Protagoras*. The statesman seems to have the same type of wisdom not only to govern himself but others as well. In my view, the passages quoted are enough evidence to conclude that Plato conceives the ideal 'divine' statesman (303b4) as somebody who has reached the level of philosophical wisdom which implies all the genuine virtues. Another question is whether such an ideal man happens to exist or not.

7 The *Politicus*: on Hostile Parts

When it comes to the description of politics as the art of weaving that belongs to kingship, the Stranger introduces a 'difficult'[23] topic with regard to virtue, namely, the idea that different parts of virtue may oppose one another. He takes extreme care over formulating the claim:

> To say that a part of virtue is in a certain sense different from another kind of virtue provides an all too easy target for those experts in disputing arguments who appeal to the opinions of the many: τὸ γὰρ ἀρετῆς μέρος ἀρετῆς εἴδει διάφορον εἶναί τινα τρόπον τοῖς περὶ λόγους ἀμφισβητητικοῖς καὶ μάλ' εὐεπίθετον πρὸς τὰς τῶν πολλῶν δόξας (306a8–10).

Young Socrates does not understand. Though cryptic, this introduction to the topic is important. The Stranger seems to be assuming that to defend the view that a so-called 'part' of virtue is *different from another kind of virtue*' is to expose oneself to an easy attack by those who like arguing in support of popular views.

In the *Protagoras*, while arguing against his interlocutor, Socrates seems to admit that virtue has parts, though at the end these parts belong in fact to that whole which he identifies, essentially, with wisdom. To say that "a part of virtue is different from another part" is to offer "an all too easy target for those experts in disputing arguments who appeal to the opinions of the many" because, I suggest, the Stranger is aware that the sophists, who always try to echo what the many think, would easily take issue with his view that virtues can oppose one

---

23 ἢ χαλεπὸν ἐνδείξασθαι πρᾶγμα ἀναγκαῖον ἄρα γέγονεν (306a5–6).

another. One might wonder whether the Stranger alludes to Protagoras and the rest of the sophists at the house of Callias. It is likely to be the case, because Protagoras defends the view that: a) there are parts of virtue; b) all the parts belong to the same kind, but c) a man can have one virtue without having the others. Clearly Socrates denied c) because he defended the view that virtue is essentially wisdom, and if this is so, if a man has wisdom he has all virtues.

There are many clues that indicate that the *Protagoras* is the dialogue Plato seems to have in mind while writing the second part of the *Politicus*. However, in the *Politicus* Plato offers a more realistic approach, when he appeals to an analogical answer to the old question about the origin of genuine virtue by use of the model of weaving.

I have suggested that the 'parts' the Stranger refers to are 'natural' virtues, namely, in-born dispositions 'towards' virtue. It is, so to speak, the 'raw material' (the 'wool' in Plato's analogy) that could be transformed into 'genuine virtue' (the piece of fabric) through a very complex process. The procedure described includes: a) the sorting out (of children?) through a test when they are at play (cleansing); b) the education of the character (carding);[24] and c) the interlacing of different, opposing characters, namely, the brave and the moderate (warp and woof) by means of two types of procedure: 'the divine bond', which implants 'true opinion about the good and the bad with a firm grounding' in their souls, and the 'human bond', which controls the unions to produce the particular births of mixed-temperament children. These natural virtues differ from 'virtue *stricto sensu*' in that they can stay at a primitive, potential level, without being turned into genuine virtue.

Let us notice that the Stranger assumes that Young Socrates shares the popular view that virtue has *parts* without endorsing that view himself: 'I imagine you think'... (οἶμαί σε ἡγεῖσθαι: 306a12). The Stranger is aware that he 'must dare to declare something astonishing' about moderation and courage (τούτων δὴ πέρι θαυμαστόν τινα λόγον ἀποφαίνεσθαι τολμητέον: 306b 6–7) which is 'not in any way the speech they are used to' (οὐκ εἰωθότα λόγον οὐδαμῶς: 306b 13), and is against 'what is said' (λέγεται: 306c1).

The thesis he ventures to propose is that courage and moderation, which are usually thought to be parts of virtue amicably disposed towards each other, 'are

---

24 El Murr (2014) 272, includes two processes : 'cardage qui distingue' (...) 'mais aussi filage qui regroupe'. I agree that the preparing of the souls for the divine bonding requires both processes: selection and a first attempt to reduce hostility among them through a number of means that promote respect and collaboration.

in some sort of way extremely hostile to each other, and occupy opposing positions in many things' (κατὰ δή τινα τρόπον εὖ μάλα πρὸς ἀλλήλας ἔχθραν καὶ
στάσιν ἐναντίαν ἔχοντε ἐν πολλοῖς τῶν ὄντων: 306b9–10). He could have said 'in
many human beings', but he said 'in many things'. This means he is taking a more
comprehensive view, which will include all the things that are called 'fine' (ὅσα
καλὰ μὲν λέγομεν: 306c7). He proposes to look into the matter with extremely
close attention to see whether this is unqualifiedly the case (i.e. that they are amicably disposed towards each other), or whether, rather, '<some> of them (accepting Robinson's addenda) are *different* from those *congenial* to them in some respect' (τοῖς συγγενέσιν ἔς τι) (306c3–5).

The claim that 'some of them are different from the ones that are akin to them'
might mean that, to the Stranger, the so-called *natural* 'virtues' are different from
their genuine counterparts, which are akin to the natural ones (in the sense that
they have the same origin as the former), since, we will learn here, the genuine
ones 'come' from the natural ones. If this is so, what the Stranger has in mind
here is that there is a difference and also a likeness from the start.

The moderate type and the courageous type of opposite qualities[25] do not mix
with each other, and those who possess them in their souls are at odds with each
other, for they praise what belongs to their own kin and censure their opponents
and engage in a great deal of hostility towards each other (306e–307d). This rivalry is the kind of play one associates with children, but it can become 'the most
hateful disease for cities' 'in relation to the organization of life as a whole'. On the
one hand, the 'orderly' are always ready in any way to preserve peace of some
kind, 'and because of this *passion* of theirs, which is *less timely than it should be*
(διὰ τὸν ἔρωτα δὴ τοῦτον ἀκαιρότερον ὄντα ἢ χρή) when they do what they want,
nobody notices that they are being unwarlike and making the young men the
same, and that they are perpetually at the mercy of those who attack them, with
the result that within a few years they themselves, their children and the whole
city together often become slaves instead of free men before they have noticed it'
(307e6–308a2).

On the other hand, the 'courageous' are described as always drawing their
cities into some war or another 'because of their *appetite* for a life of this sort,
which is more vigorous than it should be' (διὰ τὴν τοῦ τοιούτου βίου

---

25 The Stranger appeals to common language and opinion: as we admire speed and vigour and
quickness of mind and body, we speak in praise of it by using a single appellation, 'courage'.
Analogously, when someone is quiet and moderate, slow and soft, smooth and deep, we use the
appellation 'orderly'. Conversely, when these qualities occur at the wrong time and go to extremes, we call these people either 'excessive and maniac' or 'cowardly and lethargic'.

σφοδροτέραν τοῦ δέοντος ἐπιθυμίαν: 308a6–7), with the result that they either destroy their fatherlands or make them slaves and subjects of their enemies. Here the same argument holds: genuine virtue cannot be 'dragged about' by excessive appetite.

The Stranger claims that they have found what they were looking for, namely that 'parts of virtue of no small importance are *by nature* at odds with on another' (μόρια ἀρετῆς οὐ σμικρὰ ἀλλήλοις διαφέρεσθον φύσει : 308b7–8). The argument supports the 'astonishing claim' that 'parts of virtue' oppose each other, against the popular view.

The argument cannot refer to genuine virtue, but only to naturally opposed dispositions, for three reasons: a) because genuine virtue cannot be moved either by 'untimely passion' or 'excessive appetite'; b) because such dispositions are said to be in opposition 'by nature', which suggests that they are not the result of any process of education; and c) because they produce slavery and destruction, which implies lack of understanding and wisdom. No genuine virtue can produce such devastating effects, according to Plato. For these reasons, I think we have enough evidence to regard them as simply natural dispositions of temperament, even when they are called 'virtues' by the many, by Young Socrates, and in ordinary language.

On the other hand, in support of this view, they are compared to 'materials' to be classified and prepared before the work of combination begins (308c). The art of statesmanship will put to the test individuals who have an exclusively opposing disposition in their souls, to separate those with good dispositions from those with evil dispositions, and will then hand over the former to educators in order to *prepare their characters* for sharing in a disposition that is both courageous and moderate. Those whose natures are capable of becoming composed in the direction of what is noble, should they acquire education, and, with the help of expertise, of being commingled with each other, will be bonded together.[26] By contrast, 'those who are unable to share in a disposition that is courageous and moderate and the other qualities that tend towards virtue (τείνοντα πρὸς ἀρετήν) but by the force of an evil nature are thrust away (ὑπὸ κακῆς βία φύσεως

---

26 Analogously in the *Republic* only those who are born with the best natures and receive the best education have their desires measured and directed by calculation in accordance with intellect and correct belief: τὰς δέ γε ἁπλᾶς τε καὶ μετρίας, αἳ δὴ μετὰ νοῦ τε καὶ δόξης ὀρθῆς λογισμῷ ἄγονται, ἐν ὀλίγοις τε ἐπιτεύξῃ καὶ τοῖς βέλτιστα μὲν φῦσιν, βέλτιστα δὲ παιδευθεῖσιν (431c5–7), i.e. only these few can become moderate. And they become so due to their mild nature plus the exercise of calculation.

ἀπωθουμένους)[27] into godlessness, excess and injustice it throws out by killing them, sending them into exile, and punishing them with the most extreme forms of dishonour (308d9–309a3).

I should like to emphasize that the Stranger is here comparing moderate and courageous characters or dispositions to other things that '*tend* towards virtue', which clearly means that he does not regard these dispositions as genuine virtues. At 309b3 he also refers to these natural dispositions as 'tending' towards courage or moderation.[28]

These 'courageous' people are said to be *by nature* inferior to others in relation to justice and caution (311b), but when divine 'true opinions about what is fine, just and good, and the opposites of these', with a firm ground or confirmation, arises in them' (309c5–8) they will become 'just', and 'the ones with an orderly nature, if they share in these opinions will become *genuinely* moderate and wise' (τί δὲ τὸ τῆς κοσμίας φύσεως; ἆρ' οὐ τούτων μὲν μεταλαβὸν τῶν δοξῶν ὄντως σῶφρον καὶ φρόνιμον: 309d10–e6).

In my view, this interesting passage shows here again in the *Politicus* (as well as in the *Protagoras*, the *Symposium*, the *Phaedo*, and the *Republic*) that grasping the truth is essential for the attainment of *genuine* virtue. On the other hand, the relations courage-justice and moderation-wisdom make clear that the conception of virtue as being just 'one being with different aspects that are called after different names' may still have a part to play. The fact that Plato relates courage to justice and moderation to wisdom 'through the grasping of true opinion' means that knowledge is still the essential variable that produces the promotion of naturally good dispositions that had been suitably prepared by education to the stage of genuine virtue.

The Stranger speaks of dispositions that 'were born' noble, and describes the more divine bonding as the one that unites 'parts of virtue that are *by nature* unlike each other, and go in opposite directions' (τὸν σύνδεσμον ἀρετῆς μερῶν φύσεως ἀνομοίων καὶ ἐπὶ τὰ ἐναντία φερομένων 310a4–5). The final evidence that the dispositions he refers to are the natural ones we are born with, comes

---

27 The mention of bad ones that 'are thrust away by force' might seem completely opposed to the thesis of the *Protagoras* that 'passion cannot drag like a slave', but in fact there is no opposition, for, in my view, the passage in the *Protagoras* refers to the wise, and here it refers to the bad (for a detailed analysis on this see Bossi, 2008).

28 Rowe (here) distinguishes the way natural 'virtues' are disposed (before the education of the character takes place) as 'they incline': (*rhepousi*) the agent more towards courage (308a4) or 'strain more (*sunteinousas*) towards courage and the moderate' (309b2–4) from that other 'straining' (*teinousas*: 309b6) which corresponds to the binding.

from the fact that these dispositions, should no education take place, are said to be reproduced over many generations (310d–e), as if they were inherited.

Monserrat[29] claims that there is here a clear divorce between virtue and knowledge which is also apparent in *Republic* IV: while moral knowledge belongs to the genuine politician, the rest of men have only true opinions in order to control excess. There is a difference, he claims, between true opinion and truth in itself, which is assimilated to the 'divine'.

However, in our context in the *Politicus*, this is not just *any* opinion but a very peculiar one, which is called 'really true' and 'divine' and is assumed to have a 'firm guarantee'. This leads us to imagine that the distance from *episteme*, if there is any, is very small. Casertano has noticed (in his paper in this volume) that it seems that opinion is no longer downgraded with regard to 'science' or 'wisdom' as it is in the *Republic*. It is true that Plato does seem to maintain that there is a difference between those who have 'genuine virtue', which seems to be of a rather 'political' cast, and that single individual (politician, king and philosopher) who has theoretical knowledge. But if those he binds in this way do have a 'divine true opinion' about realities that seem to be quite similar to the Forms, one might reasonably wonder what that difference is.

On the other hand, the appeal to honor, shame, public opinion, and the force of law to keep both types united through *homodoxia*, and the way they are said to be cured by the *pharmakon* which is identified with the 'more divine' *techne* that is possessed by the ideal politician/king, give the impression that these people are certainly not at the top of the ranking.

8 Conclusion

While, in the former dialogues which I have explored in this paper, Plato sets the grounds for distinguishing genuine, popular and false virtue, here the analysis is more dynamic and closer to the *Republic*, as if in the *Politicus* Plato wanted to show us how he imagines real virtue could be attained, should a wise politician prove able be found, by describing the way naturally opposing dispositions, through education, law, and expertise, are readied to become genuine unified virtue when the politician realizes the proper bondings of the divine and mortal parts.

---

29 Monserrat (1999) 249; 258.

I hope I have been able to present enough evidence to argue in favour of the view that the old thesis that conceives *genuine virtue* to be essentially *wisdom* (according to the formula of the *Protagoras*) or 'united to wisdom' (according to the formula of the *Phaedo*) is not necessarily abandoned in the *Politicus*, since 'truth' is still the pivotal factor that provokes the transformation of 'character dispositions' into 'genuine virtue'. The divine bonds, 'implanted in our souls', if I may say so, echoing the *Phaedrus*, are only true opinions about the good and their opposites, but still 'opinions with a firm guarantee'.

Are these opinions tied to the divine Forms of old? Is this what the Stranger means when he refers to the divine bonds that the wise politician interlaces? Does he mean that the wise politician exercises them in dialectics? Does he mean that the politician is the philosopher? Does Plato mean that the Stranger has been playing the part of the philosopher with Young Socrates in order to make him ascend to a new stage, in which he would become both a better dialectician and by thereby also a better person?[30] I suspect my answer to all these questions is 'yes'. If dramatic resources could be taken into account, Socrates' silence throughout the whole discussion would be a last proof of Plato's consistency. But who can trust our brilliant playwright?[31]

---

[30] Monserrat (1999) 259, has very interesting observations on this topic, particularly with regard to Young Socrates becoming wise (*phronimos*) when gets old 'if he does not pay too much attention to words'. If this is to be taken seriously, I am afraid this starts to happen after having spent many years reading Plato, for he does not seem to care much about words either. On the other hand, Young Socrates' division between beasts and men is called *andreiotata* but is in fact wrong, which means that Plato is using the word to refer to his 'natural' temperament that hastens too quickly, rather than to genuine virtue. The ambiguity of the term 'virtue' here is not limited to the conclusion of the dialogue, but occurs throughout the dramatic action as well. Monserrat also points out that the Stranger works against the 'courageous' nature of Young Socrates by means of his authority (261).

[31] I am deeply grateful to Dougal Blyth for his valuable critical comments on this paper, to Thomas M. Robinson for checking the English language of the original version and to Germán Sierra for his essential help at editing the volume.

Christopher Rowe
'Moderation' and Courage in Plato's *Politicus* (305e–311c)

This paper concerns itself with the final part of the *Politicus*, from 305e to the end, when the Visitor from Elea turns to discussing 'the intertwining that belongs to kingship' (*tên … basilikên sumplokên*, a1). What the king, or the perfect states-man, 'intertwines', or 'weaves together' (*sumplekei*), turns out to be 'the disposi-tion of courageous and moderate people', *to tôn andreiôn kai sôphronôn an-thrôpôn êthos* (the passage represents the final account of the statesman):

> Then let us say that this marks the completion of the fabric which is the product of the art of statesmanship: the weaving together, with regular intertwining, of the disposition[1] of courageous and moderate people – when the expertise belonging to the king brings their life together in agreement and friendship and makes it common between them,[2] completing the most magnificent and best of all fabrics and covering with it all the other inhabitants of cities, both slave and free, and holds them together with this twining and rules and directs without, so far as it belongs to a city to be happy, falling short of that in any respect.[3]

In the first and longest section of this paper, I shall discuss what sort of *andreia* and *sôphrosunê* it is that the two types in question, the *andreioi* and the *sôphrones*, are meant to have. As the Visitor himself says, one would expect the parts of virtue[4] to be perfectly compatible, just because they are parts of the same thing, virtue; so why should their respective possessors need 'weaving together'?

---

1 Passages from the *Politicus* in this paper are cited in a modified version of my translation of the dialogue as it appears in the Hackett *Plato: Complete Works* (= Cooper 1997). Here, the Hack-ett version translates the singular *êthos* with the plural 'dispositions'; in the present context I prefer to revert to the singular, as in the original translation (in Rowe 1995), my thought being that Plato may intend a kind of prolepsis, with the singular referring to the unifying effect of the royal weaving. Cf. 308e–309a, where those 'unable to share in a disposition that is courageous and moderate …' (308e9) are excluded from the city. – There are other modifications (sometimes quite extensive) to the Hackett version elsewhere in this essay, the chief motive of which is to make the often difficult Greek of the *Politicus* more immediate intelligible; the Hackett version, like the 1995 original, was intended as a fairly 'literal' translation (i.e., one that tended to make good English less of a priority than preserving something of the structure of the Greek).

2 Reading <*hôst'einai*> in 311b9.

3 *Politicus* 311b7–c7.

4 I use 'virtue' for *aretê* throughout the paper, despite my general preference for 'excellence' (which avoids the inevitable, and often misleading, association of the English 'virtue' with mo-rality – of which there is little in Plato or his Socrates, at least when speaking in his own voice).

https://doi.org/10.1515/9783110605549-019

Evidently the *andreia* and *sôphrosunê* that belong to the *andreioi* and *sôphrones* in the context of the end of the *Politicus* are of some special, qualified kind that allows the two groups, even *qua* courageous and moderate, to be in conflict with each other. So what kind of *andreia*, and what kind of *sôphrosunê*, are they? (The Visitor suggests the question; the answer we need to work out for ourselves.) In the second section of the paper, I ask why Plato should choose these two particular types as the sphere of operation for the royal weaver's skill. When the 'fabric' he weaves is explicitly to cover 'all the other inhabitants of cities,[5] both slave and free', i.e., presumably, in addition to the courageous and the moderate, why does he pick out these two particular groups for attention? Why should he, or we, suppose, as his strategy suggests, that the relationship between these two groups is liable to be the main threat to the unity of the city? (What, for example, about the relationship between them and other free men?) In the third and final section, starting from the same passage (*Politicus* 305e–311c), I shall continue the discussion, begun in the second section, of the relationship between the city of the *Politicus* and those of the *Republic* and the *Laws*.

1 What sort of *andreia* and *sôphrosunê* are the *andreioi* and *sôphrones* of the passage meant to have?

At 306a, the Visitor proposes that he and his interlocutor, a young namesake of Socrates, should discuss the function of the true king or statesman as weaver. He immediately starts by talking about the relationship between the two groups, the *andreioi* and the *sôphrones*, which he will suggest can be in conflict with each other; and he begins with the problem:

> Visitor: To say that part of virtue is in some way different in kind from virtue provides an all too easy target for those expert in disputing statements [i.e., experts in eristics], in the context of what people generally think.
> Young Socrates: I don't understand.
> V.: I'll put it again, like this. I imagine you think that courage, for us, constitutes one part of virtue.
> Y.S.: Certainly.

---

5 The reference here to 'cities', in the plural, no doubt reflects the fact that the theory of the *Politicus* is intended to apply not just to one imagined city but to cities in general, as they could and should be.

V.: And also that moderation is something distinct from courage, but at the same time that this too is one part of what the other is part of [i.e., virtue].
Y.S.: Yes.
V.: Well, we must dare to declare[6] something astonishing in relation to these two.
Y.S.: What?
V.: That, in some sort of way, they are extremely hostile to each other and occupy opposed positions in many things.
Y.S.: What do you mean?
V.: Not in any way the sort of thing people are used to saying. For certainly, I imagine, all the parts of virtue are said to be amicably disposed towards each other, if anything is.
Y.S. Yes.[7]

The Visitor is making two separate proposals here, which are problematic in rather different ways. The first proposal is that 'part of virtue [can be], in a certain sense, different in kind from [a part of][8] virtue', which 'provides an all too easy target' for the eristically inclined,[9] but is surely, on the face of it, unexceptional. That courage and moderation should be distinct ('in kind') while being both parts of the same thing, virtue, is hardly more difficult to accept than the fact that both sheep and goats are four-footed animals fails to make sheep into goats or goats into sheep. All the same, it is a claim that clever people can easily make trouble with in the context of what people generally think.[10] And not just clever eristics, one might add: Socrates himself makes serious trouble for Protagoras, in Plato's *Protagoras*, on the same sort of issue, when he asks Protagoras whether the various parts of virtue are parts of it as the different parts of the face are parts of the face, or 'parts as in the parts of gold, where there is no difference, except for size, between parts or between the parts and the whole'.[11] He goes on pressing this second option despite Protagoras' resistance; as well he might, if he is serious about the possibility, as he appears to be, both in the *Protagoras* and elsewhere, that all

---

6 The Hackett version has 'we must take our courage in our hands and declare ...', which suggests – perhaps rightly – a reference to *andreia* here; but it is worth saying that the verb used (*tolman*) is from a different root.

7 306a8–c2.

8 The supplement appears justified by the Visitor's explanation of the first of his two proposals, in what immediately follows; his suppression of 'a part of' perhaps serves to intensify the apparent paradox.

9 i.e., those who to argue about words ('what is said', 'statements': *logoi*, 306a9) rather than about what the words are being used to say, their aim being simply to 'win' the argument by whatever means.

10 This is how I propose to take *pros tas tôn pollôn doxas*: = 'if we view things in relation to what the majority of people think', in the Hackett version, as cited above, preserving the opacity of the Greek.

11 *Protagoras* 329d6–8.

of virtue – and so all the virtues – might reduce to the single thing, knowledge. It is, I think, not impossible that this forms part of the intended backdrop to our passage here in the *Politicus*.[12]

The second of the Visitor's two proposals in the passage cited above[13] is that 'in some sort of way, they [the two parts of virtue in question] are extremely hostile to each other and occupy opposed positions in many things'.[14] The phrase 'in some sort of way', *kata dê tina tropon*, echoes 'in some way' (*tina tropon*) in the sentence introducing the first proposal ('to say that part of virtue is in some way different in kind from virtue ...'), and I think is designed to do so. The purpose is not to suggest that the two proposals are related, but rather to point out the contrast between them. In short, what the Visitor is proposing now is quite distinct from what he has just proposed: saying, as he is saying now, that *andreia* and *sôphrosunê* can be in conflict with each other is quite separate from the point that they are, anyway, distinct, *diaphora*, parts of virtue. The new proposal is not only different, but paradoxical; it isn't at all the kind of thing we usually say, which is that 'all the parts of virtue are ... amicably disposed towards each other, if anything is'.[15] So now, the Visitor asks,

> should we look, with the closest attention, to see whether this is unqualifiedly the case, or whether decidedly [*pantos mallon*] some aspects of them [i.e., of *andreia* and *sôphrosunê*] do admit of dissent in some respect from what is related to them [i.e., each other]?[16]

He goes on to treat *andreia* and *sôphrosunê* as two among a larger class of things: things: 'things that we call fine [*kala*], but then go on to locate in two opposed classes [*eidê*]'.[17] These are things like sharpness (*oxutês*), speed (*tachos*), and vigour (*sphodrotês*), which we often praise, and actually often praise by calling them 'courage':

---

12 Despite the fact that the Visitor would have no way of knowing about Socrates' conversation with Protagoras; the young Socrates would obviously be in no position to pick up any such allusion either. But we readers have an advantage over both of them.
13 I.e., 306a8–c2.
14 306b9–11.
15 306b13–c1 ('if anything is' represents the *pou* in c1).
16 306c3–5 (*andreia* and *sôphrosunê* being 'related' to each other just insofar as both are parts of virtue).
17 I.e., as it turns out, the class of the not so fine as well as that of the fine (306c7–8).

Young Socrates: How so?
Visitor: I think we say 'sharp and courageous' – that's a first example; and 'fast and courageous', and similarly with 'vigorous'. In every case it's by applying the name I'm talking
about [i.e., 'courage'] in common to all these sorts of thing that we praise them.[18]

But then again we often praise 'the kind of things that happen gently' (*to tês êre-
maias geneseôs eidos*, and

we say on each occasion that they are 'quiet and moderate', admiring things done in the
mind, and in the sphere of actions themselves, that are slow and soft, and also things the
voice does that turn out smooth and deep – and all rhythmic movement, and the whole of
music when it employs slowness at the right time. We apply to all of them the name, not of
courage, but of orderliness [*kosmiotês*].[19]

But then when we find either of the two kinds of qualities – speed, vigour, sharpness, or gentleness, quietness, slowness, softness – occurring at the wrong time,
we change our tune, and censure them instead of praising them, 'by calling them
"excessive and manic" when they turn out sharper than is timely [*oxutera ... gig-
nomena tou kairou*], and appear too fast and hard, and calling things that are too
deep and slow and soft "cowardly and lethargic"'.[20] And so the Visitor can begin
drawing his desired conclusion:

It's pretty much a general rule that we find that these qualities, and the moderate type as a
whole, and the "courage" of the opposite qualities do not mix with each other in the relevant contexts; it's as if they were the sorts of things that could be in a state of war-readiness
towards each other. Moreover we shall see that those who possess them in their souls are at
odds with each other, if we go looking for them.
Young Socrates: Where do you mean us to look?
Visitor: Both in all the spheres we mentioned just now, and no doubt in many others. For I
think because of their affinity to either set of qualities, they praise some things as belonging
to their own kin, and censure those of their opponents as alien, engaging in a great deal of
hostility towards each other, about a great many things.[21]

When people like this disagree, says the Visitor, in the course of ordinary life, it
can appear 'almost playful';[22] but

---

18 306d10–e12. ('Sorts of thing': *phuseis*, e11)
19 307a1–b3 (*kosmiotês* is here evidently treated as a synonym of *sôphrosunê*).
20 307b9–c2.
21 307c2–d4.
22 307d6 (*paidia ... tis*).

when it comes to the really important things, it turns out to be the most hateful of all diseases for cities.

Young Socrates: What are you saying – when it comes to what?

Visitor: The organization of life as a whole. Those who are especially orderly [*kosmioi*] are always ready to live the quiet life, carrying on their private business on their own by themselves. They associate with everyone in their own city on this basis, and similarly with cities outside their own, being ready to preserve peace of some sort in any way they can. As a result of this passion of theirs, which can be not as timely as it should be [*akairoteros*], they do what they want and nobody notices that they are not only being unwarlike themselves but making the young men the same, and perpetually at the mercy of anyone who attacks. The consequence is that within a few years they themselves, their children, and the whole city together often become slaves instead of free men before they have noticed it.

Y.S.: What you describe is a painful and terrifying thing to go through.

V.: But what about those who incline more towards courage? Isn't it the case that they are always drawing their cities into some war or other because of their having a desire for a life of this sort that is more vigorous than it should be, and that they make enemies of people who are both numerous and powerful, and so either completely destroy their own fatherlands, or else make them slaves and subjects of their enemies?

Y.S.: This too is true.

V.: How then can we deny that in these things both of these classes of people always admit of much hostility and dissent between them, even to the greatest degree?

Y.S.: There's no way we shall deny it.

V.: Then we have found, haven't we, what we were originally looking into, that parts of virtue of no small importance are by nature at odds with each other, and moreover cause those who possess them to be in this same condition?

Y.S. Very likely they do.[23]

The chief reason for quoting the text here at such length is to bring out the fact that throughout the whole discussion up to this point the Visitor and the young Socrates are talking about *andreia* and *sôphrosunê* in the context of ordinary experience, and ordinary language. When the Visitor says, at the end, that they have found that 'parts of virtue of no small importance [presumably, *andreia* and *sôphrosunê*] are *by nature*[24] at odds with each other', he seems to have in mind the way he has said we, or people generally, associate sharpness, speed, and vigorousness with *andreia*, and the contrary traits with *sôphrosunê*, or indeed actually identify the traits with the virtues themselves ('often ... whenever we admire speed and vigour and quickness, of mind and body, and even of voice, we praise it by giving it the single name, "courage" ...'; 'we say people on particular occasions are 'quiet and moderate'); this way, clearly, the two virtues will 'naturally' be at odds, just insofar as the associated traits are. Why 'those who are especially

---

23 307d6–308b9.
24 308b7.

orderly' are so, and why 'those who incline more towards courage' so incline is left undetermined: it might be because they are born like that, or because they have been brought up in that way, or for some other reason: as I have said, the Visitor is here talking about the world as it is, in which people are or become quieter or calmer, or more vigorous and impetuous, from a variety of causes or combinations of causes. Only in the next part of the argument does he bring the expert king and his weaving back on to the stage.

His first step in this next part is to get the young Socrates to agree to a new principle: that no expertise that involves bringing things together 'voluntarily puts together anything at all that it produces, however humble, out of bad and good things';[25] rather, 'every kind of expert knowledge everywhere throws away the bad so far as it can, and takes what is suitable and good, and from these, both like and unlike, bringing them all together into one, crafts some single kind of thing with a single capacity.'[26] The 'single kind of thing' in the case of the expert kingly weaver is self-evidently the city, which is able to fulfil its proper function because of his 'bringing together' the unlike – in the context, the moderate and the courageous – as well as the like. As for what constitute 'the bad' and 'the suitable and good' in this case, that is explained in what the Visitor and young Socrates agree on next:

> And so neither will what we have decided is by nature truly the art of statesmanship ever voluntarily put together a city out of good and bad human beings. It's quite clear that it will first put them to the test in play, and after the test it will in turn hand them over to those with the capacity to educate them and serve it towards this particular end. It will itself lay down prescriptions for the educators and direct them, in the same way that weaving follows along with the carders, and those who prepare the other things it needs for its own work, prescribing for and directing them, giving indications to each group to finish their products in whatever way it thinks suitable for its own interweaving.
> Young Socrates: Yes, absolutely.
> Visitor: In just this very way, it seems to me, the art of kingship – since it is this that itself possesses the capacity belonging to the directing art – will not permit the educators and tutors, who function according to law, to do anything in the exercise of their role that will not ultimately result in some disposition which is appropriate to its own mixing role. It calls on them to teach these things alone; and those of their pupils that are unable to share in a disposition that is courageous and moderate, and whatever else belongs to the sphere of virtue, but are thrust forcibly away by an evil nature into godlessness, excess and injustice, it throws out by killing them, sending them into exile, and punishing them with the most extreme forms of dishonour.

---

25 308c2–3.
26 308c3–7.

Y.S.: At least they say that is what they're doing.[27]
V.: And again those who wallow in great ignorance and baseness it brings under the yoke of the class of slaves.
Y.S.: Quite correct.
V.: Then as for the others, whose natures are capable of becoming composed and stable in the direction of nobility, if they acquire education, and, with the help of expertise, of admitting commingling with each other - of these, it tries to bind together and intertwine the ones who strain more towards courage, its view being that their firm disposition is as it were like the warp, and the ones who incline towards the moderate, who produce an ample, soft, and – to continue the image – woof-like thread, two natures with opposite tendencies ...[28]

The two types the kingly weaver will intertwine with each other have already been prepared for him by 'the educators', under his control. These types represent 'the suitable and good', who will have been separated off from anyone unsuitable for weaving into the fabric of the city ('the bad'). The latter will have been found out – either through the process of testing 'in play', i.e., through observation of them playing as infants, or when they show themselves unable to absorb the lessons administered by the educators – and 'thrown away' (killed or exiled). Meanwhile, those 'whose natures are capable of becoming composed and stable in the direction of nobility, if they acquire education, and, with the help of expertise, of admitting commingling with each other' pass through the education system, and emerge ready for the kingly weaver to work on, with the courageous or *andreioi* representing the warp and the *sôphrones*, the moderate, representing the woof.

So – my original question – what sort of *andreia* and *sophrosunê* are these *andreioi* and the *sôphrones* supposed to possess? On the one hand, it is not a fully developed *andreia*, nor a fully developed *sôphrosunê*,[29] because, in that case they would fit unproblematically together: the ideally good person is presumably someone who would possess all the virtues, and as such would exhibit the two virtues exactly as, where and when it was 'timely', not 'incline towards the moderate', or 'strain more towards courage', like the *sôphrones* and the *andreioi* the king and his educators have to deal with. But neither are the *andreia* and *sophrosunê* possessed by these latter a matter merely of natural traits, qualities that they were born with.[30] Or at least, their *andreia* and *sophrosunê* have become

---

27 On this problematic response from the young Socrates, see my comments in Rowe 1995 *ad loc*. At this moment, I prefer the explanation that he is referring obliquely to the fate of his elder namesake, executed on the pretext that he was 'godless'.
28 308d1–309b7.
29 Whatever these may amount to: see further below.
30 See 310a.

rather more than inborn traits or tendencies by the time the king takes them over from the educators. The latter are described as doing '[nothing] in the exercise of their role the working out of which will not result in some disposition which is fitting in relation to the mixing that belongs to the directing art [i.e., statesman-ship/weaving].' The disposition in question seems then immediately to be identi-fied as one 'that is courageous and moderate together', and associated 'with the other things that tend towards virtue';[31] those who acquire it will be ready for the statesman and his loom.

Neither mere natural virtues, then, nor fully developed *andreia* and *sôphrosunê*, but something in between: a courage which already allows for mix-ing with moderation, and a moderation that already allows for mixing with cour-age, as they would in the full-blown version, but nevertheless, both of them, still lacking, because their possessors are still inclined more towards the one than to-wards the other – in other words, respectively more inclined towards sharpness, speed, vigour and towards quietness, gentleness, and calm (so that they remain identifiable as distinct groups, the *andreioi* and the *sôphrones*). That, presuma-bly, is why the kingly weaver is still needed. He operates, the Visitor tells us, by means of two kinds of 'intertwining and bonding',[32] one mortal and human, in-volving marriage arrangements, the other divine, 'fitting together that part of their soul that is eternal with a divine bond, in accordance with its kinship with the divine'.[33] The young Socrates asks for clarification, and the Visitor responds

> I call divine, when it comes to be in souls[34], that belief about what is fine, just and good, and the opposites of these, which is really true and is guaranteed;[35] it belongs to the class of the more than human.
> Young Socrates: That's certainly a fitting view to take.
> Visitor: Then do we recognize that it belongs to the statesman and the good legislator alone to be capable of bringing this very thing about, by means of the music that belongs to the art of kingship,[36] in those who have had their correct share of education – the people we were speaking of just now?[37]

---

31 308e9–10.

32 309e10.

33 309c1–2. The part in question is presumably reason (immortal, as opposed to the mortal ir-rational parts, as e.g. at *Timaeus* 69c–70b?); the 'fitting together' is either of the reasoning part of each soul (assuming that it can be divided against itself); or of the reasoning parts of the mem-bers of the two groups; or of both.

34 Reading *en tais psuchais* at c7.

35 'Guaranteed', that is, by the knowledge of the king or statesman.

36 307d2–3 têi tês basilikês mousêi.

37 309c5–d4.

This makes it clear enough that the weaver does the work of implanting the 'divine bond' after his educators have finished their task. Exactly how he will do it is not said, but there may be a clue in the phrase 'the *mousa* that belongs to the art of kingship'. This striking phrase recalls the similar use of *mousa* a couple of pages back, where the Visitor is describing music (*mousa*), including the use of the voice, when it exhibits the qualities of the slow and moderate 'at the right time' (*en kairôi*);[38] from here, I suggest, the trail will take us back to the passage in which he included rhetoric as one of the sorts of higher specialist expertise, separate from but 'precious and related to [statesmanship]' – 'generalship, the art of the judge, and that part of rhetoric which in partnership with kingship persuades people of what is just and so helps in steering through the business of cities.'[39] Rhetoric in this role will expertly 'persuade mass and crowd, through the telling of stories, and not through teaching'.[40] On the other hand, the statesman may decide that 'some sort of force' is appropriate;[41] might this be an occasion when the voice could be used in the opposite way, 'sharply' or 'vigorously'?[42]

'Is a "courageous" soul that grasps this sort of truth not tamed', the Visitor now asks, 'and wouldn't it be especially willing, as a result, to share in what is just, whereas if it fails to get a share of it, doesn't it rather slide away[43] towards becoming like some kind of beast?'[44] 'This sort of truth' must be 'that belief about what is fine, just and good, and the opposites of these, which is really true and is guaranteed',[45] which in turn substitutes for wisdom: 'if [a moderate soul] gets a share of these opinions, doesn't it become genuinely moderate and wise, so far as wisdom goes in the context of life in a city ...?'[46] It is hard to believe that the two groups, the *andreioi* and the *sôphrones*, are supposed to emerge from their education with no beliefs at all, or that if they do (as they surely must), that these are not broadly correct; the belief or beliefs that are inculcated subsequently by

---

38 307a9–b1.

39 303e10–304a2.

40 304d1–2.

41 304d4–5.

42 Cf. the contrast in the *Laws* (IV, 722b–723b) between the persuasive 'preambles' (*prooimia*) to the laws, on the one hand and on the other the '"tyrannical" directive' (*turannikon epitagma*, translated as in Schofield and Griffith 2016) represented by the laws themselves.

43 Reading *apoklinei* at 310e2 (present tense, not future – as in the Hackett version, though the footnote there does not make it sufficiently clear).

44 309d10–e3.

45 309c5–7.

46 309e5–7.

the statesman through the expert orator are just more authoritative ('guaranteed'), but perhaps also broader in scope insofar as they include the kind of understanding of 'what is just' that is needed for the 'steering of cities'.[47]

This seems to leave us with a number of different levels of virtue, apart from whatever traces of it we may be born with ('natural virtue'): (1) virtue as we encounter it in everyday life; (2) virtue as resulting from primary education as envisaged in the *Politicus*, under the guidance of the expert statesman; (3) virtue as resulting from the acquisition of the 'divine bond' of true opinion, and (4) a level of virtue above that, one that I presume involves – or is identical with[48] – a wisdom that is not merely a wisdom 'so far as wisdom goes in the context of life in a city ...', *hôs ... en politeiai*,[49] as the Visitor describes the 'wisdom' of the 'courageous' and the 'moderate' in the *Politicus* even after they have been taken over by the expert stateman and woven into the fabric of the city.[50] But up to that point, their 'virtue' is of a still more lowly sort, even if it is superior to that of ordinary, untutored people, described in the *Phaedo* as 'the common, civic virtue, the sort that they *call* moderation, or justice, and that has come about from habit and practice and in the absence of philosophy and intelligence.[51] The *andreioi* and *sôphrones* of the *Politicus* at this stage may not have 'philosophy and intelligence' themselves, but at least their 'habit and practice' are guided by the expertise of the state educators, under the control of the wisdom of the king and statesman.

---

47 304a1–2. Cf. the 'marionette' passage at *Laws* I, 644b–645e (on which Schofield, 2016, 128–153), and especially 644e4–645a2 '... there is one of the pulls [from the marionette's tendons/strings] which each of us must always follow, never letting go of that one, and resisting the other tendons; this pull being the guidance, golden and sacred, of calculation (*logismos*), *which calls in aid the public law of the city* ...' (translation by Griffith in Schofield and Griffith 2016 [modified]: 'call in aid' is *epikaleisthai*, which is 'usually translated "is called" ... But it would seem odd to suggest that one of the basic human motivating forces is named "law" as such' [Schofield and Griffith 2016: 59 n. 41]).

48 See text to notes 11 and 12 above.

49 309e6–7 (see my comments on this phrase in Rowe 1995).

50 On different levels of virtue in the *Republic*, see Rowe (2013) and Rowe (2017a). The chief claim, relevant to the present argument, of both of these papers is that the virtues as defined in *Republic* IV – or at any rate justice, courage and moderation – are on the second of the four levels described above: see also Rowe (2007) ch.5, and section 3 of the present paper. Whether or not the accounts of courage and moderation, and of virtue, are transferrable from *Republic* IV to the *Politicus* would depend on whether or not the Plato of the latter dialogue had any lasting commitment to a tripartite analysis of the soul; there is little or no evidence in the *Politicus* that tells either way (the virtues of a city, by contrast, are plainly treated in the *Politicus* in a significantly different way from the way they are treated in *Republic* IV). On levels of virtue in the *Laws*, see Rowe (2017b).

51 *Phaedo* 82a11–b2.

2 Why should Plato choose these two particular types, the 'courageous' and the 'moderate', as the sphere of operation for the royal weaver's skill?

The Visitor does not tell us much about the education to be administered by the state educators, but what he does tell us makes it extremely tempting to identify it with the primary education sketched in the *Republic*. As Monique Dixsaut says,

> Dans cette conclusion du *Politique*, la question est reprise exactement au point où s'arrêtait l'analyse de la *République*. Un travail éducatif initial est nécessaire *pour que* les fils [the warp and the woof] puissent se prêter au royale tissage, mais il n'est qu'auxiliaire et préalable. Le premier mélange produit des êtres humains capables de devenir des citoyens, il laisse entier[52] le conflit entre deux parties de la vertu. Il permet certes au tisserand royal d'assigner à chacun sa place, dans la chaîne ou dans la trame (309b), mais il faut encore 'lier et tisser ensemble' (*sundein kai sumplekein*).[53]

If this is correct, some striking possibilities open up. The primary education described in the *Republic* is for the 'guards'.[54] If the (primary) education of the *Politicus* resembles or coincides with that of the *Republic*, then the *andreioi* and the *sôphrones* of our passage already begin to look very much like sub-divisions of the *Republic*'s guards, before these are divided into rulers (philosophers) and common-or-garden guards (the 'auxiliaries'): that is, before (long before) the

---

52 This seems to me too strong; if the educators achieve anything, it must surely include at least a lessening of the potential conflict between the two 'parts of virtue'. See 308e–309a.

53 Dixsaut (1995) 267. See also El Murr (2014) 276: 'On y retrouve ... l'opposition des tendances sur laquelle travaille la première éducation de la *République*: celle-ci, rappelons-le, a pour but de tempérer deux tendances qui, si on les laisse à elles-mêmes, peuvent dégénérer à l'extrême. La musique ... doit ainsi adoucir le caractère marquee par l'ardeur (le *thumoeidês*), pur l'empêcher de devenir bête fauve, et la gymnastique doit renforcer le caractère qui a le goût de l'étude (le *philomathes*), afin d'éviter qu'il ne s'amollisse. Il n'est donc pas interdit de penser que l'équilibre atteint par l'action du mélange, du *krasis*, qu'est l'éducation dans la *République* est celui-là même que parvient a produire l'éducateur du *Politique*' (El Murr here adds a note referring to part of the passage by Monique Dixsaut cited above).

54 i.e., the *phulakes*, commonly but misleadingly known as the 'Guardians' – 'misleadingly', because 'guardians' in English tends to suggest, not something military but (e.g.) the guardians of children. The *phulakes* of the *Republic* start off as soldiers, and most of them remain such; the higher 'guards' or rulers may have ceased to be soldiers themselves, but they can use the soldiers to watch over the city both externally and internally.

question is raised, in Book III, 412c, about who should rule in the city.[55] Socrates in the *Republic* started from the city's need for guards in the straightforward sense, and for these his original paradigm was the guard- or watch-dog, which combines spirit, speed and strength with gentleness, the latter thanks to the watch-dog's ability to distinguish friend from enemy, bizarrely attributed to his or her *philomatheia* and *philosophia*.[56] The Visitor in the *Politicus* starts from a different place, namely the basic opposition, which is nevertheless fundamental to the whole of *Republic* 375a–412c too,[57] between the fierce and the gentle, the aggressive and the reflective. The *Republic*, concerned as it is with the institution of a warrior class, satisfies itself with tempering the aggressiveness of the warriors; an excess of mildness or gentleness is only a worry to the extent that it would threaten the effectiveness of the fighting force. The *Politicus*, by contrast, addresses the potential conflict between the more spirited, more vigorous temperament and its quieter counterpart head-on; both are given equal status.

As has often been pointed out, Plato is here picking up on a traditional debate, the most extended example of which is constructed by Thucydides in Book I of his *History* (which Plato would no doubt have read). In Book II (63), Thucydides' Pericles utters a sentiment that sounds close to the one represented by the Visitor in the *Politicus*: 'the retiring and unambitious (*to apragmon*) is never secure unless drawn up in line with the active and vigorous (*to drastêrion*)'.[58] From this perspective, the question why Plato should choose to have the 'royal weaver' working with the two types at issue has a perfectly simple answer: namely, that it is, in a way, part of the cultural context within which Plato was working. There is nothing arbitrary or surprising about his suggestion that the primary source of conflict within society will be the necessary existence, side by side, of more vigorous and quieter temperaments. The parallels and contrasts with the *Republic* do, however, give another dimension to the question I am currently asking (why it is the *andreioi* and *sôphrones* in particular that preoccupy the royal weaver). The treatment in the *Politicus*, in giving the *andreioi* and *sôphrones* equal status,

---

55 It might be tempting, and I have myself been tempted, to identify the *sôphrones* of the *Politicus* with the lowest class in the *Republic*, but there are obvious objections to such a view: not least that *sôphrosunê* in the *Republic* belongs to the whole city (IV, 442c–d), not just to one class. More importantly, the evidence is heavily against supposing that the producers in the *Republic* are educated along with the guards, as the *sôphrones* of the *Politicus* are educated with the *andreioi*.

56 II, 376a–c: a passage that determines the limits of both *philomatheia* and *philosophia* as attributed to the guards until the philosopher-rulers as such are separated off.

57 Along, of course, with the need to arm the future guards against giving in to 'desires and pleasures'; I shall return briefly to these at the end of the paper.

58 See e.g. Dixsaut (1997) 259–62.

seems to signal the abandonment of at least one central element of the hierarchy of the *Republic*:[59] *andreia*, which was the defining feature of the warrior class, is now the label for a type which it is the main business of the expert statesman to mingle and merge with its opposing counterpart, not to cultivate as a class apart.

What, in all this, has happened to the producer class of the *Republic*? There seem to be two possible answers to this question: either (1) the state primary education system includes them too; or else (2) they are excluded from consideration, and by implication from membership of the city, altogether. In favour of (1) is that according to the Visitor all the citizens must be good; after all, he takes care to exclude all the bad.[60] But who exactly are 'all the citizens'? The Visitor says nothing about the make-up of the citizen body. There is, however, one place where he seems to suggest that the *andreioi* and the *sôphrones* in the city are themselves an elite, exclusive group, rather than categories that include everyone down to and including the craftsmen and producers. This is in the passage with which I began this paper, the Visitor's summing up of his account of the statesman.

> Then let us say that this marks the completion of the fabric which is the product of the art of statesmanship: the weaving together, with regular intertwining, of the dispositions of courageous and moderate people – when the expertise belonging to the king brings their life together in agreement and friendship and makes it common between them, completing the most magnificent and best of all fabrics *and covering with it all the other inhabitants of cities, both slave and free*, and holds them together with this twining and rules and directs without, so far as it belongs to a city to be happy, falling short of that in any respect.[61]

---

59 The philosopher-rulers, or course, seem to have morphed into the expert statesman, who will either be king himself or the king's adviser; I turn to the case of the lowest class, the producers, in the following paragraph.

60 See Bobonich (1995) 322: '... every citizen is to be made virtuous or good (309e–310a) and this requires that every citizen be educated and acquire the divine bond of true opinion. Since Plato has repeatedly emphasized that only the scientific ruler will have knowledge (292e1–9, 297b7–c2), only he will receive a philosophical education (whatever Plato at this point thought this was). There is, however, no sign of any further educational distinction within the citizen body. It seems that all the citizens, i.e. those not killed, exiled, disenfranchised or enslaved [308e–309a], undergo the same education and receive exactly the same bond of true opinion (309c5–e8). Once we exclude the bad on the one hand and the scientific ruler on the other, in the *Statesman* the ethical education and the content of the ethical beliefs to which the citizens are educated seem to be the same. This is strikingly different from the *Republic* where we find an enormous difference between the ethical education and the resulting ethical beliefs of the auxiliaries and those of the lowest class ...'

61 311b7–c6.

It is hard not to take this as implying that there will be free men who belong to neither of the two groups that have preoccupied the Visitor in his account of the statesman's weaving. But now if all the citizens are to be made virtuous and good, as the Visitor surely wants to say,[62] and these other free men are not to be educated in virtue, then it seems as if these others will be non-citizens, free men of inferior status. Further, if the fabric that is to be woven out of the courageous and the moderate is *ipso facto* to cover these others too ('covering with it all the other inhabitants'), perhaps they too, alongside the slaves, are there to serve the needs of the *andreioi* and *sôphrones*.

The passage is brief to the point of obscurity, and should probably not be pressed too hard. Nevertheless, insofar as we can understand it, it probably does count in favour of (2), the second of the alternatives offered just now: namely that the lowest class in the *Republic* is excluded from citizenship in the city of the *Politicus*. That Plato was capable of moving towards such a solution is demonstrated by the structure he gives to at least one of his other imagined cities: that of Magnesia in the *Laws*,[63] whose 5,040 citizens are treated both as fundamentally homogeneous[64] and as all educated together to the same level; other, free inhabitants will be the large numbers[65] of resident aliens required to do all the work that cannot be done either by the citizens or by their slaves.[66]

3 The one 'truest constitution'?

I propose, then, that the *Politicus* strips down the tripartite structure of Callipolis: the function of the philosopher-rulers is absorbed into the expert statesman, whether ruling himself or advising a ruler; the producer class is excluded, and the class of potential guards is divided into two. The structure of Callipolis, I speculate, was strictly a means to an end, namely an account of justice; that account

---

62 See 308c–d, 309e–310a (and cf. n. 60 above).
63 Even the *Timaeus-Critias*, which refers directly back to a *Republic*-type discourse, is brief to the point of silence about the role of the 'farmers and the other craftsmen' after the first page (17c); it is the guards who otherwise dominate the action, to the exclusion of anyone else.
64 The exception being that some will be wealthier than others, as reflected in the system of property-classes; but this does not affect the main point.
65 See e.g. *Laws* VIII, 848a.
66 Compare too the structure of the ancient Athens of the *Timaeus-Critias*, entirely dominated by guards possessing 'a nature that is simultaneously spirited and outstandingly philosophical, in order that they can be appropriately gentle and harsh [to friends and enemies]' (*Timaeus* 18a4–7).

was built on the tripartition of the soul, and the analogy between city and soul that was employed to help reach both of these necessitated that the city also be divided into three. In the context of the city-soul analogy, producers must be part of the city, if they are to be the counterpart of the appetitive part of the soul, and the city must be ruled directly by philosophy/philosophers for the same reason. Remove that context, and the argument against the inclusion of the producers comes into its own. After all (my speculation continues), they are not capable of education in the virtues in the first place;[67] yet the art of statesmanship is supposed to be about making people virtuous.[68] At the same time, as the Visitor in the *Politicus* suggests, to find the true king, the truly expert statesman, in any ordinary society will be a rare thing indeed;[69] best, then, not to plan on a *class* of expert rulers. But in order to fulfill the task allotted to him, of giving an account of statesmanship itself, the Visitor imagines one such wise statesman in place, and asks what his main function will be – weaving; and why – the existence of two fundamentally opposed tendencies, the very ones identified by Socrates in the *Republic*, even in those who are capable of education to virtue.

The proposal, in short, is that the best city Plato has in mind in the *Politicus* is *mutatis mutandis* the same as the best city he constructs in the *Republic*, and that the differences, large as they may appear to be on the surface, are to be explained by the difference between the contexts in the two dialogues. Furthermore, as I have suggested, the city of the *Laws* also belongs to the same pattern. The interpretation I am here proposing is no more than a radical, or more specific, version of what is probably now becoming the dominant view, that so far from representing different political solutions, Plato's three main political dialogues are talking about what is recognizably the same solution, albeit from different perspectives. On the approach I am suggesting, Plato is doing very much what the Visitor attributes to people, and by implication to societies, in general at *Politicus* 301c–d. Tyranny comes about, he says, when someone "pretends to act like the person with expert knowledge, saying that after all one must do what is contrary to what has been written down if it is best to do so, and there is some desire or other combined with ignorance controlling this imitation [*sc.* of the true expert]. Surely in those circumstances we must call every such person a tyrant?

> Young Socrates: Of course.
> Visitor: Then it is in this way that the tyrant has come about, we say, and the king, and oligarchy, and aristocracy, and democracy – because people found themselves unable to

---

67 So, at least, the *Republic* suggests.
68 All about that, according at least to *Gorgias* 521d–e.
69 See especially 301d–e.

put up with the idea of that single individual of ours as monarch, and refused to believe that there would ever come to be anyone who deserved to rule in such a way, so as to be willing and able to rule with virtue and expert knowledge, distributing what is just and right correctly to all. They think that a person in such a position always mutilates, kills and generally maltreats whichever of us he wishes; although if there were to come to be someone of the sort we are describing, he would be prized and would govern a constitution that would alone be correct in the strict sense, steering it through in happiness.

Y.S.: Quite.

V.: But as things are, when – as we say – a king does not come to be in cities as a king-bee is born in a hive, one individual immediately superior in body and mind, it is necessary – so it seems – for people to come together and write things down, *chasing after the traces of the truest constitution*.[70]

Of course *they* ('people') have no idea what 'the truest constitution' is, or what its laws would be.[71] Nor, I imagine, would Plato claim to have the necessary expertise himself. But he at least recognizes the need for an expert, and is hot on his trail; the *Republic*, the *Politicus* and the *Laws* are successive, and – I believe – mutually enlightening attempts to say what the one 'truest constitution', as constructed by fully expert knowledge, might look like.

A final note. The *Politicus* tends to leaves the impression that, for Plato, the chief and most important task of the expert statesman will be to 'weave together' the moderate and the courageous. But that, I mean to claim, is a matter of perspective and context; it derives especially from the Visitor's choice of weaving as a model for statesmanship, when he could quite readily have chosen a different model (e.g., steersmanship, or medicine – both models appear elsewhere in Plato, and indeed in the *Politicus* itself). In *Laws* Book I, a concern with the need to combine *andreia* with *sôphrosunê* and *phronêsis*[72] (see especially 630a–b,

---

70 301b10–e4.

71 I discuss this passage in Rowe (2015b). I explain people's/societies 'chasing after' what they have no idea of, or about, by reference to an idea that I take to be endemic in Plato, namely that everyone is always in pursuit of what in fact in their own best interests; presumably what applies to individuals also applies to individuals acting together in communities. (One detail in that paper needs to be clarified: it does not follow directly from 308e9–309a6 that the Visitor is excluding the producer class from citizenship, as I proposed on 161–2; it might be, as Bobonich suggests, that Plato just changed his mind about who is and is not educable [cf. n. 60 above]. But given how little information Plato gives us in the context, and the fact that the producers are excluded in both *Timaeus-Critias* and *Laws*, Bobonich's suggestion looks at best uneconomical.)

72 And also justice, for which see *Politicus* 309d10–e3.

631c–d) quickly gives way to a long disquisition on the need to avoid being controlled by pleasure,[73] and the means the city will use to train its citizens accordingly. What one might be called the hinge passage is at 633c–634b: 'courage' is to be deployed not just against pains but against pleasures. Here the *Laws*, in effect, starts where the *Politicus* left off, as the *Politicus* started from where the (political) discussion left us in the *Republic*. From this larger perspective, the weaving together of moderation and courage in the *Politicus* is only part of the job of the kingly weaver, although a crucially important one: needing an example to illustrate what the true statesman does (weaving), the Visitor/Plato reaches for one that is there ready to hand in the *Republic* – passing over, as he does so, the long discussion, in Book III, of the need to inculcate that other aspect of *sôphrosunê* in the future guards, the control over desires and pleasures (III.389d ff.), a subject that will come into its own again in the *Laws*. The novel aspect of the *Politicus* is the framing of the problem of the conflict between the moderate and the courageous in terms of character-types; and that, I suggest, viewing the *Politicus* from the perspective of Plato's political thought as a whole, is primarily a dramatization (*more Thucydideo?*) of an issue that he elsewhere sees in terms of internal conflicts of desires and beliefs.[74]

---

73 A subject dealt with, in the final part of the *Politicus*, in a mere six words (*hos ate alla esti teinonta pros aretên*, 308e10), and then only implicitly.

74 My thanks to Beatriz Bossi for inviting me to the Madrid meeting, and for the wonderful hospitality extended to the participants.

Bibliography

Aalders, G. (1969), "*Nomos Empsychos*", in P. Steinmetz (ed.), *Politeia und Res Publica*, Wiesbaden, 315–329.

Accattino, P. (1997), *Platone, 'Politico'*, traduzione e introduzione di P. Accattino, Roma/Bari.

Álvarez Hoz, J.M./Gabilondo Pujol, A./García Ruiz, J.M. (eds.) (1999), *Proclo: Lecturas del 'Crátilo' de Platón*, Madrid.

Ammann, A. (1953), *ΙΚΟΣ bei Platon. Ableitung und Bedeutung mit Materialsammlung*, Freiburg.

Annas, J./Waterfield, R. (1995), *Plato, 'Statesman'*, Cambridge.

Ausland, H. (1997), "On reading Plato mimetically", *American Journal of Philology* 3, 371–416.

Baltes, M. (1976–1978), *Die Weltentstehung des Platonischen 'Timaeus' nach den antiken Interpreten*, 2 vols., Leiden.

Baltzly, D. (2007), *Proclus. 'Commentary on Plato's Timaeus'*. Vol. III, Book 3, Part I: *Proclus on the World's Body*, Cambridge.

Baltzly, D. (2013), *Proclus. 'Commentary on Plato's Timaeus'*. Vol. V, Book 4: *Proclus on Time and the Stars*, Cambridge.

Bartnikas, V. (2014), "The State is not like a Beehive: The Self-Containment of Plato's *Statesman*", *Filosofijos istorijos tyrimai* 86, 127–137.

Berges, S. (2010), "Understanding the Role of the Laws in Plato's *Statesman*", *Prolegomena* 9, (1) 5–23.

Berti, E. (2010), "Il rapporto tra causa motrice e causa finale nella '*Metafisica*' di Aristotele", in F. Fronterotta (ed.), *La scienza e le cause a partire dalla Metafisica di Aristotele*, Napoli, 351–382.

Blondell, R. (2002), *The Play of Character in Plato's Dialogues*, Cambridge.

Blondell, R. (2005), "From fleece to fabric: weaving culture in Plato's *Statesman*", *Oxford Studies in Ancient Philosophy* 28, 23–75.

Blyth, D. (1997), "The Ever-Moving Soul in Plato's *Phaedrus*", *American Journal of Philology* 118, 185–217.

Blyth, D. (2015), "Heavenly Soul in Aristotle", *Apeiron* 48, 427–465.

Blyth, D. (2016), "The Role of Aristotle's *Metaphysics* 12.9", *Méthexis* 28, 76–92.

Blyth, D. (2017), "Aristotle's God in *Metaphysics* 12.7", *Classical Philology* 112, 138–152.

Bobonich, C. (1995), "The Virtues of Ordinary People in Plato's *Statesman*", in C. Rowe (ed.), *Reading the 'Statesman'*, *Proceedings of the III Symposium Platonicum,* Sankt Augustin, 313–329.

Bobonich, C. (2002), *Plato's Utopia Recast*, Oxford.

Bodéüs, R. (2004), *Le Véritable politique et ses vertus. Receuil d'études*, Louvain-La-Neuve.

Bonitz, H. (1870), *Index Aristotelicus. Aristotelis Opera*, vol. 5.

Bossi, B. (2000), "*Amathia, Akrasia* and the Power of Knowledge in the *Laws*: Break or Unity?", *Hermathena* 169, Winter Volume, Dublin, 99–114.

Bossi, B. (2003), "On Aristotle's Charge of Socratic Intellectualism: The Force of a Misunderstanding", in A. Havlicek (ed.), *Plato's 'Protagoras'*: *Proceedings of the Third Symposium Platonicum Pragense*, Prague, 213–232.

Bossi, B. (2008), *Saber Gozar: Estudios sobre el placer en Platón*, Madrid.

Bossi, B. (2016), "On which step of the *scala amoris* is Socrates standing in the dramatic action of the *Symposium*?", in M. Tuli/L. Elders (eds.), *Plato in Symposium, Selected Papers from the Tenth Symposium Platonicum,* Sankt Augustin, 420–426.

https://doi.org/10.1515/9783110605549-020

Bossi, B. (2017), "Ni Intelectualismo ni Socrático: Notas al argumento hedonista de *Protágoras* 351b–377", en www.academia.edu/32502161

Bouffartigue, J. (1987), "Représentations et évaluations du texte poétique dans le *Commentaire sur la 'République'* de Proclos", in P. Hoffmann/J. Lallot/A. Le Boulluec (eds.), *Le texte et ses représentations. Études de litterature ancienn*e, 3, Paris, 129–143.

Boys-Stones, G.R. (2001), *Post-Hellenistic Philosophy*, Oxford.

Boys-Stones, G.R. (2009), "Hesiod and Plato's history of philosophy", in G.R. Boys-Stones/J.H. Haubold, *Plato and Hesiod*, Oxford, 31–51.

Bravo, F. (1995), "La ontología de la definición en el *Político* de Platón", in C. Rowe (ed.), *Reading the 'Statesman'. Proceedings of the III Symposium Platonicum*, Sankt Augustin, 76–87.

Brendan Nagle, D. (2006), *The Household as the Foundation of Aristotle's Polis*, Cambridge.

Brill, S. (2017), "Autochthony, Sexual Reproduction, and Political Life in the *Statesman* Myth", in J. Sallis (ed.), *Plato's 'Statesman': Dialectic, Myth, and Politics*, Albany, 33–50.

Brisson, L. (1974), *Le même et l'autre dans la structure ontologique du 'Timée' de Platon*, Paris.

Brisson, L. (1994a), *Le même et l'autre dans la structure ontologique du 'Timée' de Platon*, Sankt Augustin.

Brisson, L. (1994b), *Platon, les mots et les mythes: Comment et pourquoi Platon nomma le mythe?*, Paris.

Brisson, L. (1995), "Interprétation du mythe du *Politique*", in C.J. Rowe (ed.), *Reading the 'Statesman'*, Sankt Augustin, 349–363.

Brisson, L. (2000), *Plato, The Mythmaker*, Chicago.

Brisson, L. (2003), with J. Pradeau (eds.) *Platon, 'Le Politique'*, Paris.

Brisson, L. (^{2}2005), *Introduction à la philosophie du mythe*, Paris, [1996].

Brisson, L. (2012), "Why is the *Timaeus* called an *Eikôs Muthos* and an *Eikôs Logos?*", in C. Collobert/P. Destrée/F.J. González (eds.), *Plato and Myth. Studies on the Use and Status of Platonic Myths*, Leiden/Boston, 369–391.

Brown, E. (2009), "Plato on the Unity of the Political Arts", available at URL: <https://pages.wustl.edu/files/pages/imce/ericbrown/unitypoliticalarts.pdf>.

Browning Cole, E. (1991), "Weaving and Practical Politics in Plato's *Statesman*", *The Southern Journal of Philosophy*, vol. XXIX/2, 195–208.

Buffière, F. (^{2}1973), *Les mythes d'Homère et la pensée grecque*, Paris.

Burnet, I. (1967), *Platonis Opera. Recognovit brevique adnotatione critica instruxit*, tomus I, Oxford.

Bywater, I. (2002), *Aristotle, 'On the Art of Poetry'*, Oxford.

Candiotto, L. (2012), *Le vie della confutazione. I dialoghi socratici di Platone,* Milano/Udine.

Candiotto, L. (2013), "Socrate e l'educazione dei giovani aristocratici. Il caso di Crizia come esempio di mascheramento operato dai difensori socratici", in F. de Luise/A. Stavru (eds.), *Socratica III. Studies on Socrates, the Socratics, and the Ancient Socratic Literature*, Sankt Augustin, 190–198.

Candiotto, L. (2018), "Purification through emotions: The role of shame in Plato's *Sophist* 230b4-e5", *Educational Philosophy and Theory* 50 (6/7), 576–585.

Canfora, L. (2014), *La crisi dell'utopia: Aristofane contro Platone*, Rome/Bari.

Capelle, A. (1933), *Platos Dialog 'Politikos'*, Hamburg, Diss. Hamburg University.

Capozzi, E. (1989), "L'analogia tra arte politica e tessitura nel *'Politico'* platonico", in *Discorsi* 9, 231–261.

Carlier, P. (1984), *La Royauté en Grèce avant Alexandre*, Strasbourg.

Carone, G.R. (2005), *Plato's Cosmology and its Ethical Dimensions,* Cambridge.

Casadesús, F. (2010), "El arte de tejer como paradigma del buen político en Platón", *Daimon*, Suplemento 3, 9–18.

Casadesús, F. (2013), "Why is it so difficult to catch a sophist? Pl. *Soph*. 218d3 and 261a5", in B. Bossi/T.M. Robinson (eds.), *Plato's 'Sophist' Revisited*, Berlin, 15–27.

Casas Martínez-Almeida, R. (2011), *Mito y paradigma en el 'Político' de Platón*, [Ph.D. Thesis] Madrid.

Castoriadis, C. (1999), *Sur 'Le Politique' de Platon*, Paris.

Castoriadis, C. (2002), *On Plato's 'Statesman'*, Stanford University Press.

Cerri, G. (2007), *La poetica di Platone. Una teoria della comunicazione* (terza edizione aggiornata e ampliata di Platone sociologo della comunicazione), Lecce.

Chantraine, P. (1956), *Etudes sur le vocabulaire grec*, Paris.

Charles-Saget, A. (1998), "Un esempio di ermeneutica neoplatonica: il Sofista Demiurgo", in F. Romano/A. Tiné, *Questioni neoplatoniche*, Catania, 29–44.

Clement, G. (1996), *Care, Autonomy, and Justice. Feminism and the Ethic of Care*, Boulder/Oxford.

Cooper, J.M. (1997), "Plato's *Statesman* and Politics", in J. Cleary/G.M. Gurtler s.j. (eds.), *Proceedings of the Boston Area Colloquium in Ancient Philosophy*, XIII, Leiden, 71–104; repr. in (1999) *Reason and Emotion. Essays on Ancient Moral Psychology and Ethical Theory*, Princeton, 165–191.

Cooper, J.M./Hutchinson, D.S. (eds.), (1997), *Plato, Complete Works*, Indianapolis/Cambridge.

Cooper, J.M. (1999), "The Unity of Virtue", in *Reason and Emotion*, Princeton, 76–117.

Corlett, J.A. (2005), *Interpreting Plato's Dialogues*, Las Vegas.

Cornelli, G. (2016), "The chameleon-like Soul and its ductility: Platonic dualisms in the *Phaedo*", *Archai* 16, 203–222.

Cornford, F.M. (1937), *Plato's Cosmology. The 'Timaeus' of Plato Translated with a Running Commentary*, London.

Cotton, A.K. (2014), *Platonic Dialogue and the Education of the Reader*, Oxford.

Coulter, J.A. (1976), *The Literary Microcosm. Theories of Interpretation of the Later Neoplatonists*, Leiden.

Crotty, K. (2009), *The Philosopher's Song: The Poets' Influence on Plato*, Lanham.

Darriulat, J. (2013), "Platon et le jeu dialectique." Accessed online on 02/22/2016 in http://www.jdarriulat.net/Auteurs/Platon/PlatonPetteia/Petteia.html

Delcominette. S. (2000). *L'inventivité dialectique dans le 'Politique' de Platon*, Cahiers de philosophie ancienne 16, Bruxelles.

Denniston, J.D. (1954), *The Greek Particles*, Oxford.

Demont, P. (1990), *La Cité grecque archaïque et classique et l'idéal de tranquillité*, Paris.

Diehl, E. (1903–1906), *Procli Diadochi in Platonis 'Timaeum' Commentaria*, Leipzig.

Diels, H./Kranz, W. (eds.) (1996), *Die Fragmente der Vorsokratiker. Griechisch und Deutsch.* Bd. 2. Zürich, Weidmann, [18th printing of the sixth ed. 1952].

Diès, A. (2000), "Notice", in *Platon. Oeuvres Complètes*. Tome IX, 1ère partie. *Le Politique*, Texte établi et traduit par A. Diès, Paris [1935].

Diès, A. (1972), *Autour de Platon*, Paris.

Dillon, J. (1973), *Iamblichi Chalcidiensis in Platonis Dialogos Commentaria*, Leiden.

Dillon, J. (1995), "The Neoplatonic Exegesis of the *Statesman* Myth", in C. Rowe (ed.), *Reading the 'Statesman': Proceedings of the III Symposium Platonicum*, Sankt Augustin, 364–374.

Dillon, J. (²1996), *The Middle Platonists: a Study of Platonism 80 BC to AD 220,* revised edition with a new afterword, Ithaca.

Dillon, J. (2000), "The Role of the Demiurge in the *Platonic Theology*", in A.-Ph. Segonds/C. Steel (eds.), *Proclus et la 'Théologie Platonicienne'*, Leuven/Paris, 339–349.

Dixsaut, M. (1995), "Une politique vraiment conforme à la nature", in C. Rowe (ed.), *Reading the 'Statesman', Proceedings of the III Symposium Platonicum*, Sankt Augustin, 253–73.

Dixsaut, M. (2001), *Métamorphoses de la dialectique dans les Dialogues de Platon*, Paris.

Dixsaut, M. (2003), *Platon. Le Désir de comprendre*, Paris.

Dodds, E.R. (^{2}1963), *The Elements of Theology*, Oxford.

Dorter, K. (1994), *Form and Good in Plato's Eleatic Dialogues*, Berkeley/Los Angeles/London.

Dorter, K. (1997), 'Virtue, Knowledge and Wisdom: Bypassing self-control', *The Review of Metaphysics* 51, No. 2, 313–343.

Dorter, K. (2013), "The Method of Division in the *Sophist*: Plato's Second *Deuteros Plous*", in B. Bossi/T.M. Robinson (eds.), *Plato's 'Sophist' Revisited*, Berlin, 88–99.

Dratwa, J. (2003), «Le statut de la Philosophie dans le *Politique*», *Revue de Philosophie Ancienne* XXI, 1, 23–50.

Duke, E.A. *et al.* (eds.) (1995), *Platonis Opera*, tomus I, recognoverunt brevique adnotatione critica instruxerunt E.A. Duke *et.al.*

Dunn, M. (1976), "Iamblichus, Thrasyllus and the Reading Order of the Platonic Dialogues", in R.B. Harris (ed.), *The Significance of Neoplatonism*, Norfolk, Virginia, International Society for Neoplatonic Studies, 59–80.

Duvick, B. (2007), *Proclus: 'On Plato Cratylus'*, London, Duckworth.

El Murr, D. (2002), "La *symplokè politikè*: le paradigme du tissage dans le *Politique* de Platon, ou les raisons d'un paradigme 'arbitraire'", *Kairos* 19, 49–95.

El Murr, D. (2006), "Paradigm and Diairesis: a Response to M.-L. Gill", *Plato Journal* 6 (DOI:https://doi.org/10.14197/2183-4105_6_3).

El Murr, D. (2009), "Politics and Dialectics in Plato's *Statesman*", in G. Gurtler/ W. Wians (eds.), *Proceedings of the Boston Area Colloquium in Ancient Philosophy* XXV, Leiden, 229–232.

El Murr, D. (2010), "Hesiod, Plato, and the Golden Age: Hesiodic motifs in the myth of the *Politicus*", in G.R. Boys-Stones/J.H. Haubold, *Plato and Hesiod*, Oxford, 276–297.

El Murr, D. (2011), "The *telos* of our *muthos*. A Note on Plato Plt. 277b6-7", *Mnemosyne* 64, 271–280.

El Murr, D. (2014), *Savoir et gouverner. Essai sur la science politique platonicienne*, Paris.

El Murr, D. (2015), "Paradigmatic Method and Platonic Epistemology", in D. Nails/H. Tarrant (eds.), *Second Sailing. Alternative Perspectives on Plato*, Espoo, *Societas Scientiarum Fennica*, 1–20.

El Murr, D. (2016), 'Logique ou dialectique? La puissance normative de la division platonicienne,' in J.-B. Gourinat/J. Lemaire (eds.), *Logique et dialectique dans l'Antiquité*, Paris, 107–133.

Erler, M. (1992), "*Anagnorisis* in Tragödie und Philosophie. Eine Anmerkung zu Platons Dialog *Politikos*", *Würzburger Jahrbücher* 18, 147–170.

Erler, M. (1995), "Kommentar zu Brisson und Dillon", in C. Rowe (ed.), *Reading the 'Statesman'*, Sankt Augustin, 375–380.

Farrell Krell, D. (2015) "'Talk to the Animals': On the Myth of Cronos in the *Statesman*", in J. Bell/M. Nass (eds.), *Plato's Animals: Gadflies, Horses, Swans, and Other Philosophical Beasts*, Bloomington, 27–41.

Festugière, A. J. (1966–1968) *Commentaire sur le 'Timée'*, 5 vols., Paris.

Festugière, A. J. (1969) "L'ordre de lecture des dialogues de Platon aux Ve–VIe siècles", *Museum Helveticum* 26, 281–296.

Fowler, H.N. (1962), *Plato, 'The Statesman'*, Harvard.

Franco Repellini, F. (2003), "Astronomia e armonica", in M. Vegetti (ed.), *Platone, 'La Repubblica', libri VI-VII*, vol. 5, Napoli.

Frederik, J./Arends, M. (1993), "Survival, War and Unity of the Polis in Plato's *Statesman*", *Polis* 12, 154–187.

Friedländer, P. (1973), *Plato, An Introduction*, transl. by Hans Meyerhoff, Princeton Legacy Library, Princeton 1973.

Gallant, T.W. (1991), *Risk and Survival in Ancient Greece. Reconstructing the Rural Domestic Economy*, Stanford.

Gaudin, C. (1981), "La théorie platonicienne de l'innocence", *Revue Philosophique de la France et de l'Etranger* 171, 145–168.

Gaudin, C. (1985), "Le paradigme du tissage dans le *Politique* de Platon. Technique philosophique et philosophie de la technique", in J.-P. Ginisti/F.Guéry (eds.), *Créer et produire des formes textiles (Actes du colloque des 13-14 décembre 1984)* Lyon, 121–132.

Gerson, L. (2005), *Aristotle and other Platonists,* Ithaca NY.

Gill, C. (1995), "Rethinking Constitutionalism in *Statesman* 291–303", in C. Rowe (ed.), *Reading the 'Statesman', Proceedings of the III Symposium Platonicum* Sankt Augustin, 276–291.

Gill, M.L. (2010), "Division and Definition in Plato's *Sophist* and *Statesman*", in D. Charles (ed.), *Definition in Greek Philosophy*, Oxford, 172–199.

Giorgini, G. (2005), *Platone, 'Politico'*, Milano.

Giorgini, G. (2016), "Progress or Regress? Plato's Account of the Beginnings of Mankind", in A. Havlicek/Ch. Horn/J. Jinek (eds.), *Nous, Polis, Nomos. Festschrift Francisco L. Lisi*, Sankt Augustin, 147–162.

Gomperz, Th. (1909), *Griechische Denken*, Leipzig.

Gordon, J. (2007), "In Plato's Image", in G.A. Scott (ed.), *Philosophy in Dialogue. Plato's Many Devices*, 212–237.

Gourinat, J-B. (2013), "'Origine du movement" (ὅθεν ἡ ἀρχὴ τῆς κινήσεως) et "cause efficient" (ποιητικὸν αἴτιον) chez Aristote', in C. Viano/C. Natali/M. Zingano (eds.), *Aitia I: Les quatre causes d'Aristote: Origines et interprétations*, Leuven, 91–121.

Grams, L.W. (2012), "The Eleatic Visitor's Method of Division", *Apeiron* 45, 130–56.

Gulley, N. (1954), *Plato's Theory of Recollection*, Classical Quarterly NS 50 (1954), 194–213.

Guthrie. G.K.C. (1978), *A History of Greek Philosophy. V. The Later Plato and the Academy*, Cambridge.

Hackforth, R. (1936), 'Plato's Theism', *Classical Quarterly* 30, 4–9.

Hadot, I. (2015), *Athenian and Alexandrian Neoplatonism and the Harmonization of Aristotle and Plato*, Leiden.

Hadot, P. (1979), "Les divisions des parties de la philosophie dans l'Antiquité", *Museum Helveticum* 36, 201–223.

Halfwassen, J. (2000), "Der Demiurg: seine Stellung in der Philosophie Platons und seine Deutung im antiken Platonismus", in A. Neschke-Hentschke (ed.), *Le 'Timée' de Platon. Contributions à l'histoire de sa réception. Platos 'Timaios'. Beiträge zu seiner Rezeptionsgeschichte*, Louvain-la Neuve/Louvain/Paris, Bibliothèque philosophique de Louvain, 53, 39–62.

Halliwell, S. (2002), *The Aesthetic of Mimesis. Ancient Texts and modern problems*, Princeton/Oxford.

Hampshire, S. (1999), *Justice is Conflict*, Princeton.

Hansen, M.H. (1983), "The Athenian 'Politicians', 403–322 b.c.", *Greek, Roman and Byzantine Studies* 24, 33–55.

Hansen, M.H. (1991), *The Athenian Democracy in the Age of Demosthenes. Structure, Principle and Ideology*, trans. by J.A. Crook, Oxford.

Helmer, E. (2010), *La part du bronze. Platon et l'économie*, Paris.

Henderson, J. (1988), *Aristophanes, 'Lysistrata'*, (Translation, Introduction and Notes), Cambridge, Focus Classical Library.

Henry, D. (2011), "A Sharp Eye for Kinds: Collection and Division in Plato's Late Dialogues", *Oxford Studies in Ancient Philosophy* 41, 229–255.

Hernández de la Fuente, D. (2016), "Fundamentos áureos de la teoría política platónica: sobre el mito del *Político* y la tradición religiosa", *Endoxa* 38, 47–74.

Herter, H. (1958), "Gott und die Welt bei Platon: eine Studie zum Mythos des *Politikos*", *Bonner Jahrbücher* 158, 106–117.

Hirsch, U. (1995), "*MIMEIΣΘAI* und verwandte Ausdrücke in Platons *Politikos*", in C. Rowe (ed.), *Reading the* 'Statesman', Sankt Augustin, 184–189.

Klosko, G. (2006), *The Development of Plato's Political Theory*, Second edition, Oxford.

Hoffman, M. (1993), "The 'realisation of the due measure' as structural principle in Plato's *Statesman*", *Polis* 12, 99–121.

Hoffmann, Ph. (2012), "La place du *Timée* dans l'enseignement philosophique néoplatonicien: ordre de lecture et harmonisation avec le *De Caelo* d'Aristote", in F. Celia/A. Ulacco (eds.), *Il 'Timeo': esegesi greche, arabe, latine*, Pisa, 133–180.

Horn, C. (2012), "Why Two Epochs of Human History? On the Myth of the *Statesman*", in C. Collobert/P. Destrée/F.J. Gonzalez (eds.), *Plato and Myth: Studies on the Use and Status of Platonic Myths*, Leiden, 393–417.

Hourcade, A. (2017), *Le Conseil dans la pensée antique. Les Sophistes, Platon, Aristote*, Paris.

Ibáñez Puig, X. (2007), *Lectura del 'Teetet' de Plató: Saviesa i prudència en el tribunal del saber*, Barcelona.

Ionescu, C. (2014), 'Dialectical Method and Myth in Plato's *Statesman*', *Ancient Philosophy* 34, 29–46.

Joly, H. (1992), *Etudes Platoniciennes. La Question des Etrangers*, Paris.

Kahn, C.H. (1995), "The Place of the *Statesman* in Plato's Later Work", in C. Rowe (ed.), *Reading the 'Statesman', Proceedings of the III Symposium Platonicum*, Sankt Augustin, 49–59.

Kahn, C.H. (2008), *Plato and the Socratic Dialogue. The Philosophical Use of a Literary Form*, Cambridge 1996, 1999³ [Italian translation *Platone e il dialogo socratico. L'uso filosofico di una forma letteraria*, Milano, Vita e Pensiero].

Kahn, C.H. (2009), "The myth of the *Statesman*", in C. Partenie (ed.), *Plato's Myth*, Cambridge, 148–166.

Kahn, C.H. (2013, 2014), *Plato and the Post-Socratic dialogue. The Return to the Philosophy of Nature*, Cambridge.

Karamanolis, G. (2006), *Plato and Aristotle in agreement? Platonists on Aristotle from Antiochus to Porphyry*, Oxford.

Kato, S. (1995), "The Role of *paradeigma* in the *Statesman*" in Rowe, C. (ed.), *Reading the 'Statesman', Proceedings of the III Symposium Platonicum*, Sankt Augustin, 162–172.

Kosman, L.A. (1992), "Silence and Imitation in the Platonic Dialogues", in J.C. Klagge/N.D. Smith (eds.), *Methods of Interpreting Plato and his Dialogues*, Oxford, 73–92.

Kutash, E. (2011), *Ten Gifts of the Demiurge: Proclus on Plato's 'Timaeus'*, London/New York.

Lamberton, R. (1992), "The Neoplatonists and the Spiritualization of Homer", in R. Lamberton/J.J. Keaney (eds.), *Homer's Ancient Readers. The Hermeneutics of Greek Epic's Earliest Exegetes*, Princeton/New Jersey, 115–133.

Lane, M. (1995), "A New Angle on Utopia: The Political Theory of the *Statesman*", in C. Rowe (ed.), *Reading the 'Statesman'*, *Proceedings of the III Symposium Platonicum*, Sankt Augustin, 275–305.

Lane, M. (1998), *Method and Politics in Plato's 'Statesman'*, Cambridge.

Larivée, A. (2009), "The *Philebus*, a protreptic?", in J. Dillon/L. Brisson (eds), *Selected Papers from the VIIIth Symposium Platonicum*, Sankt Augustin, 163–171.

Larivée, A. (2011), "Le *Philèbe*, un protreptique?" *Phoenix*, 65 (1–2), Spring/Summer, 53–65 (Extended version of Larivée 2009).

Larivée, A. (2012), "'Gender Trouble' in Xenophon and Plato", *New England Classical Journal* 39.4, 281–303.

Larsen, B.D. (1972), *Jamblique de Chalcis. Exégète et philosophe*, 2 vols., Aarhus.

Lernould, A. (2001), *Physique et Théologie: Lecture du 'Timée' de Platon par Proclus*, Villeneuve d'Ascq (Nord).

Lewy, H. (^{3}2010), *Chaldaean Oracles and Theurgy. Mysticism, Magic and Platonism in the Later Roman Empire*, troisième édition par M. Tardieu, avec un supplément: "Les Oracles chaldaïques 1891–2011", Paris, Institut d'Etudes augustiniennes [1978].

Linguiti, A. (2014), "Physics and Metaphysics", in P.Remes/S.Slaveva-Griffin (eds.), *The Routledge Handbook of Neoplatonism*, London/New York, 343–355.

Lisi, F. (2011), "La figura del Demiurgo en el *Político*: algunas reflexiones sobre un concepto problemático", in F. Lisi/M. Migliori/J. Monserrat-Molas (eds.), *Formal Structures in Plato's Dialogues: 'Theaetetus', 'Sophist' and 'Statesman'*, Sankt Augustin, 193–203.

Long, A. (2009), "Plato's dialogues and a common rationale for dialogue form", in S. Goldhill (ed.), *The End of Dialogue in Antiquity*, Cambridge, 45–59

Lovejoy, A.O./Boas, G. (1935), *Primitivism and Related Ideas in Antiquity*, Baltimore.

Marchant, E.C. (1923), *Xenophon, 'Memorabilia', Xenophon in Seven Volumes*, 4. Cambridge, London.

Márquez, X. (2012), *A Stranger's Knowledge. Statesmanship, Philosophy and Law in Plato's 'Statesman'*, Las Vegas/Zurich/Athens.

Martijn, M. (2010), *Proclus on Nature. Philosophy of Nature and its Methods in Proclus' 'Commentary on Plato's Timaeus'*, Leiden/Boston.

Martano, G. (1974), *Proclo di Atene. L'ultima voce speculativa del genio ellenico*, Napoli.

Mason, A. (2013), 'The *Nous* Doctrine in Plato's Thought'. *Apeiron* 46, 201–228.

Mattéi, J-F. (2010), *Platão*. São Paulo, UNESP [1941].

McCabe, M.M. (1997), "Chaos and Control: Reading Plato's *Politicus*", *Phronesis* 42, 94–117.

McCabe, M.M. (2016), "The Unity of Virtue: Plato's Models of Philosophy", in *Proceedings of the Aristotelian Society*, Suppl. Vol. 90, 1–25.

McCoy, M. (2008), *Plato on the Rhetoric of Philosophers and Sophists*, Cambridge/New York.

Menn, S. (1992), "Aristotle and Plato on God as *Nous* and as the Good", *Review of Metaphysics* 45.3, 543–73.

Menn, S. (1995), *Plato on God as Nous,* Carbondale.

Michelini, A.N. (2003), "Introduction", in A.N. Michelini (ed.), *Plato as author. The Rhetoric of Philosophy*, Leiden/Boston.

Mishima, T. (1995), "Courage and Moderation in the *Statesman*", in C. Rowe (ed.), *Reading the 'Statesman', Proceedings of the III Symposium Platonicum*, Sankt Augustin, 306–312.

Migliori, M. (1996), *Arte politica e metretica assiologica. Commentario storico-filosofico al 'Politico' di Platone*, Milano.

Migliori, M. (2001), *Platone, 'Politico'*, Milano.

Migliori, M. (2013), *Il disordine ordinato. La filosofia dialettica di Platone*. I. *Dialettica, metafisica e cosmologia*; II. *Dall'anima alla prassi etica e politica*, Brescia.

Mill, J.S. (1866), "Grote's Plato", *The Edinburgh Review* 123, 297–364.

Miller, M. (1980), *The Philosopher in Plato's 'Statesman'*, New York.

Miller, M. (2004), *The Philosopher in Plato's 'Statesman'*, Las Vegas/Zurich/Athens.

Miller, W. (1968), *Xenophon, 'Cyropaedia'. Xenophon in Seven Volumes, 5 and 6*. Trans. W. Miller, Cambridge.

Mohr, R.D. (1985), *The Platonic Cosmology*, Leiden.

Monserrat-Molas, J. (1999), *El 'Polític' de Plató. La gràcia de la mesura*, Barcelona.

Monserrat-Molas, J. (2003), «La mesure comme principe constitutif du *Politique* de Platon», *Revue de Philosophie Ancienne* XXI, 1, 2003, 3–22.

Monserrat-Molas, J. (2010), "Naturaleza del error y sentido de la corrección de la diéresis en *El Político* de Platón", *Daimon. Revista Internacional de Filosofía* 51, 151–169.

Monserrat-Molas, J. (2011), "Procesos cognitivos y crítica política: ¿Una política ilustrada en sentido platónico?", *Crítica* 43, 129, 2011: 31–52. [revisat a Monserrat 2012a, cap. V].

Monserrat-Molas, J. (2012a), *Al margen del 'Político' de Platón*, Barcelona.

Monserrat-Molas, J. (2012b), «'Una túnica per al poble', Un comentari a *El polític* de Plató», *Convivium* 25, 5–26.

Monserrat-Molas, J. (2013), "El retorn al polític com a fonamentació de la ciutat", *Arkhai* 11, 11–20.

Monserrat-Molas, J. (2014), "La utopia correctora. A propòsit del mite de *El Polític* de Plató", *Studia Philologica Valentina* 16, 13, 91–112.

Monserrat-Molas, J. (2016), "Règims, governs i governants: precisions al voltant d'un fragment de Plató", in A. Havlicek/C. Horn/J. Jinek (eds.), *Nous, Polis, Nomos. Festschrift Francisco L. Lisi,* Sankt Agustin, 197–205.

Morgan, K.A. (2004), *Myth and Philosophy from the Presocratics to Plato*, Cambridge.

Morrow G.R. (1939), *Plato's Law of Slavery in its Relation to Greek Law*, Urbana.

Motta, A. (2013), "L'*ekphrasis* del discorso. Una lezione neoplatonica sul miglior artefatto" *Estetica. Studi e ricerche* 1, 187–200.

Motta, A. (2014), *Anonimo. 'Prolegomeni alla Filosofia di Platone'*, Roma.

Motta, A. (2015), "Materia e forma dei miti. Su mimesi platonica e simbologia omerica", *Revista Estética e Semiótica* 5/2, 19–41.

Narcy, M. (1995), "La critique de Socrate par l'étranger dans le *Politique*" in C. Rowe (ed.), *Reading the 'Statesman', Proceedings of the III Symposium Platonicum*, Sankt Augustin, 227–235.

Natali, C. (1979–1980), "La struttura unitaria del I libro della *Politica* di Aristotele", *Polis* 3, 1, 2–18.

Natali, C. (1981), 'Il *Politico* di Platone e la natura del sapere pratico in Aristotele,' *Elenchos* 1, 109–146.

Neiman, P. (2007), "The Practicality of Plato's *Statesman*", *History of Political Thought* 28, 403–418.

Neschke-Hentschke, A. (2000), "Der platonische *Timaios* als Manifest der platonischen Demiurg", in A. Neschke-Hentschke (ed.), *Le 'Timée' de Platon. Contributions à l'histoire de sa réception. Platos 'Timaios'. Beiträge zu seiner Rezeptionsgeschichte*, Louvain-la Neuve/Louvain/Paris, IX–XXVII.

Netting, R./R. Willk/E.J. Arnould (eds.), (1984) *Households: Comparative and Historical Studies of the Domestic Group*, Berkeley.

Nicolson, P./Rowe, C. (eds.) (1993), "Plato's *Statesman*: Selected Papers From The Third Symposium Platonicum", *Polis. Newsletter of the Society for the Study of Greek Political Thought*, vol. 12, n.º 1-2.

Nightingale, A.W. (1995), *Genres in dialogue*, Cambridge.

Nightingale, A.W. (1996), "Plato on the Origins of Evil: the *Statesman* Myth Reconsidered", *Ancient Philosophy* 16, 65–91.

O'Meara, D.J. (1989), *Pythagoras Revived: Mathematics and Philosophy in Late Antiquity*, Oxford.

Ostenfeld, E. (1993), 'The Physicality of God in the *Politicus* Myth and in the Late Dialogues', *Classica et Mediaevalia* 44, 97–108.

Owen, G.E.L. (1973), "Plato and the Undepictable", in E.N. Lee/A.P.D. Mourelatos/R.M. Rorty (eds.), *Exegesis and Argument*, Assen, 340–361.

Paffenroth, K. (2014), "Agreement among the Evangelists (*De consensu evangelistarum*), translated, introduced and annotated", in B. Ramsey (ed.), *The Works of Saint Augustine. A Translation for the 21st Century*. Part 1 - Volumes 15 and 16: *New Testament I and II* (I/15 and 1/16), New York.

Palumbo, L. (1994), *Il non essere e l'apparenza. Sul 'Sofista' di Platone*, Napoli.

Palumbo, L. (2010), "Scenografie verbali di V secolo. Appunti sulla natura visiva del linguaggio tragico", in S. Giombini/F. Marcacci (eds.), *Il quinto secolo. Studi di filosofia antica in onore di Livio Rossetti,* Passignano sul Trasimeno, 689–700.

Palumbo, L. (2013a), "Portare il lettore nel cuore del testo. L'*ekphrasis* nei dialoghi di Platone", *Estetica,* 35–46.

Palumbo, L. (2013b), "*Mimesis* in the *Sophist*", in B. Bossi/T.M. Robinson (eds.), *Plato's 'Sophist' Revisited*, Berlin, 269–278.

Pasquali, G. (1908), *Proclus Diadochus in Platonis Cratylum Commentaria*, Leipzig.

Pasquali, P. (1967), *Le Lettere di Platone*, Firenze, 1938, Firenze 1967.

Perl, E.D. (2014), *Thinking Being: Introduction to Metaphysics in the Classical Tradition*, Leiden.

Peixoto, M.C.D. (2009), "La città, il saggio e gli altri uomini. Democrito pensatore della pólis", in G. Cornelli/G. Casertano (eds.), *Pensare la città antica: categorie e rappresentazioni,* Napoli, 175–190.

Penner, T. (1992), "The Unity of Virtue", in H.H. Benson (ed.), *Essays on the Philosophy of Socrates*, Oxford, 162–184.

Petraki, Z. (2011), *The Poetics of Philosophical Language. Plato, Poets and Presocratics in the 'Republic'*, Berlin/Boston.

Phillips, J. (2007), *Order from Disorder. Proclus' Doctrine of Evil and its Roots in Ancient Platonism*, Leiden/Boston.

Pomeroy, S. (2001), *Xenophon 'Oeconomicus'. A Social and Historical Commentary*, Oxford.

Pradeau, J-F. (2008), « Platão, antes da invenção da paixão », in B. Besnier/ J.-F. Moreau/ L. Renault, *As paixões antigas e medievais. Teorias e críticas das paixões,* São Paulo.

Ramelli, I. (2006), *Il 'basileus' come 'nomos empsychos' tra diritto naturale e diritto divino. Spunti platonici del concetto e sviluppi di età imperiale e tardo-antica*, Napoli.

Ramos Jurado, E. A. (1981), *Lo platónico en el siglo V p.C.: Proclo. (Análisis de las fuentes del Comentario de Proclo al Timeo platónico en su libro V: Prólogo y Genealogía de los dioses)*, Sevilla.

Reale, G. (1991), *Per una nuova interpretazione di Platone. Rilettura della metafisica dei grandi dialoghi alla luce delle «Dottrine non scritte»*, Milano.

Reale, G. (1997), "La fondazione protologica del Cosmo e della Polis ideale in Platone", in E. Rudolph (ed.), *Polis e Cosmo in Platone*, Milano, 9–38.

Reeve, C.D.C. (1997), *Plato, 'Cratylus'*, in J.M. Cooper/D.S. Hutchinson (eds.), *Plato, Complete Works,* Indianapolis/Cambridge, 101–156.

Reeve, C.D.C. (1998), *Aristotle, 'Politics'*, translated with introduction and notes by C.D.C. Reeve, Indianapolis.

Regali, M. (2012), *Il Poeta e il Demiurgo: teoria e prassi della produzione letteraria nel 'Timeo' e nel 'Crizia' di Platone*, Sankt Augustin.

Reydams-Schils, G. (2011), "Myth and Poetry in the *Timaeus*", in P. Destrée/F.G. Herrmann (eds.), *Plato and the Poets*, Leiden/Boston, 349–360.

Ricken, F. (2008), *Platon, 'Politikos'*, Übersetzung und Kommentar, Göttingen.

Ritter, C. (1910), «Beiträge zur Erklärung des *Politikos*», in Ritter, C., *Neue Untersuchungen über Platon*, München, 66–94.

Robinson, T.M. (1995a), *Plato's Psychology*, Toronto (1970, 1995).

Robinson, T.M. (1995b), "Forms, Demiurge and World Soul in the *Politicus*", *Revue de philosophie ancienne* 13, 15–30.

Robinson, T.M. (2003), "Il *Politico* di Platone: il mito e le sue implicazioni cosmologiche", *Studi Classici ed Orientali* 49, 45–57.

Robinson, T.M. (2008), "The Myth of the *Statesman* and Some Cosmological Implications", in T.M. Robinson, *Logos and Cosmos. Studies in Greek Philosophy*, Sankt Augustin, 148–162.

Rosen, S. (1979), "Plato's Myth of the Reversed Cosmos", *Review of Metaphysics* 33, 59–85.

Rosen, S. (1995), *Plato's 'Statesman'. The Web of Politics*, New Haven/Boston.

Rosen, S. (2007), *Filosofia fundadora. Estudis per a una filosofia del present*. Introducció, edició i traducció de X. Ibáñez-Puig & J. Monserrat Molas, Barcelona.

Rossetti, L. (2015), *La filosofia non nasce con Talete e nemmeno con Socrate*, Bologna.

Rowe, C.J. (ed.) (1986), *Plato, 'Phaedrus'*, Warminster.

Rowe, C.J. (ed.) (1995), *Reading the 'Statesman': Proceedings of the III Symposium Platonicum*, Sankt Augustin.

Rowe, C.J. (1995a), *Plato, 'Statesman'*. Edited with an Introduction, Translation and Commentary, Warminster.

Rowe, C.J. (1995b), "Introduction", in C. Rowe (ed.), *Reading the 'Statesman'*, *Proceedings of the III Symposium Platonicum*, Sankt Augustin, 11–27.

Rowe, C.J. (1997a), *Plato, 'Statesman'*, in J.M. Cooper/D.S. Hutchinson (eds.), *Plato, Complete Works*, Indianapolis/Cambridge, 294–358.

Rowe, C.J. (1997b), "The good, the reasonable and the laughable in Plato's *Republic*", in S. Jaekel/A. Timonen/V.-M. Riusanenen (eds.), *Laughter down the Centuries*, Vol. 3, ed. Turun Yliopisto, Turku, 45–54.

Rowe, C.J. (1999), *Plato, 'Statesman'*. Translated with Introduction, Indianapolis/Cambridge.

Rowe, C.J. (2001), "Killing Socrates. Plato's later thoughts on democracy", *Journal of Hellenic Studies* 121, 63–76.

Rowe, C.J. (2002a), "Zwei oder drei Phasen? Der Mythos im *Politikos*", in: M. Janka/C. Schäfer (eds.), *Platon als Mythologe: Neue Interpretationen zu den Mythen in Platons Dialogen*, Darmstadt, 160–75.

Rowe, C.J. (2002b), "Socrate, les lois et les '*Lois*'", *Revue Française d'Histoire des Idées Politiques* 16/2, 259–273.

Rowe, C.J. (2005), *Plato: 'Statesman', edited with an introduction, translation & commentary*, Oxford/Havertown.

Rowe, C.J. (2007=2008), *Plato and the Art of Philosophical Writing*, Cambridge.

Rowe, C.J. (2013), "On justice and the other virtues in the *Republic*: whose justice, whose virtues?", in S. Kato/N. Notomi/L. Brisson (eds.), *Dialogues on Plato's 'Politeia' ('Republic'): Selected Papers from the Ninth Plato Symposium*, 49–59, Sankt Augustin.

Rowe, C.J. (2015a), "Plato, Socrates, and the *genei gennaia sophistikē* of *Sophist* 231b", in D. Nails/H. Tarrant (eds.), *Second Sailing. Alternative Perspectives on Plato*, Espoo: *Societas Scientiarum Fennica*, 149–167.

Rowe, C.J. (2015b), "Plato versus Protagoras: The *Statesman*, the *Theaetetus* and the *Sophist*", in *Diálogos* (Departamento de Filosofía de la Facultad de Humanidades de la Universidad de Puerto Rico) XLVII/98 (special issue: La filosofía política de Platón, ed. Etienne Helmer), 143–166.

Rowe, C.J. (2017a), 'The "City of Pigs": a Key Passage in Plato's *Republic*', *Philosophie Antique. Problèmes, Renaissances, Usages* no. 17 ('Platon et la politique'), 55–71.

Rowe, C.J. (2017b), "The Athenians against the Persians: Plato's view (*Laws* III, 699b–d)", in J.F. Finamore/S. Klitenic Wear (eds.), *Defining Platonism: Essays in Honor of the 75th Birthday of John M.Dillon*, Steubenville, OH, 4–81.

Rowe, C./Broadie, S. (2002), *Aristotle, 'Nicomachean Ethics'. Translation, Introduction and Commentary*, (Trans. by C. Rowe, Introduction and Commentary by S. Broadie), Oxford.

Runia, D.T./Share, M. (2008), *Proclus. 'Commentary on Plato's Timaeus'*. Vol. II, Book 2: *Proclus on the Causes of the Cosmos and its Creation*, Cambridge.

Ryle, G. (1966), *Plato's Progress*, Cambridge.

Saffrey, H.D./Westerink, L.G. (1968–1997), *Proclus: 'Théologie platonicienne'*, 6 vols., Paris.

Sales, J. (1994), «Camins fills de les qüestions. Sobre mètodes», in *Quaderns del Centre d'Estudis Carles Cardó 2: Llibertats i liberalismes*, Barcelona.

Sales, J. (1999), «Assistir al diàleg, assistir el diàleg», in J. Monserrat-Molas (ed.), *El Polític de Plató. La gràcia de la mesura*, Barcelona, xv–xxiv.

Sandbach, F. (1977), "Five textual notes," *Illinois Classical Studies*, 2, 49–53.

Santa Cruz, M.I. (1992), *Platón, 'Político'*, Traducción, Introducción y Notas, *Diálogos*, V, Madrid.

Schicker, R. (1995), "Aspekte der Rezeption des *Politikos* im Mittel- und Neuplatonismus", in C.J. Rowe (ed.), *Reading the 'Statesman'*, Sankt Augustin, 381–388.

Schofield, M. (1990), "Ideology and philosophy in Aristotle's theory of slavery," in G. Patzig (ed.), *Aristoteles' 'Politik'*, Göttingen, 1–27.

Schofield, M. (2006), *Plato: Political Philosophy*, Oxford.

Schofield, M./Griffith, T. (eds.) (2016), *Plato: Laws*, ed.: Malcolm Schofield, tr.: Tom Griffith, Cambridge (Cambridge Texts in the History of Political Thought).

Schofield, M. (2016), '*Laws* I, 644b–645e: Plato's Marionette', *Rhizomata* 4/2, 128–153.

Schuhl, P.M. (1946–1947), 'Platon et l'activité politique de l'Académie', *Revue des études grecques*, 49–50; 46–53.

Schuhl, P.M. (²1968), *La fabulation platonicienne*, Paris.

Scodel, H.R. (1987), *Diaeresis and Myth in Plato's 'Statesman'*, Göttingen.

Seeck, G. (2011), *Platons 'Sophistes': ein kritischer Kommentar*, Munich, [online ed.: <http://books.openedition.org/chbeck/1412>, last acc. 23/6/16])

Seeck, G. (2012), *Platons 'Politikos': ein kritischer Kommentar*, Munich, [online ed.: <http://books.openedition.org/chbeck/1469>, last acc. 23/6/16].

Sheppard, A.D.R. (1980), *Studies on the 5th and 6th Essays of Proclus' 'Commentary on the Republic'*, Göttingen.

Shorey, P. (1902), *The Unity of Plato's Thought*, Chicago.

Skemp, J.B. (1952), *Plato's 'Statesman'*. A translation of the *Politicus* of Plato, with introductory essays and footnotes, London.

Skemp, J.B. (1967), *The Theory of Motion in Plato's Later Dialogues*, Amsterdam.

Skemp, J.B. (1987), *Plato. 'The Statesman'*. A Translation of the *Politicus* of Plato with Introductory Essay and Commentary, Bristol.

Sommerstein, A.H. (ed.) (1998), *Aristophanes, 'Ecclesiazusae'*, Warminster.

Speliotis, E. (2011), "*Phronesis* and Law in Plato's *Statesman*", *Ancient Philosophy* 31, 295–310.

Steel, C. (1986), "Proclus: Filosofie en Mythologie", *Tijdschrift voor Filosofie* 48, 191–206.

Steel, C. (2009), "The divine Earth: Proclus on *Timaeus* 40c", in R. Chiaradonna/F. Trabattoni (eds.), *Physics and Philosophy of Nature in Greek Neoplatonism*, Leiden/Boston, 259–281.

Steel, C./Macé, C./d'Hoine, P. (eds.), (2007–2009), *Procli in Platonis Parmenidem Commentaria*, 3 vols., Oxford.

Stratilatis, C. (2011), "A Counterpoint to Modernity: Laws and Philosophical Reason in Plato's *Laws*", *Critique* 22, 15–37.

Strauss, L. (1964), *The City and Man*, Chicago.

Szlezák, T.A. (1991), *Come leggere Platone. Un nuovo canone per affrontare gli scritti platonici*, Milano.

Taormina, D.P. (2000), "Procédures de l'évidence dans la *Théologie platonicienne*", in: A. Ph. Segonds/C. Steel (eds.), *Proclus et la 'Théologie Platonicienne': actes du colloque international de Louvain (13–16 mai 1998) en l'honneur de H.D. Saffrey et L.G. Westerink*, Leuven/Paris, 29–46.

Tarrant, H. (1998), "Introduction", in R. Jackson/K. Lycos/H. Tarrant, *Olympiodorus, 'Commentary on Plato's Gorgias'*, Leiden, 1–52.

Tarrant, H. (2000), *Plato's First Interpreters*, London.

Tarrant, H. (ed.) (2007), *Proclus, 'Commentary on Plato's Timaeus'*, vol.1, Book I: *Proclus on the Socratic State and Atlantis*, Cambridge.

Tarrant, H. (2014), "Platonist curricula and their influence", in P. Remes/S. Slaveva-Griffin (eds.), *The Routledge Handbook of Neoplatonism*, London/New York, 15–39.

Taylor, A.E. (ed.) (1971), *Plato, The 'Sophist' and the 'Statesman'*, Folkestone/London.

Taylor, C.C. (1999), *The Atomists: Leucippus and Democritus*, Toronto.

Taylor, T. (ed.) (1816), *The Six Books of Proclus, the Platonic Successor, 'On the Theology of Plato'*, London.

Teisserenc, F. (2010), *Langage et image dans l'oeuvre de Platon*, Paris.

Tordesillas, A. (1995), "Le point culminant de la métrétique", in J. Rowe (ed.), *Reading the 'Statesman': Proceedings of the III Symposium Platonicum*, Sankt Augustin, 102–111.

Trabattoni, F. (2010), *Platão*, São Paulo.

Trampedach, K. (1994), *Platon, die Akademie une die zeitgenössische Politik*, Stuttgart.

Trouillard, J. (1974), "L'activité onomastique selon Proclos", in H. Dörrie (ed.), *De Jamblique à Proclus. Entretiens sur l'Antiquité Classique*, Vandeuvres/Genève, 239–255.

Tulli, M. (1991), "Età di Crono e ricerca sulla natura nel *Politico* di Platone", *Studi Classici ed Orientali* 40, 97–115.

Usher, S. (1990), *Isocrates, 'Panegyricus' and 'To Nicocles'. Greek Orators Vol. III*, Warminster.

Van den Berg, R.M. (ed.) (2001), *Proclus' 'Hymns'*, Leiden/Boston/Köln.

Vegetti, M. (2010), *Um paradigma no céu: Platão político, de Aristóteles ao século XX*, São Paulo.

Verlinsky, A. (2008), "The Cosmic Cycle in the *Statesman* Myth. I", *Hyperboreus* 14, 57–86.

Vetta, M. (ed.) (1989), *Aristofane, 'Le donne al parlamento'*, Milano.

Westerink, L.G. (ed.) (1962), *Anonymous, 'Prolegomena to Platonic Philosophy'*, Amsterdam.

Westerink, L.G. (1987), "Proclus et les Présocratiques", in J. Pépin/H.D. Saffrey (eds.), *Proclus: lecteur et interprète des anciens*, Paris, 105–112.

Westerink, L.G. (ed.) (2009), *The Greek commentaries on Plato's 'Phaedo'. 1. Olympiodorus*, Westbury [2nd edition].

Westerink, L.G./Segonds, A. Ph. (eds.), (1990), *Prolégomènes à la philosophie de Platon*, Paris.

White, D.A. (2007), *Myth, Metaphysics and Dialectic in Plato's 'Statesman'*, Aldershot, Ashgate.

Woodruff, P. (2015), *"Mimesis"*, in P. Destrée/P. Murray (eds.), *A Companion to Ancient Aesthetics*, Oxford, 329–340.

Wydra, H. (2015), *Politics and the Sacred*, Cambridge.

Wyller, E. (1970), "The *Parmenides* is the *Philosopher*", *Classica et Mediaevalia* 29, 27–39.

Zambon, M. (2002), *Porphyre et le Moyen Platonisme*, Paris.

Zamora Calvo, J.M./Brisson, L. (2010), *Platón. 'Timeo'*, Madrid.

Zamora Calvo, J.M. (2014), "'Forjadores de mitos'. El discurso poético en el *Comentario a la República* de Proclo", *Eidos* 20, 145–172.

Zeyl, D.J. (1997), *Plato, 'Timaeus'*, in J.M. Cooper/D.S. Hutchinson (eds.), *Plato, Complete Works*, Indianapolis/Cambridge, 1224–1291.

Zuckert, C. (2000), "Who's a Philosopher? Who's a Sophist? The Stranger vs. Socrates", *The Review of Metaphysics* 54/1, 65–97.

Zuckert, C. (2009), *Plato's Philosophers. The Coherence of the Dialogues*, Chicago/London.

List of Contributors

Dougal Blyth is a senior lecturer in Classics at the University of Auckland, New Zealand. He is the author of *Aristotle's Everturning World in Physics 8: Analysis and Commentary* (Brill, 2015) and has published elsewhere on Aristotle, Plato, Cicero, Menander and Aristophanes. His interests include ancient metaphysics and cosmology, ethics and political theory, and literature and literary theory.

Beatriz Bossi is Associate Professor of Ancient Philosophy at the Faculty of Philosophy of the Complutensian University of Madrid and a member of the Editorial Committee of the International Plato Society. Author of *Saber Gozar. Estudios sobre el placer en Platón* (2008), she has edited *Plato's Sophist Revisited* with T.M. Robinson (De Gruyter, 2013). After her stay at Princeton University (2015), she has held a visiting appointment at the University of California (Santa Barbara) (2018). She has organized several conferences on Plato's Eleatic dialogues in Spain and has published widely on Plato and Aristotle.

Laura Candiotto is Research Fellow at the Eidyn Centre of the University of Edinburgh (UK). She has been awarded a Von Humboldt Senior Research Fellowship at the Free University of Berlin where she will move in March 2019. Her research merges Ancient Greek philosophy, especially Plato, and contemporary philosophy of emotions. Among her publications: "Purification through the emotions. The role of shame in Plato's *Sophist* 230b4–e5" (2018), "Plato's cosmological medicine in the discourse of Eryximachus in the *Symposium*" (2015), *Le vie della confutazione. I dialoghi socratici di Platone* (2012). She has edited *Emotions in Plato* with O. Renaut (Brill, forthcoming).

Giovanni Casertano has been Full Professor of Ancient Philosophy at the University of Naples "Federico II". *Doutor honoris causa* by the University of Brasília (2012), he is author of the following books: *Il nome della cosa. Linguaggio e realtà negli ultimi dialoghi di Platone* (Loffredo, 1996); *Morte. Dai Presocratici a Platone* (Guida, 2003); *'Sofista'* (2004; 2010); *Paradigmi della verità in Platone* (2007; 2010); *I Presocratici* (2009; 2011); *Uma introdução à 'República' de Platão* (2011); *O prazer, a morte e o amor nas doutrinas dos Pré-socráticos* (2012); *Da Parmenide di Elea al 'Parmenide' di Platone* (Academia Verlag, 2015); *Platone, 'Fedone' o dell'anima. Dramma etico in tre Atti* (2015).

Dimitri El Murr is Professor of Ancient Philosophy at the Ecole Normale Supérieure (Université Paris Sciences et Lettres / Centre Jean Pépin, CNRS); formerly Associate Professor at the Université Paris 1 Panthéon-Sorbonne and a member of the Institut Universitaire de France. He has held visiting appointments at the following universities: Durham, Brown, Milano and Cambridge. He has edited: *The Platonic Art of Philosophy* with G. Boys-Stones and Ch. Gill (CUP, 2013) and *La Mesure du savoir. Etudes sur le 'Théétète'* (Vrin, 2013). Author of *Savoir et gouverner. Essai sur la science politique platonicienne* (Vrin, 2014), he has contributed to the volume *Platon, 'Le Politique', Int. Trad. et Commentaire* by M. Dixsaut *et al.* (Vrin, 2018).

Giovanni Giorgini is Professor of Political Philosophy at the University of Bologna and Adjunct Professor of Politics at Columbia University. He has been Visiting Professor in many universities

https://doi.org/10.1515/9783110605549-021

in USA and Europe. Life Member of Clare Hall College, Cambridge, he is a member and Past President of the *Collegium Politicum*, of the scientific board of *Il Pensiero Politico* and of the board of directors of the journals *Filosofia Politica* and *Etica & Politica*. Author of *La città e il tiranno* (1993), *Liberalismi eretici* (1999), *I doni di Pandora* (2002), he has written a translation with introduction of Plato's *Politicus* (Rizzoli, 2005), numerous essays, translations and entries in encyclopaedias.

Annie Larivée is Associate Professor in philosophy at Carleton University, Ottawa, Canada. Her dissertation, written in Paris (Paris 1 Panthéon-Sorbonne) under the supervision of Monique Dixsaut, was dedicated to the care of the soul in Plato's dialogues. She has published extensively on Plato and has collaborated on a French translation of the *Statesman* recently published by Vrin. She has a special interest in Epicureanism, Late Stoicism and Cynicism as practices of self-transformation and for ancient philosophy as a way of life. Her research interests lie at the frontier of psychology and philosophy.

Maurizio Migliori was Full Professor of History of Ancient Philosophy at the University of Macerata until 2015. Though retired, he keeps on teaching. Chairman of the Board for the Specialistic Degree Course (2001–2004), Director of the Department of Philosophy and Human Science (2005–2012), he was the European Representative of the Executive Committee of the International Plato Society (2001–2007). Author of many books on Plato: *Il disordine ordinato. La filosofia dialettica di Platone* (2 vv., Morcelliana, 2013); *Platone* (2017), and on his dialogues (*Parmenides, Philebus, Sophist, Statesman*), he has also written on Aristotle: *La generazione e la corruzione* (Bompiani, 2013).

Josep Monserrat-Molas is Professor of Philosophy at the University of Barcelona, Dean of the Fac. of Philosophy and Director of «Eidos. Platonism and Modernity». Author of *El 'Polític' de Plató. La gràcia de la mesura* (1999); *Estranys, setciències i pentatletes. Cinc estudis de filosofia política clàssica* (2007), *Al margen del 'Político' de Platón* (2012), he has edited *Hermenèutica i platonisme* (2002), *Philosophy and Dialog* (2007; 2010, with A. Bosch-Veciana), *Formal Structures in Plato's Dialogues*, (Academia Verlag, 2011, with F. Lisi and M. Migliori), *Aristòtil lector del 'Fileb'. Lectures sobre el 'Fileb' platònic* (2012) and *Leo Strauss, Philosopher. European Vistas* (SUNY, 2016), with A. Lastra. His last work is a critical edition of T. Hobbes' *De Homine* (Vrin, 2018).

Anna Motta has been POINT-Fellow at the Dahlem Research School in the focus area of the Excellence Cluster TOPOI, and she is now wissenschaftliche Mitarbeiterin at the Freie Universität Berlin. Particularly interested in Plato and the philosophy of the commentators, she has published the first Italian translation (with introduction and commentary) of the *Anonymous Prolegomena to Platonic Philosophy*, and several papers on the Platonist tradition, more particularly on Neoplatonism, in international journals. Her recent monograph is entitled λόγους ποιεῖν. *L'eredità platonica e il superamento dell'aporia dei dialoghi* (Loffredo, 2018).

Lidia Palumbo is Associate Professor of Ancient Philosophy at the University of Naples Federico II. She is a specialist in ancient philosophy, with interests in Plato and the dialogic technique. Author of several essays on the Presocratics, Plato and Aristotle, she is a member of International Philosophical Societies and President of the SFI "G. Vico" Neapolitan section. Her major publications include μίμησις. *Rappresentazione, teatro e mondo nei dialoghi di Platone e* *nella 'Poetica' di Aristotele* (Loffredo, 2008) and *Verba manent. Su Platone e il linguaggio* (Loffredo, 2014).

Miriam Campolina Diniz Peixoto is Professor of Ancient Philosophy at the Federal University of Minas Gerais, Belo Horizonte (Brazil), where she directs the Research Area in Ancient and Medieval Philosophy of the Postgraduate Program. Supervised by Prof. Jean Frère at the Université Marc Bloch – Strasbourg II, she wrote her Ph.D. on Measure in the Ethics of Democritus. Member of the Latin American Association of Ancient Philosophy and of the Board of the International Association for Presocratic Studies (IAPS), she is co-author of *O visível e o inteligível na filosofia antiga* (2012) and has published several articles and chapters on ancient philosophy.

Thomas More Robinson is Professor Emeritus of Philosophy and Classics at the University of Toronto. A recipient of the Aristotle Award, he is the author of, among other books, *Plato's Psychology* and *Heraclitus: Fragments*, and is the former president of the Society for Ancient Greek Philosophy, the International Plato Society, and the Canadian Federation for the Humanities. He currently serves as an honorary president of the International Association for Greek Philosophy.

Christopher Rowe is Professor Emeritus of Greek at Durham University (UK). He is presently working on a new critical edition of the text of Aristotle's *Eudemian Ethics*, to be published by OUP as a replacement for the Walzer and Mingay edition of 1991. Among his publications are *Plato: Theaetetus and Sophist* (CUP, 2015); (with G. Boys Stones) *The Circle of Socrates* (Hackett, 2013); the new Penguin versions of [Plato] *Republic* (2012) and *The Last Days of Socrates* (2010); *Plato and the Art of Philosophical Writing* (CUP, 2007); (with T. Penner) *Plato's Lysis* (CUP, 2005); and (accompanying S. Broadie's commentary) a new translation of Aristotle, *Nicomachean Ethics* (OUP, 2002). He is currently Executive Editor of the Brill book series *Philosophia Antiqua*.

Nuria Sánchez Madrid is Associate Professor at the Faculty of Philosophy of the Complutensian University of Madrid and external member of the Centre of Philosophy of the U. of Lisbon and of the Institute of Philosophy of the U. of Oporto. Author of *A civilizaçao como destino: Kant e as formas da reflexão* (2016), she has contributed to *Kant's Lectures* (2015) and *Kant and the Metaphors of Reason* (2015). Editor of *Kant and Social Policies* (2016, with A. Faggion and A. Pinzani) and *Kant's Philosophy of Right in the XXIst Century* (2018, with L. Krasnoff and P. Satne), she is Secretary of *Isegoría* and *Con-textos Kantianos. International Journal of Philosophy*.

Gislene Vale dos Santos is Associate Professor at the Faculty of Philosophy and Social Sciences of the Universidade Federal da Bahia (Brazil). She is interested in Plato's late dialogues from an epistemological/cosmological perspective. While her Master's Dissertation explores the role of *logos* in *aisthesis* in the *Theaetetus* (2010), her Ph.D. is focused on the ontological status of the sensible in the *Timaeus* (2017).

David White is an Adjunct Associate Professor in the Department of Philosophy, DePaul University (Chicago, Illinois, USA). He has written three books on Plato, all dealing with the function of myth in, respectively, the *Phaedo*, the *Phaedrus*, and the *Statesman*. White has also written two books on Heidegger, two on Derrida, and monographs on Richard Wagner's *Ring* cycle, and the metaphysical systems in James Joyce's novels. In addition, he has two books on philosophy and children including *Philosophy for Kids* (translated into ten languages). He has also written over 50 articles in philosophy, literary criticism, and educational theory.

José María Zamora Calvo is Associate Professor of Ancient Philosophy at the Autonomous University of Madrid, Spain. Philosophy degree with honours (University of Valladolid, 1993) and Ph.D. in Philosophy with honours (University of Valladolid, 1998). Since 2008 he has been the President of the Spanish Section of ISNS-*International Society for Neoplatonic Studies* and coordinator of the UAM Research Group: "Influences of Greek Ethics on Contemporary Philosophy".

Index Locorum

https://doi.org/9783110605549-022

V.3.18.19–20	133
V.4.236.132.16–19	133
V.5–10	134
V.5.21.2	138
V.5.21.26–22.2	138
V.5.23.22–23	138
V.5.24.10–20	136
V.6, 24.22–25.1–3	152
V.6.24.23–25.19	137
V.6.25.9	132
V.6, 25.11–16	153
V.6, 25.16	152
V.6, 25.17–18	153
V.6, 25.21	152
V.6, 25.27–26.4	144
V.6, 26.5–9	144
V.6, 26.14–15	156
V.6, 26.17–20	142
V.8.29.20	134
V. 9, 31.11–12	144
V.9, 31.20–26	145
V.10.33.22–23	135
V.10, 33.25.34.1	11
V.10.35.3–11	135
V.10, 35.11–20	150
V.15.15–24	136
V.25.92.1–13	137
V.25.93.1–2	134
V.25.93.24–25	137
V.32.119.7–19	136
V.32.119.9–19	138
V.32.119.13–22	137
V.36.132.16–19	132
V.36.132.20–25	136
V.37.135.11	134
V.119.16	128
VI.3.20.7–8	134

Pseudo-Aristotle
Physiognomy
805b–806a   240

808b	240
809b–810a	240

Pseudo-Dionysius Areopagita scriptor ecclesiasticus (Dion. Ar.)
De diuinis nominibus
I 6 *Patrologia Graeca*, 3, col. 596C   137

Severus
Fr. 6 T   122

Sophocles
Elektra
1227   202

Syrianus
*In Aristotelis Metaphysica commentaria =
Commentary on Metaphysics*
26.10   137
116.20–21   137

Thucydides
History of the Peloponnesian War
I, 20   283
I, 68–71   283
I, 70   283
I, 71   284
II, 35–43   283
II, 40, 2   67
III, 82   269, 284
VI, 9   284
VI, 18   284

Xenophon
Cyropaedia= The Education of Cyrus
I, I   328
Memorabilia = Recollections of Socrates
III, IX, 10–11   28
Oeconomicus=Economics
XXI, 2–12   29
XXI   829